MARKETING

MARKETING

The Art & Science of
Business Management

A. Dale Timpe

Series Editor

Facts On File
New York • Oxford

This is volume eight in Facts On File's series, "The Art and Science of Business Management," each volume of which provides a broad selection of articles on an important business topic of our time.

Volume one: *Motivation of Personnel*
Volume two: *The Management of Time*
Volume three: *Leadership*
Volume four: *Creativity*
Volume five: *Performance*
Volume six: *Managing People*
Volume seven: *Productivity*

658.8
M3459z

Marketing
copyright © 1989 by KEND Publications

Facts On File, Inc.
460 Park Avenue South
New York, New York 10016

Library of Congress Cataloging-in-Publication Data

Marketing / A. Dale Timpe, series editor.
    p. cm. — (The art & science of business management: v. 8)
    Bibliography: p.
    Includes index.
    ISBN 0-8160-1906-1 (alk. paper)
    1. Marketing. I. Timpe, A. Dale. II. Series: Art and science of business management; v. 8
HF5415.M2946   1989
658.8—dc19   88-26838

British CIP data available on request

Printed in the United States of America
10 9 8 7 6 5 4 3 2 1
This book is printed on acid-free paper.

TABLE OF CONTENTS

v

PREFACE

The competitive strategies used by many successful companies seem to have evolved more out of a general awareness of the marketplace and an intention to build a better mousetrap than out of a formalized, comprehensive marketing strategy. Marketing is a rational process, but there is a tendency for management to confuse the irrationality of sales appeals with the rationality of marketing.

During the 1970s, the use of marketing techniques gave way to strategic planning in determining business objectives and developing products. The emphasis shifted from the customer to technology, finance, and business development. There is growing concern among managers that the lack of sharp customer focus is a serious deficiency of strategic planning. Mass markets are disappearing, resulting in greater market segmentation. In order to reach these new specialized markets, it will be necessary for companies to control information and turn it into a new, and perhaps dominant, strategic variable. Today, skillful marketing frequently depends on skillful management of information in order to respond to changes in the marketplace.

Unfortunately, manufacturing is the least understood among the functions governing market opportunities . . . yet, without a strong and highly productive manufacturing base, companies will find it difficult to respond to, much less anticipate, changes in the marketplace. Manufacturing capabilities can be a powerful weapon in the ever-present battle for market share. By understanding what the market wants and directing the manufacturing organization to maximize the related performance measures, a company's ability to market its products will be improved.

The efficiency, versatility, and reliability of their production systems have enabled the Japanese to become leaders in certain product lines and to maintain this position by continually introducing new products. Superior product quality has been one of the keys to Japanese success in American markets. Many American firms have now come to recognize the competitive importance of quality and its strategic value in positioning and selling products.

This compendium provides access to a broad spectrum of practical knowledge, research, and theory relating to marketing principles and perspectives. The diversity of insights, experiences and theoretical concepts presented here offers many useful solutions and strategies for marketers. The sources represent a wide range of professional publications, including a number not readily available to most executives. For those wanting a more detailed discussion on a particular aspect, the bibliography provides a valuable research tool.

A. Dale Timpe
Series Editor

ACKNOWLEDGMENTS

The articles in this volume are reprinted with the permission of the respective copyright holders and all rights are reserved.

Bayus, Barry L. "Word of Mouth: The Indirect Effects of Marketing Efforts" from *Journal of Advertising Research*, by permission of Advertising Research Foundation, © 1985.

Bonoma, Thomas V. and Victoria L. Crittenden. "Managing Market Implementation" from *Sloan Management Review*, by permission of Sloan Management Review Association, © 1988.

Cohen, Bernard R. "Telemarketing: Putting Business on the Line" from *Best's Review*, by permission of A. M. Best Company, © 1985.

Cohen, William A. "Historical Military Strategy Pinciples Advocated for Winning the Marketing Wars" from *Marketing News*, by permission of American Marketing Association, © 1985.

Consatantin, James A. and Robert F. Lusch. "Discover the Resources in Your Marketing Channel" from *Business*, by permission of College of Business Administration, Georgia State University, © 1986.

Coppett, John I. and Cornelius H. Sullivan. "Marketing in the Information Age" from *Business*, by permission of College of Business Administration, Georgia State University, © 1986.

Coppett, John I. and Harold E. Glass. "Manage Telemarketing Effectively," by permission of *Personnel Journal*, © 1984.

Editorial Staff of *Marketing News*. "Actionable Research Needed When Markets Change" from *Marketing News*, by permission of American Marketing Association, © 1986.

Editorial Staff of *Marketing News*. "How to Tell When Segmentation Works" from *Marketing News*, by permission of American Marketing Association, © 1986.

Eisenhart, Tom. "Marketers Trade Off for Research Productivity" from *Business Marketing*, by permission of Crain Communications, Inc., © 1988.

England, Frederick J., Jr. "Strategic Marketing Takes a Bow" from *Best's Review*, by permission of A. M. Best Company, © 1985.

Ferber, Robert C., Stanley I. Cohen and Ernst Mendels. "Drawing Road Maps to Hidden Market Segments" from *Business Marketing*, by permission of Crain Communications, Inc., © 1986.

Garvin, David A. "Product Quality: An Important Strategic Weapon" from *Business Horizons*, by permission of School of Business, Indiana University, © 1984.

Gilliatt, Neal and Pamela Cuming. "Chief Marketing Officer: A Maverick Whose Time Has Come" from *Business Horizons*, by permisson of School of Business, Indiana University, © 1986.

Gershman, Michael. "If at First You Don't Succeed, Remarket" from *Management Review*, by permission of Michael Gershman, © 1987.

Hayes, H. Michael. "Another Chance for the Marketing Concept?" from *Business*, by permission of College of Business Administration, Georgia State University, © 1988.

Haywood, K. Michael. "Scouting the Competition for Survival and Success" from *Cornell HRA Quarterly*, by permission of Cornell University School of Hotel Administration, © 1986.

Husami, Art. "Leveraging Sales Through Database Maintenance," by permission of *Direct Marketing*, © 1987.

James, Barrie G. "Deterrence—A Strategy That Pays" from *Business Horizons*, by permission of School of Business, Indiana University, © 1985.

Jarvis, Lance P. and Edward J. Mayo. "Winning the Market-Share Game" from *Cornell HRA Quarterly*, by permission of Cornell University School of Hotel Administration, © 1986.

Kastiel, Diane Lynn. "New Tools for Enhanced Sales Force Productivity" from *Business Marketing*, by permission of Crain Communications, Inc., © 1986.

Kaydos, W. J. "Manufacturing Market Share" from *Business Horizons*, by permission of School of Business, Indiana University, © 1984.

Kiel, Geoffrey. "Technology and Marketing: The Magic Mix?" from *Business Horizons*, by permission of School of Business, Indiana University, © 1984.

Langer, Judith. "Getting to Know the Customer Through Qualitative Research" from *Management Review*, by permission of American Management Association, © 1987.

Lehmkuhl, David C. "The Failure of Marketing Research," by permission of *Marketing and Media Decisions*, © 1984.

Magrath, A. J. "When Marketing Services, 4 Ps Are Not Enough" from *Business Horizons*, by permission of School of Business, Indiana University, © 1986.

Marken, G. A. "Public Relations and Sales . . . There Must Be a Measurable Relation" from *Business Marketing*, by permission of Crain Communications, Inc., © 1988.

Masten, Davis L. "Packaging's Proper Role Is to Sell the Product" from *Marketing News*, by permission of American Marketing Association, © 1988.

Moriya, Frank E. and Carl M. Vorder Bruegge. "Marketing Management in the Information Age" from *Management Review*, by permission of American Management Association, © 1987.

Naimark, George M. "The Consequentiality Index: The Key to Marketing Success" from *Business Horizons*, by permission of School of Business, Indiana University, © 1986.

Narus, James A. and James C. Anderson. "Strengthen Distribution Performance Through Channel Positioning" from *Sloan Management Review*, by permission of Sloan Management Review Association, © 1988.

Nordhaus, George. "Marketing in the Electronic Era" from *Best's Review*, by permission of A. M. Best Company, © 1985.

Oliva, Terence A., Diana L. Day and Wayne S. DeSarbo. "Selecting Competitive Tactics: Try a Strategy Map" from *Sloan Management Review*, by permission of Sloan Management Review Association, © 1987.

Pascarella, Perry. "Getting a Fix on Your Competitive Position" from *Industry Week*, by permission of Penton Publishing Inc., © 1984.

Patterson, William Pat. "The New Global Game" from *Industry Week*, by permission of Penton Publishing Inc., © 1985.

Perry, David. "Performance Advertisers Practice What They Preach" from *Business Marketing*, by permission of Crain Communications, Inc., © 1988.

Sheridan, John H. "Cracking the 'Transplant' Market" from *Industry Week*, by permission of Penton Publishing Inc., © 1988.

Varadarajan, P. Rajan. "Marketing Strategies in Action" from *Business*, by permission of College of Business Administration, Georgia State University, © 1986.

Zakon, Alan and Richard W. Winger. "Consumer Draw—From Mass Markets to Variety" from *Management Review*, by permission of American Management Association, © 1987.

Ziegenhagen, M. E. and Fergus F. O'Daly. "Where's the ARF/ABP Study Value?" from *Business Marketing*, by permission of Crain Communications, Inc., © 1988.

Part I
MARKETING
STRATEGY

1.
TECHNOLOGY AND MARKETING: THE MAGIC MIX?

Geoffrey Kiel

"Market pull" and "technology push" are not mutually exclusive paths to corporate innovation. Understanding the technology-marketing interface and integrating it with corporate strategy and organizational design is the way to maintain a productive balance between the two.

The argument is simple. Market development and technological innovation must have a symbiotic relationship for any business unit to achieve long-term success. Technological innovation without market application results in a barren squandering of resources. Yet, long-term marketing success cannot be achieved without technological innovation. Such a simple observation should be self-evident, but it requires restating, given the current debate as to whether marketing, and in particular the marketing concept, has substantially contributed to current American economic problems.

This debate has developed due to the lack of understanding of the complementary roles played by technological development and marketing in successful business strategy. There is an immense literature concerning all aspects of technology including the innovative process, technological transfer, managing research and development, technological substitution, and technological assessment. There is an equally immense literature about marketing, with detailed discussion of topics such as market segmentation, marketing research, assessing market potential, and strategic marketing management. However, for the most part, each literature has assumed away the other. Writers in technology have stated that a market, and presumably an appropriate marketing strategy, are essential for the commercial viability of a new technology. Marketing writers have paid lip service to technology as the source of new and improved goods and services but have failed to ask how technological strategy and marketing strategy are interrelated.

The failure to understand the technology-marketing interface has led to charges that market-pull processes of technological innovation are inferior to technology- or science-push processes. Furthermore, it has been argued that this movement to "market pull" is a recent phenomenon brought about by the acceptance of the marketing concept as the dominant managerial philosophy by many American corporations.

THE CHARGES AGAINST MARKETING

In 1979, Roger Bennett and Robert Cooper made the initial charges against marketing. These authors identified two means to product innovation, market pull and technology push. They stated that market-pull approaches to product innovation result from the application of the marketing concept—identifying buyer's needs and wants prior to product development. Technology push, they maintain, occurs when the ongoing process of science and research produces major technological breakthroughs, independent of market requirements. They maintained that, "'Technology push' is the antithesis of 'market pull' in product innovation. Yet history shows us that the major breakthroughs, the truly innovative products, are often the result of 'technology push.'"[1] Bennett and Cooper believe that reliance on the marketing concept, with its market pull approach to new product development, has contributed to the end of true product innovation by North American companies.

Peter Reitz added evidence to the charges by pointing out, as many other writers have done, the decline in American research and development expenditure as a percentage of GNP, and the shift away from basic research towards developmental research.[2] Marketing is accused of being a major contributory factor to this shift, stifling creativity and moving product development toward more cosmetic changes in the product line. This, in turn, has led to a decline in American international competitiveness.

These arguments against marketing were cited by Robert Hayes and William Abernathy in their strong denunciation of the attitudes and business strategies of American managers in their influential 1981 article.[3] Finally, Bennett and Cooper provided the summing up for the prosecution in the case against marketing. After summarizing the case that has been presented here, they advance the "product value concept" as an alternative to the marketing concept. The "product value concept" entails providing the market with a product which is perceived by the consumer as being superior. Furthermore, they maintain, such product value will be attained through technological and manufacturing superiority and strength.[4]

These charges against marketing came at an opportune time. American industry, reeling under the impact of heavy international competition in both domestic and international markets, high levels of unemployment, and a stagnant economy, was seeking out the causes of its decline. Yet has the correct party been charged?

IS MARKETING GUILTY?

The defense of marketing is based on three main arguments. Firstly, marketing pull and technological push are not opposing, mutually exclusive paths to innovation. These concepts have become straw men built upon a misunderstanding of the nature and roles of science and technology. Secondly, considerable empirical evidence on the innovation process proves that market-related forces are the primary influence on technological innovation. Thirdly, the view of the marketing concept put forward by its detractors is overly simplistic.

In order to weigh the charges against marketing, it is important to understand the nature and interrelationship of science and technology.[5] Science is the vast pool of knowledge created through basic research with the objective of furthering man's understanding of his world. Technology is the search for new products and processes directed by the objectives of the individual or organization undertaking the research. In corporations, this objective is the potential profit resulting from the commercialization of innovations.

In modern Western society, science is largely conducted in the universities, in the research laboratories of government institutions, and in a few very large corporations. Technology, on the other hand, is predominantly the preserve of profit-making corporations, individual inventors and entrepreneurs, and some divisions of government.

The interrelationship between science and technology is complex. On the one hand, many technological developments flow from progress in pure science. For example, the transistor was developed as a result of considerable scientific effort in solid-state physics, while a whole new realm of technology was opened up by the discovery of the DNA molecule. On the other hand, a considerable amount of science is technology driven. For example, the science of thermodynamics grew out of the need for better, more efficient steam engines; today, computer technology is driving computer science. Furthermore, technological development in one industry will often feed technological development in another. Hence, the integrated circuit has made major product innovations possible in products ranging from toys to heavy industrial equipment.

It is often impossible to forecast what components of basic science will be needed to provide technological breakthroughs. Consequently, from a societal point of view, it is essential to keep adding to the pool of basic knowledge even though, at the time of the addition, the application of this new knowledge may not be readily apparent. It is because financial return for such a function is so difficult to forecast that scientific research is largely conducted at public institutions such as universities and is primarily funded by society through government.

Furthermore, both the process of science and the process of technological innovation primarily consist of countless small incremental additions rather than single major breakthroughs. Nathan Rosenberg expressed this well by stating, "Schumpter accustomed economists to thinking of technical change as involving major breaks, giant discontinuities or disruptions with the past . . . But technological change is also (and perhaps even more importantly) a continuous stream of innumerable minor adjustments, modifications and adaptions. . ."[6]

The power of such incremental technological growth is shown by the Japanese. The Japanese did not invent television or radio, the automobile, or the integrated circuit. They left high-risk basic research to Western countries. The strength of the Japanese innovation process has been the large number of incremental innovations which they have added to these products and their production processes. An additional major strength has been their ability to search out innovations on a global basis to combine with their own research and development activities.

Consequently, the first defense of the marketing concept is that the emphasis on technology-push models of product innovation is far too simplistic. Basic research does have an important role to play. It is particularly important where the innovative thrust of an organization's R&D programs continually come up against the frontiers of science, where the existing pool of knowledge is insufficient to provide the required technological breakthroughs. However, to acclaim this research as being superior to more applied technological innovation is as misguided as claims that basic research should be abandoned by the corporate sector.

There are well-documented risks associated with research and development undertaken prior to and separate from marketing activity as advocated by the critics of marketing. Firstly, even if the research investment produces a product, there is no guarantee that it will meet consumers' needs. For example, the AT&T picture phone, developed by Bell Labs and manufactured by Western Electric, floundered on the market. Consumers were not willing to pay $285 per month for a product when there was no guarantee that the person called would have a picture phone or would even want to be seen!

Secondly, this pipeline approach to innovation is associated with lengthy innovation periods. Yet the longer it takes to get a new product to market, the greater the risk of failure due to changing market conditions, competitive responses or further technological advances. Again, a strength of Japanese industry has been its shorter time for introducing innovations to the market.

The second defense of the marketing concept draws on the considerable research evidence on successful innovations. There is overwhelming evidence from studies of more than 1,800 innovations that marketing and related production factors are the most important influences on innovation. James Utterback provides an excellent summary of these studies, which shows that between 60 to 80 percent of technological innovations over a wide variety of different products and markets have resulted from market-related forces.[7]

How can these results, drawn from many studies, be reconciled with the criticism of the marketing concept? The answer lies in the overly simplistic portrayal of the marketing concept put forward by its detractors. The view that market-pull models require extensive consumer research as a first stage and, consequently, that the approach is constrained by the consumer's limited vision of the technological future, ignores the various other means by which market requirements can be translated into technological innovation.

For example, a competitor might develop a technically superior product which then requires a competitive response. This happened in the scientific calculator market of the early 1970s and is currently occurring in the microcomputer industry. Alternatively, increasing price competition in a market may lead a firm to develop or adapt a new process technology to provide substantial cost reductions and obtain subsequent price advantage in the market. This process can be seen in industries as diverse as integrated circuits and banking services. A further example of effective market-pull strategies occurs when the need is well recognized in the industry and among customers, leading firms to invest substantially in research and development to meet this need. This can be seen in the race by Japanese, European, and American manufacturers to produce video recorders for the consumer market.

In short, the studies of innovation show that market research is only one means by which an organization can determine market requirements. The marketing concept, as a managerial philosophy, draws attention to the need to be responsive to changing markets as the key to long-run corporate success. It does not specify that the only way to find out about market requirements is through the slavish use of marketing research.

To summarize, the case against marketing is anecdotal and not supported by the considerable body of research on technological innovation. However, in dismissing the charges, I do not mean that no crime has been committed or that basic research is unimportant. Rather, the wrong defendant was tried. There is no doubt that a change in management practices is required. However, these changes must be built upon an understanding of the marketing-technology interface.

CREATING TECHNOLOGY-MARKETING MAGIC

The research literature on technological innovation clearly shows the importance of market considerations in producing viable technological innovations. Yet science and basic research are also central components of the innovation process. The challenge to management, then, is to harness both these forces to achieve corporate objectives. This requires achieving the "magic mix" of marketing and technology with the firm.

Like most aspects of modern management, there should be no "magic" in this combination of marketing and technology. Rather, the marketing-technology interface must be a planned component of both corporate strategy and organization design. With respect to overall corporate strategy, a technological strategy must be a key segment along with marketing, financial, operations, and human resources strategies. This technological strategy must encompass several areas. First, it needs to assess corporate technological strengths and weaknesses. This evaluation of strengths and weaknesses will cover both the existing technologies used by the firm as well as the firm's abilities to develop and commercialize new technologies. In short, is the firm well positioned with respect to physical research and development facilities, research personnel, and the ability to scan the technological environment?

Second, the firm must decide on the strategic balance between the internal and external acquisitions of technology. Internal acquisition through research and development has the advantage of security and exclusivity of technology. However, it contains the substantial risk inherent in lengthy development and the possibility of a zero return on the investment if the project lacks technical, financial, or market feasibility. External technology acquisition by means of licenses or takeover minimizes the risks inherent in internal technological development, but raises problems of a possible lack of access, either totally or in part, to the technology. In addition, the cost of license fees must be balanced against the investment required for in-house research.

The third critical element of the technological component of the corporate plan is the interface with the other key elements. Although the interaction of the technology component with the financial, operations, and human resources elements is of the utmost importance, the emphasis here is on the technology-marketing interface. The technology plan must be integrated with the marketing plan and both coordinated towards overall corporate objectives. For example, a particular product line might be nearing the maturity phase of the product life cycle. Marketing planning may see the need to counter strong price competition and for significant new product developments. Technological planning will then focus on the need for cost-saving process innovations as well as the development of new product features.

Such a linking of marketing and technology planning does not mean that technology plans must be subservient to marketing plans. For example, the research and development department may be working on an exciting new product which will require the allocation of marketing resources and the development of marketing plans for product launch. The central argument is that technology planning and marketing planning must be closely integrated to avoid new product failures and foregone marketing opportunities.

In addition to a marketing-technology interface oriented towards the development of new or improved products or process innovations which will affect the marketing mix, the corporate plan must ensure systematic scanning of the technological environment. The research literature supports the intuitive observation that no one firm can expect to make all the significant breakthroughs of importance to its industry. This observation assumes increased importance given that technological breakthroughs are now being made in many countries and not only in an organization's national markets. Consequently systematized technological scanning and assessment must be an ongoing corporate responsibility. This increased sensitivity and utilization of outside technology must be used to complement internal capabilities.

Again, it is essential that marketing input be introduced into this process at as early a stage as possible. This input is essential so that key policy questions such as these can be answered: What will be the impact of this technology on our existing products if it is utilized by either ourselves or a domestic or international competitor? What is the market potential for the new product which could result from this new technology? Marketing can take part in this scanning of the technological environment. Often the marketing department will be the first to hear of new products and production processes. Hence, technology scanning is a joint research and development and marketing responsibility.

Planning for technology and marketing is only the first stage in making technology-marketing magic. In day-to-day operations, it is essential to develop strong lines of communications between the technology and marketing sections of the organization. Also, it is essential to develop creative organizational systems for joint technology-market assessment. Obviously, the nature of this linkage between the research and development and marketing branches of the firm as well as the appropriate organizational systems will vary from firm to firm depending upon the firm's size, structure, and industry.

Evidence suggests that an effective means of building the research and development and marketing interface is the use of teams or dyads comprising both research and marketing personnel. However, the development of effective research-market teams requires special attention to be paid to their management. Problems of poor communication, inappropriate reporting structures, reward structures which do not reflect the long-term objectives, and motivation questions can easily turn such teams into counter-productive units. Another approach to interfacing marketing and technology is to have research and development personnel undertake their own initial preliminary market research surveys. The essential point is that this marketing-technology interface must be planned—it cannot be left to chance.

The importance of this link was amply demonstrated by Edwin Mansfield who maintains that the probability of economic success of a research and development project depends on how quickly the three key assessments are made: likelihood of technical success, likelihood of commercialization, and likelihood of market success. He notes: "In those companies whose research and development staff members do not work closely or responsively with marketing staff, the integration of research and development activity with market realities is haphazard, belated or both. Yet commercially successful innovation depends on just this sort of integration."[8]

In support of this statement he offers the evidence of three chemical companies, two of which reorganized to obtain a closer integration of research and development and marketing and a third which achieved an even worse integration than it previously had. The success at commercialization for the former two companies increased 20 percent, but the latter company showed a decline of 20 percent.

In summary, the way to achieve "technology-marketing magic" at the firm level is through integrating research and development activities as part of overall corporate planning, undertaking appropriate market feasibility studies at the earliest possible time, and developing rapport between the marketing and research and development functions.

CREATING THE ENVIRONMENT FOR TECHNOLOGY-MARKETING MAGIC

Although the individual firm is master of its own technological future, the rate and direction of technological development for society as a whole is strongly influenced by government policy. As Ellis Mottur has noted, "Although it is the private sector which ultimately must produce the innovations, it is government action—or inaction—which shapes the framework of institutions, laws, regulations and incentives which, in the final analysis, serves to stifle or to spur innovation."[9]

There are many ways by which government activity affects technological development, ranging from direct subsidization of research and development to the general economic management of the economy. However, it is beyond the scope of this article to discuss fully the role of government in fostering innovation.[10] Rather this article will provide a few brief examples of the power of government to foster a political-institutional environment conducive to innovation.

Taxation affects innovative activities in many ways. First, general tax policies, both personal and corporate, influence the rate of innovative activities through the savings ratio, level of retained earnings and, consequently, the rate of capital formation. Also, depreciation allowances and systems of investment allowances directly affect the profitability of technological investment. More specifically, taxation policy can be used as a direct tool to stimulate both basic and applied research by a variety of means such as special tax credits for research and development activity.

The government may also play a major role using direct and indirect subsidies. Although direct subsidies to industry are a controversial issue, the very fact that the government purchased various requirements from the private sector influences the nature and direction of research and development. For example, performance-standard setting in government procurements influences research and development activity, as do government expenditures on defense and space exploration. Furthermore, basic research is also influenced by the subsidization of university research programs. Consequently, the extent of coordination of such subsidization and the direction which it takes will markedly affect the overall direction and progress of innovative activity within a society.

Another important role of government in creating a conducive environment for technological development is as a supporter of small business and inventors. Small firms and independent inventors produce a disproportionate number of innovations compared with larger firms. Government can assist small, innovative firms in several ways. First, different government initiatives can ensure that a strong venture capital market is available for the small innovative businesses. Second, the tax laws can be structured to encourage small businesses, especially in allowing the reinvestment of earnings in the first few critical years of growth. Third, small businesses often need financial, marketing, and other business support and expertise to enable their early growth into national and world markets. Here again the government can provide advice and assistance.

Finally, the key role of government as the ultimate guardian of the educational system is critical if the talent to support technological development through future generations is to develop. National education policies must ensure that tomorrow's engineers, scientists, and managers are receiving a first-class education today.

Marketing, the marketing concept, and market-pull models of technological innovation are not the antithesis of success at either the firm or national level. Research evidence, as distinct from anecdotal evidence, shows the key role of market-pull models in providing the thousands of major and minor innovations which oiled American economic growth throughout the 1950s and 1960s. Furthermore, there is no reason to suggest that strategic marketing practices will not continue to play an important role in product innovation throughout the 1980s and 1990s.

This is not to say that science and basic research have no role to play. Basic research provides the building blocks of innovation. The objective, both for individual firms and society, is to maintain the creative balance between these two factors. However, the market is the final arbiter of technological success or failure and, consequently, marketing has a crucial role to play in all stages of technological innovation. The management challenge is to provide an environment conducive to both technological and market development. These are the essential ingredients for producing technology-marketing magic.

REFERENCES

1. "Beyond the Marketing Concept," *Business Horizons*, May-June 1979: 77.
2. "Revenge of the Marketing Concept," *Business Horizons*, May-June 1980: 49-53.

3. Robert H. Hayes and William J. Abernathy, "Managing Our Way to Economic Decline," *Harvard Business Review*, July-August 1980: 67-77.
4. Roger C. Bennett and Robert G. Cooper, "The Misuse of Marketing: An American Tragedy," *Business Horizons*, November-December 1981: 51-61.
5. Parts of this argument are based on Ralph Gomory's "Technological Development," *Science*, No. 4597, May 6, 1983: 576-580.
6. Nathan Rosenberg, *Perspectives on Technology*, (New York: Cambridge University Press, 1976): 166.
7. James M. Utterback, "Innovation in Industry and the Diffusion of Technology," *Science*, February 15, 1974: 620-6.
8. Edwin Mansfield, "How Economists See R&D," *Harvard Business Review*, November-December 1981: 100.
9. Ellis Mottur, *National Strategy for Technological Innovation*, (Washington, D.C.: U.S. Government Printing Office, 1979).
10. See Mottur; also Sherman Gee, *Technology Transfer, Innovation and International Competitiveness* (New York: Wiley, 1981).

2.

MARKETING STRATEGIES IN ACTION

P. Rajan Varadarajan

> Marketing strategy consists of two equally important stages: strategy
> formulation and strategy implementation. The reason that many com-
> panies are experiencing a failure of marketing strategies lies in their in-
> ability to balance these two stages.

A number of conceptual schemes and analytical techniques have been
proposed to aid managers in formulating strategy at the corporate, business
unit, and functional levels. However, a rising tide of disillusionment with the
strategy prescriptions of management consulting firms and in-house strategic
planning staff clearly indicates a need to reassess the theory and practice of
marketing strategies.

It is now becoming clear that strategy formulation has been emphasized to
the neglect of strategy *implementation*; a number of recent books and articles
have pointed out the need for a balanced perspective.[1] In an attempt to provide
that balance, this article focuses on conceptual aids for both facets of effective
marketing strategy. Beginning with a presentation of alternative conceptual
frameworks that provide insights into marketing growth opportunities at the
product-market level, we will then detail real-world examples to show the
feasibility of exploiting these opportunities. The article then concludes with a
brief discussion of marketing-strategy implementation.

GROWTH OPPORTUNITY ANALYSIS

The analysis of products and markets is an important and critical stage in the
strategic planning process. Such analysis provides the basis for deciding which
products and markets to emphasize in the pursuit into potential directions for
growth. For example, Booz, Allen & Hamilton, Inc., a leading management
consulting firm, conducted a survey of more than 700 U.S. manufacturers,
covering 13,000 new product introductions during a five-year period. They

Table 1.
Conceptual Aids for Marketing Strategy Formulation and Implementation

Strategic market planning is commonly viewed as concerned with the development of a viable match between an organization's capabilities and the opportunities and risks present in its environment. Key to formulating effective strategies is an understanding of the relationship between the variables describing the environment, the variables management controls, and performance variables. Among the strategy concepts discussed in most marketing management and strategy texts are:

Levels of organizational strategy
  Corporate level strategy
  Business unit level strategy
  Functional level strategy

Product-market growth strategies
  Market penetration
  Market development
  Product development

Integrative growth strategies
  Forward vertical integration
  Backward vertical integration
  Horizontal integration

Diversification growth strategies
  Horizontal diversification
  Concentric diversification
  Conglomerate diversification

Market entry strategies
  Internal development
  Acquisition or merger
  Joint venture

Market share management strategies
  Share increase strategies
  Share maintenance strategies
  Share harvesting strategies

Market coverage strategies
  Single-segment concentration
  Product specialization
  Market specialization
  Selective specialization
  Full coverage

Market segmentation and targeting strategies
  Undifferentiated marketing
  Differentiated marketing
  Concentrated marketing

New product development strategies
  Proactive
  Reactive
  Innovative
  Imitative

New product marketing strategies
  Rapid skimming
  Slow skimming
  Rapid penetration
  Slow penetration

Mature product marketing strategies
  Market modification
  Products modification
  Marketing mix modification

Product strategies
  Brand extension strategies
  Multibrand strategies
  Brand positioning strategies
  Brand repositioning strategies

New product pricing strategies
  Market skimming pricing
  Market penetration pricing

Distribution-promotion strategies
  Push strategy
  Pull strategy

identified the following six new product categories that constitute broad directions for growth:[2]

- *New-to-the-world-products*: New products that create an entirely new market (personal computers and videocassette recorders).
- *New product lines*: New products that, for the first time, allow a company to enter an established market (Polaroid's introduction of blank recording tapes for videocassette recorders).
- *Additions to existing product lines*: New products that supplement a company's established product lines (Kodak's introduction of Disc cameras).
- *Improvements in or revisions to existing products*: New products that provide improved performance or greater perceived value and replace existing products (Gillette's recent introduction of Good News disposable razors with pivot head to replace the earlier Good News version without a pivot head).
- *Repositionings*: Existing products that are targeted to new markets or market segments (until the early eighties, Timex watches were positioned as purely utilitarian watches that were durable. This image was reinforced by using promotional messages such as "Timex watches can take a licking and keep on ticking," and demonstrated by subjecting the brand to brutal torture tests in television commercials. However, in recent years Timex has been attempting to reposition its brands as more upscale, slick, and futuristic. This repositioning has been in response to changing watch technology, such as the introduction of digital and quartz analog watches by competitors, and changing consumer tastes).
- *Cost reductions*: New products that provide similar performance at lower costs (replacement of integrated circuits with large-scale integrated circuits and very large-scale integrated circuits in numerous types of electronic equipment).

Another technique for identifying growth opportunities is market structure profiles (MSP) gap analysis (see Exhibit 1).

In a 1957 article that has come to be viewed as a classic, one author used a 2 x 2 product-market matrix as a frame of reference to outline four basic growth strategies open to a firm: market penetration, market development, product development, and diversification.[3] Others went on to propose more detailed and/or extended versions of the 2 x 2 matrix.[4]

Before a company can effectively translate a marketing/growth strategy into specific action programs, managers must gain broader insights into opportunities for growth. Toward this end, *alternative frameworks* for defining the scope of a business, *matrix representations* of growth opportunities, and *strategy concepts* (including market penetration, market development, product development, and diversification) provide valuable insights (see Exhibit 2). The following real-world examples of marketing strategy in action illustrate effective translation of these growth strategies into action programs.

Exhibit 1.
Growth strategies selection through
market structure profile (MSP) analysis

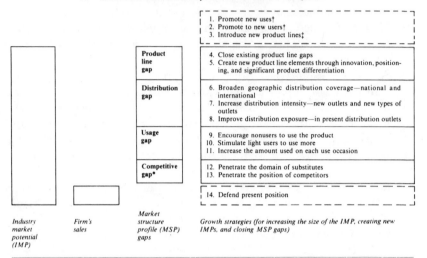

			1. Promote new uses† 2. Promote to new users† 3. Introduce new product lines‡
		Product line gap	4. Close existing product line gaps 5. Create new product line elements through innovation, positioning, and significant product differentiation
		Distribution gap	6. Broaden geographic distribution coverage—national and international 7. Increase distribution intensity—new outlets and new types of outlets 8. Improve distribution exposure—in present distribution outlets
		Usage gap	9. Encourage nonusers to use the product 10. Stimulate light users to use more 11. Increase the amount used on each use occasion
		Competitive gap*	12. Penetrate the domain of substitutes 13. Penetrate the position of competitors
			14. Defend present position
Industry market potential (IMP)	*Firm's sales*	*Market structure profile (MSP) gaps*	*Growth strategies (for increasing the size of the IMP, creating new IMPs, and closing MSP gaps)*

* Competitive gap = IMP (product line gap + distribution gap + usage gap + firm's sales).

† These growth strategies focus on increasing firm's sales through increasing the size of the IMP rather than by closing any of the existing MSP gaps.

‡ This growth strategy effectively creates new IMPs.

Source: Adapted from text (pp. 57–179) and Figures IIa and IIb (p. 59) in John A. Weber, *Growth Opportunity Analysis* (Reston, Virginia: Reston Publishing, 1976).

MARKETING STRATEGY IN ACTION

Market penetration, market development, and product development strategies are closely identified with the functional area of marketing. Market and product managers, the marketing managers, and other marketing personnel generally identify, evaluate, develop, and implement market strategies. Diversification and growth strategies, on the other hand, are more corporate in character, and decisions relating to them fall within the realm of top management.

MARKET PENETRATION STRATEGIES

Market penetration refers to a firm's attempts to increase sales of its present products in present markets. Possible courses of action include:

- Increasing the number of users (broadening the customer base) by attracting users of competitors' brands.
- Broadening the customer base by converting nonusers into users.

Exhibit 2.
Marketing strategies for growth:
An operational perspective

	Present products		New products	
	Growth strategy	*Feasible operational strategies*	*Growth strategy*	*Feasible operational strategies*
Present markets	Market penetration	1. Increasing number of users by: (a) attracting users of competitors' products; (b) converting nonusers into users. 2. Increasing the frequency of purchase. 3. Increasing the average quantity purchased per transaction.	Product development	1. *Product reformulation:* Improving present products with extra ingredients, additives, etc. 2. *Product quality improvement:* Improving the functional performance of present products, e.g., durability, speed, taste, etc. 3. *Product feature additions:* Adding new product features to current product offerings and improving present product features through attempts to modify, substitute, rearrange, or combine existing features, etc. 4. *Product line extension:* Increasing the breadth of the present product lines by: (i) introducing different quality versions of the product; (ii) introducing additional models and sizes, etc. 5. *Product replacement:* Replacing present product offerings with functionally and/or technologically superior offerings. 6. *New product development:* Introducing new products involving (a) related technology or (b) unrelated technology.
New markets	Market development	Increasing the number of users (attracting new users) by: (a) reaching new market segments within present geographic markets; (b) reaching new market segments through regional, national, or international expansion.	Diversification	(A corporate growth strategy—outside the scope of this article.)

- Increasing the frequency of purchase among present users.
- Increasing the average quantity purchased per transaction.

In practice, firms resort to a number of courses of action in order to broaden the customer base and to increase frequency and purchase quantity, such as:

- More effective promotion of present uses.
- Identifying and promoting new uses.
- Promoting more varied use.
- Promoting product use at different times of the day, in different places, and on different occasions.

Promoting New Uses: One firm that has achieved considerable success in promoting new uses for its products is Arm & Hammer. Over the years the company has successfully promoted several new uses of its principal product, Arm & Hammer baking soda, as a refrigerator deodorizer, as a bath additive, as a swimming pool disinfectant, and as a cat litter deodorizer and disinfectant. This company once even sponsored a sweepstakes contest, encouraging consumers to suggest new uses for the product. For Arm & Hammer, promoting new uses was critical to its growth because:

- As more and more women joined the work force, a corresponding decline in home baking occurred.
- The introduction of ready-to-use packaged food products that included baking soda added during the manufacturing process resulted in declining purchases of branded baking soda by households.

The first major new use promoted for Arm & Hammer baking soda was as a refrigerator deodorizer. Since practically every household in the United States owns a refrigerator, the firm was in a position to increase its sales significantly through effective product promotion.

Promoting More Frequent Use or the Use of Larger Quantities: These types of promotions have a number of successful case histories. For example, through a series of television commercials and print advertisements, Arm & Hammer educates consumers to place one carton of Arm & Hammer baking soda in the freezer compartment of the refrigerator and another in the refrigerator compartment, and to replace both boxes every two months. In contrast to the *brand level focus* of Arm & Hammer, the Florida State Citrus Commission's successful repositioning of orange juice as an ideal drink for any time of the day and not just during breakfast time illustrates effective exploitation of use frequency as related to growth opportunities at the *product class level.*

Promoting Product Use at New Times: After realizing that sales at lunchtime accounted for only 15% to 18% of its total revenue (compared to the fast-food restaurant industry average of 35%), Pizza Hut focused on increasing its share of the growing multibillion-dollar lunchtime market. Research studies indicated that customers like to eat pizza for lunch, provided they could get it quickly. This revealed a market opportunity. In response, the company developed equipment for quick preparation of personal-size pizzas for the lunchtime market. Following favorable test-market results, Pizza Hut then undertook a massive operation to redesign kitchens in Pizza Hut restaurants and to hire and train personnel. Further, in order to lend credibility to its claim that customers could eat pizza for lunch without having to wait, the company developed an advertising campaign around the theme "five-minute guarantee." Broadcast and print advertisements assured customers that if their order for a personal-size pan pizza was not served within five minutes, they would receive a coupon redeemable for a free personal-size pizza.[5]

Market Penetration—Problems and Challenges: Although firms can realize sizeable increases in sales and profits by identifying and promoting new uses, this can be a time-consuming, frustrating process, as illustrated by the case of Lysol brand disinfectant spray. Lysol has benefited considerably over the years through effective promotion of new uses. Over a number of years, starting in 1966, the manufacturers of Lysol and the Federal Trade Commission (FTC) were involved in an argument concerning the truthfulness of its new-use promotion that spraying Lysol helps prevent the spread of the common cold. Finally, in 1974, Lysol agreed to stop its flu ads and to cease making claims that Lysol might also prevent colds, throat infections, or other upper-respiratory diseases. However, the company did not stop its research. Lysol funded research at a leading medical school involving deliberate infection of college students with the common cold. Test groups of students with colds were asked to handle coffee cups, plastic bathroom tiles, telephones, and other items. A second test group of students were asked to handle those very same objects and then to rub their eyes and noses. By constructing a variety of such experiments and documenting the results, Lysol presented evidence to the FTC indicating that spraying Lysol on telephones, doorknobs, bathroom sinks and taps, and other household surfaces helps reduce the spread of the common cold. In 1983, with FTC approval, Lysol once again started airing television commercials promoting the use of Lysol in households to prevent the spread of the common cold.[6]

MARKET DEVELOPMENT STRATEGIES

Market development refers to a firm's attempts to increase sales of its present products by tapping new markets. This is generally accomplished by using two broad approaches:

- Reaching new market segments (customer groups) in present geographic markets.
- Reaching new customer groups through regional, national, or international geographic expansion.

Reaching New Customer Groups in Present Geographic Markets: When first introduced in 1979, 3M's Post-it Note Pads (the yellow stick-on note pads) were primarily targeted at the institutional market (office supplies). In 1984, as part of its market development efforts, 3M introduced Post-it Note Pads in a variety of colors targeted at the consumer market. Commensurate with the market development strategy, the product is currently being distributed through drug, discount, hardware, and grocery stores, and promoted through mass media.[7]

Aggressive pursuits of market development-related growth opportunities is an industry-wide phenomenon in certain product categories. For instance, M&M/Mars, Hershey Foods Corp., Nestle Co., and other candy marketers target some of their brands specifically at the adult market in the 18-34 age group. Besides continuously striving to improve their market position in their traditional market segments (children and teenagers), candy marketers in recent years have been targeting a sizeable portion of their effort toward this large group of young adults who, according to research studies, are more fond of candy than their parents and grandparents were.[8]

Reaching New Users Through Geographic Market Expansion: The case of Heineken beer is among the numerous case histories of successful development of new geographic markets for consumer products. Although Heineken ranks only fourth worldwide among brewers, it is the most international of brewers and has licenses or distribution in more than 150 countries. With few exceptions, Heineken beer is brewed to look the same and taste the same nearly everywhere and is positioned as a high-class beer worth the extra cost.

However, Heineken develops separate advertising campaigns for each country, taking into consideration the cultural differences and the diversity of the markets. In the United States, its advertising is designed to capitalize on America's fascination with high-quality imports. Heineken is positioned as a foreign status symbol—the Rolls-Royce of beers. In France, its advertising is designed to entice a nation of wine drinkers to drink more beer. In Italy, since beer is drunk most often with food, the advertising campaign is designed to sell Heineken as a drink for occasions that Italians don't normally associate with beer. In Britain, Heineken's marketing strategy is guided by the view that most beer-drinking Britons wouldn't respond favorably to the high class, exclusive image that the company carefully cultivates in other countries. Hence, it makes its beer with less alcohol than normal to match competitive local brews and promotes Heineken as a distinctive yet standard-price beer. Interestingly, in most parts of the world Heineken is promoted as an upscale beer for the upper crust, but in its home country, The Netherlands, the brand is promoted as a standard-price beer for everyone.[9]

Market Development—Problems and Challenges: Promoting present products to new market segments may at times present seemingly insurmountable barriers as illustrated by the case of Gerber brand baby foods. The company is aware that a sizeable number of people in the 15 to 22 age bracket are closet users of Gerber brand baby food. Once the company mailed a free sample of Gerber's Dutch apple dessert together with a free coupon for a second bottle of Gerber's dessert to 30,000 readers of teenage magazines. Of the coupons mailed, about half were redeemed, attesting to the existence of a latent market for the product. Encouraged by the results, the firm pressed ahead with its efforts to penetrate the teenage market by using a print advertising campaign in which a youthful model says to her friend, "The secret's out—Gerber isn't just for babies." Despite its best efforts, however, the company has not been successful in its attempts to promote social acceptance of consumption of baby foods by teenagers in public. An advertising agency executive associated with the task of developing the teenage market for Gerber products reportedly remarked, "The difficult part is to play down the [Gerber] name as much as possible while guaranteeing Gerber quality and yet getting people off the hook for eating baby food.[10]

A firm's attempts to grow through geographic market development can be stunted in the face of formidable and entrenched competitors. In 1963, Procter & Gamble acquired Folgers, a regional coffee company. Until 1977 Folgers was available in only 70% of the United States. When Procter & Gamble decided to expand its market coverage to all of the United States, it supported its market development strategy with massive advertising and sales promotion. In response, General Foods, the industry leader, which derives 40% of its total sales from coffee, stepped up its effort to defend its share. Over a four-year period, General Foods increased its advertising expenditures on coffee from $38.4 million in 1977 to $107.3 million in 1980. During the same period, Procter & Gamble's advertising expenditure on coffee is estimated to have risen from $14 million to $51.4 million. As of 1981, General Foods had 42% of U.S. coffee sales, the same proportion it had in 1977. Although Procter & Gamble increased its share of U.S. coffee sales from 15% in 1977 to 21% in 1981, it has been reported that the market share gain was not at the expense of General Foods, but of other firms. [11]

The problems confronting a company striving for growth through international market development can be even more formidable. For instance, Anheuser-Busch Co., the largest brewer in the United States, has met with mixed results in its international diversification efforts. Although the firm has successfully penetrated the Canadian, Japanese, Israeli, and British markets with its Budweiser brand beer, it has not been successful in its attempts to cultivate the French and West German markets. In addition, the company has been entangled in a legal battle with a Czechoslovakian brewer that claims an exclusive right to use the Budweiser name in Britain and several other European countries, including France. Courts have ruled that both companies could use the name in Britain. The company's entry into the British market is also reported to have been delayed by nearly four years due to its unsuccessful effort to link up with Britain's Allied Breweries Ltd. Anheuser-Busch finally joined forces with Whatney Mann in December 1983. [12]

Campbell Soup Company's unsuccessful attempt to penetrate the Brazilian market highlights the social and cultural barriers a firm faces in the international market development arena. In-depth interviews by company researchers are reported to have revealed that yhe Brazilian housewife felt that she was not fulfilling her role as a homemaker if she served her family a soup she could not call her own. Research also revealed that Brazilian housewives seemed to prefer dehydrated powdered soup, marketed by Campbell's competitors, because they could use it as a soup starter but still add their own flair and ingredients. [13]

PRODUCT DEVELOPMENT STRATEGIES

Product development refers to a firm's attempts to grow by selling new products to its present customers, or improved versions of its present products to its present customers. As detailed in Exhibit 2, the following action possibilities constitute the major product development strategies:

- *Product reformulation*: Making improvements in present products, such as using better ingredients, additives, and so forth.
- *Product quality improvement*: Improving the durability and reliability of present products, for example.
- *Product feature additions*: Building new features into present products.
- *Product line extension*: Broadening the product line by introducing additional sizes, models, and so forth or different-quality versions of present products.
- *Product replacement*: Replacing product offerings with functionally or technologically superior offerings.
- *New product development*: Introducing new products in present markets that are either related to or unrelated to present products.

Product Reformulation Strategy: This appears to be the most pervasive product strategy as well as the strategy of first resort in most industries. For instance, the laundry detergent industry is replete with examples of the introduction of Brand X, followed by the introduction of improved Brand X, then by new-improved Brand X, and finally by new Brand X with additives. A case in point—Bold laundry detergent has been reformulated with the addition of a fabric softener and repositioned as Bold 3, a laundry detergent that cleans, softens, and fights static. Cheer laundry detergent underwent a similar product reformulation a couple of years ago and was relaunched as new all-temperature Cheer.

Apparently, many of the product reformulations of Campbell Soup Company have been guided by the principle that all of its products, old and new, must appeal to health-conscious and sophisticated consumers. For example, in an attempt to appeal to the more discriminating palates of this target market, Campbell reformulated its Swanson's TV dinners by replacing soggy French fries with more upscale food items.[14]

Not all product reformulations are based on such careful deliberations, however. Neither are they viewed favorably by industry observers. Commenting on the introduction of gel versions of Crest and Colgate brand toothpastes, a *Wall Street Journal* article noted that "the new introductions won't make teeth whiter nor prevent cavities any better than those manufacturers' current offerings."[15] Nevertheless, such product reformulations and extension strategies are quite common in packaged consumer goods industries. (In a sense, the introduction of gel versions of Crest and Colgate were defensive moves by the concerned firms in response to inroads made by competing gel-type toothpastes such as Aim.)

Many of these industries are characterised by marginal or diminishing differences between competing brands and the absence of any significant technological breakthroughs or improvements in recent times. For instance, fluoride, once the most important feature to toothpaste buyers, is now found in practically every brand of toothpaste. This leaves marketers with little choice but to attempt to gain market share through minor changes in such areas as product formulation, appearance, and packaging, or flavor. The small percentage of new product introductions that succeed in the marketplace is another reason firms attempt to breathe new life into their products through product reformulation.

Product Quality Improvement Strategy: A firm can strive to improve quality in a number of ways:

- Performance—primary product characteristics.
- Conformance—match with specifications.
- Reliability—frequency of failure.
- Durability—speed of repair if necessary.
- Aesthetics—fit and finish.[16]

Besides focusing on improvements that relate to intrinsic product quality, a firm should also pay attention to improving perceived product quality, as Avis did with its memorable campaign, "We're number two; we try harder." Perceived product quality is a function of intrinsic product quality as well as of a number of intangibles such as corporate or brand image and reputation and the effectiveness of a firm's promotional effort (advertising, personal selling, sales promotion, and publicity) in communicating superior product quality. A firm can substantially benefit by pursuing a strategy of quality improvement if product quality can be improved, the improvement in quality is visible and can be effectively communicated to the consumer, and there are enough buyers interested in superior quality.[17]

Nevertheless, the extent to which a firm can attract competitors' customers and gain market share through pursuit of a quality improvement strategy (or for that matter, any marketing strategy) depends on the effectiveness of the counter marketing strategies and support programs of its competitor(s), as illustrated by the Heinz versus Hunt's ketchup case history. For years promotions for Heinz ketchup, the market leader, used comparative advertisements to reinforce the message that Heinz was the richest and thickest brand of ketchup in the market. More importantly, the rules of competition in the ketchup business were set by Heinz, by establishing thickness as the most salient product attribute. Hunt's, the market challenger, assigned two full-time researchers the task of developing a ketchup as thick as or thicker than Heinz. Rewarded with success in its research efforts, Hunt's went on the offensive. In advertisements using a celebrity spokesperson, Hunt's claimed, "You can't buy a thicker ketchup than Hunt's. So why pay more for Heinz?" In response, Heinz discontinued its comparative advertisements emphasizing thickness. Instead, it once again changed the rules of the game by introducing squeezable plastic bottles. Besides highlighting the advantages of the squeezable plastic bottle, current Heinz advertisements focus on taste and claim that in taste tests consumers prefer Heinz three times more often than competitors' brands.[18]

Product Feature Additions Strategy: A strategy of feature improvement aims at adding new features to enhance a product's versatility, safety, or convenience. Developments in practically every industry are replete with illustrations of successful product feature improvement strategies.

Although feature improvements can easily be imitated by competitors, certain advantages accrue to the firm which is the first to introduce new features:

- It brings the company free publicity.
- It helps generate enthusiasm and build morale among the sales force, distributors, wholesalers, and retailers.
- It helps the firm build an image of an innovator, trendsetter, and industry leader.
- It helps attract certain customer groups who tend to patronize brands that offer the most features and the most up-to-date features.
- Features can be added or dropped quickly without incurring considerable expense, or can be made optional.[19]

A comparison of the features contained in the first videocassette recorder introduced in 1976 by Sony Corporation with its most recent offering or those of its competitors, or for that matter, a comparison of any ten-year-old consumer durable good with its contemporary counterpart, serves to highlight the importance of the feature addition strategy to manufacturers of consumer durable goods.

Product Line Extension Strategy: Product line or variety extensions are routinely achieved in a number of ways: introduction of new sizes (super economy size toothpaste); forms (deodorant in liquid, powder, spray, and stick forms); composition (regular Head & Shoulders shampoo and Head & Shoulders shampoo with conditioners); flavor (Jello gelatin which originally started with six flavors is now available in more than a dozen flavors); package (HI-C fruit-flavored drinks in glass bottles, paper or metal containers); and variety (shampoo for dry, normal, and oily hair) are just some of the feasible courses of actions.

A recent case history that stands apart from these and other traditional product line extension strategies is Chesebrough-Pond's introduction of Aziza brand nail polishing pen. The fast-drying nail polish in a pen is viewed by some industry watchers as a true breakthrough in a business where me-too products are the rule. The numerous problems and challenges that had to be surmounted before the line extension became a reality are described at length in a *Business Week* article.[20]

In most industries, product proliferation (due to extensive recourse to product line extension strategies) has reached the point of offering U.S. consumers a range of choice unsurpassed in other parts of the world. Campbell's canned soup, for instance, is available in over 40 major varieties and numerous subvarieties in each major variety. For example, the firm offers more than a dozen different types of chicken soup alone. Similarly, smokers in the United States, whose number is estimated at 50 million plus, have more than 260 styles of cigarettes to choose from; these differ with respect to flavor, tar, length, package, and positioning. Marlboro, the best-selling cigarette in the United States, comes in six styles; Kool, in ten; and Newport, in eight. The high costs involved in introducing and popularizing a new brand name are reported to be one of the major considerations influencing manufacturers to introduce variations of their present brands. However, product proliferation has not slowed the pace of introduction of new brands significantly. Cigarette manufacturers justify the risk of new brand introductions on the grounds that a percent share of the market is equivalent to $170 million in revenues and that a new brand needs only a 0.5% share to be considered a success.[21]

In general, dominant firms within the industry view product variety extensions as a means to maintain or increase market share and an indispensable tool in the fierce struggle for supermarket shelf space. On the other hand, low market share firms within the industry and potential new entrants tend to view the line extension strategy of dominant firms as a calculated strategy to corner supermarket shelf space, keep out rival brands, and protect their near-monopoly position.

Industry observers of the marketing strategies pursued by most packaged consumer products manufacturers have been critical of the growing trend toward excessive product proliferation. It has even been speculated that the average consumer, who is unlikely to be interested in product variety beyond a point, is being forced to pay for the cost of endless product proliferation in numerous packaged consumer product categories in the form of higher prices on all products manufactured and marketed by the concerned firms. Unfortunately, even in industries where product proliferation appears to have reached and gone beyond reasonable limits (in view of the risks involved), firms have not shown great initiative to cut back on proliferation by eliminating some of the brands—and sizes, shapes, forms, flavors, scents, colors, and so forth—within specific brands.[22]

Product Replacement Strategy: One of the most effective strategies to maintain a leadership position is for a firm to introduce new products that are superior to its present product offerings. Often, innovative firms make their own products obsolete by replacing them with technologically, functionally, or aesthetically superior products rather than waiting for their competitors to do so. In most industries a strategy of innovative obsolescence is crucial to sales growth and sustained profitability. Gillette's successful introduction of the Trac II twin blade razor as a replacement for its conventional single blade razor, and its subsequent introduction of the Atra razor with a pivot head as a partial replacement for Trac II razors, illustrates effective implementation of product replacement strategy.

New Product Development Strategy: Product innovation is universally recognized as a strategy for building market share in mature as well as expanding markets. According to a Booz, Allen, & Hamilton survey of corporate executives and product managers of *Fortune* 1000 companies, managers expect new products to fuel industry sales and profit growth during the 1980s to an even greater extent than during the 1970s. The contribution of new products to sales growth is expected to increase by one-third, and the percentage of company profits accounted for by new products is expected to increase by 40%.[23]

Bias Toward New Versus Present Products: Firms have to guard against the specter of excessive preoccupation with existing products or with new product development, leading to a neglect of the other area. Managing present products, developing new products, and deleting unprofitable products are critical to effective product management. On one hand, the huge outlays required to introduce new products and the small percent of new products that succeed in the marketplace only highlight the need to exploit the growth and profit potential of present products to the fullest extent. Nevertheless, the Booz, Allen & Hamilton study previously cited, and numerous other studies highlight the need for continued efforts at new product development.[24]

Often, a successful new product can amply compensate for the effort, time, resources, and risk involved in new product development. A case in point, Procter & Gamble's introduction of Pampers brand disposable diapers that barely existed yesterday, but that few can live without today or tomorrow. Second only to its laundry detergents operations, Procter & Gamble's disposable diaper business accounted for 22% of its earnings and 17% of its sales during 1983.[25] More recently, the market share of its Pampers brand disposable diapers is reported to have declined from a high of 75% a decade ago to less than 33%. Part of the success of its chief competitor, Kimberly-Clark's Huggies brand disposable diaper, is attributed to that company's nationwide introduction of disposable diapers with refastenable tabs ahead of Procter & Gamble.[26]

In reference to neglect of present products, one study notes with concern that some companies show little interest in their present products and fail to fully exploit their sales and profit potential.[27] The authors of this study propose a number of questions as a framework for exploring growth products. (See the ruled insert, Framework for Exploring Growth Products.)

STRATEGY IMPLEMENTATION—A CRITICAL LINK

In face of numerous major advances in the strategy area, reported case histories of failed strategies along with the resultant turmoil in the corporate world have led to considerable disenchantment with contemporary analytical

Table 2.
Framework for Exploring Growth Opportunities

Use focus: Are there other potential uses for the product? It has been reported that a 3M Company scientist trying to develop a super-strong adhesive ended up with one that would not stick very well. The scientist's continued quest to identify a potential use for the adhesive developed led to the ultimate introduction of Post-it Notes, the popular yellow stick-on note pads.[1]

Market focus: Can a broader target market be developed for the product? Johnson & Johnson has been quite successful in its attempts to market its baby oil, baby powder, and baby shampoo to adults.

Is there a market for the unused by-products of the firm? Several lumber companies are also in the kitty litter business.

Is there a social trend that can be exploited? Juice Works, a new line of children's drinks introduced in 1984 by Campbell Soup Company is made entirely out of natural fruit juices and without added sugar, but yet is sweet tasting. Juice Works is designed to appeal to the growing market of health-conscious and sophisticated consumers.[2]

Promotion focus: Is the product a generic item that can be branded? The success of Butterball brand turkey, Perdue brand chicken, and Sunkist brand oranges attest to the feasibility of this strategy.

Is the product category underadvertised? The chocolate chip cookie business was, prior to the entry of Frito-Lay and Procter & Gamble.[3]

Is there a more compelling way for promoting the product? The sales of Procter & Gamble's Pampers brand diapers are reported to have substantially increased after a change in benefit emphasis from convenience to keeping the baby dry and happy. However, as noted earlier, Pampers has been losing share in recent years due to the success of Kimberly-Clark's Huggies brand disposable diapers with refastenable tabs. In addition, the lack of adequate differentiation between Procter & Gamble's Luvs and Pampers brands and the resultant cannibalization, is also reported to have contributed to the share decline being experienced by Pampers.[4]

Can the brand's disadvantages be turned into advantages? Smucker's brand jelly has successfully exploited this approach—"with a name like Smucker's, it has to be good."

Channel focus: Is there scope to market the product through new or unconventional channels of distribution? L'eggs was the first brand of pantyhose to be distributed through supermarkets. It should, however, be noted that Hanes Corp. has not been successful in its attempts to pursue a similar strategy in the marketing of cosmetics.[5]

Price focus: Can profits and sales volume be increased by lowering prices? Texas Instruments' dominance in the electronic pocket calculators business and Black and Decker's dominance of the hand-held electric tools market is generally attributed to their effective use of experience curve based pricing strategies. (It has been observed in a number of industries that costs fall with cumulative experience. In industries where a significant portion of the total cost can be reduced, a firm can gain a cost advantage by pursuing a strategy geared to accumulate experience faster than competitors. This strategy implies that a firm that prices its products to achieve the larger market share will have the largest cumulative experience as well, and hence, the lowest unit cost.)

REFERENCES

1. *Business Week*, "3M's Aggressive New Consumer Drive."
2. *Fortune*, "Eight Big Masters of Innovation."
3. Ann M. Morrison, "Cookies Are Frito-Lay's New Bag," *Fortune*, 9 August 1982, 64-67; *Business Week*, "The Monster That Looms Over Cookie Makers," 8 August 1983, 89.
4. John Koten, "For P&G's Rivals."
5. Bill Abrams, "Hanes Finds L'eggs Methods Don't Work With Cosmetics," *The Wall Street Journal*, 3 February 1983, 27.

approaches to strategic market planning, and the strategy prescriptions based on such analyses. For instance, based on a reassessment of the 33 strategies described in *Business Week* during the years 1979 and 1980, it has been reported that 19 failed, ran into trouble, or were abandoned, and only 14 could be considered successful. A key factor attributed to 14 of the 19 failed strategies was wrong assumptions about the business environment—ranging from interest rates to competitors' strategies.[28]

Thus, there is a growing realization among strategy researchers, strategy consultants and others that strategy formulation and implementation are

Exhibit 3.
Interdependence of strategy formulation and implementation

Strategy formulation	Strategy implementation	Remarks
1. Excellent (Appropriate strategy)	Excellent	The firm has done all that it could to assure the success of the strategy and realization of set objectives.
2. Excellent (Appropriate strategy)	Poor	Poor implementation often hampers the success of an otherwise sound strategy. Failure in the marketplace may be further accelerated when management loses faith in the soundness of its present strategy and chooses to change it.
3. Poor (Inappropriate strategy)	Excellent	Excellent execution can make up for deficiencies in strategy and provide management time to identify and correct strategic weaknesses. However, in certain situations, good implementation can hasten ultimate failure in the marketplace.
4. Poor (Inappropriate strategy)	Poor	Failure is likely to be attributed to the more visible poor implementation, and the soundness of the strategy may remain largely unquestioned. A firm might end up courting repeated failures by devising better ways to execute an inappropriate strategy.

Source: Adapted from Thomas V. Bonoma, *Managing Marketing: Text, Cases and Readings* (New York: Free Press 1984), 3-13.

closely intertwined and that major shortcomings in either area are likely to affect the overall success of a strategy.

As indicated in Exhibit 3, poor implementation can hamper the success of an otherwise brilliantly conceived strategy. Likewise, the implementation skills of a company can make up for deficiencies in strategy and provide time for management to identify and correct strategic weaknesses.[29] Highlighting the importance of strategy implementation, one author notes that "just as there are structural strengths and weaknesses that contribute to a firm's success or failure, there are implementation strengths that contribute to differences in firm performance."[30]

One study indicates that at least three organizational factors must be considered in the context of strategy implementation: structure, implementation process, and leadership skills.[31] Thus, structuring an organization consists of a sequence of steps and activities including: defining the tasks that must be performed, assigning responsibility for carrying out these tasks, allocating resources, coordinating the actions of individuals and groups responsible for strategy implementation, and ensuring timely feedback of relevant information to facilitate corrective decision making.

The authors of this same study note that a strategic change can either be implemented by a *forcing process* (a directive is issued to the employees of the organization detailing the actions they are required to carry out) or by a *participative process* (employees contribute ideas, goals, and implementation methods). The relative effectiveness of these two processes and their appropriateness in particular situations are contingent on a number of factors including organizational climate, employee commitment to the organization and its goals, and the extent to which the new strategy differs from the present strategy.[32]

Yet another factor relevant in the context of strategy implementation is the leadership style used by the manager. The cognitive style, or the way the manager defines and solves strategy-related problems, the ability to negotiate and bargain with people over whom the manager has no formal authority, and other leadership abilities of the manager affect the effectiveness of strategy implementation.[33]

CONCLUSION

In most large firms, there are three distinct levels of strategy: (1) corporate-level strategy, concerned with questions about what businesses to compete in; (2) business-level strategy, concerned with how to compete in a particular business; and (3) functional-area strategy, concerned with how to get the most productivity from resources employed in various functional areas. A number of conceptual schemes and analytical techniques have been proposed to aid managers in formulating strategy at these three levels. Notwithstanding major advances in the area of strategy formulation, it is apparent that the right strategy alone cannot help a company move forward. Managers have begun to realize their need for an integrated theory of management that assigns strategy in its proper place and also considers other factors that have to be managed.[34]

Indicative of the metamorphosis that is taking place in the strategy area is the 7-S framework proposed by McKinsey & Company, a leading management consulting firm. The 7-S framework is based on the premise that it is not just strategy that moves a corporation forward, but a number of factors. These factors, the seven S's—strategy, structure, system, staff, skills, and superordinate goals—supposedly interact with one another and with the firm's environment to determine how the company moves.[35]

Also indicative of this trend is the increased emphasis on strategy implementation at the corporate level, the business-unit level, and the functional level.[36] Clearly, the era characterized by an all-consuming focus on strategy formulation is giving way to a new era that emphasizes the need for a balanced perspective of strategy formulation and strategy implementation.

REFERENCES

1. See for example, Thomas J. Peters and Robert H. Waterman, Jr., *In search of Excellence: Lessons from American's Best-Run Companies* (New York: Harper & Row, 1982).
2. Booz, Allen & Hamilton, *New Products Management for the 1980s* (New York: Booz, Allen & Hamilton, Inc., 1982).
3. H. Igor Ansoff, "Strategies for Diversification," *Harvard Business Review* (September-October 1957): 113-124.
4. See for example, David T. Kollat, Roger D. Blackwell, and James F. Robeson, *Strategic Marketing* (New York: Holt, Rinehart and Winston, 1972), 21-23.
5. *Marketing News*, "Pizza Hut Asserts Presence in Lunch Market," 29 April 1983, 4.
6. Bill Abrams, "Lysol's Maker Keeps Fighting FTC Over Advertising Claims," *The Wall Street Journal*, 24 February 1983, 29.
7. *Business Week*, "3M's Aggressive New Consumer Drive," 16 July 1984, 114-122.
8. *The Wall Street Journal*, "Candy Makers Step Up Fight Over America's Sweet Tooth," 13 June 1985, 29.
9. Richard L. Hudson, "Competition Gets Scrappy in Heineken's Beer Markets," *The Wall Street Journal*, 24 August 1984, 24.
10. Gail Bronson, "Baby Food It Is, But Gerber Wants Teenagers to Think of It As a Dessert," *The Wall Street Journal*, 17 July 1981, 29.
11. Anne Mackay Smith, "Both General Foods and P&G Look Like Coffee War Victors," *The Wall Street Journal*, 29 October 1981, 25.

12. *Business Week*, "Bud is Making a Splash in the Overseas Market," 22 October 1984, 52-53; *The Wall Street Journal*, "Anheuser-Busch Tries to Find New Markets as Drinking Declines," 28 March 1985, 1, 22.
13. *Business Week*, "Campbell Soup Fails to Make It to the Table," 12 October 1981, 66.
14. *Fortune*, "Eight Big Masters of Innovation," 15 October 1984, 76.
15. Bill Abrams, "Warring Toothpaste Makers Spend Millions Luring Buyers to Slightly Altered Products," *The Wall Street Journal*, 21 September 1981, 33.
16. David A. Garvin, "Product Quality: An Important Strategic Weapon," *Business Horizons*, March-April 1984, 40-43.
17. Philip Kotler, *Marketing Management: Analysis, Planning and Control*, 5th ed. (Englewood Cliffs, NJ: Prentice-Hall, 1984), 368.
18. Betsy Morris, "Thwack! Smack! Sounds Thrill Makers of Hunt's Ketchup," *The Wall Street Journal*, 27 April 1984, 1, 17.
19. Kotler, *Marketing Management*, 368.
20. *Business Week*, "How Chesebrough-Pond's Put Nail Polish in a Pen," 8 October 1984, 196-200.
21. Margaret Loeb, "Giving Smokers Added Value Is Tobacco Firm's Latest Idea," *The Wall Street Journal*, 30 August 1983, 27.
22. Kent MacDougall, "Market-Shelf Proliferation—Public Pays," *Los Angeles Times*, 27 May 1979, 1, 34.
23. Booz, Allen & Hamilton, *New Products Management*.
24. Ibid.
25. Faye Rice, "Trouble at Procter & Gamble," *Fortune*, 5 March 1984, 70.
26. John Koten, "For P&G's Rivals, the New Game Is to Beat the Leader, Not Copy It," *The Wall Street Journal*, 1 May 1985, 31.
27. *The Wall Street Journal*, "Ten Ways to Restore Vitality to Old, Worn-Out Products," 18 February 1982, 23.
28. *Business Week*, "The New Breed of Strategic Planners," 17 September 1984, 62-68.
29. Thomas V. Bonoma, *Managing Marketing: Text, Cases and Readings* (New York: Free Press, 1984).
30. Michael Procter, *Competitive Strategy: Techniques for Analyzing Industries and Competitors* (New York: Free Press, 1980).
31. Frank T. Paine and Carl R. Anderson, *Strategic Management* (New York: Dryden Press, 1983), 50-52.
32. Ibid.
33. Ibid.
34. Walter Kiechel III, "Corporate Strategists Under Fire," *Fortune*, 27 December 1982, 34-39.
35. Robert H. Waterman, Jr., "The Seven Elements of Strategic Fit," *Journal of Business Strategy*, Winter 1982, 69-73.

36. Lawrence G. Hrebiniak and Willian F. Joyce, *Implementing Strategy*, (New York: Macmillan 1984); James M. Higgins, *Strategy: Formulation, Implementation and Control*, (New York: Dryden Press, 1985).

P. Rajan Varadarajan is professor of marketing at Texas A&M University in College Station, Texas.

3.
PRODUCT QUALITY: AN IMPORTANT STRATEGIC WEAPON

David A. Garvin

Superior product quality has been one of the keys to Japanese success in American markets. Many American corporations are now beginning to recognize the competitive importance of quality. The author defines product quality and explains how it can be used in positioning and selling products.

For many years, the experience curve has dominated discussions of competitive strategy. High production volumes and low costs have been viewed as the keys to financial success. Recently, however, new strategies have become popular, bringing with them a surge of interest in the competitive implications of product quality.

Undoubtedly, some of this interest has been stirred by the success of Japanese products in this country. Many of them have quickly gained large market shares by offering superior quality and reliability. The outstanding financial performance of several American firms regarded as quality leaders—Boeing, Caterpillar Tractor, and Hewlett-Packard are three obvious examples—has also been effective in focusing attention on this area.[1]

Yet relatively little is known about the use of superior quality as a competitive weapon. The term itself is the source of much confusion: Does high quality imply Rolex watches and Steinway pianos, or do Toyota automobiles and Polaroid cameras also qualify? A better understanding of the term is necessary before strategic issues can be addressed.

TRADITIONAL APPROACHES

Quality is one of those slippery concepts, easy to visualize and yet exasperatingly difficult to define. Traditionally, one of three approaches has been followed:

Quality is conformance to requirements.[2] According to this view, product quality is synonymous with meeting specifications. A well-made Mercedes is a high-quality automobile, and so is a well-made Chevette. The critical issue is whether the final product conforms to the design and performance standards that have been set for it, and not the content or validity of those standards.

Quality is fitness for use.[3] This approach is more user-oriented. Stripped to the essentials, it boils down to the claim that "quality lies in the eyes of the beholder." Different users have different needs, and to the extent that a product is designed and manufactured to meet those needs, it is of high quality. For business travelers, the highest quality airline is usually the one with the best record of on-time arrivals and departures; for vacationers, it may be the one with the finest food, the quickest in-flight service, or the most interesting movies.

Quality is innate excellence.[4] This definition reflects the belief that though styles and tastes change, there is something enduring about works of high quality. They provide a standard against which other products are judged. Excellence, according to this view, is both absolute and universally recognizable; whatever it consists of—and the writers in this camp are distressingly vague on that point—we all know it when we see it. Michelangelo may not be your favorite sculptor, but it's hard to deny the quality of his work.

Each of these definitions is helpful in some respects but is lacking in others. The first, for example, minimizes the performance differences among products. Somehow it doesn't seem right to say that a Mercedes and a Chevette are of equivalent quality; the former, after all, offers a smoother ride, and handles better at high speeds. The second definition is equally incomplete. Quality isn't entirely relative, for there is wide agreement that the more consumers get of certain product attributes, the better. Durability is a good example —who, after all, would prefer a washing machine that lasts only five years to one that lasts fifteen? Nor is the third definition of much help. While it recognizes the universal aspects of quality, it is lacking in specifics. To argue that the hallmarks of quality are "intensive effort" and "honesty of purpose" tells us little about how to produce it.[5] What is needed is a syntheses of the above approaches, based upon more careful separation of the various elements of product quality.

The accompanying list of eight dimensions of product quality provides such a framework. Each dimension is self-contained and distinct, for a product can be ranked high on one dimension while being low on another. Quality is not a single, recognizable characteristic; rather, it is multifaceted and appears in many different forms.

ELEMENTS OF EXCELLENCE

First on the list is *performance*, which refers to the primary operating characteristics of a product. For an automobile, these would be traits like

Table 3.
Dimensions of Product Quality

- Performance (primary product characteristics)
- Features ("bells and whistles")
- Reliability (frequency of failure)
- Conformance (match with specifications)
- Durability (product life)
- Serviceability (speed of repair)
- Aesthetics ("fits and finishes")
- Perceived quality (reputation and intangibles)

acceleration, handling, cruising speed, and comfort; for a televsion set, they would include sound and picture clarity, color, and the ability to receive distant stations. While the basic measures of performance for a particular product are usually clear, as are the rankings of competing brands on any one measure of performance, identifying the best (highest quality) brand overall is considerably more difficult. Here, an element of subjectivity enters in, for different groups of users are interested in different performance characteristics. For some, the fastest car is the best; for others, the most comfortable. In this case, quality does lie in the eyes of the beholder.

Much of the same is true of product *features*, the "bells and whistles" that are often added to products to spice them up. Free drinks on a lengthy plane flight, permanent press as well as cotton cycles on a washing machine, and automatic tuners on a color television set are all secondary to the basic product or services being offered. Yet for some consumers, these features imply improved performance, and thus, higher quality.

Reliability and *conformance* are more widely accepted as measures of quality. A reliable product is one that we can count on; the odds of its failing within a specified period are small. Two common measures of reliability are the mean time to first failure (MTFF) and the mean time between failures (MTBF). Conformance, on the other hand, is a measure of consistency: a reflection of how well a product matches up against pre-established specifications. Does it do what it's supposed to do, or are there frequent disappointments? This is an especially important element of service businesses, where incorrect bank statements, lost mail, or delayed airline flights are often cited as examples of deteriorating quality.

Durability, a fifth dimension of quality, is a characteristic of products alone. While services are consumed at the time of purchase, many goods provide a stream of benefits over time. Durability thus reflects the economic or physical life of a product; it is commonly measured by the number of hours, years, or miles that a product can be used before replacement is required.

Both repair frequency and product life are related to the user's primary concern, availability. Consumers are worried not only about a product's breaking down, but also about the elapsed time before service is restored. Product design is also relevant, for some products lend themselves to repair by homeowners or local handymen, while others require the assistance of expensive and hard-to-locate specialists. A product's *serviceability* or speed of repair is therefore an important independent element in maintaining a quality image. For example, Caterpillar Tractor's guarantee that replacement parts will be shipped anywhere in the world within 48 hours has undoubtedly enhanced its reputation for reliability. The product may break down, but you know that it will soon be fixed.

The final two dimensions of quality, *aesthetics* and *perceived quality*, are the most subjective. How a product looks, feels, sounds, tastes, or smells is clearly a matter of personal judgement. That these elements affect buying behavior is certain—witness the attention paid to the superior "fits and finishes" of Japanese automobiles. Perceptions of quality, based on advertising or on the excellence of other products produced by the company, have a similar impact. Both shape first impressions, which are critical in assessing an unknown product. The strong quality image of Maytag's new line of dishwashers—initially based on the performance of its laundry equipment, rather than on any solid evidence of the superior reliability or durability of this particular product—is a perfect example of the "halo effect" in action.

These eight dimensions of quality incorporate all three of the traditional definitions, as well as a number of other elements. In addition to being more inclusive, the framework suggests an important strategic consideration that might otherwise be overlooked: One can compete on quality in a number of different ways.

FINDING THE NICHE

Being the quality leader in a market does not require one to be first on all eight dimensions of quality. In fact, this is seldom possible, unless exorbitant prices are charged. A firm is likely to be more successful in pursuing a strategy of high product quality if it selects a *small number of dimensions on which to compete, and then tailors them closely to the needs of its chosen market.* Consider the following examples:

- Japanese automobiles have succeeded in this country not by offering outstanding performance or safety, but by emphasizing reliability and superior "fits and finishes." Both were sadly neglected by U.S. manufacturers, who were more interested in luxury, features, and the regular introduction of new models.
- Steinway & Sons, the piano maker, has long been known for the quality of its instruments. All are carefully hand-crafted and offer a distinctive "feel," clarity of sound, and tone. Yamaha, a Japanese competitor, has

taken a different approach: Its emphasis on automation has resulted in an extremely consistent product, with few variations in workmanship or performance. Both firms have been quite successful, despite their radically different ideas about product quality.

* Among manufacturers of pocket calculators, Hewlett-Packard stands out for its features and advanced performance. Its appeal has been primarily to scientists, engineers, and other sophisticated users, a strategy requiring careful attention to product design and close monitoring of market needs. Texas Instruments, a leading competitor, has focused instead on reliable low-cost production; its energies have been more often devoted to process engineering and tight manufacturing control.

The implication of these examples is clear: Firms should carefully define the dimensions of quality on which they hope to compete, and should then focus their energies in that area. Such a choice is necessary because each element of quality imposes different demands on a firm. A company may produce high durability by employing sturdy and oversized components, yet may still suffer from poor conformance if the assembly process is not carefully managed. Proliferating features may interfere with streamlined service, just as an eye-catching design may impede a product's basic performance. While some firms are able to succeed on several of these dimensions at once—Maytag washers are both the longest lasting and the least in need of repair—this need not be true.[6] Of the three most highly rated air conditioners in a recent *Consumer Report* test of product performance, two had excellent reliability, while the third had the highest failure rate in the industry.

Managers, then, need to be more attentive to the nuances of product quality, and more selective in approach. They also need more reliable market information to tell them how good or bad their quality really is. Too often, decisions in this area have been fueled by flimsy assumptions or imprecise data. Many firms *think* they know what quality means in their industry; few have taken the time to survey customers to actually find out. If a company hopes to compete effectively on the quality of its products, a deeper understanding of the consumer's perspective is a necessary first step.

REFERENCES

1. These three firms received the highest rankings on quality in a survey of U.S. corporate reputations. See "Ranking Corporate Reputations," *Fortune*, January 10, 1983: 38.
2. Philip B. Crosby, *Quality Is Free*, (New York: New American Library, 1979): 14-15.
3. J. M. Juran, ed., *Quality Control Handbook*, 3rd. ed. (New York: McGraw-Hill, 1974): 2-2, 2-3, and Corwin D. Edwards, "The Meaning of Quality," *Quality Progress*, October 1968: 36-39.

4. Barbara W. Tuchman, "The Decline of Quality," *New York Times Magazine*, November 2, 1980: 38-41, 104, and Robert M. Pirsig, *Zen and the Art of Motorcycle Maintenance*, (Toronto: Bantam Books, 1974): 184-185, 205-209, 223-224.
5. Tuchman: 39.
6. Jeanne Johnson, "Maytag-ability," *Quality*, January 1983: 16.

David A. Garvin is an assistant professor of Business Administration at the Harvard Business School.

4.
HISTORICAL MILITARY STRATEGY PRINCIPLES ADVOCATED FOR WINNING THE MARKETING WARS

William A. Cohen

In developing marketing strategies for competitive markets, it makes sense to build on concepts formulated by military geniuses of the past. It's not surprising, then, that captains of industry occasionally search military strategy for lessons which can be applied to business operations.

Given man's extensive experience at making war, a considerable body of practical and theoretical knowledge of military strategy exists.

It's not surprising, then, that captains of industry occasionally search military strategy for lessons which can be applied to business operations. For example, a guide to strategy by a 17th Century samurai warrior sold more than 100,000 copies in 1982, making it a business best-seller.

Chinese General Sun Tzu wrote *The Art of War* more than 2,000 years ago, and it still is in print and being studied. But no concept is better-known or more celebrated by military strategists than the principles of war, and those principles have applications for contemporary marketers.

Napoleon said the principles of war have "regulated the great captains" since the beginning of recorded warfare. But those principles have been modified many times, and they vary depending on whose list you're looking at.

The U.S. Army and its counterpart in the United Kingdom acknowledge nine principles, but three of them are not the same. The Soviet Union adheres to five principles, and Sun Tzu cited six.

Even the different branches of the U.S. armed forces adhere to different principles. The U.S. Army switched from the principle of coordination to unity-of-command after the U.S. Air Force gained its independence in 1947, but the Air Force retained the original principle.

To eliminate duplication and include only those principles with applications to marketing strategy, I have developed a list of 12 principles. They are:

39

1. Objective.
2. Initiative.
3. Concentration.
4. Economy-of-force.
5. Maneuver.
6. Unity-of-command.
7. Coordination.
8. Security.
9. Surprise.
10. Simplicity.
11. Flexibility.
12. Exploitation.

1. *Objective.* The principle of objective states every strategy must have an objective, and the objective should be the attainment of a specified and decisive goal.

    The objective should be specified so it is clearly understood by everyone responsible for or participating in its attainment. It should be decisive so the cost of attainment in resources and time is minimized.

2. *Initiative.* This implies action instead of reaction and underscores the advisability of maintaining an offensive attitude to control the time and place of action. Defensive attitudes should be considered temporary expedients which exist until a counteroffensive can be mounted.

3. *Concentration.* Some consider this to be the fundamental concept of all military strategy. It was summarized by Confederate Gen. Nathan Bedford Forrest, who said winning battles was a matter of "getting there firstest with the mostest." In business it means allocating resources to achieve a competitive advantage at a decisive point.

4. *Economy-of-force.* No one can be strong everywhere, and no general or business executive should try. Minimum resources should be allocated to secondary efforts.

5. *Maneuver.* This refers to positioning resources to assist in accomplishing the objective you have set. In military terms it refers to physical positioning, but it also can be applied to economic or psychological factors. It also incorporates the concept of timing.

6. *Unity-of-command.* For every assigned task there is one responsible manager. This ensures unity of effort, which is necessary to get maximum power output from available resources.

7. *Coordination.* This emphasizes cooperation between company organizational units and the integration of tasks in planning the overall strategy, as well as implementing it. It minimizes the dangers of suboptimization while facilitating economy-of-force and concentration.

8. *Security.* You must never let a competitor acquire an unpredicted advantage. Security requires accurate intelligence about the competition

and in-house security, both physical safeguards and guarding information about your capabilities and intentions.

9. *Surprise*. Surprise may emanate from deception, secrecy, variation in methods, innovation, audacity, or speed of action, and it can compensate for inferior resources. Total ignorance of your intentions is not necessary; you merely must be able to accomplish your purpose before the opposition can react effectively.

10. *Simplicity*. Simple, direct plans are necessary because operational conditions and pressures by personnel make even the most simple plan difficult to execute. It needs to be emphasized from the planning stage through execution.

11. *Flexibility*. The maxim is "Everything that can go wrong, will," and alternative objectives are advisable when the original strategy fails. Allow as much as possible for uncertainty by planning in advance alternate solutions to potential problems.

12. *Exploitation*. "Pursue the enemy with the utmost audacity," advised Gen. George S. Patton, and this principle refers to maintaining forward momentum. When winning, don't relax; continue to maintain pressure until success is maximized.

The principles of marketing strategy can be applied in several ways to the practice of marketing, and three examples follow.

A structure comparison/analysis can be used to determine why a campaign succeeded or failed. After a campaign, strategic and tactical actions can be analyzed, and what went wrong and what went right can be described in terms of the principles of marketing strategy.

New strategic concepts can be developed. Most current concepts were developed on the firing line—product differentiation, market segmentation, and positioning. But new strategic concepts can be developed and tested against actual marketing experience.

For example, a study of the principles enumerated here—especially concentration, economy-of-force, and maneuver—might lead to a strategy of taking an indirect approach to a stronger competitor and avoiding head-on competition.

The principles of marketing strategy also can be used to develop operational strategies. One approach might be to develop a weighting system for each campaign and each principle used in decision-making models. Depending on the relative importance in the given situation, a subjective importance-value in points would be assigned to each principle, with the highest value-principles being incorporated into one strategy.

Another way would be to use the principles of marketing as a checklist against which the intended strategy would be compared and modified, if necessary. Some deviance from the principles might occur, but not before an evaluation is made to ensure that the situational justification was sufficient.

The history of warfare and the use of strategic principles traces back at least 7,000 years. In developing strategies for competitive markets, it makes sense to build on concepts formulated by military geniuses of the past. The principles of marketing strategy are an adaptation of prior military strategic thinking which can improve our strategic thinking about marketing.

William A. Cohen is professor of marketing at California State University in Los Angeles.

5.
PACKAGING'S PROPER ROLE IS TO SELL THE PRODUCT

Davis L. Masten

> The role of a package is not merely to hold the product—it is to *sell* the product. Research can help determine which package will be the best sales tool for your product.

Many companies have learned that spending time and money on packaging is one of the best possible investments.

The Kroger stores enjoyed a 200% increase in first-year sales of a private-label cheese product after the package was redesigned.

After Memorex redesigned its audio- and videocassette tape packages, profits increased more than $1 million during the first year. The new package allowed the company to enter previously closed distribution channels.

Since McCormick/Schilling redesigned its gourmet spice line in 1985, it has generated a double-digit increase in sales.

An effective package is never a substitute for a quality product. However, assuming you offer a good price, effective packaging can:

- Enhance the ways consumers think of the product.
- Increase the visibility of the product and the company.
- Reinforce the brand image in the store and at home.
- Retain current customers and attract new ones.
- Enhance the cost effectiveness of the marketing budget.
- Increase the product's competitive edge and profits.

The role of a package is frequently misunderstood; often it is viewed simply as a container to hold a specific amount of a product. The proper role of a package is to sell the product. It is a sales tool that either can attract and motivate customers to buy the product or alienate them.

To be motivating, a package must visually articulate a positive product personality (the total set of ideas and impressions, both rational and emotional, that consumers form about a product).

At the point-of-purchase, the package *is* the product to the consumer. It must deliver a compelling "buy me" message; at home, the package should convey a potent "use me" message.

The degree to which a package delivers a compelling sales message depends on the gestalt of the package—the overall impression it conveys.

However, that gestalt consists of individual components, and all of them must be equally strong. One weak component can undermine the strength of the package. The primary components are:

• The container: Today, consumers demand functional and convenient containers, and are irritated by containers lacking these qualities. Convenient, functional containers are consistently purchased over their inferior competitors.

Some recent examples of winning containers include the Quaker State plastic motor oil bottle, the Heinz squeezable catsup package, the liquid Tide self-draining cap, and the Colgate toothpaste pump.

Innovative designs from the global marketplace—the pump dispenser, aseptic packaging, squeezable and recappable bottles, ultralight plastic, and plastic pouches—demonstrate convenience and cost effectiveness. They are worth studying.

• The elements of the design: Graphics, illustrations, color, typeface logo or symbol, and brand name are package elements; together they communicate the visual message of the package.

Careful design and use of each element is imperative to communicate a message consistent with product objectives as a sales tool.

For example, Scotch transparent-tape packages communicate high quality, functionality, reliability, and value. The familiar Scotch plaid is used in two colors, both of which communicate quality, yet with a subtle distinction. Red communicates quality, green communicates premium quality.

The container is sturdy, reliable, easy-to-use, and disposable. All elements work together to communicate the desired message, and these products dominate the U.S. market.

In many companies, packaging decisions still are made subjectively. If the president of the company or the head of marketing likes a package design, often that design is adopted.

Occasionally, a subjective decision is accurate—the package does function effectively as a marketing tool. Yet, in the majority of the cases, the decision is inaccurate. Few executives can determine whether a package design will effectively sell the product.

For that information, you must go directly to the consumer.

Consumers, not marketers or CEOs, are the target market, and they should drive the evaluating process. Their feedback can tell you the degree of effectiveness of your package in communicating strong favorable associations about the product, and whether the package is visible and readable.

They alone can tell you whether the package will motivate consumers to buy the product. Using their feedback facilitates clear, focused, timely decision-making.

Research can tell whether a package is an effective sales tool and what, if anything, must be done to enhance the package to gain a greater competitive edge.

Few consumers are aware that a package affects their decisions to buy. If asked directly, they will tell you that the cost of the product, its endorsements, and its quality determine their buying decisions.

However, the psychological sensations generated by the package itself are a key determinant in any buying decision, for the consumer transfers those reactions to the product itself.

If the package produces positive sensations such as high quality and good value, the product itself will be perceived as one of high quality and good value. This is called "sensation transference," and a package that evokes positive sensation transference has a significant advantage over competing brands that do not.

To obtain objective data about the psychological sensations generated by a package, you must ask consumers indirect questions.

For example, you might present five package designs for the same product, each with a slightly different logo. You would not ask consumers "Which logo is best?" because the answer would represent only intellectual opinions. Instead, you would ask indirect questions: What is the highest quality product? Which seems to be the best value?

Asking such questions of a representative sample of the marketplace can provide invaluable quantitative data, which, as a basis for deciding packaging issues, greatly enhances the decision making process.

It also significantly increases the probability of choosing a package that will be an effective sales tool, meet your marketing objectives, and increase your profit margins.

Before beginning package modifications or creating a package for a new product, you should do some homework.

First, determine the company's marketing, communications, and product objectives. This should be an interdisciplinary process, with top management, marketers, packaging managers, manufacturing directors, and research and development specialists involved.

Then, with those objectives in mind, begin to formulate a packaging strategy.

Look around for innovative, cost-effective approaches to packaging. Perhaps the product that's been in a glass bottle could be packaged in ultralight plastic instead.

Collect a wide variety of product samples, photographs, or advertisements of products in categories of interest. Focus on the key elements of the products and determine the strengths and weaknesses of each.

Set priorities for communicating your product's personality through package elements, and determine which elements could be acted on immediately.

Determine research questions and develop a strategy for getting the answers from a statistically valid market sample. Test the package's gestalt. Test the elements of the package one by one. Understand the strengths and weaknesses of each. Test the functional aspects and convenience factors of the container.

Define design objectives. Combine all of the information gathered through research and combine it with your company objectives to arrive at design criteria. This will allow your designer to focus on strategic and market needs, and to translate the criteria into alternative designs.

Test those designs against each other to determine quantitatively which will result in maximum sales. Then test the strongest design against the competition.

These research steps take time and cost money, yet, the cost is minimal when compared to the cost involved in product development and advertising, and the benefits are significant.

You will take a package to market that you know has a high sales potential and a high probability of increasing profits.

Davis L. Masten is president of Cheskin & Masten located in Palo Alto, California.

6.

THE CONSEQUENTIALITY INDEX: THE KEY TO MARKETING SUCCESS

George M. Naimark

The Consequentiality Index should determine the nature and extent of all marketing efforts. Its accurate determination helps to invest limited resources where they will do the most good.

The primary goal of all marketing efforts is to effectively communicate to the marketplace the major benefit the customer will get from a given product or service. The Consequentiality Index (CI) is the measure of the true significance of a product or service to the potential customer. It is *not* what the vendor thinks or hopes will be meaningful to the customer; it is, instead, the customer's view of the importance of the selling proposition. The customer determines the CI by positioning the promised benefits in his or her own hierarchy of needs.

As Figure 1 demonstrates, communication begins with the CI but does not end there. The equation in Figure 1 presupposes that all the other business aspects, all those items that are not included in the equation, are in place and

Figure 1.
The Components That Influence Success

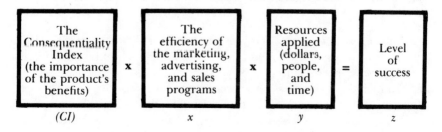

The Consequentiality Index (the importance of the product's benefits)		The efficiency of the marketing, advertising, and sales programs		Resources applied (dollars, people, and time)		Level of success
(CI)	x	*x*	x	*y*	=	*z*

functioning well; that is, that pricing is appropriate, profit adequate, manufacturing timely, distribution effective, and so on.

In effect, the CI should control everything else a company does—and the way it is done. It should be the major initial focus and the subsequent determinant of the nature and extent of all of the marketing efforts. As Figure 2 suggests, the CI actually controls the very quality of our business lives.

Although the traditional goal of a company's research and development efforts is to produce products with the highest possible CI's, this goal is seldom achievable. Unfortunately there is no nontoxic, totally effective, orally administered cancer cure. The more frequent situation is this:

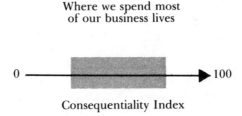

APPRAISING THE CONSEQUENTIALITY INDEX

How can the realistic assessment of a product's CI help a company? The CI, when accurately appraised, can be a substantial aid in developing programs and

Figure 2.
The Influence of the Consequentiality Index

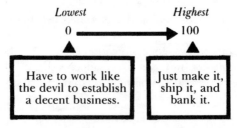

allocating resources. Figure 1 demonstrates the usefulness of the index in the planning process. For example:

- If the CI is very high, x and y can be low and still yield a decent z.
- If the CI is low, x and y must be higher to achieve a healthy z. (Consider alternative investments.)
- An inefficient x requires a stronger y and vice versa.
- If the CI, x, and y are all high, a great z is almost inevitable.
- If the CI and x are low, seriously consider investing y elsewhere.

The CI must be realistically determined, however difficult this may be. It should not be based solely on intuition or instinct.

Market research must almost always be used in making this determination. Although it is less reliable with products that are revolutionary, market research is particularly helpful when the product is a fairly obvious extension of something familiar.

Failure to establish a CI—or significantly misjudging a product's true CI—can be a major cause of failure. It can also lead to inadequate exploitation of a real winner (when, for example, a good product is abandoned because of an inappropriately low CI assessment).

The "emperor's new clothes" syndrome must also be avoided in establishing a CI. That is, early enthusiasm or subsequent substantial investment should not obscure current realities. Even cute puppies can become unsalable dogs. Recognize them for what they are.

Resources are always limited, while the opportunities for their "investment" are essentially unlimited. Therefore, it is important to ask some questions. Are we spending our time, money, energy, creativity, and enthusiasm where it counts most? Or are we dissipating our limited resources on low leverage activities? An inevitable mismatch between available resources and investment opportunities suggests that, while resource allocation decisions are being made continuously, they are not being made thoughtfully. A realistic assessment of the Consequentiality Index can have a positive influence on marketing success.

George M. Naimark is president of Naimark & Barba, Inc., of Cedar Knolls, New Jersey.

7.
GETTING TO KNOW THE CUSTOMER THROUGH QUALITATIVE RESEARCH

Judith Langer

> Qualitative research can provide a company with valuable insights into how consumers view their products or services. It can also provide an early barometer of consumers' changing values and lifestyles.

To say that qualitative research provides a way of learning who a company's customers and prospective customers are is a cliché. This is, as we all know, one of the primary uses of focus groups and in-depth interviews. The initial impetus for many qualitative research studies is the desire to find out about the target group: What kinds of people are they, how do they talk, how do they think, how do they see themselves, how do they live, how do they feel about the product?

In some cases the client already has a quantitative, statistical, demographic profile of customers, but wants to "flesh it out, bring it to life." Beyond knowing users' median age and income, the client cannot picture these people, and therefore does not know how to communicate with them or design products for them. In other cases, there is a total information vacuum, and qualitative research is the first step.

I would like to discuss:

- The emotional, gut-level learning qualitative research offers.
- Where client's resistance lies and how to break through it.
- How to get more from qualitative research to understand the consumer.

THE GUT-LEVEL GRASP

The immediacy of the qualitative research experience provides clients with a gut-level grasp of their customers. I'm talking about deep, broad-ranging, experimental, intuitive insights into who these people really are—beyond a list of their attitudes, words, and behavior. This gut-level grasp can give clients a sense of what is unique about their customers—the self-perceptions, the drives, and the needs that affect everything they do. It is a basic, comprehensive view that allows the client to enter into the customers' experience and world.

Some examples from our research:

• The small-business market is a fast-growing one, now representing a significant proportion of American business. These owners and managers are typically aggressive, dynamic, and informal; they reject neat plans and systems. For them, there is no separation between work and personal life. Their business *is* their life, their employees their family. Addressing them in the same way one would *Fortune 500* corporate managers means failing to communicate or, worse, backfiring.

A print ad for a financial institution addressed to small businesses which we showed in focus groups did not explicitly and immediately say it was talking to small businesses—so respondents *assumed* it wasn't, because they *expect* to be ignored by large financial institutions. Asked why they thought the ad was meant for what one respondent called "the upper echelons" of business, they said the wording was too sophisticated. Further, the illustrations showed people in suits, and no women were in the ad. (Several owners and managers in the group were women.) Verbally and visually, then, the cues for this market missed their target.

• Larger-sized women, our research showed, speak for themselves with sharp, cutting humor as "fat ladies" who could be mistaken for "trees." Criticizing stores for showing only skinny mannequins, one woman said, "There are no fat dummies—except us." Their discomfort and self-dislike is clear, along with their irate, hurt response when anyone *else* views them this way. Understanding this twin embarrassment and struggle for pride is the key to reaching this market.

• In a study of cat owners, women spoke with great affection about their pets, describing them as "members of the family," and relating many fond stories. The brand manager, observing his first groups with cat owners, was astonished. "I had no idea that people loved cats so much," he said afterwards. Because of its firsthand power, qualitative research can bring home a message that other sources of information, even highly credible ones, may not communicate as effectively.

• As part of a larger study, two focus groups were held on money management and financial services. The first session, with men and women over 55, was a lively, spirited, intelligent discussion among people who were involved and highly knowledgeable about their money. The second session, among respondents 30 to 54, seemed oddly flat by comparison. These people knew less, cared less; they were busy with other areas of their lives.

Observing from behind the one-way mirror throughout was a small group of clients in marketing, advertising, and research, all in their twenties and thirties. "I can't believe the older people were so sharp," one client remarked in surprise at the end of the evening. This group unsettled the young clients' picture of "senior citizens" as rigid, old-fashioned, slow-witted, unsophisticated.

Why did a focus group do what *Time* magazine, *The New York Times*, and *The Wall Street Journal*, not to say quantitative surveys, had failed to do? My hypothesis is that this other information had been received on an intellectualized level, while the focus group had an emotional impact on the gut level that made it get through. The picture of those respondents in their fifties and sixties may well stay in the clients' memories, counteracting and possibly replacing the former stereotypes of "senior citizens." As a result, these marketers may now approach the 55-plus group with new respect for their sophistication and savvy. In this era of cross-segment marketing, it also suggests that knowledgeable investors cut across age groups.

Qualitative research can bring the point home not just by counteracting perceptions, but, equally important, by reinforcing feelings. The Gillette Company asked us to conduct research on "quality," a major issue in the 1980s. What does quality mean to consumers; when do they and don't they look for it; how do they recognize it? A focus group with women showed that consumers are more demanding and "educated" about quality than in the past. This comment was typical:

"I think as consumers we're becoming more aware of what goes into a product. For myself, I have become more aware of the ingredients—food or clothing or whatever. I feel that I'm not the same shopper I was perhaps six years ago. That was just fad buying. Now I look at something."

Marketing, market research, and research and development people observed the group; the videotape of the session has since been shown to others in the company. Hans Lopater, Gillette's research director, says that the focus group made what top management has been saying more tangible and believable.

This wasn't another generalized corporate lecture. These were real people who cared, who could tell the difference, who shopped what they believed. Understanding the importance of quality in today's competitive marketing environment, one can argue, can affect not only a company's attitude, but ultimately its bottom line.

MAKING THE ABSTRACT REAL

Qualitative research, then, has a powerful emotional force. Seeing and hearing consumers only a few feet away has an impact that no set of statistics or written report alone can have. It makes the abstract real because it is human, individual. Qualitative research offers not just an intellectual comprehension of consumers, but also a vivid, visceral recognition that affects, on a very deep level, how companies see, feel about, and deal with their customers from then on.

The powerful impact of qualitative research is, of course, exactly what makes many researchers and marketers wary of the technique. The danger, it is often said, is that marketing personnel observing a session will listen selectively to one individual (usually the one who says what they already felt), then rush off and make major decisions based on this person's comments. Even after large-scale quantitative studies have been conducted, it is argued, those observers will believe isolated examples of what they saw in the groups ("Remember the women in yellow in Columbus?") rather than the statistical research. Some companies, in fact, go so far as to ban all qualitative research or all focus groups because of this danger. The danger, I agree, is real. The problem may not be the qualitative research *per se*. As researchers, we routinely issue—and believe—caveats about the limitations of sampling and questioning methods. The danger, instead, as many corporate researchers will admit, is that non-researchers will run off and make policy decisions based on a handful of people. The answer is *not* to consider the qualitative hypotheses as absolute fact, but rather to accept that they just *may* be true. The new picture of the consumer is a possibility to consider and to explore further.

BODY LANGUAGE

To use qualitative research to its full benefit, it is essential to recognize that words are just a starting place. Pay attention to the intensity in respondents' voices, their body language, and their self-presentation, not just what they say. Are they excited and involved, or are they angry, upset? These responses can tell you a lot about your chances of persuading them.

• In several studies with consumers about possible new financial services which entailed outside companies being able to withdraw money from their checking accounts, a few respondents in each group typically reacted very negatively. It wasn't just that they said they dislike the idea; they pulled back from the table, shook their heads, pursed their lips tightly and, with evident vehemence, declared, "I would *never* let anyone get into my checking account." The mistrust, the sense of invaded privacy, suggested this was a highly resistant group, difficult, if not impossible, to convert.

• How people dress also can offer an important message about who they are and how they see themselves. In a study of female deodorant users, we conducted separate focus groups with users of a brand positioned specifically for young women, and users of other brands (most of them advertised to both sexes). Simply looking at the respondents showed how dramatically different the groups were in their self-image. The users of the female-oriented brand wore clothing that was distinctly, even stereotypically, feminine—either innocent (pink and white, ruffles), or sexy (lots of jewelry and makeup, low necklines, Playboy T-shirts, etc.). Non-users generally wore sporty and more tailored outfits. These divergent styles suggested very different advertising approaches would be needed for each group.

Such observations, I believe, cannot be formalized and packaged into quantitative studies. Qualitative research allows us to see in consumers what they themselves may not be aware of and, therefore, what they cannot report in straightforward questioning. Also, what is important and relevant in one category (how people dress or their energy level, for instance) may be meaningless in another. One standard set of psychographic variables would be simplistic and inadequate. Instead, we have to be open and receptive while observing respondents: What it is that is noteworthy; what stands out about these people; what is the dominant feeling and impression they leave behind?

LOOKING AT LOYALTY

All heavy users of a specific product or service are not alike—some are there because the current alternatives are worse; some have a love-hate relationship, complaining while secretly being pleased; and some are diehards who would never consider any other choice (a point that Coca-Cola, for instance, overlooked).

• In a study of discount stores in a Southern market, shoppers spoke highly of a major chain where they bought regularly. The store, they said, did what a discount store should do—offered good quality merchandise at decent prices. Any dissatisfactions? Yes, lines were long and the dressing rooms cramped, but, respondents said, you have to expect such frustration in the quest for bargains.

What about a regional chain on the other side of the river which, the client knew, planned to move into the market relatively soon? Well, *that* is a really *wonderful* store. Several women went 20 miles out of their way to shop there and others, who had seen the commercials, couldn't wait for it to open. It was everything a discount store should be and more—the people were friendly, the everyday prices were great even when there was no special sale, the merchandise of excellent quality—and so on.

Listening to this enthusiasm, it became clear that the current market leader, despite its apparently high rating, was potentially very vulnerable.

• On the opposite end of the spectrum, loyalty can be surprisingly intense and unquestioning. In a study of cooking oil, when respondents were asked about a major brand, most of the women embarrassedly admitted they had always used the brand their mother used. There was both a strong emotional connection with the brand and a longstanding habit pattern that seemed virtually impossible to overcome. Most of the women had not even looked at any other brand or paid attention to competitive advertising claims. Further, they were convinced that using a different brand would mean risking cooking failure.

The point, then, is that the market leader would be smart to reinforce these family feelings that their success had been built on. Any competitor would be smart not to be overly rational about its product attributes, but to build its own relationship with the prospective user and to find daring new ways to entice them to try the brand.

LOOKING FOR NEW TRENDS

Qualitative research provides an early barometer of consumers' changing values and lifestyles. A basic limitation of quantitative research is that respondents are allowed to answer almost totally within the confines of multiple-choice questions, questions a researcher was smart enough to think up in advance. The open-ended, interactive nature of qualitative research means that consumers do not merely react within set confines—*they* bring up issues, directly or indirectly.

When the recession was at its height, for instance, we found that the standard market-research questions, "What is your favorite brand?" simply wasn't working. Respondents recruited as one brand's users often said in groups that they had just bought something else. A brand might have been a shopper's "favorite," but last week she bought a different one because there was a coupon. The economic squeeze had shaken up old shopping patterns, making the question fairly meaningless. The focus group responses indicted change was in progress.

· To help a small magazine develop ideas on how to expand its readership, we interviewed its current subscribers and, in separate sessions, the people it hoped to attract—young professionals (a.k.a. yuppies). Rather than focusing narrowly on respondents' present media behavior and attitudes, we took what we call the "step back" approach, examining the context of consumers' values. This is a purposefully broad view.

The discussions were opened by asking respondents what their values are and how they've changed. This simple, yet challenging, question let loose a flood of response.

We discovered there is a segment of what might be called "searching yuppies." Fitting the demographic requirements on paper (though, of course, rejecting the label), these professionals did indeed embrace the goal of "success" and the comfortable lifestyle it brings. They were, however, highly aware of the evolution in their values from the 1960s, when they opposed the system and hoped to bring about a better world. Trying hard to convince themselves—and others—that they had grown, not sold out, they were eager to hold on to some sense of idealism. At the very time that they are enjoying their success, they have come to question it.

Searching yuppies were filled with anxieties, conflicts, questions: Is that all there is; How do I find time for relationships and myself; Have I been so focused on career that I've forgotten my personal life, and so on. The overriding gut-level impression of these people was that they were groping for meaning in their lives. The search for a new balance is a dominant concern.

This picture, then, was quite different from the usual one of cocky, uncon-cerned, narrowly ambitious professionals. It suggests, too, some possible new trends to look for: a move away from workaholism both by men and women; greater concern with personal relationships, including an element of despera-tion on the part of some career-oriented professionals who previously ignored this part of life; the reemergence of idealism, but within the established system.

Fascinating, of course, but how could this be useful to the magazine? Under-standing these people's philosophies and their concerns could be helpful in several ways: suggesting what segments might be prospects in the future; stimulating ideas for future editorial direction; and learning how to communi-cate with potential readers about the magazine.

SOURCE OF CLIENT RESISTANCE

A few years ago we conducted a study of designer jeans. The fashion phenomenon had already, as the client admitted, passed its peak; the market had, so to speak, bottomed out. Respondents were all designer jeans purchasers, but they did not all match the client's expectation of highly fashion-conscious, trendy, physically attractive women. Some, for example, were overweight. The client wanted to change the respondent specifications, requiring that all the women wear sizes six to ten only and that they all read fashion magazines. If we had done this (we didn't), we would have been look-ing only at a select segment of jeans buyers.

Why did the clients reject what they saw? They wanted to believe they had glamorous, exciting customers who mirrored the disco life-style of their advertising. And, I think, they resisted the message that designer jeans were no longer a fashion-leader item, that they were a mass-market item accepted by the fashion followers.

Sometimes clients reject what they see because the customer is *more* sophisticated than they expected. For a discount department-store chain, we screened for women who shopped regularly at that type of store. Expecting to observe a group of women all with low incomes and education, this client was upset because some of the shoppers were too upscale. They shopped often at discount stores and found good places to find name brands at reduced prices. What we were witnessing was middle-class customers adapting themselves to a bad economy and reduced financial power, using their consumer savvy to get more for their money. They were shopping more in stores that not too long ago they had looked down on. The qualitative research was an early barometer of the economy's impact on store loyalties.

In many such target groups, I must emphasize, the client agreed that these respondents were indeed users of their products. Nevertheless, they denied they were "customers."

Client resistance often stems from corporate ego. Many clients want to believe their customers are attractive, appealing, sophisticated people who understand and care about their products. Conversely, in some categories, clients look down on their customers, viewing them as unintelligent and easily manipulated. Such corporate pictures are well-established and transmitted as part of the corporate culture, sometimes on an unconscious, unstated level. Because of the strength of this preconception, clients sometimes reject whatever they see in the research that clashes with their preconceptions, even if they have no other current sources of information to suggest that the research is wrong.

The "this-isn't-my-customer" response is more common with qualitative research. It is easier to blame the qualitative recruiting and the moderator. In a quantitative study, clients rarely see the respondents in person, so there are no images to clash with their preconceptions. The statistics in a study seem impersonal, detached from the researcher reporting them, harder to attack.

If the focus group respondents do not match your picture of your customer, question whether that picture is based on real information or corporate wishful thinking. Allow the focus groups to challenge your assumptions, to raise new questions and possibilities. Most of all, be open to all you can learn about your customers. In this era of cross-marketing, companies need all the information—both, intellectual and gut-level—they can get.

Table 4.
Client Checklist

Here's an eight-point checklist companies should keep in mind before conducting qualitative research on who their customers are:

1. Don't expect your customers to look like the models in your ads. Fitness seekers don't all look like Jane Fonda—they are *trying* to.
2. Don't expect your customers to like you. Sitting behind the mirror can be blitz group therapy. Your ego and your company's ego are in the hands of a few customers. It can be upsetting and anger-provoking to hear what they have to say. Be prepared.
3. Don't expect customers to care as much about your products as you do. It represents only a small part of their lives.
4. Don't expect your customer to be people just like you—or, on the other hand, to be unlike you.
5. Don't expect people to be consistent, and don't label them as hypocrites when they aren't.
6. Use your qualitative researcher as a consultant to put the study in context—are these customers satisfied or dissatisfied, compared to what the researcher has seen in other categories?
7. Remember, if they buy your product, they *are* your customers—whether or not you like the way they look, talk, think, or feel about you.
8. Be honest about your expectations. There is no clean slate. Everyone has preconceptions about their customers. Ask where you expectations come from—research or prejudice.

Judith Langer is president of Langer Associates, Inc., a New York-based marketing research firm and publishers of the Langer Report, a marketing research newsletter.

8.

THE NEW GLOBAL GAME

William Pat Patterson

As advances in technology help reshape the world into a global economy, the rules of competition are changing. Consumer tastes are becoming increasingly similar throughout the world, which means that global marketing could become increasingly effective for consumer products.

The world economic order created and sustained by the Industrial Revolution, and brought to its keenest cutting edge following World War II, is fading. Old power structures, alliances, and consumer values—all the old gods that underpinned international politics and global competition—are being reshaped. And the forces driving these changes—including advanced communications systems—have set in motion some far-reaching economic, political, and psychological tremors.

In the accompanying paranoia, nations have resorted to finger-pointing, grumbling, and veiled threats. And tensions are certain to grow as the new "global game" unfolds.

Thomas Campbell, a Stanford University law professor, sees the world steadily drifting toward a paralysis of trade. "It could be as severe as that which fueled the Great Depression," he warns. "The world is on the verge of reverting into hostile camps. All the efforts that nations have made since World War II in opening up trade are now in peril."

Charles L. Brown, chairman of AT&T Co., also sees the world at the crossroads. "We can follow an expansive approach and seek increased international cooperation," he says. "Or we can opt for a restricting approach and withdraw behind the walls of protectionism and national pride."

GLOBAL MARKETS

At stake in all of this is the future of the "global" corporation, which scholars view as distinct from the multinational corporation. The global corporation, they point out, tends to view the world as a homogenous market rather than as a collection of separate markets with unique requirements.

Prof. Theodore Levitt at Harvard Business School, one of the most respected marketing minds in the country, has long been a champion of the global corporation and the "globalization" of markets. "What we are dealing with here," he declares, "is an implacable force. A tide and not a wave."

Others, citing protectionist tendencies, suspect that the tide will never reach shore. But Prof. Levitt contends that protectionist moves "are really symptoms of the intensification of global competition—not long-term barriers to it."

In his book, *The Marketing Imagination* (The Free Press, 1983), he describes a "homogenization of the world's wants—almost everybody everywhere wants all the things they have heard about, seen, or experienced via the new technological facilitators that drive their wants and wishes." The result, he says, is a "global commonality." People will sacrifice traditional regional preferences in product features for comparable products offering high quality at lower prices—the "generic" product, mass-produced and world-distributed.

For large international companies, he suggests, this portends a trend away from multinational (or "multi-domestic") organizations—in which subsidiaries employ different strategies for different markets—and the rise of the global corporation "which sells the same things in the same way everywhere."

Another leading proponent of globalization—and also a Harvard Business School professor—is Michael E. Porter, author of *Competitive Strategy and Competitive Advantage* (The Free Press). But he sees things a bit differently. "I agree that products are becoming more homogenized," he says, "but I also think that needs are increasingly being met in a segmented way—and this has to do with the cost of customizing products coming down." Some companies, he notes, are employing a "global-segmentation" strategy which emphasizes market segments rather than geographic differences. "A company can, for example, pick the minicar segment and serve that worldwide and become a real powerhouse."

Such ideas aren't new to executives with an international perspective. "Today," declares Jose J. Dedeurwaerder, president of American Motors Corp. (AMC), "companies have to develop global concepts—not only in sales and marketing, but also with suppliers and manufacturing plants, if they are to survive." And Toyota Motor Corporation's "Global 10" strategy is predicated on the belief that the company needs at least 10% of the world auto market to remain healthy.

TECHNOLOGY'S THRUST

Of course, there has always been competition for international markets. But what is new is a shift in perceptions—a growing tendency to view the world as *one market, not many.* Moreover, the global game is being played with greater intensity; there is a higher level of government involvement in structuring the rules; and it is becoming important to penetrate new markets quickly as old ones become saturated.

Driving all of this at an incredible speed is high technology. Communications satellites and copper cable (soon fiber-optic) span the globe. And 1986 will witness the first installation of equipment for the much heralded Integrated Services Digital Network, a worldwide public telecommunications system that will simultaneously transmit voice, telex, and packet-and-circuit-switched data.

When the network is widely implemented—about 1990—it will include digital links between telecommunications companies around the world; and it will open the door to a whole new level of global communication. (A CEO will be able to telephone managers of a European or Asian subsidiary for what it now costs to call cross-country in the U.S.) In the meantime, some of the advantages are already evident in the use of global communications for 24-hour-a-day banking. BankAmerica Corp., for example, in 1984 invested $200 million to create a worldwide communications network linking the bank's 100 offices and corporate branches in Europe, North and South America, and Asia.

Other segments of the financial community are jumping on the bandwagon. Talks are underway to link the stock exchanges of New York, London, and Tokyo. Observes Harvard Prof. Levitt: "One of the most powerful and yet least celebrated ways in which we see commerce being driven toward global standardization is through the monetary system and the international investment process."

Japan has leaped into global finance with both feet. Of the 10 largest international banks, five are Japanese. Three are American, one is British, one is French.

But for all its power, the world of finance has a less tangible impact on countries than decisions involving the locations of plants and the production of goods. So the use of world-shrinking technology by giant manufacturing companies—which have the ability to move plants or to change distribution patterns—is more likely to give nations continuing migraines. "Countries are in charge of territory," points out David B. Abernethy, professor of political science at Stanford. "Huge companies pose a challenge to national sovereignty. And so there is always a tug of war between the two."

Since the implementation of advanced communications systems gives companies greater control over far-flung subsidiaries, one of the effects of technology is the centralization of corporate power. It portends more decisions by "faceless" strangers, immersed in computer printouts, thousands of miles from the affected site—decisions over which a host-country government will be less likely to exert influence.

Yet, somewhat paradoxically, another effect of technology is to encourage dispersed manufacturing operations—and, hence, to distribute corporate power. Therefore, depending on a company's internal policy and strategy, it may mean more rather than less local autonomy.

Companies that make high-technology products are particularly able to exacerbate international tensions by playing one country against another. Unlike mineral- or agricultural-dependent companies, high-tech firms are not resource-bound. They can easily pull up stakes. "High-tech companies are beholden to no one," observes Prof. Abernethy.

LABOR 'CHIPS'

The only playing card that some countries have is their pool of low-cost labor; but with factory automation, this is becoming less of a bargaining chip. Moreover, the spread of technology has created a worldwide labor pool—one in which workers in one country actively compete for jobs with workers elsewhere. A case in point: Workers in Barbados now earn $2.50 an hour keypunching data into American Airlines computers. Previously, the task was done by 200 U.S. workers in Tulsa, who earned $6.50 an hour. (Unions call such job transfers "telescabbing.")

The portability of jobs is a serious concern in the labor ranks—even if some workers don't show it. Trying to create new jobs, West German metalworkers struck for a 35-hour workweek at a 40-hour pay scale. But in a global economy, with the workers in all countries competing, such demands may prove to be a form of economic suicide. And with 600 million non-Americans expected to enter the Free World's labor pool between now and the end of this century, U.S. workers are certain to experience growing competitive pressures.

DISPERSING

The specter of massive unemployment is, of course, a major driving force behind protectionist laws and regulations around the world. In turn, government intervention (including the erections of *barriers to exit* for domestic industries) has become the leading cause "of the new complexity we see in the move to globalization," says Harvard's Prof. Porter. He is referring to dispersed manufacturing in which companies established production facilities within market countries.

Observes AMC's Mr. Dedeurwaerder: "If you want to sell into the developing and newly industrialized countries that form the growth markets of the future for many products, you've got to realize that these governments will require you to make capital investments first." Mexico, for example, imposes a 60% local-content requirement on automotive manufacturers; Brazil insists on 85%. "These two countries account for three-fifths of all automotive demand in Latin America," the AMC president points out. "And other countries are fast following suit."

Thomas Hout, vice president of the Boston Consulting Group, management consultants, sees dispersed manufacturing as a signal that globalization has stalled. Several years ago, Mr. Hout co-authored with Prof. Porter a *Harvard Business Review* article ("How Global Companies Win Out") that suggested that international success will require companies to shift from multidomestic approaches—with subsidiaries competing differently in different markets—to global organizations that pit their entire worldwide clout against the competition. The article published in 1982, envisioned global companies serving world markets from just a few centralized manufacturing sites.

But, through dispersed manufacturing, companies now are reverting to a more multi-domestic stance, Mr. Hout observes. "Globalization describes only one classic behavior of business," he says. "It is not an inexorable march of the cycle." He now believes that the spread of engineering and design skills throughout the world, as well as the need for faster responses to market changes, "make it less likely that a global-scale strategy will be valuable."

Prof. Porter disagrees. Thanks to flexible manufacturing and computerization, he says, "the new economics of production allow companies to place facilities in various parts of the world so as to minimize the cost of transport and government pressures. In-country manufacturing allows companies to respond to local needs faster and at less cost—but *still based on a global strategy.* The new frontier for management of the global corporation is how to coordinate dispersed facilities."

TARGETING THE U.S.

Although global competitors can pick and choose among markets, most find that being a worldclass player requires a strong presence in the U.S. The European market is nearly as large, but it is not homogenous and the rules change from country to country. Consider telecommunications: The U.S. market is expected to total $20.8 billion this year—more than one-third of the $57 billion world market—says Arthur D. Little Inc., a Cambridge, Mass., consulting firm. Adding to the attractiveness of the U.S. is its high-growth potential and political stability.

As a result, foreign companies are investing heavily here. The U.S Commerce Department reports that European investment in the U.S. totaled $92.5 billion in 1983, up from $82.2 billion in 1982. And Japanese firms have been flocking to U.S. soil. The Japanese Economic Institute, San Francisco, counts 342 Japanese-owned or controlled manufacturing companies currently operating 522 U.S. plants, employing some 90,000 Americans. In California's

Silicon Valley alone, more than a dozen firms affiliated with Japanese parents employ 6,000 people. "Every Japanese supplier thinks the same way," says Shinji Ohnishi, vice president and general manager of Hitachi American Ltd.'s semiconductor division, San Jose, Calif. "It's important to produce here—not 100% but a certain percentage."

COALITIONS

So, as high technology has brought diverse nations into a kind of global village, it has also engendered a global economic mating game. In the auto industry, says AMC's Mr. Dedeurwaerder, "no one company can afford to go it alone anymore. The capital investments are too large, the world market is too complex, and technology changes too quickly."

Kenichi Ohmae, managing director of the Tokyo office of McKinsey & Co., an international consulting firm, believes that global companies "must establish a strong insider position—not just an assembly operation or a marketing arm—in the U.S., Japan, and Europe." These Free World markets have some 600 million consumers; and increasingly they are seeking the best product at the best price.

In his book, *Triad Power: The Coming Shape of Global Competition* (The Free Press), Mr. Ohmae points out that the R&D costs for product breakthroughs are so high that, once achieved, "the product's global potential must be quickly exploited." As a result, he expects more and more trans-national coalitions—or consortiums—involving Japanese, U.S., and European companies.

Boston Consulting's Mr. Hout, however, thinks the phenomenon may be a short-lived one. "We're seeing a fair number [of trans-national coalitions] now simply because a lot of industries have shaken out," he says. "I don't see many of these coalitions as being anything permanent."

Permanent or not, the increased intensity and complexity of the global game have generated increased telecommunications traffic between nations. And the steady stream of digitally pulsed information has been a prickly thorn in the sides of national governments. Countries are afraid of losing control, especially where "sensitive" information is concerned.

The trans-border data-flow issue must be settled, however, if true global communications is to occur. "In the long run," Harvard's Prof. Porter expects, "the societal benefits of convenient and inexpensive worldwide communications . . . will be great enough that the public will demand it." In fact, after years of negotiation, the U.S. and European members of the Organization for Economic Cooperation & Development reached a preliminary agreement "to avoid the creation of unjustified barriers to the international exchange of data and information and to seek transparency in regulations and policies."

CONFRONTING WEAKNESSES

The world is moving forward to "a greater global convergence in all things," observes Harvard's Prof. Levitt. And this convergence is holding a mirror up to national weaknesses. America, for example, has a high creative thrust and introduces many breakthrough products, but many U.S. industries have been slow to update manufacturing processes and technologies.

Harry Brooks, professor of technology and public policy at Harvard, notes that the U.S. has only 7% of the world's population and yet controls half of the Free World's gross national product. "This probably isn't a viable situation for any prolonged period," he observes. "Even so, I believe the U.S. still retains the capacity to stay in front of the rest of the industrialized world—but not way in front." And simply maintaining a slight edge, he contends, will require placing a high priority on science, technology education, and productive investment.

It's no secret that U.S. competitiveness has been eroding. That trend prompted the creation of the President's Commission on Industrial Competitiveness, which issued its final report in 1984. Among other things, the report pointed out that, since 1965, seven out of ten U.S. high-tech industries have lost world-market share. (See Figure 1.)

Figure 1.
Losing Ground in High Tech
(U.S. Shares of World High-Technology
Exports, 1965 and 1980)

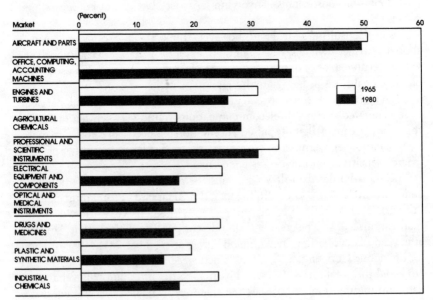

Source: U. S. Dept. of Commerce

The commission called for creation of a cabinet-level Department of Science & Technology, a new Department of Trade, and passage of an omnibus trade bill. And some observers have wondered whether such actions would constitute the first stage in establishing a national industrial policy that eventually might stifle creative juices and the American penchant for risk-taking.

Dr. Albert Bowers, chairman and CEO of Syntex Corp., Palto Alto, Calif., is leery of the implications. "The government must become a partner to American business—and not an impediment," he insists. "We need a public policy to regain our leadership." The difficulty, he admits, will be in finding a suitable way to establish a national consensus.

RALLY ROUND THE GIANTS

As the global game heats up, so much is at stake that, in Europe and Asia, there is a growing sentiment for "Japan Inc." arrangements—that is, governments and corporations joining forces to work their will on the rest of the world. Instead of individual corporations dueling with one another in a free market, countries are beginning to wage economic war and distort market forces to their own advantage.

And every country has its national champions—its corporate giants that are expected to lead the attack on global terrain. Two of the U.S. champions are AT&T Co. and IBM Corp.—each of which has the "mega-mass," the breadth of markets, and the technological capability to play the global game to the hilt. More than a few analysts believe that part of the motivation for dropping the Justice Department's antitrust suit against IBM and permitting AT&T to enter previously restricted markets (including computers) was to unleash the two Goliaths so they could compete more forcefully worldwide.

It is interesting to note what happened after the companies were un-shackled. Once the threat of an antimonopoly breakup was lifted, IBM adopted a low-cost manufacturing policy and broke many old corporate taboos by going outside to develop and distribute its personal computer. The acquisition of ROLM Corp. gave IBM a foothold in telecommunications. It shored up its microprocessor capability by acquiring a piece of Intel Corp. and, last year, acquired Sytek Inc. to help in developing local area network technology.

Meanwhile, AT&T forged a link with Olivetti Corp., Europe's No. 2 information-processing company, by buying a 25% stake. It launched a joint venture with Philips of the Netherlands. And then made an unsuccessful bid for Inmost Corp., a British semiconductor manufacturer.

Did the unleashing of IBM and AT&T represent conscious actions on the part of the U.S. government? Harvard's Prof. Levitt isn't so sure. "Most strategies," he maintains, "are not conscious and don't have to be. There is something that emerges. It's more a matter of an accumulation of wisdom in the sense of knowing where you want to go and how. Unspoken rules and presumptions develop—and all this accumulates into a strategy without it being specifically stated."

AWAKENING

Conscious strategy or not, it does seem that U.S. policymakers have awakened to the fact that they must begin viewing the world in global economic terms. And recent actions have reinforced that perception elsewhere. With Congress in a foul protectionist mood, Japanese Prime Minister Nakasome implored his countrymen to help reduce the trade imbalance between Japan and the U.S. by buying more U.S. goods. That was dramatic, but more effective was a meeting held later between Japan's foreign trade minister and top executives of 60 leading Japanese companies. The executives were told to make an "all-out effort" to increase imports of U.S. products.

If that was mere political window dressing, it nonetheless suggests that Japan has got the message that the global game will no longer be played by its rules alone.

Perhaps the next message that will be delivered is that there is only one earth and we all live on it—that all people, their environments, and their economies are interconnected. That we can't afford any big losers. And that we all have to win together.

GLOBAL OR MULTINATIONAL?

Marketing executives are far from unanimous in their assessments of global marketing and the "global corporation"—a company that sells identical products the same way in various parts of the world.

Only 5% of 120 senior marketing executives polled in a nationwide survey believe that the era of the multinational corporation has given way to the "Age of the Global Corporation." However, 31% felt that global marketing *can be more profitable* than multinational marketing for many product categories, although only 9% are now using global strategies for most of their products. The survey was conducted earlier this year by Peterson Blyth Cato Associates, a New York design and marketing communications firm, and Cheskin & Masten, a Menlo Park, Calif., research firm.

In general, the respondents confirmed that consumer tastes are becoming increasingly similar throughout the world—and that global marketing could become increasingly effective for consumer products. But, for now, industrial and high-technology products are rated more likely candidates for global-selling strategies.

The product categories deemed "most appropriate" for global marketing (and the percentage so responding) were:

1.	Computer hardware	70%
2.	Airlines	66%
3.	Photography equipment	63%
4.	Heavy equipment	61%
5.	Machine tools	59%
6.	Consumer electronics	42%
(tie)	Computer software	42%
7.	Automobiles	40%
8.	Sports equipment	33%
9.	Major appliances	31%
10.	Hardware	29%
(tie)	Wine & spirits	29%
11.	Nonalcoholic beverages	27%
12.	Tobacco	26%

Part II
GETTING A FIX ON A COMPETITIVE POSTURE

9.
GETTING A FIX ON YOUR COMPETITIVE POSITION

Perry Pascarella

> The key to marketing success lies more now than ever in knowing what you are, where you are, and who's there with you. Companies in the 1980s need a much more sophisticated view of competetive advantage than was previously required.

Have all the landmarks of your business vanished? Do you long for a return to the comfort of: fast growth, incremental change, no big surprises, regional or national boundaries around your industry, and a stable group of customers, competitors, and suppliers?

More than ever, the key to success now lies in knowing precisely what you are, where you are, who's there with you, and how radically different things may be tomorrow.

"The essence of strategy in the 1980s is a much more sophisticated view of competitive advantage than was previously required," says John S. Clarkeson, vice president at Boston Consulting Group (BCG), a specialist in corporate strategy.

Most strategies are fashioned without studying the competitive situation, says William Rothschild, staff executive for business development and strategy at General Electric. He calls it "mapping the battlefield." In his book, *How to Gain and Maintain the Competitive Edge*, he lists five steps for analyzing one's position:

1. *Determine your customers' needs and wants.*
2. *Study both "current and potential competitors"* in your "served and related unserved markets."
3. *Study the "entire economic situation,* "understanding all the actors and where the industry makes its money." (This includes studying suppliers to the industry and the firms that serve as intermediaries between you and the user.)

4. *Group competitors according to their degree of specialization* and their degree of *globalization*.
5. *Do an in-depth analysis of competitors' strategies* in product development, distribution, promotion, pricing, service-support, finance, and human resources.

KNOW THYSELF

Often, management doesn't know which of its businesses is most profitable, says Robert W. Gunn, principal in A. T. Kearney Inc.'s New York office.

"Sometimes they don't know *where* their competence is," he says, recalling that a large retail company which prided itself on being strong because of its distribution facilities discovered through careful analysis that it was competent branch managers and their buying skills that actually made for its success.

Too many companies *think* they know their own strengths, and let that determine what businesses they will be in, says Marcus Bogue, president of Planning Economic Group, a Woburn, Mass., consultant. "But it doesn't matter how good you are; it only matters how *relatively good* you are. If someone else is better than you are, it doesn't matter how good *you* are."

It's easy to delude oneself about the basics of competitive advantage, cautions Tom Wind, vice president with A. T. Kearney. "Be careful how you define the customer and his needs. Be precise about what you bring to the party," he says.

Strategic analysis should begin with a look at themselves, says Kearney's Mr. Gunn. "Where are you applying value against the marketplace? Where do you differentiate yourself?"

Strategic analysis may sound like a good chore to assign to a staff person. It could be regarded as a data-manipulation job that line managers—and certainly top executives—don't have time for.

To the contrary, it can only be done by people who know the business thoroughly. The process needs input from people who can see the big picture, who know customers' wants and competitors' strengths in detail, who know the old technologies, and who can see the potential for new ones. And it requires top management willingness to challenge itself—and its system.

This means that a company must continually be tuned in to new information about itself, the way others perceive it, and the way competitors are serving the market. Alan Zakon, chief executive officer at BCG, says: "A firm can remain adaptive to its environment only be seeking out new data, looking honestly at it, and continually assessing what actions—if any—should be taken. Individuals must be encouraged to bring up *new information* that does not fit the existing strategy and 'the way we do things.'"

At Emhart Corp., the diversified Hartford, Conn., manufacturing firm's general managers are guided through an "objective-setting" phase of planning, notes Marcus White, director of strategic planning. At this point, each of them defines his business, isolates and identifies his competitive strengths and weaknesses, identifies the attractiveness of his industry, and lays out options that follow from his position.

An understanding of what Emhart's objectives should be is fostered through ongoing discussions throughout the year, explains Mr. White. "We don't surprise people very much around here. We like to signal long in advance the types of directions we think the company ought to be taking."

Emhart's managers then turn to "functional programming"—identifying the implications for each of the managers of various departments. This does not lead to many changes, Mr. White says. Generally, those people are doing what their management has pointed them toward doing, but the exercise tends to focus their attention more on the long-term strategic element than on day-to-day tactical matters.

WHEN TO STAY OUT

Emhart is determined to compete only in "attractive" industries— those that lack powerful suppliers, powerful customers, substitute products, government threats, or threat of new entrants. Its management believes that a large number of firms in a slow-growing industry in which there are high fixed costs is a sign of an overly competitive environment.

In assessing the pressures within an industry, Emhart's managers consider how many firms are in it, whether they're growing rapidly or slowly, how fast the industry is growing, whether there is a high or low level of fixed costs in the industry, whether there is excess capacity, the size of the "exit barriers," and whether demand is price-sensitive.

The characteristics of attractive industries are defined by top management; then each manager looks at the business he serves—and decides whether these are attractive or not.

Analysis generally occurs on two levels, says Kearney's Mr. Wind. There is the *one-shot* analysis in which everybody gets together to make strategic decisions, and the *ongoing* kind which should be part of the line-management decision-making process.

"Triggering points" determine when a company should be especially interested in doing a strategic analysis, says Kearney's Mr. Gunn. Consideration of an acquisition or the arrival of a new top manager often signals a good time to reassess the business.

"We try not to make the analysis an annual or semi-annual event," says Emhart's Mr. White. "We try to keep this thing going full tilt all the time. You don't consider strategic planning as an isolated, once-a-year activity."

In the past, some consultants fostered the belief that they could come in and hand a company a "magic potion." The consultants did the analysis—in fact, they "superanalyzed," says Mr. Gunn. Now, companies are trying to place the process in the hands of *line managers*. The consultant's role is becoming that of an "enabler" to guide management teams through the process.

DIFFERENT DRUMMERS

Most managers credit themselves with knowing their competitors, but sometimes they don't know them well enough—their strategies, their intentions. "A common problem," says BCG's Mr. Zakon, "is the assumption that competitors do things the 'same way that we do.' That is a huge trap. In evaluating a competitor's cost position, for example, most companies really evaluate what their own cost would be if they had the location, labor, power costs, and so on of their competitors. Rarely is enough attention paid to whether competitors are doing business in a *different way*."

When analyzing competitors, says Kearney's Mr. Wind, it's important to be precise. You have to ask how competitors compete in ways that really have an impact on you. People have been guilty of not analyzing their competitors at all, says Planning Economics' Mr. Bogue. "And when they do analyze them, they have been all too guilty of analyzing them in the static—'Where are they now?'—as opposed to 'Where are they going?'"

GETTING STARTED

Mr. Bogue suggests that executives start by studying who's doing what to whom. Who has what position? In what segments of the market? Who's winning and who's losing? Then ask: Why? Are competitors structurally configured in such a way that they have an advantage in a particular segment of the market? Will that segment grow faster than some other segment?

A manager may know an industry's past well, yet fail to gauge the present and the future. Market needs, for example, may shift and scuttle yesterday's advantage, Kearney's Mr. Wind points out. He tells of an insurance company that had capitalized on its ability to advise people on how to protect their property. But that know-how became widespread and competitors began showing customers how to protect their balance sheets—how to cut the cost of buying insurance.

"The competition isn't necessarily just those who make the same product for a given market," says Mr. Wind. "It's also who can dislodge you."

Pointing to a coffee mug on his desk, he says: "If you're a mugmaker who extends liberal credit, that may be your competitive advantage; you don't need to watch all the cupmakers, only the ones who can match your credit terms."

Kearney's Mr. Gunn observes that it's important to determine whether a competitor can really capitalize on its advantages. "Can it deliver on its strengths? A company may not have the management commitment to do that."

One good source of intelligence is your company's purchasing agent if he deals with suppliers who also sell to your competitors, says Mr. Gunn. Another good source is your cadre of product engineers who run into your competitor's engineers, Mr. Wind adds. Not so high on the list are salesmen. Although salesmen are a source for a great deal of information, they tend to come back with lots of stories that help them with their own sales, but not strategically useful information, cautions Mr. Wind.

AVOIDING BIASES

If a company has a strong value system and a sense of corporate mission, its managers are not likely to spend a lot of time worrying about their competitors' every move, because they'll know where they are going and why they perform well. "If you monitor your performance against your mission, there is no need to be constantly reacting," says Mr. Wind.

The more a company searches for new information and tries to anticipate surprises, the more likely it is to avoid biases and being whipsawed by minor shifts in the marketplace. John R. White, senior vice president with Arthur D. Little, Inc., Cambridge, Mass., observes: "We have to be very clear in distinguishing between the rejuvenation of an industry where there is actually a significant growth in demand and where turmoil and change are caused by the introducing of new technology.

"The CEO has to be aware of the possibility of competitive response and be careful that he doesn't commit irreversible capital investment on the [assumption] that this growth is going on forever. He has to be prepared for a flattening of that curve."

Strategic analysis can reshape the basic structure of the organization. Alexander Oliver, vice president at Booz, Allen & Hamilton, Inc., explains: "The economics may argue that you should be centralizing in order to get the *economies of scale*. And yet the market needs may argue that you move in the direction of decentralization to get the *market responsiveness* you need. There's a series of delicate balances, which comes back to the need for business judgment. You really have to understand the business—and the way the business is evolving—in a way which traditional strategies didn't."

It's important, too, to recognize when you are in a business that is going nowhere. BCG's Mr. Clarkeson says: "For a wide range of industries the *stable* condition is more likely one of *stalemate*. The skills and resources necessary to achieve minimal levels of economic performance are widely available, and no competitor is able to gain sufficient advantage over the others. The pace is usually set by the competitor with the lowest labor costs or the lowest expectations of return.

"An organization must learn to recognize the signs of imminent stalemate—to avoid getting bogged down in a form of trench warfare that no one can win. The fact that much of the equity of American industries trades well below book value indicates the pervasiveness of this investment trap."

NEW TOOLS

The next generation of strategy-development tools "should enhance the corporation's ability to anticipate and interpret change in the competitive environment," says Mr. Clarkeson. "The original portfolio approach distinguished winners from losers; the new approach must distinguish *which races are worth entering.*"

At Emhart Corp., strategic analysis is conducted within the context of the firm's mission and culture. A systematic look at its own strategy in late 1978 and early 1979 revealed that the firm's distinctive competence was in managing mature, long-lived businesses that can be improved through technology.

Classical planning theory says that a company generating positive cash flow and underutilizing its potential debt should be investing in embryonic businesses. But such acquisitions are risky, expensive, and not in keeping with Emhart's culture. If an Emhart unit has a strong competitive position in a highly attractive industry, it is funded aggressively. By the same token, the firm would throw in the towel on a business that has a weak position in an unattractive industry. A weak unit in an *attractive* industry is funded if it develops strategies for overcoming its weaknesses.

"Our main thrust is being a differentiated producer," says Emhart's Mr. White. "We make very specialized products for specialized markets. A product may include various service characteristics. It may include quality characteristics. It may include corporate-reputation characteristics which are not necessarily subject to traditional accounting [measurements]."

BUILDING VALUE

Until recently the thrust of many corporate strategies was to boost volume. Little attention was paid to cost or to efficient use of resources. *Today, an increasing number of companies are carefully studying the high cost of being the low-price supplier.* While they may compete on price, they do not rely on that as the sole differentiating factor. In fact, some have learned that "low price" can be the road to ruin.

An increasing number of managers are working to differentiate their products in ways other than price. They are seeking to build value as perceived by the customer.

Emhart's executives believe that if a product is truly differentiated, the customer becomes relatively insensitive to price. In fact, increased price sensitivity may be a sign that a product is losing its advantage of differentiation.

NEW CHALLENGES

Industry faces greater challenges than ever before, believes John Boylan, executive vice president at J. I. Case Co., Racine, Wis., a construction-equipment manufacturer. "*It must now do more than build the best product possible for the cost.* It must also pay attention to factors such as providing extensive after-sales support, anticipating what the customer wants—even if what he wants doesn't agree with what we would like to manufacture—and knowing what the customer will want 5, 10, and even 15 years from now."

The purpose of strategic analysis is to expand a firm's options. In his book, *The Marketing Imagination*, Harvard Business School Prof. Theodore Levitt says: "It is wrong to say that the most important and creatively challenging act of corporate decision-making is about choices regarding what's to be done. *The most important and challenging work involves thinking up the possibilities from among which choices may have to be made.*"

In the end, then, strategic analysis leads to synthesis—the leap in insight that puts the pieces together to create a distinct competitive advantage.

Perry Pascarella is executive editor of Industry Week *magazine.*

10.
DETERRENCE—
A STRATEGY THAT PAYS

Barrie G. James

Attack strategies are used to acquire market share and *defense* strategies to protect market territory. But *deterrence*—the indirect approach—is the ultimate business strategy. Deterrence offers companies the opportunity to win conflicts in the marketplace without resorting to direct battles with competitors.

Military strategy is attracting growing management attention because of its relevance to current market conditions. Probably at no time in the recent past has business been so competitive, placed so much emphasis on survival and growth under adversity. In fact, business is now on a war footing. In declining markets, business succcess rests either on timing disengagement and withdrawing in good order or on finding a new way to win. In static or low-growth markets, success depends on taking share away from competitors and protecting existing share from competitive aggression. In high-growth markets, companies are confronted with the need to carve out and hold a share in the market in the face of strong opposition from myriad of competitors, all eager to obtain the spoils of growth.

While the attack-defense strategies are widely practiced in business, one military strategy—*deterrence*, the indirect approach—is largely ignored by management and strategists. However, if properly devised and executed, deterrent strategies offer the highest return. They can circumvent costly resource battles with competitors in the marketplace and preserve intact the company's security, sovereignty, and power.

An excellent example from recent military history is Israel's deterrent strategy with Jordan. Following the 1967 Arab-Israeli war, the Israelis have been successful in persuading the Jordanians to avoid military confrontation. By building up their sophisticated air and ground capability, the Israelis have made certain that the risks of military action outweigh the benefits.

WHAT IS DETERRENCE?

Deterrence is a strategy to prevent conflict by persuading a rational competitor that you are willing and able to punish noncompliance with your clearly expressed and understood wishes. Deterrence is a strategy for an acceptable peace rather than for war. It depends more on intuition and emotion than on logic. Because it means inducing a competitor to cooperate through voluntary restraint, deterrence is a battle won in the mind of the competitor through psychological pressure rather than physical combat.

Market conflict occurs when a company anticipates that the risk is low in relation to the gains from a planned aggressive move or from an impulsive act. An effective deterrent strategy must discourage combat in either form. It must deal effectively with direct attacks, extremely provocative acts, and aggressive adventures by competitors.

- *Direct attacks.* Chesebrough-Pond's correctly anticipated that, by launching a new product into a market of small importance to a major manufacturer, it could achieve spectacular results. Chesebrough-Pond's launched Rave into the then $40 million U.S. market for home permanents, a market dominated in the mid-1970s by Gillette's Toni. Rave, a superior product with no ammonia and no smell, was backed by a small but skillful marketing program. The market increased to $100 million by 1981, and Rave took brand leadership away from Toni.
- *Extremely provocative acts.* An extremely provocative act was Duracell's entrance into the battery market in the United Kingdom, a market dominated by Eveready with an 85 percent share.

  Duracell gambled correctly that Eveready would emphasize its traditional strength in the declining zinc-carbon battery segment rather than in the growing alkaline segment and would maintain its traditional distribution through specialist retailers rather than open up mass merchandising through supermarkets. Within two years, Eveready's market share had fallen to 65 percent. By using new technology and mass distribution techniques, Duracell, the newcomer, had reached 22 percent.
- *Aggressive adventurism.* Starting in the early 1960s, Japanese car manufacturers correctly anticipated that their cumulative strategy for enveloping the European car market country by country would not be deterred by either competitors or European governments until the aggressive adventure was essentially complete.

ELEMENTS OF EFFECTIVE DETERRENCE STRATEGIES

Four key elements are present in all effective deterrent strategies in both war and business: credibility, capability, communication, and rationality.

CREDIBILITY

Credibility means one company's convincing its competitors that, to further its aims or to maintain its market position, it is willing to inflict unacceptable losses on that firm. The competitor is also persuaded that it has something to gain from restraint. If the second firm is willing to accept the risk of punishment, it obviously does not regard the threat as credible.

Texas Instruments (TI) successfully used its credibility to win a battle for future supply. In 1981 TI announced a price for random access memory (RAM) chips to be marketed in 1983. Within a week Bowmar offered a lower price for RAM chips with the same characteristics. Three weeks later Motorola followed with an even lower price. Two weeks after Motorola's offer, TI announced a new price one-half of that offered by Motorola. Because of its proven credibility as the lowest cost producer of RAM chips, TI won the battle even before the product was manufactured.

In contrast, in the mid-1970s, Fokker, the Dutch airframe manufacturer, signaled British Aerospace that it would not tolerate BAe's projected HS-146 aircraft competing directly with Fokker's existing F-28 short-haul jet airliner. Fokker indicated that more than 40 percent of the total cost of both its F-27 and F-28 aircraft was supplied by British companies and that both contracts were at risk if the HS-146 project went ahead. BAe correctly gauged that the threat was not credible. Fokker's cost for redesigning, retooling, and recertification of both aircraft, using non-British equipment, would have been prohibitive. The HS-146 project went ahead. In mid-1985 Fokker announced the end of the production run for the F-28 and started development of the larger F-100 aircraft. BAe began quantity deliveries of the HS-146 to major customers, including Air Wisconsin, Aspen, and PSA.

CAPABILITY

A company uses capability when it convinces a competitor that, in addition to being willing, it has the means and the resources to carry out the threat of punishment.

Because of high start-up costs and a limited customer base, IMS has been able to deter competitors from entering the pharmacy and hospital audit markets for drug products on virtually a worldwide basis. On the other hand, A.C. Nielsen with its dominant position in the U.S grocery sales and television audience measurement markets, was unable to deter competition. Despite Nielsen's imposing technological prowess, innovative use of sophisticated data handling and analysis, and formidable legacy of historical data, AGB of the U.K., Times's Sales Area Marketing, McGraw-Hill's Data Resources, and Control Data's Arbitron Subsidiaries, were not deterred by its capabilities. All successfully penetrated Nielsen's markets.

COMMUNICATION

A company uses communication to clearly signal a competitor of its intention to further its aims or maintain its position, and it makes the competitor fully aware of the benefits of cooperation and the punishments that may be meted out for noncompliance.

Boeing successfully used deterrent communications to avoid a physical contest with other airframe manufacturers over its 747 aircraft. The development cost to the 747, some two billion dollars, was then the largest private funding of a civilian jet airliner. In the late 1960s, there was a limited demand for routes for an intercontinental airliner with 350 or 400 seats. Developing a large, expensive aircraft with such a limited sales volume would have been economic suicide for another aircraft manufacturer. From its introduction into airline service in 1970, Boeing's 747 has remained without a direct competitor.

In contrast, U.S. truck manufacturers in the period from 1979 to 1981 were unsuccessful in communicating the poor operating economies and low margins of the medium-sized truck market in the U.S.A. Therefore, they were unable to deter market entrance by Daimler-Benz, IMAC, Renault, and Volvo. The economic situation in Europe meant that these companies were facing problems in their home markets and looked to the U.S. as a way of revving depressed demand. Because of ineffective communication, the U.S. manufacturers were forced to fight additional new competitors in a weak truck market.

RATIONALITY

A company, although acting arbitrarily and unreasonably, uses rationality to avoid arousing emotion on the part of a competitor. It puts the competitor at a disadvantage because, to avoid forgoing the benefits of cooperation, the competitor has been persuaded to act rationally, reasonably, and objectively. Although rationality is the key to an effective deterrence strategy, actual potential competitors do not always act rationally.

IBM's introduction of its advanced Displaywriter line of word processors in mid-1980 did not force all its twenty-odd competitors to act rationally when faced with a superior product and the power of IBM's sales and service organization. Some firms counterattacked by introducing new, better, and less expensive models as a direct response. Other firms, faced with shrinking profit margins and volumes, acted rationally and looked for mergers or left the market.

DESIGNING DETERRENT STRATEGIES

Deterrent strategies in business consist of a number of marketing, production, financial, technological, and managerial substrategies designed to prevent competitors from upsetting market equilibrium. These strategies create significant entry barriers to the market and erect profit-taking hurdles.

MARKETING DETERRENTS

Distribution. Japanese companies have successfully used the complexity of the distribution system in Japan to deter potential competitors from doing their own distributing. Instead, competitors use the local system or a Japanese partner. This strategy produces another layer of costs for the foreign competitor to absorb and removes the new company from direct contact with the customer. Therefore, foreign firms are less competitive than their Japanese counterparts.

Promotion. A hallmark of Procter & Gamble in the U.S. is its massive advertising and promotion budget. In 1981 it spent more than $500 million on media alone. Its use of its budget to buy and maintain market share acts as a strong deterrent to many companies seeking to enter or increase share in markets dominated by P&G products.

Franchise. Over the years Hewlett-Packard (H-P) has built a strong reputation with such major manufacturing companies as Boeing and General Motors by supplying high-quality electronic test and measurement instruments. H-P's reputation among such companies was sufficient to deter them from purchasing rival mini-computers; instead, they bought H-P models from a firm they knew and trusted.

Customer Relations. In the late 1960s IBM announced its 370 series computer far and wide. Two to three years before the 370 series was commercially available, IBM promised that it would have a level of performance far exceeding current competitors. This product announcement deterred customers from purchasing existing competitive computers and enticed them to wait for the new advanced 370 series.

Service. Pitney-Bowes' 92 percent share of the postage meter market in the U.S. is due in part to the 7,500-person sales and service force that calls on thousands of small firms. Despite encouragement from the U.S Justice Department, few firms want to enter a market so dominated by one company's product and its sales and service force.

Quality. Following TWA's withdrawal in the mid-1970s, Swissair successfully deterred U.S.-based carriers from competing profitably on scheduled Swiss-U.S. air routes. Swissair discouraged potential competitors by skillfully maintaining prices, matching demand closely with capacity, and offering exemplary in-flight cabin service.

Pricing. In the soft contact lens market in the U.S., Bausch & Lomb deterred competitors by drastically reducing prices and pushing for wider distribution. It changed the product from a specialty to a price-sensitive mass-market item. The majority of competitors were small firms who were financially unable to match the changed economics of the market and the new distribution system; therefore, they sought buyers for their companies.

PRODUCTION DETERRENTS

Capacity. By building production capacity to meet world demand, Hoffmann-LaRoche successfully deterred existing and potential competitors in the bulk vitamin C market. By creating the specter of the lowest-cost supplier who was able to meet and win any price war, it so intimidated competitors that many withdrew from the market. By 1980 Hoffmann-LaRoche had cornered some 60 percent of the world market for vitamin C.

Utilization. In the free-for-all following airline deregulation in the U.S., a few regional carriers such as Piedmont, Southwest, and U.S. Air increased capacity with more frequent routes, to deter competition. Because the airline with the most flights on a route gets a disproportionate share of traffic and the load factor determines profitability, many new airlines were deterred from competing on routes dominated by Piedmont, Southwest, and U.S. Air.

Equipment. Kodak's monopoly on film for its new Disc camera forced film processing companies either to purchase special, relatively expensive processing equipment from Kodak or to hand over their Disc film processing business to Kodak's own facilities. Either way, by deterring direct competition, Kodak could maintain a strong profit position in the Disc film processing business.

FINANCIAL DETERRENTS

Costs. Because of the high costs of participation, existing semiconductor firms have successfully deterred new competitors from entering the industry. In the early 1970s, new manufacturing facilities cost up to $5 million. By 1982 a single new plant for building advanced VLSI 64K RAM chips cost between $60-$120 million, exacting a high entrance fee for new competitors.

Economics. Federal Express is the leading low-cost air courier service in the United States. Federal Express's overnight letter service was introduced in 1981 at a low price with the aim of becoming profitable on volume in a 12-month period. Because it was difficult to make money when pitted against the lowest-cost competitor, who was using marginal costing and penetrating pricing, competitors were deterred from entering the overnight letter market.

TECHNOLOGICAL DETERRENTS

Innovation. All but the largest new companies have been deterred from entering the pharmaceutical industry. Risks are high—the number of products reaching the market is small. The business cycle is long-run—the discovery to marketing time averages twelve years. Costs are high—development costs range between $50-$100 million per product. In fact, with the exception of Janssen and Syntex, no company totally new to the drug market has succeeded in becoming a medium-sized pharmaceutical firm in the last 30 years.

Information. To provide itself with lead time over competitors who wish to supply compatible equipment to plug into new IBM computers, IBM is believed to delay the release of new product specifications. This policy deters an immediate response from plug-compatible competitors.

MANAGERIAL DETERRENTS

Acquisitions. Firms use both vertical and horizontal integration as a deterrent. By integrating backward, a firm can secure control over production and supply sources. Tube Investments in the U.K. integrated backwards by buying into steel-making when the industry was first denationalized in 1953. Tube Investments deterred its competitors by obtaining security of raw materials and the profits made by its previous suppliers. By integrating forward, a firm can secure control of distribution or other benefits. Genentech, a leading biotechnology company, is integrating forward from research into production. By limiting the transfer of critical purification know-how, it will deter current clients from becoming future competitors.

In horizontal integration, firms seek to corner the market to deter competitors. In the U.S., fast-food market firms seek the first franchise in new shopping malls to deter other fast-food companies from opening up competitive outlets. All integration strategies have the potential to deny competitive access to raw materials, know-how, and customers. Therefore, they can be powerful deterrents.

Mergers. In 1983 Thomson-Brandt of France acquired 75 percent of AEG-Telefunken's television and videotape recorder subsidiary. The merged entity held 25 percent of the West German and 20 percent of the European color TV markets and 10 percent of the West Germany video recorder market. Thomson-Brandt's strategy was designed to build a large European consumer electronics group with 1982 sales of $2.6 billion, a force capable of competing with and deterring further Japanese penetration into the European consumer electronic market.

Alliances. None of the three leading jet aero-engine manufacturers—General Electric (GE), Pratt and Whitney (P&W), and Rolls-Royce—were willing to fund alone the development of a new fuel-efficient engine to power a 150-seat airliner. The estimated development cost was $1.5 billion. But none could face the prospects of competing against the two other manufacturers for the same market. Each of the firms attempted to form alliances with smaller firms (GE with Snecma; P&W with MTU and Fiat; and Rolls-Royce with

Kawasaki, Mitsubishi, and IHI) in an effort to deter the others from entering the market.

In early 1983 Pratt & Whitney formed a consortium with Rolls-Royce. Together with MTU and Fiat, Pratt & Whitney would design and build the gearbox and turbines. Rolls-Royce and its Japanese partners would, in turn, build the fan and compressors for the new engine.

THE VALUE OF DETERRENCE

Deterrent strategies in business attempt to induce stability by encouraging prudence on the part of competitors. Rather than signifying that the combatants can inflict *equal* damage on each other, this stability reflects their ability to inflict unacceptable losses on one another in the worst case and, under less violent circumstances, a greater loss for the challenger. To deter a competitive thrust effectively, a firm must present a credible and visible case. It must convince competitors that challenges to the market equilibrium will be met and that, beyond a certain point, the challenge is not in the long-term best interests of the aggressor. If a company is not prepared to fight a war in the marketplace, it cannot rationally or credibly threaten another company, and its own survival will be threatened if it adopts a deterrent strategy.

The most critical factor in a deterrent strategy is gauging the capabilities and intentions of a challenger. Because full information can never be obtained, this process must be imprecise. Capabilities in terms of management, products, and resources constantly change and are not entirely tangible. Nevertheless, they can be determined with some degree of objectivity. Intentions are a state of mind and can be gauged only subjectively. Measuring intention means judging the interests and objectives of a competitor and the temperament and will of its management.

Companies frequently appear to be unaware that, in addition to a physical component, market conflict has psychological dimensions. Being able to predict and effectively counter competitive moves is a major strategic task. Business, unlike the military, has conducted little research to identify the intentions of a competing management and its psychological behavior. Yet such a study would enable a firm to use its capabilities fully in order to deter a challenge.

As the examples suggest, deterrent strategies are highly successful in avoiding fratricidal battles in the market. They enable companies to win without resorting to the debilitating physical contest of resources in the market.

Most military practitioners and theorists, from Sun Tzu around 500 B.C. to the present-day, have believed implicitly in the strategic value of deterrence. Napoleon said that all his "care will be to gain victory with the least shedding of blood." Most deterrent strategies in business appear to be adopted unconsciously as part of an overall strategic response rather than as a conscious competitive policy. Unfortunately, business appears to be wedded to the attack-defense syndrome of market conflict, thereby forgoing the considerable benefits of deterrence.

Because current market conditions require innovative strategic approaches to combat competition, companies that actively pursue deterrent strategies have an opportunity to gain a high pay-off at the expense of companies adopting more traditional approaches to market conflict.

Barrie G. James is head of marketing development in the pharmaceutical division of CIBA-GEIGY AG, in Basel, Switzerland. He is the author of three books, the most recent being, Business Wargames.

11.

SELECTING COMPETITIVE TACTICS: TRY A STRATEGY MAP

Terence A. Oliva
Diana L. Day
Wayne S. DeSarbo

When developing strategy, a manager considers how various tactics will affect both short-term performance and broad strategic direction. The skilled manager can keep these factors in mind while simultaneously gauging what the competition is up to. The authors describe a mapping technique that will help managers achieve this goal.

A company's competitive environment—that is, the industry characteristics and the behaviors of competitors in a given business—is the key determinant of that company's strategy and performance. However, as any manager can attest, knowing this simple fact and acting on it are two different things. Clearly, to survive in a competitive environment, a strategic planner must not only identify an industry's relevant performance measures, but also develop tools to understand the relationships among them.

We have developed one such tool: a "strategy map" that describes how performance measures (such as return on investment and market share), strategy tactics, and actual competitors' performance are related. In theory, given sufficient business data, a strategy map of this kind could be generated for any industry. In this article we will:

- present a map for an actual industry, showing competitors' locations, relevant measures for determining performance, and a "compass" that can help managers develop competitive strategies,
- discuss why this particular configuration is useful, and
- explain how strategy maps can be generated.

WHAT IS A STRATEGY MAP?

Perhaps the best way to understand a strategy map is to examine one for an existing industry. The use of actual corporate data precludes identifying the industry mapped out in Figure 1, but Table 1 shows its general characteristics. Mature and fragmented, it resembles the following industries: metal cans, adhesives and sealants, folding paperboard boxes, bricks and structural clay tile, and cement. We chose this general type for three reasons: a large percentage of industries are fragmented; the largest single group of industries is mature and industrial; and fragmentation is strategically interesting (in other words, problematic).

Figure 1 shows fourteen competing businesses—identified by the numbers—and eight performance measures—identified by the points. (We

Figure 1.
Strategy Map of an Actual Industry

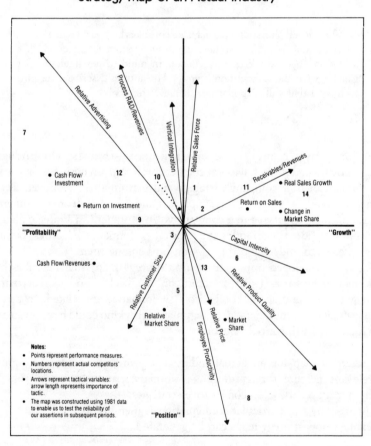

Notes:
- Points represent performance measures.
- Numbers represent actual competitors' locations.
- Arrows represent tactical variables: arrow length represents importance of tactic.
- The map was constructed using 1981 data to enable us to test the reliability of our assertions in subsequent periods.

Table 1.
Characteristics of Industry Examined

Table 1   **Characteristics of Industry Examined**

Highly Fragmented
- Only 18% of industry sales were from the top four sellers

Mature Stage of the Product Life Cycle
- Low growth—7%
- Cost-price squeeze—mean = −9%, sd = 4%
- Industry instability is low—.19
- No new products

Simple Technology, Easy to Imitate
- No patents for processes

Few Economies of Scale
- Direct costs relative to the three largest competitors —mean = 101%, sd = 4%
- Cost disadvantage ratio = 1.0
- Minimum efficient scale of plant = 11

High Transportation Costs
- No imports and exports
- Regionally served markets

Businesses Key Link to Markets for Their Companies
- Forward integration for the company—mean % of purchases internal = 85%, sd = 8%
- Forward integration for the business— mean % of sales internal = 7%, sd = 2%
- Relatively large industry

will consider the arrows and the axes presently.) The map is developed in such a way that the closer a business is to a performance measure, the better it does on that measure (and vice versa). For example, business 14 does very well on both real sales growth and change in market share, while 9 and 12 do better on return on investment (ROI), and 11 does better on return on sales (ROS). Firm 4, on the other hand, does relatively poorly on everything.

To see how such a map can be developed, consider a simple, intuitive example. Suppose you have the performance information shown in Table 1 for two competing firms. You simply develop a graph showing the location of the firms relative to the performance measures. Figure 2 meets that requirement. Of course, as the number of firms and performance measures increase, the development of a map by hand becomes difficult, if not impossible. While the map in Figure 2 is not really worth the effort, the one in Figure 1 is, since you can "see" what is going on better than if you were looking at the data in tabular form (say, in a spread-sheet like Lotus 1-2-3).

It is clear from Figure 1 that a number of tradeoffs *must* be made when pursuing the different performance measures. That is, the only way business 14 can improve its ROI is to suffer some reduced performance on real sales growth and

Table 2.
Hypothetical Performance Data on Two Competing Firms

	ROI	ROS
Firm 1	5	20
Firm 2	20	5

change in market share. We caution to point out that this condition is industry specific; such a tradeoff may be unnecessary in other industries. However, this pattern *is* consistent with both theory and practice for many industries. And, as most managers will attest, it is extremely difficult to improve all performance criteria at the same time. The map allows a manager to gauge what trade offs he or she will make in pursuing a given strategy—or what trade offs a competitor is making—and therein lies its major benefit.

The distribution of the performance measures in Figure 1 suggests what overall strategies businesses might pursue. The horizontal dimension appears to be profitability versus growth: cash flow/investment, cash flow/revenues, and return on investment are toward the left end of the axis; returns on sales, real sales growth, and change in market share are toward the right end of the axis. As one moves from left to right, growth is pursued at the expense of profitability, and vice versa. Measures of competitive position—market share and relative market share—appear near the lower half of the vertical axis, which we have labeled "position." There is no readily defined strategy associated with the upper half of the vertical axis.

We can now broadly classify the strategies that competitors appear to be following. Businesses 7 and 12 are enjoying higher profitability; business 12 is pursuing growth through high real sales growth and a large change in market share; and businesses 3, 8, and 13 have high market shares. Business 4's manager, on the other hand, has a major strategic problem. Businesses 3 and 10—which are not as far out as 4, but are not close to any measure—are poor performers.

At this point, a manager looking at the map (exclusive of the arrows) has a

Figure 2.
Map Drawn from Data in Table 2.

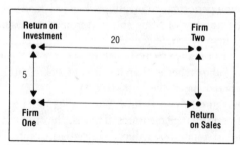

fairly good idea of the competitive environment's structure, as well as of the competing businesses' relative distribution within that environment. In fact, the clustering of several businesses indicates the existence of what Porter calls strategic groups.[1] This evidence, in turn, gives the manager a yardstick for comparison and can suggest new positions that may be reasonable to aim for. The question then becomes, "What tactics are necessary to change—and improve—my competitive position?"

HOW BUSINESS LOCATION RELATES TO TACTICAL VARIABLES

In Figure 1, the arrows represent tactical variables that, taken together, determine business performance. Examples include price, advertising, and research and development. Arrow length represents the individual variable's impact on performance—in other words, the importance of the tactic for movement in the direction of the arrowhead. We refer to this set as the "strategic compass."

In this particular industry, employee productivity, process R&D revenues, relative advertising, and relative product quality appear to have the largest impact on performance. This finding makes sense, since the industry is mature and fragmented. For example, one would expect process R&D to be more important than product R&D because of product maturity and the drive toward efficiency in the latter stages of the product life cycle.

The angle that the strategic vector (arrow) makes with each major axis corresponds to the relationship between the tactical variable it represents and the axis dimension. For example, a growth strategy would involve increasing both receivables and capital intensity (gross book value). This relationship makes sense: the business is adding marginal customers by increasing receivables; it is expanding the plant by increasing capital intensity to handle the business it hopes to generate. This particular strategy is appealing, because all businesses in this study were operating near maximum capacity and so needed to expand their plants in order to grow.

Conversely, a profitability strategy would entail reducing those two strategy variables and simultaneously increasing relative advertising and process R&D/revenues. Decreasing receivables/revenues should help reduce the marginally profitable customers; decreasing capital intensity will dampen its well-known detrimental effect on profitability. Increasing advertising, on the other hand, can inexpensively achieve product differentiation when products and their technologies are basically simple. In addition, increasing process R&D/revenues should improve production efficiency.

Finally, a market-share leadership strategy would focus more on heavy-use customer groups (i.e., high relative customer size) and employee productivity, and less on vertical integration and relative sales force. It seems reasonable to decrease attention to vertical integration: Both the product and its manufacturing are relatively simple. And, since these businesses are the last link in their companies' vertical chain, there are few opportunities to add value either backward or forward through additional manufacturing. On the other hand, using a relatively smaller sales force for higher market-share positions seems counterintuitive. However, at the mature stage, businesses can maintain superior market-share positions with relatively fewer salespeople. That is, by selectively focusing on heavy-demand segments of their market, they should be able to "get more for less."

As should be evident from the preceding discussion, the strategy map gives a clear picture of the specific nature of the industry it represents. To the degree that mature fragmented industries are similar, the map in Figure 1 is representative of a type. From an analytical viewpoint, the map relates competition, strategy (in the form of tactics), and performance in a single gestalt, which to our knowledge is not accomplished by any other technique.

CHANGING LOCATION

Strategic mapping allows the manager to simulate different strategies' probable impact on performance—and therein lies its power. Consider the case of business 10. Figure 3 shows its performance relative to its thirteen competitors in 1981. (Data has been disguised for confidentiality.) Table 3 gives the specific performance values for the business. It is apparent that business 10 is a below-average performer at best. The manager may conclude that a change in location would make sense. Specifically, he or she may want to move toward a profitability strategy via increased cash flow and ROI (for example, increasing ROI to 15 percent and changing cash flow from negative to positive). However, since market share is already low, the manager wishes to move without sacrificing share. The map gives us an intuitive feel for what will have to happen. That is, the new location will probably be in the third quadrant of the map, since this position would tend to balance the key performance measures involved (cash flow/investment, ROI, cash flow/revenues, relative market share, and market share). Suppose that the manager wishes to see what

Table 3.
Business 10's Actual 1981 Performance Data

Market Share	5.00
Change in Market Share	0.00
Relative Market Share	20.00
Return on Investment	0.60
Return on Sales	0.30
Cash Flow/Revenues	-1.40
Cash Flow/Investment	-2.50
Real Sales Growth	21.00

Figure 3.
Business 10's 1981 Performance Compared to the Highs and Lows for the Industry

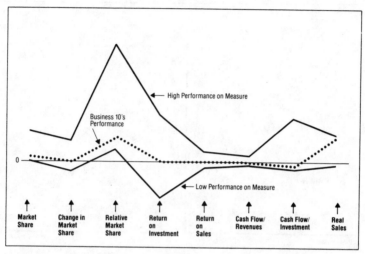

would happen if the business moved to location T in Figure 4. Table 4 shows the disguised data for business 10's tactical variables. The middle column represents the variables' current levels, which are responsible for the business's current location. The other two columns represent reasonable changes (up or down) that the business can make in setting strategy for the given time period (in the case, one year).

Location T's coordinates from the map (for clarity in the drawing we have not presented the scale) are fed into the computer program. Using the parameters set in Table 4, the program adjusts the tactical variables until it gets as close to the desired location as possible. Location S represents that point. Table 5 shows the appropriate changes in tactical variables, as well as simulated performance levels, for location S. At this point the manager can evaluate the changes that must be made in tactics, along with the expected results in performance.

Examining Table 5 more closely, we see that the suggested strategy would create the increase in market share, ROI, and cash flow called for by a profitability-oriented strategy. It would also require keeping relative advertising at the current level; lowering relative product quality, relative sales force, and receivables; and raising relative price, employee productivity, process R&D, capital intensity, relative customer size, and vertical integration—in other words, moving the business toward a low-cost position in a focused market. The suggested changes in the tactical variables, and the accompanying movement of the business, are consistent with the prevailing theory of how businesses stuck in a fragmented industry should behave.[2] Notice that trade offs

Figure 4.
Strategic Map Showing Target (T) Location for Chosen Strategy

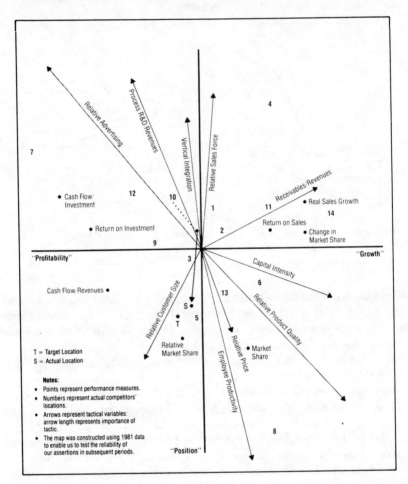

in performance do occur. For example, both real sales growth and ROS decline. We knew from the map that in all likelihood this would happen.

Obviously, other desired locations would generate different performance results and strategic changes. However, unreasonable moves would not be possible. For example, if business 4 tried to move to location T, its ability to make the required adjustments in tactical variables would be severely limited. In fact, if T were specified, the closest possible location would still be in the first quadrant. We hasten to point out that there may be a good reason for business 4's present location—all businesses in this industry are at the bottom of the vertical chain, so their performance goals may be determined by other corporate considerations.

Table 4.
Discrete Strategy Levels Tested for Business 10
(Disguised Data)

Tactical Variable	Levels		
	Low	Current	High
Relative Product Quality	40.00	60.00	100.00
Relative Price	9.60	10.00	10.40
Relative Advertising	3.00	4.00	5.00
Relative Sales Force	4.00	6.00	8.00
Employee Productivity	21.00	28.00	35.00
Process R&D/Revenues	.00	.00	.40
Receivables/Revenues	6.80	8.88	10.80
Capital Intensity	35.00	58.00	78.00
Vertical Integration	32.00	36.39	41.00
Relative Customer Size	1.00	2.00	3.00

Note: Discrete levels of the tactical variables have been used. This is realistic in the sense that managers would not look at an infinite number of possible combinations of changes, but rather would think in discrete quanta. For example, price changes are typically adjusted along discrete strata, rather than infinitely along the entire possible range.

CREATING A STRATEGY MAP

Strategy maps are generated using a technique known as multidimensional scaling, which is commonly used by marketing specialists to create product maps.[3] The program listing used here is called GENFOLD2. Developed by DeSarbo and Rao, it is available to those interested in using this approach.[4]

Table 5.
Business 10's Target Strategy and Resulting Performance

Strategy	
Relative Product Quality	40.00
Relative Price	10.40
Relative Advertising	4.00
Relative Sales Force	4.00
Employee Productivity	35.00
Process R&D/Revenues	.40
Receivables/Revenues	6.80
Capital Intensity	78.00
Vertical Integration	41.00
Relative Customer Type	3.00
Performance	
Market Share	7.464
Change in Market Share	2.464
Relative Market Share	28.337
ROI	15.752
ROS	− 3.086
Cash Flow/Revenues	1.996
Cash Flow/Investment	3.635
Real Sales Growth	− 5.320

• *The Data.* Clearly, a manager using this approach needs to have industry data on the competition's performance and on the relevant tactical variables. However, the key issue is defining the relevant information for your firm's industry or market. No single source of data can or should be used for every business. For firms with highly developed competitor intelligence systems, the information is already being gathered. For firms without such a system, this approach presents an opportunity to develop one.[5] In the latter case, managers can start by using public resources, particularly government documents and trade sources. One very good starting point is Information USA Inc., which publishes *The Data Informer: For Information-Hungry Decision Makers.*[6] Corporate business databases are becoming more readily available, but may be restricted either to project participations or to certain industries or markets.

For this demonstration, we used data drawn from the Profit Impact of Marketing Strategies (PIMS) projects, an annual, large-scale, statistical study of environmental, strategic, and performance variables for individual strategic business units.[7] Our example draws from what is known as the yearly fragmented, mature industry identified by use of a four-digit SIC code. We used fourteen businesses that had complete data on all of the performance and tactical variables over a four-year period. That period of time was not needed to develop the map, but rather to help validate the results. More than fourteen businesses exist in this industry; we used just fourteen for two reasons. First, the data was complete. Second, since this is a mature, fragmented industry where competition tends to be constrained within a local area (as opposed to the entire U.S. or world market), the use of a subset would not distort the results. Obviously, the appropriate number of businesses to use will depend on the specific situation confronting the manager.

Table 6.
Tactical and Performance Variables Used in the Study

Tactical Variables	Performance Measures
Differentiation	**Market Position**
Relative Product Quality	Market Share
Relative Price	Relative Market Share
Relative Advertising	
Relative Sales Force	**Profitability or Return**
	ROI
Efficiency and Asset Parsimony	ROS
Employee Productivity	
Process R&D/Revenues	**Cash Flow**
Receivables/Revenues	Cash Flow/Revenues
Capital Intensity	Cash Flow/Investment
Scale/Scope	**Growth**
Vertical Integration	Change in Market Share (%)
Relative Customer Size	Real Sales Growth (%)

Note: For operational definitions of these terms, consult the Appendix.

We chose the tactical variables shown in Table 6 because they represent the best selection available in the database for these businesses and because they are consistent with Porter's generic strategies. The Appendix gives specific operational definitions. They were distilled from a larger list of twenty-nine theoretically and empirically appropriate variables. We used both correlation and the theoretical analyses to identify tactical variables whose impact on performance was essentially the same. For example, employee productivity and manufacturing costs/revenues were almost perfectly negatively correlated over the eight performance measures used.[8] We chose between the two based on how each correlated with other variables, and on what seemed reasonable according to theory and practice.

The performance measures we used fall into four categories typically discussed in the literature: market position, profitability, cash flow, and growth. We chose two measures for each category. (These are also shown in Table 6 and defined in the Appendix.) The measures include the main ones that managers typically use for evaluating performance at the business level. When we ran a regression analysis to verify a significant relationship between tactical variables and performance measures, the average R was .85.[2]

The foregoing represents careful preprocessing of the data to get the best possible set of variables. Obviously, for different industries, different variables may be relevant. It is important to select them carefully and to use common sense about what the numbers really mean. One cannot simply throw in all possible variables, then have the computer pick out what it "thinks" is the best subset. The higher the quality of the measures used, the more specific the results will be. For example, if actual prices are used, then an actual price will be suggested in moving to a specific location. Managers must also consider the data's time frame. If a change in a variable would not be effective for several periods, the data must be adjusted appropriately.

• *The Program Analysis.* The data relating to tactical and performance measures entered into the computer is used to generate maps with different numbers of dimensions. This variety is necessary because, depending on the complexity of the material, a one-, two-, or three-dimensional map may best configure the industry. The two-dimensional solution given in Table 2, for example, can also be shown in one dimension. (A variation in possible frameworks is characteristic of maps and mapping in general.)

Typically, the choice of configuration depends on a combination of things. The two major criteria usually are, first, common sense—whether a particular map is consistent with managerial intuition and experience—and second, how much of the variation in the data is accounted for by a particular map. For our data set, we chose two dimensions because this representation made most sense in terms of the literature and our knowledge of the variation (94.83 percent). In this case, both the one- and three-dimensional solutions were less helpful on both accounts.

• *Validation.* After a map is developed, its results must be validated.

Practitioners have an advantage here, in that they can run small-scale tests. However, we suggest starting even earlier by running a few tests with the given data.

We did so by rerunning the analysis holding out business 10. (We selected that particular business because its fit with the analysis was neither very good nor very poor. We determined the fit by investigating the variance-accounted-for statistic by business, which is an output of the program.) The analysis, run with the thirteen remaining businesses, produced a variance-accounted-for value of 96.74 percent. Next we inserted the data for business 10 (the holdout) into the solution that had been based on the thirteen businesses. When we compared the two configurations using canonical correlation as an approximate measure, the correlation exceeded .99 on all dimensions, which simply means that the two maps matched up almost perfectly.

We used a second approach to examine how well we could predict business 10's performance merely knowing its tactical-variable values. Again using the map developed from only thirteen businesses, we calculated the business's predicted locations and its subsequent performance, then compared our results with the actual values. Since we had collected four years' worth of data on the businesses, we were able to perform a predictive validation for business performance.

Table 7 shows business 10's tactical variables for the years 1981 through 1984. Major changes include:

- increases in relative product quality from 60 to 80 between 1981 and 1982, and maintained at 80 for the subsequent years;
- increases in employee productivity each year;
- dramatic increases in process R&D expenditures in 1983 that were basically maintained in 1984; and
- decreases in capital intensity each year.

Table 7.
Actual Changes in Business 10's Tactical Variables 1981-1984

Tactical Variable	1981	1982	1983	1984
Relative Product Quality	60.00	80.00	80.00	80.00
Relative Price	10.00	10.00	9.00	10.00
Relative Advertising	4.00	4.00	4.00	4.00
Relative Sales Force	6.00	6.00	6.00	6.00
Employee Productivity	28.66	35.88	38.27	41.77
Process R&D/Revenues	0.00	0.00	1.20	1.10
Receivables/Revenues	8.84	9.29	9.29	9.70
Capital Intensity	58.00	54.00	48.00	45.00
Vertical Integration	36.29	40.56	36.90	35.77
Relative Customer Size	2.00	2.00	2.00	2.00

Figure 5.
Actual Movement of Business 10: 1981-1984

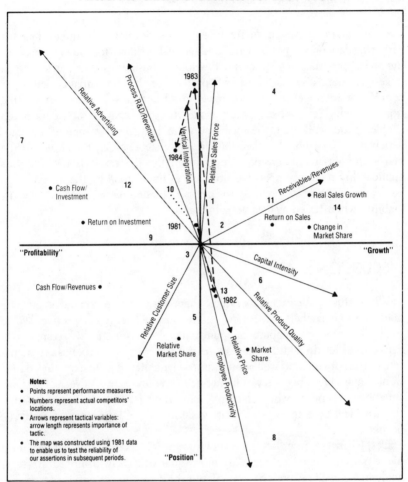

Notes:
• Points represent performance measures.
• Numbers represent actual competitors' locations.
• Arrows represent tactical variables: arrow length represents importance of tactic.
• The map was constructed using 1981 data to enable us to test the reliability of our assertions in subsequent periods.

These strategic changes over time are depicted by the firm's path in Figure 5. In 1981, business 10 is located near the origin. In 1982, the location changes to a new point in quadrant 4, reflecting one-year increases in product quality and employee productivity. Notice how this movement pushes the business in the outward direction of the two corresponding arrows. In 1983, the business moves from quadrant 4 to quadrant 2 as the result of a dramatic increase in process R&D expenditures that occurred in 1983. Again, this increase moves the business in the direction of the process R&D arrow. Finally, in 1984 the business moves back toward its original 1981 position. This change is due to a slight decrease in process R&D expenditures and further increases in employee productivity. A comparison between these movements and the actual values reveals virtually no difference in results.

• *Summary.* To recapitulate briefly, one develops a strategy map by gathering data on key performance and tactical variables for the industry, noting the appropriate lag structure. Obviously, businesses that participate in large-scale databases like the PIMS project, or that have highly developed competitor intelligence systems, have an advantage—they are not starting from scratch. Personal computers make the gathering of such data much simpler. Once collected, the user inputs the data to the computer program, which may be obtained as described in reference 4. Next, the choice of the map's appropriate dimension is made. Finally, the result is tested for its applicability to the competitive situation as understood by the manager, its ability to make good predications on a holdout sample, and, ideally, its viability when tested against actual data.

DISCUSSION

While this application of strategic mapping is a step forward in helping managers to make better decisions, its use must be kept in perspective. We do not believe that any computer program can or should function as a competitive decision maker. In addition, a map's usefulness over time depends on the nature of the data used, as well as on industry dynamics. The map produced here would have a life expectancy of about one to one-and-one-half years. For stable situations, or ones in which data is developed over a long time period so that the historical trajectory of the industry is understood, longer periods would be possible.

Despite these reservations, it should be clear that the strategy map overcomes a major problem in most quantitatively oriented strategic analysis—namely, it presents the relationships among performance measures and the tactical variables that determine strategic thrust. In fact, most other current research tends to focus on what the performance measures or tactical variables are, but not on how they fit together to create the competitive environment. By integrating these relationships into a single map, the manager gets a feel for the forces at play in the competitive environment and for how those forces affect performance. However, the bottom line is, "Are the results a reasonable, accurate, and insightful portrayal of industry relationships?"

While this question is difficult to answer in an absolute sense, we can check reasonableness against what we know about the industry. For example, in our data the location of the performance measure is fairly straightforward. That is, ROI and cash flow measures tend to operate in the same direction, while real sales growth, ROS, and change in market share cluster together, but in the opposite direction. Similarly, market share and relative market share also hang together. Hence, their arrangement in the environment appears to make both intuitive and theoretical sense.

Perhaps more interesting are the *importance* and *direction* of the tactical variables. These, too, make sense as they stand for a fragmented, mature industrial industry. For example, if the general strategy is to maximize profits in such an industry, then we would expect the key variables for achieving this goal to be increased process R&D/revenues, relative advertising, and relative customer size—and these are the longest arrows. That is, process R&D improves differentiation inexpensively; and relative customer size focuses the business on the heavy-user category of customers. Hence, if we used Porter's generic strategies, this one would be characterized as low-cost leadership to a specific target segment, heavy users.

Other tactical-variable relationships are also both interesting and consistent with conventional wisdom for this type of industry. For example, sales force and customer size work in almost opposite directions, as one would suspect. Vertical integration is interesting in that it is not near any performance measure. This finding is consistent with the literature, which suggests that vertical integration, in and of itself, does not have an impact on performance. Rather, its effect is conditioned by other factors in the industry.[9]

It should be apparent that the strategy map is an extremely useful tool that can tell managers even more than we have discussed here. In particular, the relationships among the tactical variables are rich sources of information. Considered fully, they will provide new insights about the nature of specific industries and markets.

APPENDIX: PIMS VARIABLES

Tactical Variables

- **Differentiation.**
Relative Product Quality—Percentage volume from superior products minus percentage from inferior products.
Relative Price—Weighted average of three largest competitors = 100 percent. Example: If this business's price averages 5 percent above those of leading competitors, then the value is 105 percent.
Relative Advertising—Relative to the three largest competitors, did this business spend from "much more" to "much less" on advertising using a five-point ordinal scale.
Relative Sales Force—Relative to the three largest competitors, did this business spend from "much more" to "much less" percentage of its sales on sales force effort using a five-point ordinal scale.

- **Efficiency and Asset Parsimony.**
Employee Productivity—Value added divided by the ratio of net sales (+ lease revenues) to sales per employee ($1,000).
Process R&D/Revenues—Indicates all expenses for improving the efficiency of the manufacturing and distribution. The figure is disguised in the database by a factor unique to each business.
Receivables/Revenues—Average receivable for the year, net for allowances for bad debts.
Capital Intensity—Gross book value of plant and equipment divided by new sales (+ lease revenues).

- **Scale/Scope.**
Vertical Integration—Value added divided by net sales (+ lease revenues).
Relative Customer Size—Breadth of this business's served market, relative to the weighted average of the three largest competitors on a three-point ordinal scale from "narrower than competitor" to "broader than competitor."

Performance Measures

- **Market Position.**
Market Share—Percentage market share for this business.
Relative Market Share—Percentage market share for this business divided by percentage market share for the top three competitors.

- **Profitability or Return.**
Return on Investment (ROI)—Net operating income divided by average investment (book value).
Return on Sales (ROS)—Net income divided by net sales (+ lease revenues).

- **Cash Flow.**
Cash Flow/Revenues—Net income times (.5) minus average investment (year n) minus average investment (year n-1); divided by net sales (+ lease revenues).
Cash/Flow Investment—New income times (.5) minus average investment (year n) minus average investment (year n-1); divided by average investment.

- **Growth.**
Change in Market Share—The sum of the absolute values of the yearly changes in percentage market share for this business, largest competitor, second largest competitor, third largest competitor; divided by number of years in the span.
Real Sales Growth—Percentage change found by dividing net sales (+ lease revenues) by percentage index of price (1973 = 100 percent).

REFERENCES

1. M. E. Porter, *Competitive Strategy* (New York: The Free Press, 1980).
2. Ibid.
3. See Y. Wind, *Product Policy: Concepts, Methods, and Strategies* (Reading, MA: Addison-Wesley, 1982), 83-91.
4. For program listing, contact Professor W. S. DeSarbo, Department of Marketing, The Wharton School, University of Pennsylvania, Philadelphia, PA 19104; W. S. DeSarbo and V. Rao, "GENFOLD2: A set of Models and Algorithms for the General Analysis of Preference/ Dominance Data," *Journal of Classification* (1984): 146-186.
5. There are several texts in this area, including L. M. Fuld, *Competitor Intelligence: How to Get It, How to Use It* (New York: John Wiley & Sons, 1985).
6. *Information USA Inc.*, 4701 Willard Ave., #1707, Chevy Chase, MD 20815; (301)657-1200.
7. For more information regarding PIMS, see C. R. Anderson and F. T. Paine, "PIMS: A Reexamination," *Academy of Management Review 3* (1978): 602-612; and S. Schoeffler, "Cross-Sectional Study of Strategy, Structure, and Performance: Aspects of the PIMS Program," in *Strategy + Structure = Performance*, ed. H. Thorelli (Bloomington: Indiana University Press, 1977), 108-221.
8. This result would be expected from the arithmetic relationship between the two.
9. See E. Anderson and B. A. Weitz, "Make-or-Buy Decisions: Vertical Integration and Marketing Productivity," *Sloan Management Review*, Spring 1986, 3-20.

Terence A. Oliva is Visiting Associate Professor of Marketing at The Wharton School, University of Pennsylvania. Diana L. Day is the Ebrenkranz/Greenwall Assistant Professor of Management at The Wharton School, University of Pennsylvania. Wayne S. DeSarbo is the Howard and Judy Berkowitz Associate Professor of Marketing at The Wharton School, University of Pennsylvania.

12.
DISCOVER THE RESOURCES IN YOUR MARKETING CHANNEL

James A. Consatantin
Robert F. Lusch

> While institutions in the marketing channel are often treated as
> elements of the external environment, they are in reality off-balance-
> sheet resources that management should develop. The Marketing
> Support System is a business philosophy that helps senior managers see
> marketing channels as resources to be managed.

Marketing channel and distribution problems of a recurring nature are experienced by many firms, perhaps most, because many chief executive officers,
presidents, and marketing vice presidents are myopic when it comes to their
firm's resources. Although they recognize that they are off-balance-sheet
resources. Consequently, the tactics for using middlemen and managing
marketing activities are not strategically based.

A myopic view of resources prevents the marketing channel, through which
goods reach their buyers, from working as effectively as it should because (1)
management fails to recognize that management of relationships among
organizations is as important to the effectiveness of the total marketing process
as the management of customer relationships is to the marketing concept; and
(2) there is a vast difference between the tactical process that centers on the
activities related to *distributing to* trading partners in the marketing channel
and the strategic factors centering on the function of *marketing with* them.

This article introduces the Marketing Support System (MSS) concept. MSS
is a business philosophy that helps senior managers see marketing channels as
resources to be managed.

The MSS concept underlies the strategic management of processes in the
marketing channel. MSS holds that the function of institutions in the marketing channel is to support the marketing effort of those involved in the channel.
It is based on the fact that those institutions collectively serve one another as
key off-balance-sheet resources and that integration of strategies affecting in-

terorganizational marketing relationships among those resources enhances the effectiveness of the channel process. A series of contemporary examples, involving well-known business enterprises, will best illustrate the MSS concept.

SOME COMPANIES AND THEIR PROBLEMS

Procter & Gamble had one set of problems with its wholesale customers: The McKesson Corporation had a different set of problems with its retailers. Yet, both sets of problems were solved when the companies recognized, then acted on, the difference between *distributing to* their customers and *marketing with* them.

The problems centered on supplier-customer market relationships. The solutions, reached under the guidance of former Chairman O. B. Butler of Procter & Gamble and the late Thomas E. Drohan, chief executive officer (CEO) of the McKesson Corporation, were achieved by identifying the nature of the problems.

One $7-million-dollar customer characterized Procter & Gamble's distributor relations this way: "P&G has always treated us as a necessary evil."[1] The customer was pointing a finger at an industry-wide problem that arises from the uncoordinated effort of complementary marketing channel institutions to achieve common goals. But P&G's Butler identified both the problem and the solution:

"We gain nothing from confrontation between manufacturers and wholesalers and between wholesalers and retailers. We need to approach our differences in viewpoint from a different perspective. I think we the manufacturers will sit down with you the wholesalers and try to decide how to [resolve our differences] as if we, in fact, were not only divisions of the same company but [as] if the retail outlets we serve were also divisions of that same company."[2]

McKesson's problem arose from a different aspect of the customer relationship problem. While P&G aimed at better service to smooth the process—and improve profits—McKesson addressed the inability of its customers, independent drug companies, to compete with the integrated marketing effort of the large retail chains. In a letter to the authors, Drohan said that "consideration of selling our drug wholesaling business back in 1975 and 1976 was never publicly articulated, although it is certainly true that some consideration had been given to it internally." The option chosen was "to join the independent retailer . . . in his marketing and total business efforts to compete with the chains."

Almost a decade ago, Leslie A. Hubbard, a former director of distribution and customer services at Black & Decker, noted a continuing shift in the nature of customer demand. He reported, "They seek increasingly to mesh their logistics systems with our own. We saw this coming three to four years ago."[3]

Black & Decker developed a strategy to interface its logistics techniques with its internal needs and with the needs of its customers and carriers. To do this, the company modified virtually every logistics activity and task, including distribution center locations, transportation policies, and methods of managing information.

Another chairman-CEO of a large company became personally involved in improving marketing relationships with its trading partners in order to provide better service to is customers. Lewis Lehr of 3M suggested the development of a "Partners in Quality Program" to match the company's standards and goals with those of the firms it does business with.[4]

The situation of K Mart and McLean Trucking Company involved a completely different reason for and approach to distribution management. K Mart had a vertically integrated private transportation system. Charles F. Rowe, K Mart's director of Transportation, could not get enough transportation equipment, so he began looking for a for-hire carrier to take over the long-haul portion of his transportation operations. A contract between the two companies called for Salem, a subsidiary of McLean, to provide long-haul service to K Mart; K Mart continued to handle its own short-haul shipments.[5]

In effect, three things happened: Some transportation resources were shifted from the balance sheet of one company to the balance sheet of the other, a new middleman was created, and the two companies became off-balance-sheet resources of one another.

These examples illustrate how the MSS concept can be tied to both marketing channel management and management of resources. Proctor & Gamble's Butler, as a manufacturer, pointed his finger at a "confrontation" type of relationship with wholesalers. McKesson's Drohan, as a wholesaler, cited the inability of retailers to survive under the existing system; 3M's Lehr, also a manufacturer, targeted flaws in the overall marketing system, including transportation; Black & Decker's Hubbard focused on the need for integrating company and customer logistics systems for better marketing support; while K Mart's Rowe as a retailer, highlighted inadequate private transportation resources.

These varying viewpoints are both symptomatic and symbolic of what appears to be a serious oversight or, as stated earlier, an incomplete perspective on resources. Manufacturing, wholesaling, retailing, and transportation companies typically do not see themselves as off-balance-sheet resources of one another. Nor do they typically include one another in planning the development of their resource packages. This results in insufficient attention to developing strategies for effectively managing firms in the marketing channel—to the end of *marketing with* them in contrast to *distributing to* them. While established marketing concepts tell us to market with target markets, MSS tell us to deal with interorganizational support of common marketing efforts by complementary firms. The experience of these companies shows that MSS opens to independent firms many of the same opportunities to improve their marketing effectiveness that are open to vertically integrated organizations.

MANAGING WITH MSS

We think of resource management as "the mother concept" of other concepts related to strategic management. Resource management meshes the functional theory of resource with certain managerial frameworks, including strategic planning and MSS.[6] It states that the relevant elements in the environment are resources of (or resistance to) the organization, and that the resources can be expanded or contracted in response to both managerial effort and cultural change.

For managers this means that all of the so-called constants and uncontrollable elements of the environment are potentially variable; that they are subject to being actively managed, as distinct from being passively coped with; and that the organization's resources include not only those that are shown on the balance sheet, but also such off-balance-sheet resources as people, concepts, complementary firms, and actual and potential customers.

Firms as Marketing Resources: One of the key features of MSS is its concept of marketing firms as marketing resources to be managed. The alternative view is that such firms are freestanding elements of the external environment hired to perform certain necessary tasks. Procter & Gamble apparently received the environmental signal that all was not well with its distributor relationships. CEO Butler met the issue head-on in a talk to members of the Food Marketing Institute: "I know there are times when it seems to some of you that we are not willing to listen. I hope we can reverse that feeling because we are at least as anxious to listen to you as we are to millions of individual customers."[7]

Procter & Gamble's response to those signals from the marketing channel has gone far beyond an avuncular "There, there!" from the chairman. Using the advertising theme, "At P&G, we hear you," Procter & Gamble told trade members about some important changes in its practices. Even more significantly, recent advertisements allude to major change in strategy concerning marketing relationships with channel members. In taking these steps, the company has acknowledged that the new realities of marketing support require that marketing firms in the channel be recognized as resources to be wisely used—the first feature of MSS.

Relationship of Complementary Firms: Another key feature of MSS is recognition that firms engaged in marketing channel-related activities have complementary and interdependent relationships with one another in order to serve a target. This contrasts sharply with the alternative concept of more-or-less discrete institutions that distribute to or through one another in order to market their products.

Perhaps the most important implication of this feature of MSS is that it recognizes what actually takes place in the marketing channel. All of the transactions involve institutions that should be marketing with one another—not just distributing to, acquiring from, or transporting for one another. Also, while each engages in certain activities, all have only the one marketing channel function, that of supporting the marketing effort required to serve target markets. In addition, each intermediary is a means to the overall marketing end of serving target markets—their reason for being. Finally, the activities that each performs are part of the continuous marketing process as distinct from a series of discrete and unrelated steps.

McKesson's adaptation to the realities of market support illustrates how the interdependent relationships in the channel resulted in the company's strategic approach to marketing with both its suppliers and customers. In 1976 McKesson even considered selling its largest business, drug wholesaling, because the company was limping along on a return-on-equity of about 11% and a profit-growth rate of about 2% per year—well below the inflation rate. The tendency of manufacturers to act as their own distributors precluded a faster growth rate.

As a start, McKesson developed a two-pronged strategic approach to establish new relationships with both its suppliers and customers and to create a new posture for itself as a middleman. First, it improved its own operations to "make the company so efficient at distribution that manufacturers could not possibly do as well on their own." The result of this approach is that the company is "redefining the function of the middleman."[8] This approach was designed to make McKesson such a valuable resource to both suppliers and customers that it would become part of their marketing teams. Also, it positioned McKesson as a company that marketed with its suppliers and customers instead of just distributing to them. After McKesson redefined its functions as a middleman and restructured its supplier-customer relationships, profits rose from the 2% per year average before 1976 to 20% per year by 1981. Also, over the past 10 years its return on equity averaged 19% per year, up from the previous 11%. By 1985, it had experienced over the preceeding five years a compound growth rate in sales of 16% with profits rising 17% per year.[9]

Perspective of the Marketing Channel: A third feature of MSS is the functional role it assigns to the firms in response to the strategic question, "What business are we in?" The function that each firm fulfills is to support the marketing efforts of complementary channel firms. This type of response develops strategic channel relationships. MSS does not imply the abandonment of the operations-based activities approach. To the contrary, that approach is strengthened because MSS provides a resources-oriented strategic foundation for the operations-based activities of wholesalers, carriers, and others. With that foundation, otherwise discrete activities become an integrated part of the marketing process.

We saw this activity-strengthening process at work as McKesson began to make itself indispensable to its manufacturers and as it began to position itself as an extension of both its suppliers and its customers. We saw the activity-strengthening aspect again in a specialized logistics setting. Black & Decker began to match its logistics techniques with both its internal needs and those of its customers and carriers. Hubbard acted on signals from Black & Decker's customers who were seeking "to mesh their logistics systems with our own." The strategic changes mentioned earlier were accompanied by changes in the way certain tasks were performed. For example, the distribution center changes were accompanied by adjustments in internal systems and types of equipment. The new transportation strategy led to new shipping patterns, delivery schedules, and carrier choices. The computer system changes resulted in improvements in order processing and inventory management.

Hubbard said that his company viewed "the distribution organization as a strategic support arm of our marketing divisions."[10] The company and its customers, carriers, and suppliers all gained from the new strategic posture and the improved nature of the logistics activities.

While 3M's "Partners in Quality Program," cited earlier, is broad-based and covers several areas, one facet of it deals specifically with transportation. To get the program underway with its carriers, 3M invited 85 senior transportation executives to its headquarters to explain the concept of 100% compliance with negotiated performance standards. According to Roger M. Nelson, systems quality specialist, 3M considers the carriers to be partners in quality because "they are really an extension of 3M."

Hundreds of logistics managers, probably including those of McKesson and Procter & Gamble, have routinely applied the functional features of the marketing support system concept to logistics matters for at least two decades. Many times their motive was to improve the effectiveness of their own logistics and marketing programs. Even so, to make those improvements the logistics managers had to consult with suppliers, customers, carriers, warehousemen, and other departments of their own firms. Despite the one-sided approach of supporting their own firm's marketing efforts, the fallout of changes flowing from that approach caused the support to be extended to others in the channel. Now, those logistics managers do not depend on fallout from internal adjustments; they consciously integrate the internal with the external.

Marketing Relationships: The fourth feature of MSS is that it does for the design of strategic marketing relationships among marketing channel firms what the marketing concept does for relationships with target markets. Those relationships are primarily output relationships designed to enable customers to take possession of their purchases in the expected form and at the desired time and place. In short, target markets are results-oriented and care little about the nature, effectiveness, or efficiency of the marketing process that provides the satisfactory results. The marketing concept focuses on both the possession-results orientation of target markets and the alignment of departments of the firm to deliver satisfaction. However, it is silent on matters concerning the relationships among the firms jointly responsible for delivering that satisfaction.

To illustrate this fourth feature of MSS, we recall that Butler told the wholesale grocers what they, Procter & Gamble, and retailers should do to establish effective relationships that would enable them to act as if all three groups were integrated parts of the same firm. Either directly or by allusion, he touched on all four of the features we assign to MSS. First, he clearly saw wholesalers and retailers as marketing resources instead of as organizations engaged in necessary activities. This came through when he said that Procter & Gamble needed the knowledge and creativity of middlemen to determine how certain things affect the consumer and the system, so they can collectively embrace the best one. Second, when he said that manufacturers, wholesalers, and retailers need to try to resolve their differences as if they were operating divisions of the same company, he was in effect saying that they were a continuum of firms marketing with one another to serve a target market.

Third, while Butler did not directly address the functional approach, the third feature of MSS, his several references to each of the channel members working for the same firm, alluded to the need for mutual support of the marketing effort of each. That support concept is the outgrowth of the functional approach. Finally, his comments as a whole dealt with the fourth feature of MSS, which holds that the MSS concept is to strategic relationships among marketing channel firms what the marketing concepts are to strategic relationships with the target market.

IMPROVING PERFORMANCE WITH MSS

Three characteristics of the marketing support system concept make it a valuable tool for improving performance. It *supports* the common marketing effort of complementary firms, it *facilitates* the several marketing processes, and it may result in greater *rewards* to the resources dedicated to the effort as a result of improved efficiency. Some of Procter & Gamble's recent ads have stressed the fact that they have helped wholesalers reduce costs.

The discussion of the features of MSS in the context of changes in the channel relationships between McKesson, Procter & Gamble, Black & Decker, and 3M and their trading partners showed that MSS is a concept that is both workable and profitable. Because that discussion was result-oriented, it did not address a means of attaining the improved performance. The elements of the strategy formulation process provide the foundation of the means-ends relationship. Together those elements make up the strategic planning that includes setting objectives, deciding on resources required to attain those objectives, and determining policies that govern the acquisition and use of resources.[12] Some subtle but profound changes in managerial perspectives on resources are called for.

Planning Premises: Since resources are the means by which ends are attained, the most significant change required in planning premises is to acknowledge that each firm is dependent on complementary channel organizations as resources for aid and support of its marketing efforts.

The activities these firms perform are not their excuse for being. They exist to fulfill their function of providing support for the marketing system, and their activities are the means by which marketing ends are attained. The interdependence of these firms implies that each should develop plans to obtain the support of the others and see to it that the support is rewarded. We have shown that a few firms have adopted this posture and have included their complementary firms in their strategic planning process.

Procter & Gamble, noting a lack of harmony with its customers, adjusted its concept of interorganizational relationships, reduced conflict, lowered costs, and increased the profitability of all concerned. It was so proud of its revised approach that it has developed an advertising campaign based on it. One part of that campaign centers on testimonials from customers about savings that resulted from the customers and Procter & Gamble working together. For example, one ad features a picture of William O. Christy, CEO of Certified Grocers of California, over the new Procter & Gamble logo ("Procter & Gamble" at the top of a circle; "We hear you" at the bottom). The theme is a $0.26 per case saving. Christy says, "It's reassuring to have . . . Procter & Gamble helping us lessen the cost of doing business in so many ways." Another ad features John Baldwin, president of Dillon Stores. He says, "Procter & Gamble, we look forward to other changes like this which will give us new profit opportunities."[13]

Common Interest in Marketing Objectives: The premise that marketing channel firms are interdependent leads to the second phase of strategy formulation—the recognition that marketing firms have a joint interest in marketing objectives. For example, even though there may be a conflict over the terms of trade, retailers are just as interested as producers in seeing that goods sell. Carriers have nothing to move if goods do not sell, and wholesalers will be creating assortments of nothing.

Setting objectives is the next step of strategy formulation. In addition, each firm should mesh its objectives with the objectives of its trading partners when possible. McKesson's profitability depended on the survival of its independent druggist customers, so it worked with those customers to devise ways to reduce costs and meet sales objectives.

Off-balance-sheet Resources: The third step in formulating strategy is to decide on resources required to attain the planning firm's objectives. To develop a marketing support posture, each of the complementary firms should recognize that all are off-balance-sheet resources of the others. They are more than just elements of the external environment to be coped with; they are resources to be managed. Each is more than just another organization to acquire or distribute goods; each is a resource to be marketed *with*. While each of our examples illustrates this step, the K Mart/McLean situation provides the most dramatic illustration. K Mart, in effect, quit using some of its balance-sheet resources (road equipment), while McLean created a brand new off-balance-sheet resource (Salem) for K Mart. At the same time, it put road equipment on Salem's balance-sheet and Salem on K Mart's balance-sheet.

Marketing Policies: The final step in formulating strategy is to develop inter-organizational marketing policies for resource use to enhance the marketing effectiveness and efficiency of all concerned. Black & Decker and its customers worked out arrangements like this in the logistics area, as have scores of other logistics trading partners. Also, 3M has negotiated performance standards with carriers and expects zero defects as just one part of its overall program.

With these four elements in place, the channel institutions that serve one another are able to manage their relationships in much the same way that their counterpart divisions in vertically integrated firms do.

Problems With MSS: There are two basic problems in formulating and implementing strategy for a marketing support system. While interorganizational cooperation is the basis for MSS, we cannot imagine a situation where all firms would be in complete agreement on all objectives and all implementation measures all of the time. Nor can we imagine all firms being in complete disagreement on these matters all of the time. Logic, common sense, history, and good management provide the solution: cooperate on those points where there is agreement; negotiate agreement where there is conflict; and lower the boom with the use of power when negotiation fails. This is a time-tested approach used by managers of complementary divisions of vertically integrated firms.

The second problem centers on the large number of organizations involved. While resolution is not simple, it becomes easier when negotiations are carried on within the framework of the so-called 80-20 rule. For example, 3M dealt with only 85 carriers. Or take a manufacturer, for example. A relatively small number of each of its suppliers, wholesalers, retailers, carriers, and warehousemen typically account for a relatively large portion of the business done. Negotiations can be carried on with some of these trading partners to develop basic methods of cooperation, and the result will probably fit the needs of the remainder. Modifications can be made when the communication system indicates they are called for.

When Procter & Gamble, McKesson, 3M, and others worked through these problems, they showed that solutions were possible.

PUTTING MSS TO WORK

If MSS is so desirable, why hasn't it become commonplace? We cannot answer that question with certainty. But neither have we heard of anyone that had an answer to that question when the marketing concept, the integrated logistics concept, the concepts of managerial accounting, strategic planning, Keynesian economics, and supply-side economics were introduced. We will look at some possible explanations before outlining an approach to making MSS operational.

Strategic Planning Overlooked MSS: As our ideas about resource management and interorganizational relationships began evolving, we asked ourselves why MSS was not a part of the strategy of every firm. One possible answer is that management got off course because strategic planning overlooked the marketing channel in general and relationships with complementary firms in particular were considered to be operational matters and got left out of the strategic planning process. Again, we are not sure why, but there appear to be several explanations or rationalizations:

- Because in dealing with channel matters, firms talked the operational questions, "What activities do we perform?" rather than asking the strategic question, "What business are we in?"
- Because conventional wisdom held that the complementary firms were part of the uncontrollable external environment and were not on the balance sheet; therefore, they were not resources.
- Because firms were overwhelmed with trying to develop strategy for target markets and with day-to-day channel crises, they did not take the time to think strategically about relationships with other channel institutions.
- Because channel strategy was thought to be concerned with such things as the types, number, and image of middlemen, it was not considered to be a subject for top-level formulation.

Historically, there are probably as many firms that have applied the marketing system concept as there are that applied some other new concepts before they caught on. Contemporarily, there are probably managers who took the concept to their bosoms while Procter & Gamble, McKesson, and 3M were still trying to define their problems.

Even so, except for many manufacturers' logistics departments, we believe that the broad spectrum of business has largely ignored the ideas underlying MSS. Because a few companies, including some we have not identified, have begun to apply MSS, we hope that Emerson was right when he said, "There is no force so powerful as that exerted by an idea whose time has come."

WHY MSS NOW?

Nearly two decades ago, Norman Judelson of American Standard (a manufacturer of plumbing, heating, and related systems) was quoted as saying that the purpose of planning is to make happen what we want to have happen.[14] Environmental signals, organizational rationalization, and managerial ferment indicated that this is a time to review what is happening and what is not happening in order to determine what should be made to happen.

What is marketing doing for and to the marketing channel? The output segment of the channel is governed largely by the marketing concept or some variant of it, and it is apparently working well by effectively delivering output-satisfaction to target markets. However, output is only part of the input-throughput-output continuum.

Off-balance-sheet resources on the throughput side are not being managed effectively; these logistics—wholesaling, retailing, and other resources—are just being used. The input to the marketing channel consists not only of the product or service, but also of the throughput segments whose activities deliver form, place, time, and possession utilities to the target markets. With relatively few exceptions, the management of nonintegrated firms, assumes that if company activities are performed efficiently, these functions will be fulfilled effectively. As the CEOs of Procter & Gamble and McKesson pointed out, that is not a valid assumption.

What can MSS do for and to the marketing channel and marketing? MSS can permeate and favorably affect all levels of management. Several forces can provide not only more effective inputs to the marketing channel, but also more effective throughputs and outputs in these ways:

- Functionally, because MSS relates to the total environment of marketing and responds to the question, "What business are we in?"
- Strategically, because in recognizing that the complementary firms are resources, a basis for improved marketing relationships is created.
- Managerially, because MSS provides for the integration of marketing policies of all involved, from the supplier to the recycler.
- Operationally, because MSS provides for trade offs in costs and services in the input sector.

MSS is not perfect. It is just better than what we have. It replaces conflict with cooperation and recognizes the use of power when cooperation fails.

Making MSS Operational: The MSS concept implies that the relevant institutions involved in the marketing channel are means to marketing ends and do not exist as ends unto themselves. Also, we have determined that each institution should be more to others in the marketing channel than just another group that in its own way converts raw materials into goods and services to put in the hands of the target market.

Three steps are necessary to integrate MSS into the strategic and operational framework of channel institutions. Taking these steps will solve the functional identity problems of all involved, and will define the "reason for being" of both the institutions in the channel and the firms in each institutional group:

1. Define what the firm is in terms of the marketing channel.
2. Spell out what the firm is here for in terms of being a means to marketing ends.
3. Find ways to help the firm take the lead in being what it is and to excel in doing what it is here for.

Table 5.
Ten-Point Plan for a MSS

WHAT WE ARE

We are in business to support your marketing effort; our resources are dedicated to that end.

We are more than just another company to process your goods through the marketing channel; we are a marketing support system.

We are an off-balance-sheet marketing resource of your company, and we consider you to be one of our resources.

WHY WE ARE HERE

To discover opportunities. We are here to help you discover and exploit opportunities to improve your customer service—and your profits. Tell us your marketing plans; we'll mesh ours with yours.

To discover problems. We are here to help you discover potential customer service problems—before they erode your profits. Tell us your customer service objectives; we'll use our resources to help you attain them.

To solve problems. We are here to help you *solve* existing customer service problems that are hurting your profits. Tell us about your marketing process; we'll try to design our operations around it.

For strategic reasons. We are here to help you design and implement your strategy for getting your goods to your target market. Tell us about your marketing opportunities; we'll help you exploit them.

For operational reasons. We are here to help you design and implement your tactics for getting your goods to your target market. Tell us about your operational problems; we'll work on them as if they were our own—because they are.

To improve your profit. We are here to help you manage your costs associated with getting your goods to your target market. Tell us about your operating process; we'll help you manage your costs.

To serve wants and needs. In short, because we are a marketing support system, we see ourselves as your resource (and you as ours), working as an extension of the arms of your firm in channel matters and serving the wants and needs of you, your customers, and your customers's customers. Tell us about those wants and needs; we'll help you meet them.

The ten-point program should help a firm in any of the manufacturing, wholesaling, retailing, transportation, warehousing, or their relevant industries position itself as a marketing support system. The program is outlined from the perspective of a firm in any of the relevant groups addressing itself to any, or all, of the other groups.

CONCLUSION

MSS is an idea whose time has come. Treat the cause of the problem by viewing complementary firms in the marketing channel as resources to be managed; then, treat the symptoms:

- Review your perspective of channel relationships—as Procter & Gamble did.
- Design "supplier service policies" to parallel customer service policies—as McKesson did.
- Upgrade your promises to complementary firms and your expectations of them—as Black & Decker did.
- Focus your attention on performance standards to improve quality—as 3M did.
- Get quick results by an audit of operating needs, especially with your carriers and warehousemen—as K Mart and McLean did.
- Above all, go back to the basic of strategic planning as they were outlined by early writers on the subject. This means that planners do not plan—they assist managers in the planning process—and that operating managers are involved in both strategy formulation and implementation.

REFERENCES

1. "Why P&G Wants a Mellower Image," *Business Week*, 7 June 1982, 60.
2. Owen B. Butler, speech to National-American Wholesaler Grocer's Association Convention, 9 March 1983.
3. Jack W. Farrell, "Where Logistics Thrives on Adversity," *Traffic Management*, May 1976, 36-37.
4. James Aaron Cooke, "In Search of (Carrier) Excellence," *Traffic Management*, May 1984, 34.
5. Denis Davis, "New Directions for Trucking," *Distribution*, November 1979, 34.
6. W. Nelson Peach and James A. Consatantin, *Zimmermann's World Resources and Industries*, 3rd ed. (New York: Harper & Row, 1972).
7. Owen B. Butler, speech to the Food Marketing Institute, 7 January 1982.
8. "Foremost-Kesson: The Computer Moves Distribution to Center Stage," *Business Week*, 7 December 1981, 115.
9. "For Drug Distributors; Information Is the Rx for Survival, *Business Week*, 14 October 1985, 116.
10. Farrell, "Where Logistics Thrives on Adversity," 36-37.
11. Cooke, "In Search of (Carrier) Excellence," 34.
12. Robert N. Anthony, *Planning and Control Systems: A Framework for Analysis* (Boston: Harvard University, 1965), 16.
13. *Progressive Grocer*, February 1985, 7.
14. Ernest C. Miller, *Marketing Planning* (New York: American Management Association, 1976), 89.

James A. Consatantin is a professor of business administration at the University of Oklahoma in Norman. Robert F. Lusch is a professor of marketing at Arizona State University in Tempe.

13.
WINNING THE
MARKET-SHARE GAME

Lance P. Jarvis
Edward J. Mayo

Because the hotel industry is a mature business, hotel companies must
work to hold or increase their market shares. A survey of "chain loyalty"
can help by identifying the most promising market segments and indicating the most effective marketing strategies.

Indications of the hotel industry's maturity are unmistakable. Growth in the
demand for lodging services has leveled off, and there is no prospect of
sustained high-growth rates in the foreseeable future. Indeed, the growth in
rooms demand was so modest in 1985 that a net increase of 70,000 rooms
helped to bring occupancy rates *down* 3.5 percent between 1984 and 1985.[1]

This relationship between the addition of new rooms and the decline in
occupancy rates is an indication that the industry's former strategy of pursuing
a growing market by rapidly building new hotels—a strategy that was highly
successful in the past—will no longer work. As Kotler and Singh suggested,
companies in a mature industry must pursue market-*share* gains, rather than
market-*growth* gains.[2] In this environment, any improvement in one company's market share will come primarily at the expense of competitor's market
shares. Defending one's existing market share and seeking opportunities to expand it by attracting competitors' customers will be the foundation of any
clearly focused marketing strategy.

Shifts in market share result directly from changes in patronage patterns.
Building more hotels might be one way to influence customers to alter their
buying habits, but a fundamental understanding of how and why patronage
patterns change is valuable for developing a strong marketing strategy.

A major factor in patronage patterns is what package-goods marketers call
"brand loyalty"—traditionally thought of as a customer's repeat purchase of a
given company's product. For the hotel industry, we prefer the term "chain
loyalty," to indicate a guest's returning to a given company's hotel properties,
wherever they are located. (Independent hotels can also enjoy brand loyalty,

when guests return repeatedly to that property.) In this article, we present a method of assessing hotel guests' chain loyalty, and we suggest ways to use the information gained from this assessment to build market share.

LOYALTY FOLLOWING

Customers who are loyal to a given lodging organization (or property) are the least likely of all hotel patrons to change from one chain to another as they travel, despite advertising appeals, sales promotions, discounts, or other efforts by competitors. These loyal customers constitute the repeat business that is the solid core of a hotel firm's business. If this core is large enough, the need to protect these customers from other firm's efforts to win them can dictate marketing strategies that emphasize retention of customers rather than the acquistion of competitors' customers. Companies with a softer customer base, on the other hand, would be more likely to pursue a strategy of trying to pull customers away from other hotels.[3]

In either case, however, the main strategy is to build a loyal following of as many customers as possible. So, first of all, we must develop a clear understanding of what "loyalty" means. Some marketers might say that customers are loyal if they have stayed in a given firm's hotels during, say, eight of their last ten nights away from home. Brand loyalty is often defined this way, in terms only of a customer's patronage behavior.[4] But, as we shall show, a definition of loyalty based on mere purchase behavior is not sufficient, because purchase behavior says nothing about the underlying motivations for that purchase. We will instead identify several distinct types of loyalty, based on *consumer attitude* as it relates to purchase behavior.

Who's loyal? Say, for instance, that Abercrombie is a traveler who has stayed at a Heaven Inns property for eight of his last ten nights away from home. Can we say that he is loyal to Heaven Inns? The answer really depends on the reasons that Abercrombie has stayed at a Heaven Inn. Say that he is really indifferent about which hotel chain he patronizes. During the past six months, however, Heaven Inns has been running a special promotion for a free night's accommodation after a guest stays nine nights. Abercrombie is one night away from collecting the premium.

Consider the following other hypothetical cases of Heaven Inns customers, all of whom have been staying regularly at the chain's properties.

Bumstead is a frequent business traveler to Boise, Idaho. Bumstead prefers to stay at Sheraton Hotels. But as there is no Sheraton in Boise, Bumstead stays in the Heaven Inn there as a substitute.

Columbo, an employee of Worldwide Widgets, stays at Heaven Inns whenever he is on company business, because the firm extends favorable corporate rates to Worldwide Widgets. Columbo follows the company's policy of using Heaven Inns whenever possible.

Davis stays at a Heaven Inn whenever she can. She has tried other chains, but she has found that Heaven Inns suits her needs.

Despite the fact that these four customers have consistently been staying at Heaven Inns, only Davis could be described as truly loyal to Heaven Inns. Given a free choice, the first three would probably give their lodging business to another chain. But Davis would be less likely than the others to switch chains.

What accounts for the difference in purchasing preference? For Davis, a psychological factor—a strong liking for the services of Heaven Inns—underlies the consistent purchase behavior. While Davis has become committed to Heaven Inns, the other three have no such psychological bond. Their patronage, though consistent, is not the result of any liking of or commitment to Heaven Inns.

True loyalty, therefore, is different from simple repetition of purchase. Hotel managers who do not recognize this difference are likely to equate repeat patronage with customer satisfaction, when the two are not necessarily related. Furthermore, these managers might conclude that their repeat customers are somehow safe from competitors' efforts to capture this business. To gauge real loyalty, however, hotel managers must consider not only customer patronage behavior, but also customers' attitudes as well. Managers who fail to take this step may devote considerable effort and money to the quest for new customers, while failing to take the necessary step of working to keep existing patrons.

GAUGING LOYALTY

The interplay of the two critical elements of chain loyalty— patronage behavior and customer attitudes—can be depicted as a chain-loyalty matrix, as shown in Exhibit 1.[5] In this matrix, each cell represents consumers who will respond to a different set of marketing strategies, based on their levels of patronage and of commitment. We will explain the characteristics of and strategies for the customers in each cell.

TRUE LOYALTY

True loyalty is evident in customers who nearly always stay at a given company's properties and also have a strong, positive attitude toward the company. In effect, truly loyal customers have compared the alternatives and have decided that one lodging chain best suits their needs, at least for the time being. In general, the greater the proportion of truly loyal customers, the less vulnerable is a chain's market share to depredations by other companies. We can say that its core market is relatively solid.

In the examples above, only Davis meets both criteria. She is relatively im-

Exhibit 1.
Chain-loyalty matrix

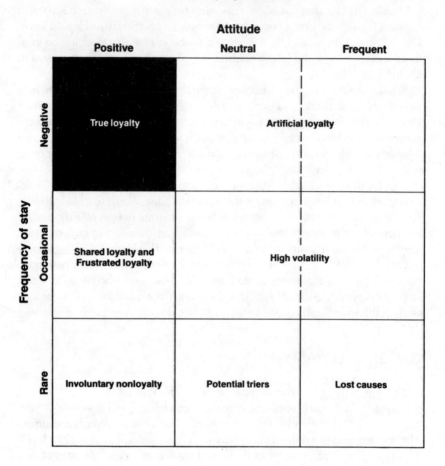

	Attitude		
	Positive	Neutral	Frequent
Negative	True loyalty		Artificial loyalty
Occasional	Shared loyalty and Frustrated loyalty		High volatility
Rare	Involuntary nonloyalty	Potential triers	Lost causes

(Frequency of stay — vertical axis label)

pervious to marketing efforts of other lodging companies. Indeed, her loyalty to Heaven Inns may cause her to screen out other companies' advertising and sales.

Strategy. Like Davis, customers who are grouped in this cell are barely susceptible to competitors' efforts to win their lodging business. Nevertheless, it is essential that the lodging chain *actively defend* its position among its loyal guests. An active defense entails sustaining, improving, and communicating a company's performance to its guests, so that the customers' existing perceptions of and loyalty to the firm are reinforced. An active defense of market share also requires an emphasis on quality control, the close monitoring of competitors' activities, and expansion into new markets where feasible.

ARTIFICIAL LOYALTY

Artificially loyal customers can be quite regular guests at a given lodging company's properties, so these customers are easily mistaken for the truly loyal. These customers, however, do not have a pronounced positive attitude toward the chain. In fact, they may not like the chain at all. Instead, they are staying at the chain's properties for reasons other than their personal feelings toward the company. These reasons may include one or more of the following:

- The guest may be indifferent about which lodging chain he patronizes, but ends up staying frequently at a given chain's properties more or less by chance.
- The chain's property may be the only one acceptable to some travelers at a given destination, as in the instance of Bumstead. Given a choice, she would stay at a different company's inns, but there is no choice.
- Rather than face the risk of trying a different lodging organization (and face a set of unknown procedures and policies), the guest may stay at a given chain's properties simply because he is familiar with them.
- The choice may be made out of habit or inertia, even when a traveler is not especially pleased with the chain's properties.
- The traveler may consider the chain the best of a poor set of alternatives available at the destinations to which he travels regularly.
- Sales promotions, premiums, or other financial inducements may provide sufficient incentive to attract an individual who would otherwise stay elsewhere, as in the case of Abercrombie.
- The lodging choice may be made by someone other than the traveler.

Despite their superficial resemblance, the artificially loyal customer is different from the truly loyal customer. Artificially loyal customers represent "soft" market share. Most of the attitudes that underlie these customers' lodging choices make this business vulnerable to competitors' efforts. Moreover, because these customers are so consistent, the loss of their business is a serious prospect.

Strategy. Defending one's market share by reinforcing existing attitudes, a good strategy with truly loyal customers, will not work with artificially loyal customers. Their feelings toward the company range from neutrality to active dislike. So the best strategy is to try retaining these customers by reducing the number or attractiveness of opportunities for switching. In the short term, premiums or other continuity incentives can be effective (as in the case of Abercrombie). But the essential long-term strategy is to solidify these individuals' business by developing in them more positive feelings toward the lodging chain (i.e., to move them toward true loyalty).

The specific actions necessary to improve these attitudes depend on the reasons for these guests' choice of a lodging chain. Attitudes toward a lodging organization are based on a set of beliefs or knowledge, which come either from firsthand experience (staying at the hotel) or from second-hand sources (e.g., advertising or word of mouth). To create more positive customer attitudes, a lodging organization must identify the beliefs that contribute to existing neutral or negative attitudes. Marketing research plays a vital role in this effort.

A guest's ambivalent or negative feelings toward a lodging chain can, for example, result from the belief that the chain does a poor job of providing one or more services that the guest deems important. Or that the chain doesn't provide the important service at all. Or that the chain's checkin or checkout policies are inconvenient. Or that maintenance is never up to par. In any case, once the beliefs contributing to the attitude are understood, managers can determine what actions can alter these beliefs about their lodging organizations. These actions may include changing the service mix, improving the properties, or simply communicating existing services to correct consumers' erroneous impressions.

SHARED AND FRUSTRATED LOYALTY

Some customers may have a positive opinion of a lodging firm, yet patronize the company's hotels only sporadically. These guests may have a *shared loyalty* between two lodging firms, patronizing each about equally. The guest may also have *frustrated loyalty*—they would prefer to patronize a particular lodging chain, but some factor stands in the way (e.g., the chain has no vacancies, someone else makes the person's lodging decisions).

Strategy. Because these consumers already harbor positive feelings toward the lodging company, this cell represents great opportunity. The strategy for the hotel company is to expand the opportunities for these travelers to stay more often at its properties.

For attracting individuals whose loyalty is shared, premiums, price incentives, and other sales-promotion offers are particularly effective. A chain could, for instance, offer its business clients favorable rates for pleasure travel. Such additonal benefits provide yet another reason to make a lodging purchase that the individual already views favorably.

The factors fostering frustrated loyalty are often temporary. If a significant number of people want to but cannot stay at a particular company's inns, the company has a substantial opportunity to increase business. The firm should investigate whether expansion of existing facilities or addition of new ones is indicated.

VOLATILE GUESTS

Individuals who are occasional guests and who hold neutral to negative feelings toward a lodging company are *highly volatile*. A firm whose clientele chiefly comprises these volatile guests has a market share that is extremely soft and vulnerable to competitors. Like the artificially loyal guest, these customers hold no favorable impression of the lodging company, and they stay at its properties for reasons other than personal preference. Unlike the artificially loyal guest, however, volatile guests are more likely to change their patronage from one lodging chain to another.

Strategy. These guests represent a highly volatile "swing" group of customers. The principal strategic focus should be on retaining these guests and increasing the frequency of their patronizing the firms' hotels. Like customers who hold shared loyalty, lodging companies can offer the volatile guests premiums or continuity incentives. The company should make every effort to promote new benefits to this group.

But the lodging firm's managers must take an additonal step with this group: they must understand the reasons for the group's neutral or negative feelings, and work to remove the causes of these feelings. Only then can this group's business be considered solid. Once again, attitude research should be used to identify needed changes.

If most of the volatile guests hold neutral feelings toward the chain (instead of negative feelings), the firm has a particularly good opportunity. These people are already occasional guests, so the firm could research the additional services or improvements in existing services needed to augment these guests' positive feelings toward the firm.

INVOLUNTARY NONLOYALTY

Consumers who are *involuntarily nonloyal* hold a favorable attitude toward a given hotel company, but they have not often been able to follow up that loyalty by staying at the chain's properties. Like the cases of frustrated loyalty, these infrequent guests might not find one of the chain's properties in the locations they visit, or the lodging decision might be made by someone other than the traveler. Another reason for infrequent patronage might be price; the traveler might consider the cost of staying at this well-regarded chain as too high.

Strategy. The principal focus here is to encourage individuals to give the chain more of their business—something they would presumably do if they could. Again, to the extent that involuntary nonloyalty stems from a shortage of rooms or absence of properties at desired locations, these individuals represent unfulfilled demand, and chain expansion may be indicated.

If price is an issue, the firm might consider temporary price reductions to encourage the guest to sample the chain's hotels. This strategy can be expensive if the guest will not come back at the regular rate. Furthermore, this strategy will allow some current customers to take advantage of the discount, permitting them to rent rooms at a price lower than they would be willing to pay. For this reason, the consideration of a price-cutting strategy must balance the value of attracting these customers against the financial consequences of price reductions.

POTENTIAL TRIERS

Potential triers rarely or never stay at the firm's properties and they hold no opinion about the firm, positive or negative. In this instance, the neutral attitudes usually reflect a lack of knowledge about the chain. In fact, many customers in this category have never patronized one of the chain's properties. Well-targeted advertising can create awareness of the chain, while coupons or price incentives can encourage a trial stay.

LOST CAUSES

Consumers who don't like a lodging firm and don't patronize it are *lost causes*. There may be any number of reasons that these people shun the chain. They may have had an unfavorable experience, they may believe that no hotel company suits their needs (and dislike them all, therefore), or they may dislike the look-alike tendencies of many chains and seek out independents instead.

Strategy. This is a low-priority group for marketing efforts. Given the numerous opportunities elsewhere, this cell offers the poorest opportunity for a payoff. Negative attitudes are difficult and costly to change, so any success among the lost causes would require considerable time and money. More favorable opportunities to solidify and increase the existing business base are available elsewhere.

MARKET ANALYSIS

The following example shows the usefulness of information gleaned from the chain-loyalty matrix. As part of its strategic-planning process, Heaven Inns, a regional lodging chain, commissioned a consumer-research study among frequent business travelers, who constitute its primary target market. A representative sample of 350 business travelers provided information concerning, among other things, their recent patronage behavior and their attitudes toward Heaven Inns and one of its main competitors.

From these data, researchers developed a chain-loyalty profile for both lodging organizations, as shown in Exhibit 2. The percentages shown in the matrix refer to percentages of the target market. Thus, any individual business traveler

Exhibit 2.
Sample chain-loyalty matrices for two competitors

Attitude toward Heaven Inns

Frequency of stay:	Positive	Neutral	Negative	Total
Frequent	True loyalty 10%	Artificial loyalty 3%	3%	16%
Occasional	Shared and frustrated loyalty 20%	Highly volatile 4%	4%	28%
Rare	Involuntary nonloyalty 16%	Potential triers 31%	Lost causes 9%	56%

Attitude toward competitor

Frequency of stay:	Positive	Neutral	Negative	Total
Frequent	True loyalty 3%	Artificial loyalty 6%	7%	16%
Occasional	Shared and frustrated loyalty 7%	Highly volatile 13%	6%	26%
Rare	Involuntary nonloyalty 12%	Potential triers 23%	Lost causes 23%	58%

is represented in the matrices for both lodging chains. In fact, examination of the row totals of each chain-loyalty matrix indicates that both chains enjoy approximately the same market share among frequent business travelers.

Heaven Inns' marketing share consists of customers who like its properties, for the most part. Better than six of ten guests who usually stay at a Heaven Inn display true loyalty, and some 70 percent of those who occasionally patronize Heaven Inns' properties have a positive attitude toward the chain. Its market share, then, seems relatively solid.

The chain's major competitor, on the other hand, faces a considerably different market-share situation. Most of the competitor's market share is vulnerable; levels of true, shared, or frustrated loyalty are low. More than 75 percent of the chain's customers hold a neutral or negative opinion of its hotels.

Based on the chain-loyalty analysis, Heaven Inns' management identified three segments of the market that promised the greatest rewards in terms of market-share growth. The firm developed the following strategies to maintain existing share and build new market shares.

SOLIDIFYING LOYALTY

First, Heaven Inns implemented a program to defend its position among guests who were truly loyal. Identifying its frequent business-traveler guests by name, the firm sent direct-mail advertising to these individuals. The company intended to reinforce the already positive attitudes that existed among these travelers.

Research had shown that the customers' favorable opinions were partly a result of the chain's excellent quality-control policies. To strengthen this control, Heaven Inns implemented an incentive program for its housekeeping departments and intensified its corporate inspection procedures.

WOULD-BE LOYALTY

Heaven Inns recognized a strong opportunity in the 20 percent of the market classified as holding shared or frustrated loyalty. The study suggested that most of the customers in this segment were splitting their patronage between Heaven Inns and its major competitor. Furthermore, the analysis of the competitor's market showed that three-fourths of its occasional guests were in the highly volatile segment. This finding indicated substantial softness or vulnerability in that portion of the competitor's occasional guests.

Heaven Inns' management decided that its primary objective would be to increase the frequency of patronage by its customers who shared their loyalty with another chain—thereby making these customers truly loyal. To do this, the chain began aggressive promotion of a continuity program that offered every seventh night free. The company also offered its business customers heavily discounted rates for vacation and weekends travel.

Next, Heaven Inns began to explore ways to differentiate its product from its closest competitors. The firm considered, for instance, adding a physical fitness facility to each property or arranging complimentary use of a local health club for guests.

EXPANDED KNOWLEDGE

Heaven Inns' research revealed that 31 percent of business travelers knew little or nothing about the company, probably because they had never stayed at one of its properties. These "potential triers" represented a significant source of potential new business.

To take advantage of this opportunity, the company adopted policies that would encourage these travelers to try the chain's inns. Rather than offering across-the-board price incentives, however, the company implemented a coupon program, coupled with targeted advertising in business publications and en-route media (e.g., in-flight magazines).

Short-term costs. Heaven Inns' management recognized that the programs designed to solidify a shared loyalty or to encourage travelers to try Heaven Inns would also be used by other parts of the company's market. The coupons intended for new guests would also be used by the company's regular guests, and these persons would certainly be able to take advantage of the free-night promotion. This meant that the company would lose some revenue during its promotions. This short-term loss was nearly unavoidable, but management determined that the potential for new business was worth the expense.

A WHOLE NEW BALL GAME

The low growth rate anticipated in the lodging market strongly suggests the need for a company to pay attention to its market share. This attention must be divided in two directions, however. A company must work on protecting its existing market share, and it must capitalize on opportunities for building its market position.

In the past, those companies attuned to playing the market-share game have taken a bricks-and-mortar approach by building new rooms and new properties. As this article has shown, expansion is not necessarily the most productive or cost-effective way of maximizing market share.

Packaged-goods marketers who have competed in mature markets have long recognized the importance of customer loyalty. It is usually easier and less costly to retain an existing customer than it is to attract a new one. A brand having many loyal customers is generally a profitable one. Accordingly, it is not surprising that marketing efforts are focused specifically on the cultivation of customer loyalty.

The framework presented here gives hotel-company managers a useful tool for focusing on the behavior of their markets as that behavior relates to loyalty. With little alteration, the matrix presented here can be applied by restaurant chains, as well as independent hotels and restaurants. Through this type of market research, management can identify unique target markets, assess the vulnerability of existing market share, and determine the most profitable opportunity for enhancing market-share position.

REFERENCES

1. Saul F. Leonard, *U.S. Lodging Industry* (Philadelphia: Laventhol & Horwath, 1986).
2. Philip Kotler and Ravi Singh, "Marketing Warfare in the 1980s" *Journal of Business Strategy*, Winter 1981, 30-34.
3. Joseph P. Guiltinan and Gordon W. Paul, *Marketing Management: Strategies and Programs* (New York: McGraw-Hill, 1985), 153-174.

4. Jacob Jacoby and Robert W. Chestnut, *Brand Loyalty: Measurement and Management* (New York: John Wiley & Sons, 1978), 28.
5. The chain-loyalty matrix is adapted from the brand-vulnerability matrix in: Y. Wind, *Product Policy: Concepts, Methods, and Strategy* (Reading, MA: Addision-Wesley, 1982), 160-166.

Lance P. Jarvis is an associate professor of marketing at the University of Central Florida. Edward J. Mayo is an associate professor of marketing at Western Michigan University.

14.
SCOUTING THE COMPETITION FOR SURVIVAL AND SUCCESS

K. Michael Haywood

"Putting the book" on your competition is a sound business strategy. Competitive intelligence is an essential ingredient in the strategic-planning process. The difference between good and bad decisions often lies in the information available. Here is what to look for and where to look.

Late in the 1929 baseball season, Connie Mack, manager of the Philadelphia Athletics, was convinced of three things. The A's would win the American League pennant, the Chicago Cubs would cop the National League flag, and Howard Ehmke needed a rest. Ehmke, a right-handed pitcher with a sore arm, had won only seven games for the A's. Mack told Ehmke: "Take the rest of the year off, and go watch the Cubs."

When the Cubs met the A's in the first game of the World Series, they faced Mack's surprise weapon—Howard Ehmke. He struck out 13 Cubs that day, and the A's went on to win the series in just five games.

Ehmke is sometimes credited with being the first advance scout in major-league baseball. Today, almost all sports teams "put the book" on their opponents, often through complex computer charting.[1]

You can, too. Businesses also put the book on competitors, as Peters and Waterman reported in their survey of top-notch businesses: "The excellent companies clearly do more and better competitor analysis than the rest."[2] Competitive analysis is one secret of success for many firms. This article will explain why your firm should make competitive analysis a regular practice, how you can start a program of monitoring competitors' activities, and the types of information that should go into a competitive audit.

A LINK TO STRATEGY DEVELOPMENT

Many hospitality businesses cast an occasional eye on competitors, but they do not always seek in-depth information about them. Competitive analysis entails the *systematic* retrieval and evaluation of information about competitive strategies. Michael Porter observed that the lodging and food-service industries are so fragmented that a competitive advantage can be gained only after a company's management thoroughly understands the structure of the industry and the position of competitors.[3]

Denny's Restaurants, for instance, used competitive analysis as part of its decision earlier in this decade to aim for the mid-price market. Denny's determined that all major players in the coffee-shop sector were saddled with problems, so the firm set out to reposition itself as a family restaurant. It expanded by acquisition in certain geographic regions, stepped up its renovation and design program, redeveloped its menus, and boosted its marketing and advertising budget. In this instance, intelligence efforts led Denny's to develop a strong offense.

CONSTRAINTS

Few hospitality firms are inclined to conduct this type of competitive analysis, however. The nature of the hospitality business fosters a focus on daily operations and immediate customer contact. But exclusive attention to internal operations may create a short-term point of view as well as a false sense of confidence, even when competitors are about to overtake a business.

Some hospitality companies—particularly small operators—assume that the costs of competitive analysis are beyond their financial capabilities. The expense of competitive analysis is no reason to assign it low priority, because it can yield invaluable information.[4] But as I shall show, much competitive information can be obtained for little or no cost.

Although gathering information on competitors smacks of spy rings and shady deals, competitive analysis has nothing to do with corporate espionage. Most of the information you'll gather is public, and much of the rest is freely available through informal contacts. After all, Ford and Chrysler are said to be GM's first two customers for any new car that rolls off the assembly line.

BENEFITS

There are compelling reasons for conducting competitive analysis.

- It enlarges a company's understanding of the customer, and sheds light on how customers—faced with multiple choices—make decisions about which hospitality businesses will best fulfill their needs.
- It is a source of new ideas and a confirmation of an operator's own ideas. It fosters product development and innovation.
- It facilitates better prediction about the future, and helps an operator prepare contingency plans for future crises.

- It enforces discipline in playing the competitive game, forcing an operator to evaluate any prospective course of action in the light of possible responses by competitors.
- It focuses an operator's attention on the need to choose which points of the operation will be emphasized.
- It fosters an acceptance of change—a realization that the business will necessarily be different tomorrow and that complacency is the surest road to failure.
- It helps point up competitors' weaknesses. A company that builds strength in the area in which its competitors are weak is likely to expand its market share.

BITS AND PIECES

Uncovering information on competitors is not as difficult as it might first appear, although the information generally comes in bits and pieces. You can start by reading the trade press, which publishes industry statistics, biographies of industry leaders, new-product information, profiles of companies, news of marketing efforts, financial results, and much more. The local business press might also print news of building proposals, new openings, and the like. Most companies seem to like publicity, although one industry leader, McDonald's, generally shuns company profiles and other revealing publicity.

National and local trade associations are also sources of information, both in the published information they supply and in the personal contacts that you can make during their meetings. Sometimes people reveal in conversations sensitive information that they would never want printed. You can also sometimes pick up information on competitors' plans during seminar presentations and discussions.

Firms that do business with your competitors usually have an excellent sense of their strengths and weaknesses. Vendors will probably not disclose privileged information, but they can tell you about general buying trends, levels of new-product use, experiences with new kinds of kitchen equipment, and so on.

Professional recruiters and personnel agencies might give some indication of the labor situation in a given company. Local trade schools, colleges, and universities will know when companies are recruiting, and what positions are being filled. Simple help-wanted advertising will tell you a great deal about what kinds of jobs competitors are filling. Personnel announcements also give you a clue as to the level of talent a company has. Whether appointments are being made from within or from outside can also reveal much about a company's philosophy and personnel situation.

Propriety's edge. A common information-gathering tactic is simply to hire persons who have worked for competitors. While these people will not necessarily reveal all of their former employers' secrets, they will certainly bring a fresh perspective to their new employer.

You can also analyze competitors' advertising and marketing programs, taking note of media used, timing, type of offers, and prices. An understanding of the messages communicated, their continuity, and the relationship of the messages to other competitive information can be strategically valuable. Some media firms specialize in gathering and selling this sort of data.

Consultants. Consulting firms, government agencies, and college faculty members conduct analyses of the food-service and lodging industry and of specific sectors and firms. Some consulting firms monitor certain parts of the industry, making their data available to others (often at substantial cost). Since your competitors often use the same consultants, you (and they) may learn additional information through direct contacts with these firms.

Publicly traded companies must issue reports to their stockholders and to analysts on Wall Street. If you hold some of your competitors' stock, you will receive this information—which is, of course, public. Statements by corporate executives reveal management attitudes and values, trends, performance, and future directions. You can compare annual financial disclosures to those of years past. Information held by the U.S government can be obtained through the Freedom of Information Act, but, under this law, your request itself becomes a public document. (A firm in Rockville, Maryland, FOI Services, specializes in making requests under this law to shield the identity of those seeking information.)

Customers. One of the best sources of information is your customers, who also patronize your competitors' establishments. You can talk to your customers in informal conversations, or learn their views through more formal structured interviews or surveys. A market survey of patronage habits in your community can be conducted via mail or telephone. Many firms engage college marketing students to gather this type of information.

You can also assess your competitors' products firsthand, be eating at their restaurants and staying at their hotels. You can determine price-value relationships, ingredients, costs, and a variety of performance measures. But developing an objective evaluation of competitors' customer demographics, staff competency, and product strengths and weaknesses requires far more than the simple collection of brochures and menus.[5] Moreover, since observations like these are a good way to collect information on the competitors, many companies have discontinued plant tours. (Companies can go too far in protecting their concepts; I recall a colleague's being booted out of a small dessert eatery simply for photographing the interior.)

FRAMEWORK FOR COMPETITIVE ANALYSIS

You must pursue competitive information in a methodical fashion, if it is to be useful to you. Large firms will benefit from the five-step program I will explain next; smaller firms need not use such a sophisticated approach. The steps are as follows:

1. Set up a structure for gathering competitive information;
2. Identify direct competitors;
3. Gather competitive information through a competitive audit;
4. Evaluate competitive information; and
5. Feed this information into your planning processes.

Creating a structure. Without top-level support, a company probably cannot maintain a useful competitive-intelligence system. Once management decides to proceed, it should create a structure for gathering and using the competitive information. To begin with, management should decide why the information will be gathered and what kind of information is needed. From these decisions will follow the assignment of responsibility for maintaining the information system. Because the type and extent of competition may vary from one locale to the next, the best plan is usually to have each unit manager be responsible for collecting his or her own competitive information. Chains operating regional clusters of units may want to vest responsibility for disseminating information in an area manager. Ultimately, one person in the head office will compile all reports from the field.

The degree of importance attached to competitive analysis will determine the amount of time to be spent on this activity. Regardless of the time involved, employees must be committed to the process, and understand why competitive analysis is essential. You can work out with your employees an arrangement for gathering, storing, and disseminating the information.

At minimum, your information-gathering system should include, for each competitor, a file that is kept up to date, a useful format for recording information, a way to disseminate the key information, regular meetings to discuss the information, and a security system to prevent the release of sensitive information.

Identifying rivals. The process of determining your direct competitors can be complex. To begin with, you can list all the hospitality businesses operating in your geographic area. Because you are not competing directly with all the restaurants and hotels in town, however, you should then classify these businesses, distinguishing the primary competitors from firms that affect your business only tangentially. Use such measures as type of establishment, target market groups, type and timing of patronage, and location.

Your trading area—the vicinity from which you draw most of your customers—depends on your market niche. A luxury center-city hotel might define its competitors as other high-ticket hotels within a five-mile radius. But airport hotels might present some direct competition, and must be included even if they are farther away or if their pricing structure seems different. Moreover, the hotel's management should take note of whether some potential customers are selecting university facilities for conferences.

For a fast-food restaurant, the competition might easily be defined as other fast-service restaurants within three or five miles. But all other restaurants with a $3 to $6 dinner check might be competing for the same customers and should also be included.

Functions and benefits. The most effective way to identify competitors is by matching the hotels or restaurants with the specific needs their customers are trying to fulfill, or by the benefits each competitor is offering the customers. Say that you want to attract well-to-do, dual-career couples who are entertaining important business clients during the evening. Consider the competitive choices these people have: a meal prepared at home by the hosts, a catered meal eaten at home, a catered meal served at a facility like a bed-and-breakfast inn, a fancy hotel restaurant, an exclusive independent restaurant, the company's executive dining room, or a country club. All the firms that can meet this demand are your direct competitors.

The process of identifying competitors can be likened to mapping a battlefield. By locating the relative positions of the major competitors on the "map" relative to target groups of customers, you can gain a better understanding of the strategic and tactical decisions that may be necessary to outfox the competition. Once your have identified your competitors, you can focus your attention on gathering information about them.

Dynamics. The problem with identifying your major rivals is that the field is always changing. One company may be ascendant this year; next year, it's been purchased and its components sold piecemeal. The really important competitors are those that can meet the needs and wants of customers now and in the future. Identifying rivals is a matter of determining which firms the customer will choose to patronize, because the customer makes the final determination of business success. For this reason, you must watch new and existing businesses and regularly reassess the question of which ones are your direct competitors.

COMPETITIVE AUDIT

After you have identified your competitors, you start gathering information. This could involve an in-depth analysis of competitors' product and market mixes, pricing policies, promotional techniques, positions in the product life cycle, and their past, present, and anticipated behavior. You can also assess how well each competitor is doing and their strengths and weaknesses.

Clearly, it is possible to gather reams of data on each competitor. You must, therefore, conduct an early "triage" operation of the information, deciding exactly what is worth keeping. All the effort you spend on data gathering is wasted if you cannot answer the essential question about your competitors. The many kinds of information you should consider collecting are listed in Figure 1.

Location. Note each competitor's location and size in relation to those of your firm. If a market is dominated by large firms or chains, small firms might find it difficult to compete effectively. In a market consisting of small firms that

Figure 1.
Keeping Track of Competitive Information

A complete competitive-information system will comprise a wide variety of information. The list below suggests what such a system should include.

Location:
   Location of competitor
   Advantages and disadvantages of the site
   Proximity to other competitors
   Effect of location of head office

Size:
   Number and size of units or properties
   Typical per-unit sales volume
   Number of employees

Background:
   Company founder: biography, business philosophy, management style
   Evolution of company: period of glory, setbacks
   Problem-solving methods
   Type of ownership
   Financial performance: sales, profitability, market share, occupancy, turnover

Executives:
   Personal traits: energy level, perseverance, self-discipline, initiative, level of
      enthusiasm, leadership skills, reputation, age, management style
   Job history: length of service, degree of commitment
   Knowledge, experience, judgement: managerial ability, skill levels, education,
      savvy, business judgement

Market status:
   Current rank or standing
   Trend of company business
   Status as market leader, trend setter, or follower
   Penetration of market with units, properties, sales personnel, products, or services
   Strength of company's loyalty among specific customer groups
   Dependency on current customers or market groups (noted seasonally)

Corporate objectives:
   Desired internal performance: market share, growth, profitability, cash flow, return
      on investment
   Desired levels of customer satisfaction, product quality, and performance
   Strength of company's objectives and degree to which they are communicated
   Past successes in achieving objectives
   Possible future choices of products, services, markets
   Priorities and guidelines in allocating resources
   Competitive intentions regarding each component of the business
   Identifiable events that have triggered company's intense retaliation
   Means company uses to detect market trends
   Structure of company; appropriateness to mission and objectives
   Company's ability, speed, and response to activities of market competitors;
      adaptability

Customers:
Typical customer mix and variation over time
Average customer expenditures for different time periods
Actions designed to attract specific kinds of customers and success thereof
Strength of company's grip on specific market area: coverage and penetration, company or brand-name awareness, media coverage
Customer's view of company's products, services, facilities, reputation, price-value relationship strengths, and shortcomings
Way in which other firms have enticed competitors' customers away

Physical facilities:
Age of units, maintenance levels, state of obsolescence
Size of capacity of units, appropriateness, and need for expansion or renewal
Cost-efficiency of units in regard to maintenance and energy
State of repair and attractiveness of interior design, decor, furnishings and equipment
Overall ambience, unique features
Efficiency of service-delivery systems

Performance of products and services:
Extent to which products create desired effect or perform intended function (atmosphere, comfort and convenience, appropriateness, flexibility, tastefulness, presentation)
Consistency, dependability, and safety (speed, waiting time, cleanliness, neatness, attention to detail)
Efficiency (operational systems, customer flow, policies and procedures, services, delivery systems, checkin and checkout)
Trade offs customer might make when purchasing

Salability of product or service:
Physical and functional attractiveness and distinctiveness
Unique selling proposition, or any other important, exclusive, or promotable feature
Price in relation to competition
Demand for product or service

Defensibility of product or service:
Protection of company's name, facilities, product line (e.g., menu) by copyrights, licenses, franchise agreements
Proprietary advantages, access to special sources of supply or trade secrets

Functional factors:
Overall labor situation: costs and rates, employee attitudes, union activities, job-classification flexibility, fringe benefits, access to skilled employees, training programs, skill level and technical expertise, recruitment loyalty, turnover, and absenteeism
Age and appropriateness of equipment
Equipment limitations
Competitive sophistication
Relationships with suppliers, access or control of sources of supply
Location of major suppliers
Use of special buying practices

Adaptability and flexibility of production space
Adequacy of capacity
Management ability to keep quality up and costs down
Extent and use of research in menu development, cost control, kitchen design, con-
cept development, facility evaluation, etc.

Marketing prowess:
Management: number of people, size of budget, existence of annual marketing plan,
distribution of marketing expenditures, effectiveness of decision-making, effectiveness of forecasting
Products and facilities: Current product-service-facility mix, and contribution of
each to sales and profitability; existence of program of product development and
deletion; management concentration of a given product or service; stage of
product life cycle; distinguishing features, advantages, or benefits; image
presented by current decor and furnishings
Pricing: methods and image, leadership role, reaction to other companies' price
changes, objectives and strategies, elasticity of demand, sensitivity of customers,
credit policies and payment plans
Promotion: sufficiency of advertising budget in relation to marketing objectives; use
of campaign objectives for promotional expenditures; use of outside marketing
agencies (e.g., travel agencies, advertising agencies); creative and media strategy;
frequency of advertising and type of media used; use of direct mail, point-of-sale,
or cooperative promotions; use of public relations; staff training in suggestive
selling

Finances:
Means of financing growth: external, internal, or both
Debt load
Credit rating
Seasonal and cyclical cash requirements
Short- and long-term borrowing capability
Extent of any past financial difficulties
Effectiveness of physical control of food, beverage, and other items
Systems of monitoring costs and cost performance
Effectiveness of accounting systems

---

cater to distinct tastes, larger firms might check for reasons that large firms are
not competing in the market.

Philosophy. You should also record competitors' prevailing philosophy and
approach to business, as a function of history and as it is currently expressed. A
study of a company's history can provide clues to its reactions to future market
changes.

The personal traits, know-how, experience, and ambitions of current
managers affect a company's success or failure. While it may not be possible to
evaluate all the managers in a firm (particularly a large company), a profile of
key executives is essential.

GUESSING GAME

Wouldn't it be marvelous to know the precise corporate objectives, strategy, and positioning of your competitors? Unfortunately, that is an unrealistic goal, because no company will knowingly present its game plan to its rival or define exactly what it intends to do or become, or to specify the kinds of results it seeks. Nevertheless, by studying what a competitor can or might do, you can develop a counter-strategy that might blunt your competitors' moves.

To release a customer from a competitor's grip, you need to know as much as you can about each competitor's customers, and the reasons for their purchase decisions. You should also examine the facilities and environment maintained by each competitor. At the same time, you should evaluate each competitor's products for performance, saleability, and "defensibility."

After completing a product analysis, you also should assess the labor, equipment, and technology involved in production. Next, keep track of the competitor's marketing programs to determine how well the marketing mix is managed. Last, you should consider competing firms' financial resources, taking note of their access to money and their management of existing capital.

EVALUATING DATA

As you can see from Figure 1, you'll have much information to assess. It must be sorted and judged according to the credibility of its source. Then you can draw inferences and make interpretations. The major problem is that of compiling good information and applying it to decision-making. Many factors can interfere—namely, the initial information may be inaccurate, distorted, garbled, or deliberately ignored (if it doesn't fit the management's preconceptions), information sources may be unreliable, or the information may not be relevant, timely, or in a useful form.

One way to reduce the amount of bad information going into the system is to evaluate the source content of each item. The following letter-number scheme used by military intelligence is one excellent way to make this evaluation.

SOURCE RELIABILITY:

A—completely reliable
B—usually reliable
C—fairly reliable
D—not usually reliable
E—unreliable
F—reliability cannot be judged

INFORMATION ACCURACY:

1—confirmed
2—probably true
3—possibly true
4—doubtful
5—improbable
6—accuracy cannot be judged

After judging the accuracy of each item, some companies put the information into one of three categories: background or basic description, current activities, or future speculation. Basic descriptive information contributes to the in-depth profile of the competitor. A major U.S. hotel chain, for instance, keeps a file on each of its major competitors, including exhaustive descriptions of personnel, holdings, performance, strategic thrusts, room-rate policies, and the like.

Current-report information gives you an idea of what is occurring at the moment. Executives in the hotel chain I just mentioned meet regularly to discuss current industry and competitive developments identified through their competitive-information system. They use this information to speculate on competitors' possible future actions.

Speculative information is difficult to process. In a perfect grand strategy, the unexpected should never happen. But information gathering has not yet approached such perfection, so it is necessary to develop a set of indicators or essential information points that allow operation of an effective forecasting or warning system. Examples of indicators in such a warning system could be the hiring of a new vice president for real-estate development or a staff expansion in the franchise division. Depending on past events, each of these hirings may signify a renewed emphasis on expansion or a strategic change in unit- or property-ownership patterns. Other indicators of renewed vigor or a change in direction could be new senior management, a switch of advertising agencies, an increased marketing budget, or a major recruiting drive. These indicators, added to the usual financial- and resource-based indicators, may have real significance when viewed in light of existing knowledge of the competitor's specific capabilities and weaknesses.

The value of an integrated collection plan is that it is a first step in the development of sound estimates or forecasts of a competitor's capabilities and intentions. The essence of competitive-intelligence process is the creation of a set of indicators that can be applied to a competitor's actions. To be valid, such indicators can be established only on a base of accurate descriptive studies, coupled with current information. Predictions based upon bias or hunch are of little value, as are those based on the premise to "what we would do if we were in their shoes."

GAINING COMPETITIVE ADVANTAGE

Merely gathering information on competitors does not provide the answers needed to outperform them. By researching the competition, you can gain information that allows you to follow them closely. But you still need to answer such "what-if" questions as: How can we increase our share of the market? What should we do if competitor X cuts prices? What can we do that we're not doing now? The answers to these questions involve integrating competitive information with a clear vision of your firm's strengths and weaknesses.

But competitive information can take you only so far. It can show you your competitors' strengths, but if you choose to match them in these areas of strength, you merely meet them head-on. The best of competitive information is to ascertain the competition's weaknesses, so that you can build strength against those weaknesses and gain an upper hand in that portion of the market. Patronage is not necessarily won by offering excessively appealing benefits to customers. It results from skillfully outmaneuvering your competitors to gain a patron's purchase.

Identifying your competitors' Achilles' heel is not easy, however. In some markets, most operators will have the same weaknesses. This is particularly likely when no operators are conducting adequate market research, and everyone is simply following the leader. These operators may not be aware of products and strategies being tried in other markets. An operator who regularly visits other areas or reads trade magazines might be exposed to new competitive tactics and benefits therefrom.

You may see the limitations of the competition, and the consequent opportunities for you, relatively early in the competitive-analysis process. As an opportunity becomes clear, you should determine your firm's ability to fulfill that need. You may soon observe that some of your competitors are failing to deliver on the promise of their concepts or that they are simply missing a market opportunity. On the other hand, you may discover that your competitors are in such a strong position that you cannot justify continuing with your present strategy.

Although many operators neglect it, competitive intelligence is an essential ingredient in the strategic-planning process. The difference between good and bad decisions often lies in the information available to the decision-maker and the decision-maker's ability to make sound judgements about the eventual consequences of competitors' current moves.

REFERENCES

1. Phil Patton, "Baseball's Secret Weapon," *The New York Times Magazine*, July 8, 1984, 25-27, 49-52.
2. Thomas J. Peters and Robert A. Waterman, Jr., *In Search of Excellence:*

   Lessons from America's Best-Run Companies (New York: Harper & Row, 1982), 197-198.
3. Michael E. Porter, *Competitive Strategy* (New York: Free Press, 1980).
4. Robert Hershey, "Commercial Intelligence on a Shoestring," *Harvard Business Review*, September-October 1980, 22-24, 50.
5. For example, see: K. Michael Haywood, "Assessing the Quality of Hospitality Services," *International Journal of Hospitality Management*, 2, No. 4 (1983), 165-177.

K. Michael Haywood is an associate professor at the School of Hotel and Food Administration at the University of Guelph.

Part III
MARKETING MANAGEMENT

15.
CHIEF MARKETING OFFICER: MAVERICK WHOSE TIME HAS COME

Neal Gilliatt
Pamela Cuming

To embrace the concept of the chief marketing officer (CMO) is to invite intuition and creativity into the boardroom. In an era of rapid technological change, cultural diversity, and consumer impatience with unresponsive institutions, these mavericks are the key to business success.

Many years ago, Samuel Maverick, a Texas rancher, gave five hundred head of cattle to a hired hand. The hired hand neglected to brand the cattle. The maverick cows, as they came to be called, scattered, seeking greener pastures. Today, organizational mavericks, like their bovine predecessors, seek new markets, products and approaches. Their willingness to take an independent stand and to challenge the status quo is essential if an organization is to be innovative in its response to change in the marketplace.

Organizational mavericks, unfortunately, are often either ignored or resisted by people who have a vested interest in maintaining the status quo. We believe that successful corporations are those that encourage non-traditional forward-thinking mavericks. Further, we contend that a maverick is needed at the top level if an organization is to incorporate a marketing perspective into the strategic planning process. We recommend that a chief marketing officer (CMO) be added to the executive office.

THE MARKETING PERSPECTIVE

The executive suite in most organizations is inhabited by the chief executive officer (CEO), the chief operating officer (COO), and the chief financial officer (CFO). Conspicuously absent is the chief marketing officer (CMO). If this omission leads to an insufficient emphasis on the market as strategic plans are formulated, the results can be devastating. Fascination with financial analysis, technology, and production can blind an organization to emerging trends. Management solely by analysis can stultify an organization as its visionaries become increasingly unimportant.

The organization that loses sight of emerging market trends and cultural shifts eventually will become paralyzed. Continued organizational vitality depends on considering the marketplace perspective when decisions are made in such diverse areas as product, price, resource allocation, acquisitions, divestitures, and technology. If this perspective is to guide decision making, the inputs of marketing must be deeply imbedded in the corporate ethos. Among the key management personnel, there needs to be an individual with vision who imbues the culture of the business with a marketplace point of view.

Because marketing is an art and not a science, it is best practiced by people who are creative, intuitive, and comfortable with change and ambiguity. Bureaucracy, with its efficient management of routine, is not the natural home of the effective marketing officer. Retention of a market perspective requires that the culture emphasize innovation over routine and that it accept risk and uncertainty as a way of life. The internal champion of the marketplace must, therefore, be somewhat of an organizational deviant or maverick, an individual who challenges the status quo, encourages fluidity, and fights rigidity, while still attending to the "bottom line."

A marketing perspective is essential to success. The ability to listen to the marketplace and to take innovative, imaginative actions based on an in-depth understanding of the consumer differentiates effective corporations from those that fail to realize their potential. Consider the Coca-Cola Company's move in the late 1960s to relinquish the popular advertising campaign, "Things go better with Coke," for a new strategy built around "It's the real thing." What motivated that move? Was it simply weariness with an old promotion? The desire to refresh the advertising? The hope of presenting an old product to the public in a new way?

All those factors undoubtedly came into play as the decision was made to invest tens of millions of dollars in the new advertising campaign. This specific change, however, was triggered by a firm belief that the buying public had undergone (or soon would undergo) a transformation in attitudes and life-styles.

Coca-Cola executives and their advertising agency correctly anticipated the "back to basics" mentality. The shift in attitudes and values forced modifications in many industries. Automobile buyers began to shun cars with fins and flash in favor of more functional styling and high-quality fits and finishes. Clothing fashions changed as people began to value comfort over glamour. The shift from "things go better" to "the real thing" defined that change clearly and simply.

Anticipating such a change in attitude and life-style is an art, but it is an art based upon the hard, tough work of making visible the invisible. The ability to predict social, cultural, and psychological change and the willingness to base operational decisions on these predictions: These are the hallmarks of successful organizations. The marketplace perspective must be as conspicuous in the top management group as are the financial and the operations perspectives.

In companies with a marketplace perspective, a predominant criterion for any action or reaction is the ultimate effect on the consumer. The statement seems obvious enough. After all, companies that fail to respond to consumer needs and preferences will go out of business eventually. And yet many companies accept mere financial survival failing to realize fully their sales potential. In some cases, their survival is ensured by their status as a regulated monopoly.

AT&T provides a prime example of an organization that did not have to develop a market orientation in order to survive. Regulation and the absence of competition did the job for it. With deregulation, AT&T has been thrown into the competitive arena. The greatest challenge it faces is not whether it can out-research and out-manufacture its competitors, but whether it can out-market them. Doing so will require that the members of the top management team redefine their jobs and become consumer watchers.

THE NEED FOR A CMO

Business literature today is replete with popular stories and thoughtful, academic studies heralding the resurgence of concern about marketing. For example, George S. Day of the University of the London Business School, proposes that "in the 1980s marketing has an opportunity to reassert its influence through contributing to the theory and practice of strategic management."[1] The 1984 Coopers & Lybrand/Yankelovich, Kelly, and White report states, "Marketing strategy is the most significant planning challenge in the 1980s regardless of industry type or size of company."[2] A special study in 1985 followed up on this report. Entitled "The New Marketing Shape of American Corporations," it further emphasized the shift in business planning priorities towards more strategic marketing.[3] And Theodore Levitt contends that there is no effective corporate strategy that is not oriented to marketing.[4]

Isn't it surprising, then, that in so many U.S. business organizations there is no specific provision in the executive suite for a marketing point of view? There are chief financial officers (CFOs) and chief operation officers (COOs) but, at least to our knowledge, few chief marketing officer (CMOs). In fact, the trend has been away from including a marketing officer in the executive suite. Since the early 1970s the percentage of multibusiness manufacturing companies with a senior marketing executive at the corporate level has dropped from around 50 to 30, according to a 1984 Conference Board Report.[5]

According to John Howard of Columbia University, the concept of CMO has been rejected because the marketing officer is unable to interact effectively with the heads of other functions and because well-established and widely understood marketing concepts and principles are absent.[6]

The Marketing Science Institute argues that the desire to quantify marketing efforts contributes to the problem. "The CEO with a nonmarketing background wants a more vigorous demonstration of what return he gets from the marketing investment . . . . and is more likely to expect marketing to be a *science* rather than an art."[7]

Lacking such overall concepts and unable to quantify the return on investment in marketing, many organizations relegate the marketing function to the divisional level. They restrict marketing to such tactical activities as field sales management, merchandising, sales training, sales research and reporting, sales promotion, product advertising, distributor/dealer relations, and national account management.

With all of these tactical bases covered, organizations convince themselves that they have a full-blown marketing function. In reality, they have a series of activities that do not necessarily provide a *marketing perspective*.

When there is a corporate marketing director, that person is often a coordinator for business unit marketing functions and the center for corporate advertising and corporate communications. The director is usually not expected to participate in corporate strategy decisions, nor does this person rank as a member of the inner executive group.

Of course, in many successful enterprises the marketplace perspective is deeply embedded in corporate tradition. In other firms, a sense of the marketplace stems from the fact that one or more of the top executives grew up in marketing. These firms may fill the role of a CMO while not showing the position on the organizational chart. But even if the CEO and COO have marketing backgrounds, the constraints and pressures of their jobs often make it difficult for them to find enough time to reflect on the marketplace per se.

The appointment of a CMO makes it far more likely that strategic decisions will reflect the marketplace perspective in addition to financial realities, operational constraints, and technological opportunities. In effect, establishing such a position gives the function of marketing a formal power base. With this base, the CMO can modify the direction of the company and influence the allocation of resources based on insights gained from a deep understanding of the consumer.

THE ROLE OF THE CMO

The primary responsibility of the CMO is to imbue the culture of an organization with a marketplace perspective by injecting *strategic marketing* into the planning process of the organization.

Strategic marketing is, in a sense, a hybrid of strategic planning and classical marketing. Classical marketing starts with an *analysis of needs and desires of selected market segments* and proceeds to formulate the organizattion's goals in accordance with those needs and desires. Strategic planning, on the other hand, emphasizes the *analysis of the organization's resources* and, given the macroenvironment, the ways to best utilize those resources. Competitive analysis, portfolio analysis, political risk analysis, cash use and generation analysis, and cost reduction studies are all the province of strategic planning. An understanding of the consumer, both present and prospective, is the province of classical marketing. Strategic marketing, then, is the marriage of strategic planning and classical marketing.

The CMO needs to be involved throughout the strategic planning process. The marketing perspective is essential as the organization defines or redefines what it is seeking to be, to achieve, and to become.

The CMO's involvement intensifies as the next level of strategic planning begins. Having defined the business, the organization must then specify its intended competence or domain regarding its customers and markets, its products or services, and technologies to be utilized. The strategic definition is elaborated as the organization establishes objectives around the acquisition and utilization of its resources—human, financial, and physical—and around ways to manage interactions with critical environmental groups such as unions, government bodies, and competitors.

It is in defining the mission of a company or business unit and in carefully developing that definition that a company can begin to construct these meaningful differentiations that are the heart of a successful marketing strategy. As Theodore Levitt points out in his latest book, *The Marketing Imagination*, marketing success is much more than statistical analysis. Break-through insights come out of a deep understanding of customer behavior, in terms of where it is now and where it is going. The subsequent classification of this behavior into useful market segments or clusters of segments begins to provide a structure for practical action.

The CMO, then, is more than a prophet of consumer preferences. This person must be centrally involved in strategic decision making with regard to the definition of the core business, as well as decisions to acquire or divest, and thereby to change the nature or scope of the business.

Organizations that are run by financially-minded strategists emphasize potential profitability, market share, cash generation potential, and cash use demands as they make decisions to acquire or divest. The extent to which the decision will diffuse or confuse the corporate image is rarely given sufficient consideration. The complexity of compromises, negotiations, and legal decisions that attended the AT&T breakup ripped asunder the long-time, carefully nurtured confidence in "Ma Bell." The cost of the multiple divesture in terms of image loss and image rebuilding has yet to be calculated.

Further, decisions to acquire or to divest need to take into account the organization's market niche. Acquisition decisions need to reflect the organization's understanding of a consumer group. When Coca-Cola acquired

Columbia Pictures, for example, it used its understanding of consumer preferences regarding leisure hours and entertainment modes. The acquisition, in effect, fit the culture of Coca-Cola. The criterion of cultural fit would probably have received far less attention had the acquisition process been driven by persons lacking a marketing orientation.

In addition to being involved in the strategic planning process, the CMO needs to be involved as decisions are made regarding:

- Products/services,
- Customers and markets,
- Pricing,
- Technology,
- Competition,
- Environment,
- Financial resources,
- Physical resources, and
- Human resources.

Only if the CMO is influential in these areas will the strategic marketing perspective become operational.

The nature of the CMO's involvement in these areas will vary enormously according to the size, the product-line diversity, and the organizational style of the enterprise. In decentralized companies, corporate concern is focused on policies, culture, and the overall design of the business structure. But even in such businesses, corporate decisions delimit divisional efforts and must therefore incorporate a marketplace perspective.

Products/services. The CMO must be able to influence decisions regarding products. Should a line be rationalized or eliminated? Should a line be diversified? Is a new product introduction in order? Should the company enter the accessory market? Although financial, operational, and environmental constraints have to be considered, the anticipated response of the market should be the driving force behind any product decision.

The marketing perspective was critical to Coca-Cola's decision to introduce Tab, the first dietetic soft drink, in 1961. The decision to withhold the use of the precious trademark, Coke, was the result of sound marketing judgement. No one knew, then, how big this new category would become. Twenty-three years later, low-calorie soft drinks represented more than 17 percent of the market and were still growing. This suggested that the time had come to use the trademark on a new, low-calorie product. Thus, Diet Coke was born and was an immediate success.

Some may claim that a marketing orientation renders an organization excessively reactive to the consumer and that technological innovation suffers as a result. The premise behind this argument is that an innovative product frequently will itself create a new, previously unimagined market. We agree with this premise wholeheartedly. If it were not true, the age of microelectronic typewriters never would have dawned.

Consumers did not seek out corporations and ask them to devote their R&D dollars to create word-processing systems. However, sensitivity to office pressures and costs stimulated exploration of the new technology and the development of "user friendly" products that have revolutionized the office. Note that technology alone has not assured success for all firms in the field. The firms, products, and systems emerging as leaders in this business have married marketing and technology.

To claim that a marketing orientation is essentially reactive with regard to product development is to misunderstand strategic marketing. The job of the CMO is to understand customers—their attitudes, work habits, leisure time, aspirations, life-styles, and needs—and contribute this understanding to the new product process. Strategic marketing is far more complex and visionary than the more traditional market research function. To create a product prototype and subject that prototype to consumer review and critique is only a small part of the strategic marketing function.

Customers and markets. Decisions made regarding *distribution channels* and methods and the *market segments* that should be pursued obviously fall within the natural province of the CMO. The definition of market segments poses a challenge to both reason and imagination. Traditional statistical segments may stultify any breakthrough. Without the perspective of a CMO, such understanding may never penetrate the executive suite.

Pricing. The organization's *pricing strategy* needs to reflect not only financial formulations but marketplace sensitivities and desires as well. In corporations in which the pricing strategy is formulated at the corporate as opposed to the divisional level, it is easy to see how the CMO could be involved in the generation of an overall price strategy. Should the organization attempt to be the lowest-cost producer? Or should the organization attempt to become the premium provider of what is regarded as a luxury, top-of-the-line item? Where is the market going? Can the company differentiate itself through price? What are the competitors doing? All of these are appropriate concerns for the CMO.

Human resources. Finally, the CMO needs to be able to influence acquisitions and allocation decisions in the area of human, physical, and financial resources.

It is not sufficient to imbue only top management with a marketplace perspective. Such perspective must permeate the entire organization. It is the job of the CMO to monitor the extent to which employees at every level in the organization reflect active concern for the customer. Only if the CMO is involved in making decisions regarding personnel management can he or she promote a service mentality throughout the organization.

The CMO needs to be a guardian of the corporate culture, ensuring that the organization maintain a sufficient level of risk-acceptance and innovativeness to enable a timely response to changes in the marketplace. Figure 1. outlines

---

Figure 1.
Hallmarks of Market-Sensitive Organizations

Behaviors That Are Encouraged

Positive attitudes toward change
Energetic approach to problem solving
Perception that change is an opportunity
Enthusiasm and a bias for action
Experimentation
Cooperation and collaboration across functional and divisional lines
Open communication and spirited discussion of different points of view
Orientation toward results rather than activities
Problems dealt with from a systems point of view rather than a segmented or
    functional point of view
Loyalty to and pride in the organization as a whole

Behaviors That Are Discouraged

Protective (CYA) strategies
Rigid adherence to job descriptions, regardless of need
Apathy and lethargy
Resistance to change
Complaints and nonproductive gripe sessions
Thinking in terms of existing categories
Turf protection and empire building
Withholding of information
Fear, insecurity, and pessimism
Underutilization of talents and capabilities
Emphasis on particular parts of problems and opportunities rather than on the whole
Dysfunctional levels of competition

---

behaviors and attitudes that are encouraged and discouraged in innovative, market-sensitive organizations.

Encouraging the mergence of desired behaviors and discouraging the display of unwanted behaviors often requires a shift away from a *bureaucratic* culture, which emphasizes the efficient management of the routine, and the embracing of a more *entrepreneurial* culture, which enthusiastically seeks to manage the challenge of the new and the nonroutine.

The CMO must participate in guiding the cultural evolution of the company. Doing so may require involvement in decisions regarding organization structure, performance review and reward systems, the design of jobs, and the patterns of organization communication and information exchange, both formal and informal.

Physical resources. The CMO should also be involved in decisions regarding the physical plant, when such decisions have an impact on the image of the corporation or upon the organization's customers. A healthy insurance firm specializing in coverage for the aged and infirm commits a vital marketing error when it constructs a new office in which customers must climb a flight of stairs in order to pay their premiums.

Financial resources. The CMO's involvement in financial allocation decisions naturally grows out of involvement in other areas. Spending decisions must reflect the marketplace if the organization is to continue to be economically viable. Stories abound of organizations that had a "winner" and yet lost. Instead of spending in order to maintain an image, they funnelled the profits from that winner into another line. As a result, the image suffered, and the winner began to lose its brand differentiation. It takes money and time to inspire the public year after year to ask for "Kleenex" when they want a tissue, or for "Smirnoff" when they want vodka.

The process does not end there, however. Because the marketplace is so complex, so changing, so *human*, the CMO has a continued role in the planning process. As a senior of social trends and consequent marketplace changes, the CMO stimulates a continual reassessment of organization direction. Unlike the marketing director or sales manager, the CMO must have an impact upon *every* area of the business. The complexity and importance of the role requires that the position be formalized within the executive suite.

Modifying the organizational chart to incorporate the role of the CMO is difficult, given the very human tendency to resist changes that threaten existing turf and jurisdictional boundaries. Even more difficult is finding an individual who is suited for the job in terms of intellect, temperament, attitude, and skill.

A PROFILE OF THE CMO

The CMO must be prepared and able to function as an organizational maverick. This person must be able to take an independent stand and be willing to refuse to conform. Obviously, the CMO must not be such a maverick that communication with the other organizational decision makers is a problem. And the CMO must understand and accept the facts that no business survives without profit and that tight controls are necessary to achieve and maintain financial success. The word "maverick" is used to underscore independence, innovation, artistry, and understanding of people. These are the characteristics the CMO must bring to an enterprise.

In order to influence decisions ranging from products to the use of the organization's financial resources, the CMO must also be able to command the respect and attention of such diverse personalities as the CFO, the COO, the head of sales, the director of personnel, and the technologist or scientist who heads the R&D function. The CMO has to have the same command of marketing expertise as the COO and CFO have of operations and finance. Herein lies the challenge, for few businesses have this type of CMO.

Communications skills and a tolerance for being different are not all that is required. The CMO must have the intellectual ability to understand and to anticipate changes in the marketplace and in society. What is required is a prophet and a seer who is simultaneously pragmatic enough to recommend a specific form of organizational response.

To perform effectively in the role of CMO, then, an individual must:

- Think strategically,
- Be intellectually curious,
- Have the ability to pull information from data,
- Be comfortable with innovation,
- Be socially curious,
- Have superb interpersonal skills, and
- Be courageous.

Strategic thinking. People who are able to maintain a strategic perspective are comfortable thinking in the long term. They are able to see beyond the immediate; today's crises and operational demands do not absorb all of their attention. Further, they are comfortable with the abstract and have a high tolerance for ambiguity. They are able to accept the notion that the environment is turbulent and unpredictable, and they seek opportunity within change. Finally, they are able to perceive the interrelationships between the many variables that make up an organization. They are able to maintain a total corporate orientation as opposed to a product, regional, or functional viewpoint.

Intellectual curiosity. The ability to understand broad social trends depends on an awareness of changes in all facets of our society: political, economic, legal, technological, psychological, social, and familial. Keeping abreast of these changes requires not only a high level of awareness but also an active pursuit of multiple sources of knowledge. An individual who reads only engineering journals, or only psychological journals, or only nuclear news is unlikely to have a broad enough perspective to be able to understand emergent trends in the marketplace.

It is impossible to have a strategic marketing orientation without an understanding of emergent social trends. Intellectual curiosity enables the CMO to be oriented to the future and aware of the impact of short-term operational decisions on the long-term market viability of the organization.

For example, the intellectual curiosity of Heublein executives made them sensitive to the shift in consumer attitudes toward health and fitness. They understood that drinking patterns would change to reflect not only a concern with health, but also the shift toward social drinking in the home as opposed to bars. Intellectual curiosity propelled the successful strategy of building the vodka category through new drinks with more ice and mixer and less alcohol, like the Bloody Mary and the screwdriver.

Pulling information from data. The mental prowess of the effective CMO goes beyond intellectual curiosity. Coupled with an insatiable desire to learn is the ability to perceive the message hidden within statistics. In today's computerized environment, such a marketer will of course be comfortable with the most contemporary research and analysis tools.

To continue the Heublein example, its executives became aware that alcohol consumption rates per capita were on the decline. They understood that the issue was not the number of drinks but the relative alcohol content of each drink. The data (consumption rate per capita) were simply interesting, if true. The information, however, that was hidden in the data was indispensable to a viable corporate strategy. While a more analytically oriented thinker might have perceived only a problem, Heublein executives were able to view the trend as an opportunity.

Comfort with innovation. To be effective, the CMO must be more than comfortable with change. He or she must be a catalyst of innovation within the organization. The focus of the office is on what the organization *might be* doing, not on what it is doing or always *has done.* Promoters of change tend to be self-confident people who trust their own instincts and their ability to survive regardless of what the future may bring. The stimulus for change also tends to come from people who have an experimental nature, who take pleasure in the exploration of new concepts, technologies, and approaches. The security of the known is of less interest to the effective CMO than is the challenge of the untried.

The CMO anticipates changes in the buying public. Responding to a change in consumer needs and preferences generally requires innovation on the part of the organization. But organizations as a whole tend to resist change. The CMO needs to be able to counteract these resistances and to push the organization into a more risk-accepting mode.

Social curiosity. The CMO must be at home at both the opera and the local discotheque. The CMO must be curious enough about people, and interested enough in their lives, to take the subway, to visit the bars, to walk the streets. Although it may be acceptable for the CFO to take a limousine to work and to spend the day in conversation with like-minded and like-status colleagues, the CMO cannot behave in this way.

Henry Ford's success stemmed directly from his in-depth understanding of the mentality of the farmer and the ordinary working person. This understanding probably grew out of his own exposure to their life-styles and from surrounding himself with people who enjoyed spending time with the "common man." Unfortunately for Ford, when the "common" American changed with the prosperity of the 1920s, it was General Motors and then Chrysler who first grasped the change.

The effective CMO enjoys the company of a wide variety of people. Unblinded by stereotypes of class, race, or age, the CMO is curious and wants to learn about people with different values and backgrounds, dreams, and problems. He or she is interested in people who pursue alternative life-styles. The CMO who succeeds invests energy in understanding, not in evaluating, others.

Superb interpersonal skills. The ideal candidate for the position of CMO is bright, aware, and perceptive, able to persuade others to follow his or her lead while maintaining sound interpersonal relationships. In effect, the successful CMO leads through the power of trust and friendship, not through the power of force or fear. People both enjoy and are inspired by the CMO. In spite of status and success, the CMO is quietly self-confident, not arrogant or abrasive. He or she is able to assert opinions and beliefs clearly, but not at the expense of others. Astute listening skills enable the CMO to understand the point of view of others, and astute persuasive skills enable the CMO to convince others.

The effective CMO enjoys the power of presence. Thought, appearance, manner, and energy combine to effect a charisma that stimulates others to attend and to follow. Chrysler's Lee Iaccoca provides a ready example of the importance of presence, or charisma, to the attempt to imbue the organization with a marketplace point of view.

Courage. Mavericks are, by definition, courageous. They have the self-confidence and the stamina to stand alone, to reject the status quo, to fight for a new course of action. The CMO must have the courage to tell the CEO that a favorite line of business should be rationalized or to suggest to the CFO that the company risk a large sum of money in an untried product area or on a novel advertising campaign. John Scully of Apple Computer displayed such courage when he launched the multimillion dollar campaign to introduce the Macintosh.

The CMO is the champion of change, the promoter of risk-taking strategies. Because the new involves an element of the unknown, there is always the possibility of error due to misjudgement or to a shift in market trends or competitive strategies. It takes insight to anticipate the market; it takes courage to act on those insights.

EVALUATING THE PERFORMANCE OF THE CMO

Finding a suitable candidate for the job of CMO is difficult. Even more difficult is evaluating the performance of such a person. The measure most often used to assess the effectiveness of top management is, very simply, the "bottom line." Did the CFO anticipate that the yen would drop in relation to the dollar? Was the decision to invest in a particular stock a sound one? Are products being delivered according to schedule and within the cost constraints indicated in the budget?

There are clear and definitive answers to questions like these. They offer standards against which to measure the performance of the COO and the CFO. These standards are not appropriate measures of the performance of the CMO.

The job of the CMO is to anticipate trends and to alert the organization to these trends early enough to enable an appropriate response. Changes in buyer behavior evolve slowly, so slowly that years elapse before an organization can determine the impact of the visions of the CMO on the "bottom line."

Because short-term performance measures cannot be applied to the CMO, organizations are forced to take a leap of faith in accepting and acting upon the visions of their organizational maverick. This is difficult for management to do, particularly in an era of fascination with numbers and analytical models. And yet, to do otherwise is to render the CMO ineffective.

Strategic marketing is an art; it is not a science. It can be practiced only by a creative individual. Creativity flourishes in an environment in which there is freedom to experiment, freedom to fail. Short-term financial measures inhibit the creativity process, forcing the CMO to predict short-term changes in buying habits as opposed to the longer-term cultural trends that require a more significant response for the organization.

To embrace the concept of the CMO is to invite intuition and creativity into the boardroom. Many will argue against issuing such an invitation. Mavericks, after all, make people uncomfortable. And yet it is the empowered mavericks who are the key to success in an era of rapid technological change, cultural diversity, and consumer impatience with the unresponsive institution. The time for the CMO has come.

REFERENCES

1. In *Priorities for Research in Strategic Marketing* (Cambridge, Mass.: Marketing Science Institute, 1983).
2. *Business Planning in the Eighties: The New Competitiveness of American Corporations.* The firms termed this the "result of an in-depth study of the planning function in American corporations." It was a sequel to their 1983 study, *The State of Corporate Planning*, which concluded that the majority of executives perceived marketing as the key competitive battleground.
3. *Business Planning in the Eighties: The new Marketing Shape of American Corporations*, which gave the "results of the third in a series of special studies on the business planning function in American corporations."
4. See *The Marketing Imagination* (New York: Free Press, 1983).
5. David S. Hopkins and Earl L. Bailey, *Organizing Corporate Marketing* (New York: The Conference Board, 1984): 5.
6. "Parlin Award Winner Calls for a Marketing Involvement in the Managerial Revolution," *Marketing News*, June 22, 1984: 12.
7. Frederick D. Wiersema, *Strategic Marketing and the Product Life Cycle* (Cambridge, Mass.: Marketing Science Institute, 1981).

Neal Gilliatt is president of a New York City management consulting firm. Pamela Cuming is president of Dialectics Inc., a consulting firm in Encinitas, California. She is the author of The Power Handbook *and* Turf and Other Corporate Power Plays.

16.
MANAGING MARKET IMPLEMENTATION

Thomas V. Bonoma
Victoria L. Crittenden

Many assume that if a market strategy is sound, its implementation will be smooth. Not so. In a four-year study, the authors found that marketers need to better understand how plans translate into actions and into marketplace results.

Marketing strategy concerns itself with "what" questions—what aviation segment should we serve?—while marketing implementation deals with "how" questions—how do we reach CEOs of medium-sized companies to sell them business jets? By and large, academics have concentrated on strategy issues and neglected implementation ones.[1] This is true despite the fact that the implementation of even well-formulated strategies is fraught with problems.

This neglect of marketing implementation problems reflects the widespread assumption that strategy drives practice, and that practice does not affect strategy. We disagree with this assumption. Our field research indicates that, in many firms and in many situations, the habitual mode of executing strategy eventually shapes its formulation. Our purpose here is to suggest preliminary generalizations about good marketing practice, in the hope that eventually marketing *practices* will be formulated with the same clarity that now characterizes strategy formulation.

MARKETING IMPLEMENTATION: A TAXONOMY

The existing work on marketing implementation points to the importance of the structure through which strategies are executed.[2] Other work suggests that managers' skills are a key indicator of effectiveness.[3] The literature does not make clear though, *what* structures, and especially what skills capture the essence of the marketing manager's job.

We conducted thirty-seven interviews with top marketing and general managers to gain a better understanding of key concerns in marketing practice. The interviews were "patterned"—that is, we asked semistructured questions in some areas (such as on marketing control systems) because the literature indicated that these factors were probably important to effectiveness. We asked open-ended questions in other areas (such as implementation skills or cultural aspects of marketing practice) because their importance was not so well established. We then created a taxonomy, based on those interviews and on the existing literature, to categorize marketing implementation problems.

STRUCTURAL VARIABLES

Operations problems in marketing occur at one of four structural levels. The first level, marketing *actions*, includes low-levels execution problems. Selling, new product development, trade promotion, and distributor management are all marketing functions in which important practice problems occur. For example, how does a marketing manager monitor the effectiveness of the trade show program? How does this manager decide between spending money on a trade show and spending it on the sales force?

At the second level, marketing *programs*, management is concerned with integrating subfunctions to serve a special customer segment or to manage a product line. "Key account management" is one currently popular marketing program; many firms are using this concept to tailor their marketing mix to major customers.[4] "Brand management" is another; using this approach, packaged goods companies treat all marketing subfunctions for a product or product line together.[5] The programs level involves all of marketing subfunctions, and so raises the issues of cohesiveness and coherence inherent in any project-management task.

At the marketing *systems* level, managers are concerned with formal control and decision-aid devices. Compensation and decision-support systems were both mentioned often during our interviews; other, nonmarketing systems like order entry and inventory control have powerful effects on marketing implementation, as well.[6]

The final level is marketing *policies*—the broad rules of conduct (formal or informal) articulated by top management to guide marketing conduct. Marketing policies are prescriptive statements that specify how things ought to be done. Two types of marketing policies exist: identity and direction. The former embodies the cultural values about customer interactions and marketing performance that exist within the organization. The latter covers marketing strategy and the conduct of marketing leadership—policies of direction offer broad guidelines about the marketing direction in which the firm wishes to go.

In the course of our interviews and clinical case development, this marketing structure emerged as a set of constraints, or unconstrained habits, that at once foster and inhibit marketing implementation efforts, much as human habits foster complex action but dig behavioral "ruts" from which it can be difficult to escape.

MANAGERIAL SKILLS

Crosscutting these four structural levels are managers' behavioral skills at four central implementation processes: interacting, allocating, monitoring, and organizing. Individual marketers exercise these skills, which are distinct from corporate ritualizations of similar activities (structures). Thus, while there is a formal organization—a structure of habitual hierarchical interactions—a manager's approach to organizing a marketing task may be informal and at some variance to the formal structure. Similarly, managers have monitoring skills that are different from the firm's monitoring systems. The former may foster informal allocations of time, money, and people that are substantially different than what the formal manpower plan or budgeting system dictates.

Interaction skills include managers' own behavior styles and the management of other people's behavior. The marketing job by nature involves influencing others within the company, often without having any formal power. For example, a product manager wishing to convince the sales force to devote more attention to his or her line must rely purely on persuasiveness. Such central variables as negotiation, conflict management, and persuasion were captured by managers' allusions to the importance of being an effective interactor.[7]

Interaction skills are important in another way too. Marketing staff deals with a parade of "outsiders," including customers, distributors, manufacturers' reps, ad agencies, and consultants. Managing each of these parties depends heavily on personal interaction skills, because the interests of outsiders are not ordinarily the same as those of the firm. Whether conceptualized as exchange notions, as personal competence, or as power and influence, good interaction skills are essential to marketing management.[8]

Allocation skills involve a manager's capacity to budget time, people, and money.[9] Without a doubt, the most important commodity allocated by marketers is their own time. What the top marketer pays attention to, so will others. Allocation problems occur at all levels of marketing practice. At a functional level, for example, how should staff be assigned across marketing programs? At a policy level, how can managers use their skills to formulate policies that control demonstration rides for business jets, yet do not constrain sales management?

Monitoring skills involve the construction and maintenance of feedback mechanisms used to measure, and sometimes to control, marketing activities.[10] Our subjects identified four monitoring tasks regardless of a marketer's scope of responsibility: tracking time, money, people, and markets.

A number of important problems arise in this area because the information that the firm's intelligence system makes available for monitoring purposes may lead to very different conclusions than the "back of the envelope" ratios good marketers construct to get around formal control-system inadequacies.

Finally, *organizing skills* refer to managers' informal "networking" behavior that attempts to supplant or defeat the formal organization structure in order to better execute marketing tasks. A marketer will often be given assignments for which the formal organization chart is irrelevant. (For example, Lysonski reports on the product manager who remarked, "I feel like a real politician at times—I'm always lobbying for support from other departments."[11]) The tendency to "box" management functions so that production does not talk to R&D, R&D does not talk to marketing, and sales does not talk to anyone, creates functions at cross-purposes and reporting chains empty of accountability. Marketers organize to get the marketing job done despite territorial boundaries and "local" interests.[12] Organizing is not the same as interacting. The former involves networking and managing group dynamics, while the latter refers to one-on-one behavior.

Most important, skills are not structures. Managers' skills often are invoked to get around, short-circuit, or otherwise subvert perceived system inadequacies. While a competitive monitoring system may exist, for example, managers' monitoring skills are often directed at obtaining competitive or internal data that the system does not seem able to supply.

Table 1 represents a taxonomy that crosses the structural and the skills variables. Each box gives an example of the type of marketing operations problem likely to occur given the structure/skill combination. Each example is taken from an actual operations problem observed during our four-year clinical research project. The project was designed to more clearly delineate the nature of actual marketing implementation situations; assess the completeness of the taxonomy, which had been developed from open-ended interviews and from the existing literature; and explore the dynamics of marketing implementation in the field.

CLINICAL CASE RESEARCH

The clinical research program observed managers as they dealt with implementation problems. The intent of the research was exploratory and qualitative. We hoped that by studying marketing implementation problems anthropologically, we would gain access to a kind of "deep knowing" that could both improve the theory and comment on the usefulness of the inquiry area.[13]

We developed forty-four case studies on marketing implementation problems. (The firms involved were different from those included in the interviews described above.) We selected cases from a much broader, but nonrandom, group of opportunities presented by management invitation, con-

Table 1.
Marketing Implementation: A Taxonomy

SKILLS

STRUCTURE	Interacting	Allocating	Monitoring	Organizing
Actions	How are production and R&D colleagues encouraged to devote more time or effort to a single brand?	How is sales force territory allocation best done by a printing company?	How are salespeople best evaluated and compensated by a bulk chemicals firm?	How should the new product planning function of a market follower be organized in a high-loyalty business?
Programs	How can sales and marketing effectively collaborate on a new national account program?	How should the prospects be selected for demonstration rides in a corporate jet?	How is a successful ad agency team best managed within a brand group for a new pipe introduction?	How should a sales force be reorganized to emphasize a marketing shift from "dumb" to "smart" terminals?
Systems	How should ownership of a competitive pricing intelligence system be divided between sales and marketing in an ethical drug company?	How should a regional bank set up centers, lock boxes, and computer services to maximize market share in a new cash management program?	How does a mine machinery manufacturer monitor a major trade promotion expenditure?	How should customer service engineers be redeployed to avoid hardware-software "by passing" in a computer graphics manufacturer?
Policies	How should a recall of a defective building component be managed by a major steel producer?	How should dollars and service resources be allocated to service key accounts by segment and country for a computer-aided design manufacturer?	How does a major securities firm regularly audit the marketing function?	How should the market team be reorganized because a company changes its "theme"?

sulting, and "cold calls" to firms. We studied eighteen cases on firms in consumer industries, sixteen on firms in industrial businesses, and ten on firms in commercial businesses. A wide range of industries was included. Business units (the basic analysis unit for the cases) ranged in size from a start-up firm to the country's largest corporation.

The cases were constructed from direct observation over a four-year period. Each case followed a similar development process. After initial contact with either the chief executive or the chief marketing officer, the researcher explained the project and interviewed the executive about current marketing implementation problems. Each case then examined a specific existing problem that, as construed by the interviewer, occupied one of the cells in Table 1. All cells had at least one case study; for many, we developed two or more cases. The data sites were not chosen randomly; we attempted to identify sites where strategies were adequate and clearly specified, but where "something else" was causing problems. [14]

We do not attempt to present an organized analysis of the case studies, which in any event is available elsewhere. [15] Rather, we present some of the more informative and provocative findings with respect to the structure/skills dynamics.

OVERALL FINDINGS AND TAXONOMY PLAUSIBILITY

The forty-four cases fit neatly but not exclusively into the matrix given in Table 1. That is, while we encountered no case that could not be categorized, implementation problems often fit into more than one place. This argues that Table 1's typology is exhaustive for the problems studied, but is perhaps a better device for conceptual understanding than for exclusive categorization.

More interesting, perhaps, is the nature of the implementation problems experienced by managers. In just over one-half of the sample, the primary problem concerned either marketing systems or marketing policies. (Inadequate systems were by far the most common problem.) This was true when we selected a site that we thought represented a different problem altogether—often "our" problem existed, but so did severe system and policy problems.

Two systems routinely caused or contributed to execution difficulties: ones associated with *monitoring* marketing efforts and ones associated with *allocating* marketing resources across tasks. Regarding monitoring, all but five of the forty-four managements were uninformed about what many marketing scholars would consider rudimentary feedback and control measures, like profitability by product, by segment, or by account. As a consequence, much marketing was done in a bell jar-like information vacuum. Regarding allocation systems, the marketing budgeting system was a constant problem for management. Routinely, a pattern of overallocation to mature programs was coupled with severe underallocation to new ones. This pattern caused serious problems both in marketing management and in strategic growth.[16]

The problems we encountered in the "policies" category were bred on (a) unclear *identity* policies concerning the firm's theme and culture, and (b) weak or ineffective top management leadership. In the former category we encountered firms that had a major innovation, but could not price for value received because the firm's systems, attitudes, and even sales force management were all geared toward commodity behavior. This was a problem of culture and theme.

The next most frequent cause of operations problems was the program management created to serve key accounts or to sell a product line. These problems accounted for almost 30 percent of those we observed. However, what on the surface looked like and were counted as programs problems, turned out on closer examination to have more basic causes. Either the firm did not have the routine tools in place to execute the low-level functions (e.g., pricing) of which programs were composed, or else its lack of theme and direction caused a proliferation of programs, going off in different directions, that management simply could not implement.

The presence of many marketing programs, or of an intensive and formal marketing effort, was in no way associated with good marketing practice. In fact, a proliferation of programs seemed to be used by management as an attempt to disguise deeper shortcomings, as when a computer vendor partially introduced six separate programs over the course of nine months, then pulled back from each when early results were not up to management expectations.

Finally, almost 20 percent of the sample experienced execution problems with low-level marketing actions. The three most frequent problem areas were sales force management, pricing, and distribution management. Sales force management is still done poorly in many companies despite the relatively large amount of work that has been done to codify its practice. Pricing, especially the implementation of pricing moves, was almost uniformly done poorly. And channel management remains the perplexing and conflict-ridden business it always has been for managers.

All of the managerial skills did relate to how well management coped with problems. More interesting than the confirmation of the skills, though, was that the data suggested an unexpected definition of quality in marketing practice. Market share and other traditional variables seemed to have little relationship with the "goodness" of management's short-term practices; further, "good" implementers did not experience less severe or less frequent crises than "bad" implementers. It was not *the absence of operations problems* but rather *the quality of coping with them* that seemed to measure marketing productivity.

THE DYNAMICS OF THE MARKETING PROCESS

The case data, as well as the earlier analysis of marketing strategy and im-plementation, strongly indicated that strategy and implementation affect one another. Treating only the provocative half of this causal loop, we suggest the following.

• *The firm's structures for marketing implementation, and the skills of its managers, will frequently determine strategies.* Strategy formulation is affected, constrained, inhibited, and often prohibited by the structures the firm has in place and the skills of its managers. In one case study, a volume-oriented, low-priced producer of plastic pipe was prevented from using a skim-price strategy for an innovation because of the skills of its sales force and because of the management's measurement systems—*not* because it was a "bad" strategy. In another, marketing policies and systems allowed investment only if strong growth was proven to be essential. This policy caused marketing management to retrench a chain of promising stores because "heavy up" spending would have been required to ensure their success. In all the cases, we saw a repeated pattern of the "how" constraining, shaping, and changing the "what."

THE RELATIONSHIP BETWEEN STRUCTURES AND SKILLS

An interesting set of propositions arises from the relationship between structures and skills.

• *There is normally a tension, rather than a synergy, between the firm's marketing structures and the skills of its managers. Whether this tension is productive or harmful depends on environmental factors.* Marketing implementation is a joint function of the level at which practice occurs and the skills of the managers doing the job. Marketing structures often cause or exacerbate implementation problems. Managers exercising execution skills can "bridge the gap" between inadequate structure and good practice. The opposite is also true. That is, poor execution skills may inhibit im-plementation but effective structures can mitigate that problem.

• *The interaction between marketing structures and management skills is partially predictable using the rate of marketing change.*

• *In low-change markets, structures and their associated systems dominate skills. Quality marketing practices result more often, and more cheaply, when strong systems and weak management skills are combined.*

• *In high-change markets, the reverse is true. Firms with weak structures and highly skilled managers get more desirable marketplace results, more cheaply, than do firms with strong structures.*

It is important to note that market *change* does not mean market *growth*, although high-growth rates are one form of change. Rapid change can occur in other ways as well, as when a computer vendor and an aluminum manufacturer included in the case research each found their dominant products made obsolete by technological advances. Another example of a rapid-change market is one in which the industry's standard buying patterns change (e.g., hospital buying consortia).

• *The complexity of the tasks that marketing faces suggests whether structure or skills should dominate.*

• *Routine, repeatable tasks (i.e., low complexity) are done more efficiently under strong structures with less strong execution skills.* For example, a firm producing a single, standardized product is probably more efficient if the strength is on the structural side.

• *Highly complex tasks (e.g., if a multiproduct firm is producing to individual customer specification) require stronger execution skills and a weaker structure than routine tasks.*

The preceding suggests the interactions between structure, skills, market change, and task complexity pictured in Figure 1. When market change and complexity are low, structural variables dominate skill variables. When market change and marketing-task complexity are high, skills dominate structures. The primary problem with strong structures in rapidly changing markets involving complex tasks is that reliance on rules and procedures limits the firm's ability to adapt quickly to marketplace needs. On the other hand, if skills dominate structure in more stable markets with low-task complexity, the firm cannot increase efficiency by relying on rules and standard operating procedures.

These propositions pose some general rules for the relationship between structures and marketing skills. The case data clearly suggested that there is

Figure 1.
Structure/Skills Dynamics

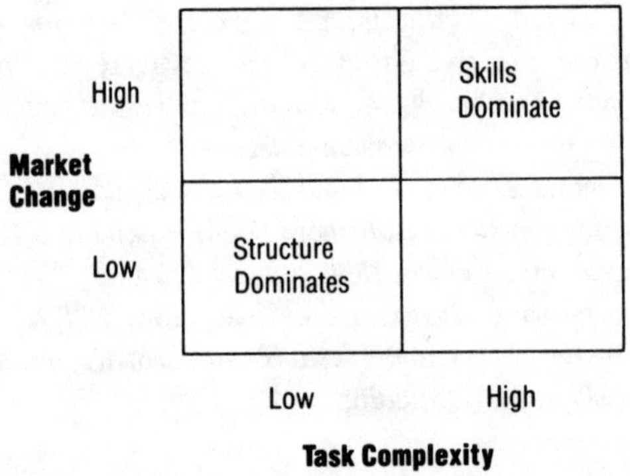

Market Change		Low	High
	High		Skills Dominate
	Low	Structure Dominates	

Task Complexity

tension between the structures the firm puts in place to guide marketing execution and the skills of its managers. Usually, this tension is counterproductive because: (a) most firms find themselves in changing markets; (b) the structures (especially systems) in place to guide the execution of marketing strategies, like all habits and routines, lag behind reality; and (c) managers are often put in a position of subverting the "system" with their own skills, often in violation of structural guidelines, to assure quality practices.[17]

Propositions, 2, 3, and 4 can be linked to early and late stages of the life cycle.

• *In the turbulent periods of the product or market life cycle (e.g., introduction, rapid growth, and late maturity/decline), management skills will dominate marketing execution structures in better-performing firms. In mid-life cycle, structures dominate skills.*

OTHER PROPOSITIONS

Our interviews, case descriptions, and study of the literature suggested several other propositions.

• *The number of marketing programs in a firm, compared to relevant competitors, will be inversely related to the quality of marketing practices observed.* The case data made clear that sound policies at the top, and well-executed actions at the bottom, were vital to marketing success. It was by no means clear, however, that a proliferation of programs was necessary or even desirable. Indeed, many managements seemed to substitute programs they could not execute for such fundamentals as clear pricing and strong distribution. Contrary to a widely held view that strong attention to marketing, measured as a large number of different marketing programs, is necessarily related to good marketplace results, we observed many instances where programs were being used as an intentional or unintentional "cover" for the lack of more basic marketing abilities. Of course, it is important that firms be compared with relevant competitors in any further investigation of this proposition.

• *Marketing organizations with explicit routines or systems (e.g., distributor management systems) designed to treat the trade as a customer will show a higher degree of marketing productivity than those without such programs.*

The proposition requires little explanation; however, it is important to note how widespread problems with the distribution channel were, and how often these problems impeded the execution of strategies. Most firms seemed to be engaged in a kind of unmanaged "guerrilla warfare" with their channel intermediaries, and only a few consistently managed to form a partnership with them.[18] Invariably, those that did had fewer problems executing their strategies. Although we did not collect specific data that would allow us to defend this statement, this proposition could probably be repeated with the words "sales force" substituted for "trade."

MANAGERIAL PRACTICE

Underlying the variables in the taxonomy are several serious execution problems that have direct implications for managers.

• *Management by Assumption.* Management assumes that *someone, somewhere* in the corporation will do the analysis necessary for making knowledgeable pricing, sales promotion, or distribution decisions. Unfortunately, the function in question is often ignored until a crisis happens.

• *Global Mediocrity.* Management tries to excel at all of its marketing activities, rather than picking one for special concentration. The firm does many things adequately, but is not outstanding at anything. Ultimately, it finds itself without a competitive advantage.

• *Empty Promises Marketing.* Management creates programs it does not have the subfunctional capability to execute. Declaring that a program exists and appointing a competent individual to manage it is usually not enough for subfunctional success. The existence of too many programs generally means that none is pursued with a vengeance.

• *Program Ambiguity.* Lack of clear identity and direction result in a multitude of programs and no unifying theme. Clever programs fail because of an absence of shared understanding about identity (i.e., theme) and strong leadership.

• *Ritualization, Politicization, and Unavailability.* Errors of ritual arise when the firm's systems mandate a particular course of action because "things have always been done that way." Often, good judgement dictates a different course, yet habitual pathways are chosen.

Management intelligence is often undermined by the politicization of data and information. Often, daily records are not prepared until the end of the month (when much may already be forgotten), or not turned in until inflammatory data are removed.

Systems installed to make managers' lives easier quickly become unsuitable for current environmental conditions, or place the data in the hands of those completely removed from its significance. Many marketing managers do not have the data necessary to analyze profitability by segment, product, account, and order.

Marketing practice problems span the breadth and depth of management concerns. The five problems here typify the problems encountered in our research, and they could serve as starting points for more in-depth individual firm analysis. Considering such problems simultaneously with the taxonomy might well lead to improved marketing execution. However, this is not to suggest that good marketing practice leads to an absence of execution problems and crises. No firm will ever plan so well that things do not go wrong in the field.

The study of marketing practice at once informs the marketer about the problems managers encounter in implementing proposed strategies and leads to awareness of how those practice problems circle back over time to affect the strategies themselves. It is not enough to have a science of making plans; it is also necessary to understand how they are translated into actions and into marketplace results.

REFERENCES

1. F. E. Webster, Jr., "Top Management's Concerns About Marketing," *Journal of Marketing,* Summer 1981: 9-16.
2. A. D. Chandler, Jr., *Strategy and Structure: Chapters in the History of the American Industrial Enterprise* (Cambridge: MIT Press, 1961); L. G. Hrebiniak and W. F. Joyce, *Implementing Strategy* (New York: Macmillan, 1984); J. R. Galbraith and R. K. Kazanjian, *Strategy Implementation Structure, Systems, and Process,* 2d. ed. (St. Paul: West Publishing, 1986).
3. J. R. P. French, Jr., and B. Raven, "The Bases of Social Power," in *Studies in Social Power,* ed. D. P. Cartwright (Ann Arbor: University of Michigan Press, 1959); R. M. Stogdill, *Handbook of Leadership* (New York: The Free Press, 1974); J. B. Miner, *The Human Constraint: The Coming Shortage of Managerial Talent* (Washington, DC: Bureau of National Affairs, 1974); E.E. Lawler and J. G. Rhode, *Information and Control in Organizations* (Pacific Palisades, CA: Goodyear, 1976).
4. B. P. Shapiro and R. T. Moriarty, "National Account Management: Emerging Insights" (Boston: *MSI Special Report #82-100,* 1982).
5. J. A. Quelch, "It's Time to Make Trade Promotion More Productive," *Harvard Business Review,* May-June 1983: 130-136.
6. V. Sathe, *Controller Involvement in Management* (Englewood Cliffs, NJ: Prentice-Hall, 1982).
7. See, respectively, D. Druckman, ed., *Negotiations: Social Psychological Perspectives* (Beverly Hills: Sage Publications, 1977); J. T. Tedeschi, T. V. Bonoma, and B. R. Schlenker, *Conflict, Power and Games* (Chicago: Aldine, 1973); and C. I. Hovland, I. L. Janis, and H. H. Kelley, *Communication and Persuasion: Psychological Studies of Opinion Change* (New Haven, CT: Yale University Press, 1953).
8. See, respectively, G. Homans, *Social Behavior: Its Elementary Forms,* 2d. ed. (New York: Harcourt Brace Jovanovich, 1974); T. F. Gilbert, *Human Competence: Engineering Worthy Performance* (New York: McGraw-Hill, 1978); and Tedeschi, Bonoma, and Schlenker (1973).
9. J. L. Bower, *Managing the Resource Allocation Process: A Study of Corporate Planning and Investment* (Boston: Division of Research, Harvard Business School, 1970).
10. For studies examining reactions to feedback mechanisms, see M. F. Foran and D. T. DeCoster, "An Experimental Study of the Effects of Participa-

tion, Authoritarianism, and Feedback on Cognitive Dissonance in a Standard Setting Situation," *The Accounting Review* 49, October 1974: 751-763; and P. Brownell, "A Field Study Examination of Budgetary Participation and Locus of Control," *The Accounting Review* 57, October 1982: 766-777.

11. S. Lysonski, "A Boundary Theory Investigation of the Product Manager's Role," *Journal of Marketing*, Winter 1985: 26-40.

12. For a discussion on boundary spanning roles, see H. Aldrich and D. Herker, "Boundary Spanning Roles and Organization Structure," *Academy of Management Review* 2, April 1977, 217-230.

13. C. A. Geertz, *The Interpretation of Cultures* (New York: Basic Books, 1973).

14. Developing each case required a substantial amount of time at each site. We reviewed and incorporated all available background literature, spent between forty and one hundred hours on-site, and assembled field notes and background data. In writing case studies, we disguised confidential data but preserved relationships among data. Several companies were the subject of more than one case study.

    The forty-four cases were drawn from twenty-five corporations, thirty business units, and two hundred and fifty managers. Fifteen of the cases were compiled with the aid of a research assistant or outside expert; twenty-nine were simply investigations into marketing implementation by one of the authors.

15. T. V. Bonama, *Managing Marketing* (New York: The Free Press, 1984); T. V. Bonoma, *The Marketing Edge: Making Strategies Work* (New York: The Free Press, 1985).

16. Lodish makes a very similar claim about sales force allocation. See L.M. Lodish, "'Vaguely Right' Approach to Sales Force Allocations," *Harvard Business Review*, January-February 1974: 119-124.

17. T. V. Bonoma, "Marketing Subversives," *Harvard Business Review*, November-December 1986: 113-118.

18. Ibid.

Thomas V. Bonoma is professor of business administration at the Graduate School of Business Administration, Harvard University. Victoria L. Crittenden is a doctoral candidate in marketing at the Graduate School of Business Administration, Harvard University.

17.
LEVERAGING SALES THROUGH DATABASE MAINTENANCE

Art Husami

> In good times or bad, marketshare can be increased when one company identifies, qualifies, follows up and closes more sales prospects than its competitors. This article contains some do's and don'ts for lead generation through efficient database maintenance.

In good times or bad, marketshare can be increased when one company identifies, qualifies, follows up and closes more sales prospects than its competition. That's a basic marketing axiom that many feel is easier said than done.

While attending a strategic marketing course at Stanford University's graduate school of business, I surveyed about 50 chief marketing executives who were also attending the course. I then surveyed 20 additional marketing executives in major high-technology firms.

The survey asked: 1) If they thought a cost-effective lead-generation program would be helpful, 2) If they had such a system running efficiently, and 3) If not, why not?

Only three respondents reported having an ongoing satisfactory system. All but six of the industrial marketers said that such a system would enhance their sales and profits. More than 50 indicated they had attempted such a system, at least once, but could not keep it going.

The following reasons were most frequently cited for the failure of a lead-generation program:

- The individual campaigns to generate leads became uncoordinated and random.
- The number of raw leads coming in was either too low to keep the program going or so high it was overwhelming.
- Raw leads backed up and became stale.
- The person assigned to fulfill and forward the leads got distracted by other tasks.

- After requested information was sent to the prospect, there was no personal follow up; the benefit of the lead was lost.
- The sales organization received all leads with no pre-screening. After fruitless follow-up on a few, they decided the leads were not qualified and stopped following up on them.
- Leads were not tracked to determine the effectiveness of the programs and the status of the leads. Leads were not pursued to the optimum level. There was no feedback to either refine the program or justify its continuation. Qualified leads were not captured into a marketing database for either periodic prodding or tracking.
- Maintenance of the qualified prospects base became random or died. Many executives mentioned lonely first editions of what was intended to be a quarterly newsletter.
- The prospect list was simply added to and duplications were not deleted. The database became too big, too old and non-productive.

The marketing department of a national provider of high-technology products and services to the electronic industry wanted to establish a cost-effective lead-generation system and current-prospect database. Its business cut across many vertical markets—high-tech engineers, computer engineers, radio frequency engineers, electrical engineers, etc.—at the office manager level.

The provider was mailing quarterly price lists to 40,000 general managers but was unsure if the mailings were actually reaching qualified prospects. The marketing department sent out 40,000 letters, asking for the return of non-deliverables; 12,000 were returned.

The 28,000 letters that successfully reached general managers offered them the opportunity to subscribe to a quarterly newsletter featuring technical information as well as general interest information, such as how to get the best seat on an airplane or how to get the attention of your associates.

The prospect could become a charter member of an information exchange club and a subscriber if he could qualify himself by completing a questionnaire. If he did not qualify, he could subscribe for $5. The questionnaire asked for company size, which of 60 industries the prospect belonged to, and which of 16 groups of products would interest him.

For completing the questionnaire, the prospect could select two of eight articles reprinted from the *Harvard Business Review*. He could purchase additional selections for $10 apiece.

The first qualifying mailing drew 3,000 responses. When the first newsletter was published, it was mailed to new subscribers and non-responders. The latter group also received a letter saying "look what you're missing." An additional 3,200 responded, providing qualifying data.

The marketing department advised the salespeople of the database cleanup process that was taking place. Salespeople were asked to review non-responders and get qualifying information from those prospects they wished to retain on the database.

From a sales force of 50 people, 2,000 cards were returned. At the same time, the salespeople were given the opportunity to become familiar with the list. They were made to feel it was their own list.

Four years and 16 issues later, the list has been built back to 45,000 prospects—all qualified. The following are essential factors for continued success of the program and related comments:

- The sales force must be convinced that these leads will help them find prospects and generate sales. If not convinced, the sales force will ignore the leads and spend time trying to prove the system does not work.
- The leads must be telephone qualified before being submitted to a salesperson. While this may seem expensive, it is cost-effective and essential to secure the support, follow up and eventual close by the sales force.
- The sales force must have complete access to and control of the qualified prospect database. They should feel the list is theirs. They should be responsible for reporting changes, and initiating additions and deletions to the list.
- Each salesperson should be responsible for all pending leads forwarded to her, until she reports back on them.
- There should be a system for tracking leads and reporting on their status, cost per lead, qualification level and amount of sales directly related to the system. These results should be reported according to program and salesperson.
- The prospect base should be mailed to and tracked regularly. The sales force should feel that the system is helping them maintain the interest of their customer base.
- Prospect data may be excellent grounds for market characterization and research.
- Inquiries resulting from a campaign should be fulfilled and followed up promptly, while the prospect's interest is still high.
- Lead-generation campaigns should conform to the company's image. The message should be brief, simple and inexpensive. It should include an offer that will appeal to the target audience and induce them to respond.
- Individual lead-generation programs should be targeted at well-defined market segments as dictated by an overall marketing plan. The frequency and magnitude of lead-generation programs should be determined by the number of qualified leads needed to continue to support the sales force.
- An ongoing system serves as an excellent tool to steer the sales force toward specific markets and to focus lead-generation efforts on these markets. The resulting qualified leads will trickle through the system, and the sales force will find itself calling on that market segment as it follows up on the leads.

It's easy for other concerns and responsibilities to take precedence over this system. When using a company's data-processing facilities to maintain and store the prospect base, marketing people often have to yield to other more immediate company activities such as billing and production runs. This can cause delays that force compromises and sometimes jeopardize the continuity of the system.

It's common for marketing professionals to slight or ignore the fundamental responsibility of leveraging today's selling efforts. They often become preoccupied with more interesting and equally important aspects such as product planning, strategic planning, competitive analysis and image advertising.

Art Husami is president of Prospect Systems, Long Beach, CA.

18.
MARKETING IN THE INFORMATION AGE

John I. Coppett
Cornelius H. Sullivan

Successful marketing frequently depends on skillful management of information. Here are some recent innovations in communication technology that will have a profound impact on marketers.

"A few years ago we did not even know where the data processing department was located," admitted the marketing vice president of a large Chicago distributor. "Now I believe we are the single largest user of systems, particularly communications."

Marketing is one of the business functions most dramatically affected by emerging information technologies. Because marketing is so inherently communications-intensive, networking technologies are particularly useful. This article illustrates major opportunities to exploit communications systems to support the marketing functions.

BEYOND TELEMARKETING

Time-honored communications tools for marketing include media advertising, direct mail, telephone selling, trade show exhibits, and, of course, face-to-face presentations. Each method has its strengths and weaknesses. Commercials and newspaper ads, for example, reach large numbers of people. But these messages are fairly indiscriminate, and must always be kept simple. On the other hand, a large amount of information can be conveyed at a meeting, but the cost is high.

Conventional communications techniques no longer exhaust our range of options. More recent marketing vehicles include national account management, demonstration centers and showrooms, industrial stores, catalog sales, and telemarketing. These, too, each have distinct advantages and occasional trade offs and drawbacks. When used appropriately in conjunction with earlier approaches, the new avenues expand and enrich the overall marketing communications portfolio. Together they produce a "new economics of selling" and a need to manage our marketing communications mix deliberately and carefully.[1]

But this is just the beginning. Innovation in communications technology is accelerating, as the result of regulatory changes, the entrepreneurial spirit, declining prices for systems, a rapidly expanding installed base of communicating devices, and the marketplace demand for more cost-effective channels.

In particular, three kinds of communications technology appear to be gaining the attention of marketers. One is *store and forward technology*, specifically electronic mail and voice messaging systems. Products of the office automation boon, these systems make it possible for people to create messages and deposit them in electronic "mailboxes" until such time as they are picked up by designated recipients. It is unnecessary for the parties to the conversation to communicate at the same time, thus avoiding the game of telephone tag. Using group codes, it is as easy to send a message to dozens—or hundreds—of recipients as it is to send the message to one person. And, because the messages are deposited immediately but remain indefinitely, the timeliness of the communication is kept flexible. Pace and volume can be leisurely and light or instantaneous and heavy, depending on the severity of the current week's brush fire.

A second category of technology is *conferencing*. Conferencing includes at least three basic varieties. At one extreme is *audio conferencing*—voice transmission among three or more meeting participants in different locations. At the other extreme is *full-motion video teleconferencing*. In between are a variety of audiographics conferencing alternatives, which generally combine *voice transmission with a supplemental information flow*, such as facsimile, an electronic blackboard, data-file transfers, or some other graphics or image exchange.

All three of these conferencing technologies free participants from the need to be in the same place in order to exchange information. But they do require that everyone participate at the same time. That is to say, the communication is *synchronous*. An interesting hybrid of store/forward and conferencing technologies is frequently referred to as *computer mediated conferencing*. This is an asynchronous system.

Computer mediated conferencing allows a group of people to communicate with one another on a particular subject by reading existing messages and depositing new ones on that subject, each at his or her own leisure. Over time this technique simulates a meeting or conference but allows any number of participants and permits people to contribute when they can, rather than when the meeting is scheduled. The basic distinction between an electronic mail system and a computer conferencing system is that electronic mail and voice message system mailboxes generally are assigned to *people*, while computer conference mailboxes are assigned to *subjects*. Anyone who wants to peruse or contribute to one of the subjects on the system (a conference) signs on and reads the messages attached to that subject or conference. On some systems, conferences can beget other conferences at the discretion of the participants.[2]

A third kind of technology of great interest to marketing executives is hard to give a name to yet, but it clearly consists of the already great and still accelerating base of *computer terminal devices* appearing in front of secretaries, professionals, engineers, analysts, foremen, supervisors, branch managers, small-business owners, middle management and senior management, school children, and home owners. The sophistication of these devices ranges from what is amusingly (and somewhat inaccurately) called dumb terminals and video games machines to desktop word processors, personal computers, and multifunction workstations with almost as much processing power as the largest mainframe computers' of less than 20 years ago.

By no means are all of these devices now serving as communications terminals. In fact, only a small fraction is regularly used for telecommunications. However, many of them have communications capabilities or could be upgraded for that purpose in a fairly straightforward fashion. Herein lies their enormous potential for marketing purposes. Given applications and the incentive, customers and employees at computer terminal devices can be networked into a new medium.

Why bother with the new technologies? Farsighted marketers in American business see three kinds of uses for these innovations. One is to offer new ways to communicate with customers—new technologies can supplement or improve existing channels to the marketplace. A second application is for the marketing chain of command. The field sales force is (and always has been, and should remain, as much as possible) "out of the office." When sales representatives are gone they are selling; when they are in, they are doing something else—it may be important, but it is not selling. Some of these technologies make that simple fact of life much easier to live with. Finally, the technologies are finding uses as peer-to-peer communications tools, enhancing the ability of a large organization to communicate from one function to another, as well as from one business unit to another.

Innovations such as telemarketing and the industrial store add options to the marketing communications portfolio. They increase flexibility and hold down expenses of marketing programs. The potential benefits of the new messaging, conferencing, and workstation technologies also include those benefits, but there are additional reasons for considering their use. The new technologies can be used to differentiate products from the competition or may even become the basis for new products and services. These technologies can also add to the quality of relationships with customers and to the quality of work life for employees. Finally, as we shall see, new technologies can produce new forms of organizational design. Benefits are never automatic. Consider the following examples, and then we will return to the question of how to plan for these information age technologies in order to realize their full potential.

ELECTRONIC ORDER EXCHANGE

A critical information flow at any company is the stream of orders from customers for products or services. If a way can be found to speed up the flow, stabilize and solidify it, or make it easier, more pleasant, or more convenient for customers to initiate this vital information transfer, most marketers will jump at the chance. Beginning in financial services and distribution, but now spreading into many other fields, this is precisely what is happening. The enabling technology is electronic document transmission. Files of data constructed at customer sites are transmitted on a daily basis to vendors in place of the familiar paper forms and telephone calls.

One approach is to put a terminal in the customer's office. In a well-known case, American Hospital Supply (AHS) of Evanston, Illinois, has exploited the fact that hospital procurement administrators are relatively insensitive to price but extremely conscious of out-of-stock items and the availability of medical supplies from distributors. (It simply does not do for surgery to halt in the middle for want of gauze or a retractor.)

To accommodate hospital priorities, AHS extended its order-entry system onto the customer site, placing a terminal in front of the administrator, and making it as easy as possible for that individual to do business with AHS, while also realizing the goal of extreme reliability in logistics and supply. Customers of AHS can inquire about the availability of products, review purchase histories, place orders, and obtain statements. Information about a product is an important element in evaluation of the product itself.

Virtually every major insurance company in the United States is at some stage of developing a similar system for its network of agencies and brokers. Like airline reservations systems, these agency links will typically present the products of the provider insurance carrier in the most favorable light. In an effort to reward high-performance agents, the systems are sometimes provided free of charge. They are often coupled with other applications of interest to brokers and agents, such as word processing, office automation, general business accounting, and customer file account management software. A nagging marketing problem for the providers of these systems is the ironic fact that they are given to a firm's most loyal independent agents, yet inherently the systems facilitate comparison shopping of the rates offered by competing carriers.

A different approach is to put a hand-held device in the hands of every member of the field sales force. A good example of this is the Keebler Company of Elmhurst, Illinois. An innovator several years ago when its firms installed intelligent terminals at all distribution centers for daily order entry, Keebler has recently gone one step further to equip its entire 1,300-person sales force with battery-operated cassette data terminals.

Each sales representative takes his or her terminals to customer stores during the day and keys in product orders on the spot. After accumulating orders on the terminal, sales representatives need not return to the distribution center to submit the paper forms for later transcription. Nor do they let the orders gather dust in their cars until they get around to dropping them off at the office. Rather, they simply go home. During a prearranged time frame in the evening, staggered to level the calling load, each salesperson dials Keebler's corporate computer in Elmhurst on a 800 number and transmits sales input data. Shipping, picking, and billing documents, as well as sales reports and inventory updates, can then be produced expeditiously. With this communications system, Keebler has increased the number of accounts that the average salesperson can handle, improved accuracy in the ordering process, decreased returns, and, most important in the baked-goods industry, cut another day off the order-cycle time.

CUSTOMER SERVICE AND RELATIONSHIP MANAGEMENT

In this postindustrial age, many firms find themselves in a service business, regardless of how they started out. Effective marketing under these circumstances requires careful attention to the close connection between the sales process and customer service. The next sale is generally a result of satisfactory services performed in connection with the previous sale.

An excellent example of the role of information age networking in marketing is a tale of two banks—one in New York City, the other in Chicago. The Chicago bank was aggressive on pricing and set growth targets well above the industry average. The New York bank was highly respected in banking circles for its long-standing, high-quality relationships with corporate and personal accounts. As one vice president of the New York bank put it, "We are definitely not the low-priced alternative; no one expects us to be."

Both banks, along with the rest of the financial services community, saw growth potential in noncredit services for customers, such as wire transfer and cash management products. In both cases the banks developed marketing strategies that would place noncredit services in the forefront of their attempts to secure profitable relationships with corporate customers.

The New York bank built a new network to provide corporate treasurers with a variety of services, including financial information, modeling applications, and the opportunity to initiate money transfers. Meanwhile, the Chicago bank offered the same functions but as extensions of their existing in-house network, the one already used extensively by loan officers. Concerned about the security implications associated with allowing nonbank employees to access the corporate computer, the New York bank did not permit customers to use internal systems.

Continuing to use the same electronic mail, cash reporting, and money transfer systems that had been originally developed for internal use, the

Chicago bank's loan officers were able to keep in closer touch with their customers. The technology created a sense of more personal service. The systems became traditional relationship-building tools. The New York bank, although prudent in considering security risks, managed with its disjointed communications arrangement to drive a wedge between its customers and its lending officers. They were unable to send electronic mail or data files and reports to one another. While the New York bank blocked the close relationship and interaction between the account officer and the customer, the Chicago bank was able to supplement its aggressive pricing with an impression of a New York-style relationship—their customers now had the best of both worlds. Two years later, the Chicago bank was voted one of the five best-managed corporations in America.

MARKET RESEARCH

Promotions play a large role in consumer business marketing strategy. Accurate and timely measures of results are crucial. Another marketing opportunity that stems from the information age is the use of point-of-sale devices to capture data needed for detailed sales tracking during a promotion in test markets and control groups. Accurate tallies of sales by product, size, class, date, and time of day by location is a gold mine for the market researcher.

A pioneering example of the use of networking for merchandising was developed for the casino and gaming industry in general, and Bally Manufacturing in particular. Relying on monitors in slot machines, arcade games, and other point-of-sales devices, an operator of a series of arcades or casinos can gather at one location an enormous amount of data about transactions. The network provides information about defective devices, large or frequent payoffs from a particular machine, and tampering. It can accumulate a variety of statistics, such as volume of use by specific location and time of day. With this network, it becomes possible to manage effectively and merchandise scientifically.

What Bally first did in casinos is already happening in other retail industries. Supermarkets have been installing point-of-sale devices in great numbers recently, at first merely because of customer pressure. Once the devices are in place, however, management begins to take advantage of the fact that these systems accumulate a wealth of data. Specifically, supermarkets are using their networks of point-of-sale devices to track detailed sales and promotion results in a far more accurate, timely, and flexible fashion than before. Similarly, other chains and franchise operations, such as McDonalds and The Limited, now closely monitor sales by line of business, location, and time of day. As sales information networking appears in these kinds of businesses, merchandising decisions become better-informed and more effective.

TRAINING AND EDUCATION

Training the sales force is an expensive and difficult job when products and services change faster than representatives can be rotated through a physical training facility. A New York brokerage house, for example, supplements its conventional annual training program with more frequent *teletraining* sessions. Teletraining refers to the use of conferencing rooms for interactive discussions of new financial instruments and account executive skills.

But the notion of using communications networks for educational purposes need not be limited to internal staff training. One large commercial bank has an extensive network of affiliates and correspondents. Semiannually, the bank convenes this group at its headquarters or at a resort hotel to discuss financial issues, describe new services, and foster a closer relationship with these important customers. Although highly effective, the meetings are necessarily infrequent and are followed by long periods when a newsletter is the only means of communication besides individual contacts by loan officers. To foster better ties and supplement the traditional information exchanges, the bank is developing a computer conferencing system. The conference allows bank economists, operations managers, and loan officers to communicate productively with correspondents. Several conferences are being established on subjects such as interest rates, economic indicators, industrial engineering, and production statistics in different industries. The system allows participants to ask questions and venture opinions. Bank employees monitor messages, insert comments, and guide each conference constructively. The plan is to establish additional conferences to provide preliminary information on complex financing opportunities. Conferences may even be used later as an administrative vehicle for loan participations.

ORGANIZATIONAL INNOVATION

Matrix management schemes became popular a generation or so ago in American business. The schemes rather quickly fell into disrepute, largely because they did not work very well, particularly in large organizations. The problem seems to have been that array structures required enormous new amounts of information exchange. Conventional communications channels simply could not handle the load. In plain terms, there were not enough hours in the day to hold all the meeting and telephone calls necessary to coordinate discussion and resolve issues in which a substantial portion of the entire management structure of a company became involved.

With the help of store/forward technologies, it may be possible for matrix management to enjoy a renaissance. The concept was not a bad one; its problem was feasibility. Given the power of new enabling tools, we can now realistically reconsider different organizational structures on their merits.

Professional firms, such as law offices, engineering firms, and management consulting firms, frequently employ a matrix management structure, and they are finding that electronic mail and voice messaging systems are extremely helpful. A brand management matrix in a marketing organization may be similarly affected.

INFORMATION AGE PRODUCTS

One final, and extreme, way for companies to participate in the information age is by actually getting into the communications business. A good example of a firm in transition is McGraw-Hill. Through over 200 separate business units, McGraw-Hill has taken a position in almost every aspect of information technology delivery, particularly as an information provider and purveyor.

McGraw-Hill's traditional business was the purchase from authors of manuscripts that were to be printed, bound, and sold to bookstores. Noting several years ago that the proportion of total information dissemination accounted for by conventional books was declining in the information age, McGraw-Hill began to diversify, staying in the information dissemination business but adding other data bases and media and distribution channels. At this point, their fastest-growing businesses use tapes, floppy disks, and telecommunications lines instead of books and bookstores to provide access to their published data.

One interesting product, developed as a joint venture with Visicorp, the company that brought the world its first automated spreadsheet, is a communications program that enables people at personal computers and word processors to dial into the mammoth McGraw-Hill data bases, search for statistical information on any of thousands of subjects, extract a desired portion of the data base, and bring it back to the desktop workstation in a format that the Visicalc spreadsheet can use and manipulate. Simply put, the product is a combination of *information* and intelligent *access* to that information. What McGraw-Hill and Visicorp realize is that networking links to the outside world multiply the power of professional productivity tools.

THE DARK SIDE OF INFORMATION
AGE MARKETING

From looms and steam engines to combines and computers, almost every technological innovation meets with some philosophical resistance. Generally, the fears turn out to be unfounded. In one case, however, the Luddites may actually have a point. The technology in question is telephone robotics or automated telemarketing, and the legitimate fear is that arrays of mechanical telephone number dialers will ring people up at random, harass them, invade their privacy and serenity, and become an insidious and deadening nuisance. It is bad enough when a person calls unexpectedly and without invitation to hawk a product, but at least the consumer has a meager satisfaction of knowing that the caller is investing an equal amount of time on the attempted sale and therefore, theoretically, has given some thought to the appropriateness of the call. But a machine that spews out an unwanted pitch is purely inhuman and embodies all the worst elements of the information age.

These machines come in a variety of sizes and levels of sophistication. The simplest ones merely dial numbers from a list or at random and play a recorded message to whomever answers. Enhancement includes the ability to measure the length of time before the called party hangs up (presumably indicating level of interest in the product), ability to handle many outgoing lines simultaneously, callback features, and the ability to record what the called party says in response. The most sophisticated systems can actually engage the poor recipient of the call in a pseudo conversation, ask questions, sometimes even try to understand responses, and then take appropriate action, such as branching to another message, switching to a live operator, or (less often) hanging up.

Telephone robotics were originally developed for collections and dunning. Here one man's harassment may be another man's poetic justice. When used in conjunction with toll-free numbers to provide additional follow-up information after an advertisement, or to take orders, the devices may be perfectly acceptable. But in the case of outward calling, particularly when based on random telephone number selection, we come face-to-face with the nadir of modern marketing practices. Never mind cynics who say that they have had more intelligent conversations with these devices than they sometimes have with human telephone interviewers. The point is that we shall have no one to blame but ourselves for government regulation of marketing activities if we fail to act responsibly to prevent abusive application of this technology. Run—do not walk—away from telephone robotics.

GUIDELINES FOR ACTION

These examples demonstrate the range of changes taking place in marketing during the information age. While the mission of the marketing function remains constant, strategies and tactics are shifting to exploit new opportunities opened up by innovations such as store/forward switching conferencing, and the growing base of desktop workstations. "The excellent companies *really are* close to their customers," wrote the authors in *In Search of Excellence.* "Other companies talk about it; the excellent companies do it."[3] Effective use of networking technologies is turning out to be one of the most important ways to sustain and enhance a customer orientation.

As is often the case with leading-edge firms, however, some of the companies mentioned here were not entirely aware of what they were doing at the time. Intuition and judgement played a role. Some actually stumbled onto success (while many others simply stumbled). Effective programs to achieve similar results in a more deliberate and less risky fashion must retain a variety of traditional elements, such as analysis of communication costs, specification of needs, and ongoing monitoring of results. Additionally, more novel program elements come into play for information age marketing. Here are some of the guidelines:

Manage the Portfolio: The new technologies, when combined with existing ones, as well as with others which are as yet only on the horizon, create a substantial and growing portfolio of information exchange options for marketers to use. Understanding their capabilities, choosing appropriate elements from the portfolio in response to marketing needs and developing the most effective mix becomes a major aspect of effective marketing.

Probe for Competitive Advantage: The firms previously mentioned have freed themselves from the myth that information technology is at best a cost-reducing tool. When these companies look at systems, they see revenue potential.

Design for the Future: A new life cycle for systems is becoming apparent. The first step in automation makes it possible for clerical people to do what professional employees had done before. The next step lets the customer do the work. This is already the experience of American Hospital Supply and many insurance companies and banks. Other industries appear to be following suit. This trajectory has clear design implications for systems if they are to remain useful from one stage to the next.

Nurture Diffusion and Adoption: Exploitation of emerging information networking technologies for marketing purposes catapults a company into a high-technology posture with customers. Be prepared to provide a full range of ongoing training, support, encouragement,
enhancement, and overall management of any systems provided.

REFERENCES

1. Benson P. Shapiro and John Wyman, "New Ways to Reach Your Customers," *Harvard Business Review*, 59:4, July-August 1981: 103-110.
2. For an introduction to different kinds of conferencing, see Robert Johansen and Christine Bullen, "What to Expect from Teleconferencing," *Harvard Business Review*, 62:2, March-April 1984: 164-174.
3. Thomas J. Peters and Robert H. Waterman Jr., *In Search of Excellence: Lessons From America's Best-Run Companies*, (New York: Harper & Row, 1982).

John I. Coppett is professor of marketing and chairman of the Marketing Department at the University of Houston, Clear Lake, Texas. Cornelius H. Sullivan is president of the Information Technology Planning Corporation in Chicago.

19.
MARKETING MANAGEMENT IN THE INFORMATION AGE

Frank E. Moriya
Carl M. Vorder Bruegge

> The time has come for marketers to make full use of information technology's potential. Utilizing the latest technology for aggressive marketing management is prudent, if not imperative, in view of today's realities.

For 30 years consistent improvement in "information-age" technology and the evolution of the marketing function as the prime mover in business enterprises have been parallel, but unrelated phenomena. This will not be true in the future. American industry is struggling anxiously to apply computer/communications technology as the linchpin of competitive strategy in worldwide markets. Utilizing the latest technology for aggressive marketing management is prudent, if not imperative, in view of today's realities.

WHAT'S HAPPENING TO "INFORMATION-AGE" SYSTEMS?

A proliferation of magazine and trade journal articles, news items, speeches, and stated corporate strategies is clear evidence that technology is a basic underpinning of corporate competitive strategy. The nature of these strategic efforts generally falls into four basic categories, as follows.

1. The most common strategy is *to add value to the information ingredient of the product or service.* One example is General Electric's household appliance service database, which is accessible to customers by a toll-free number. As a more sophisticated example, Citibank offers corporate loan clients video terminals with access to the banks proprietary worldwide money-market database of up-to-the minute exchanges. The effectiveness of this

strategy in acquiring new customers left Citibank's competitors scrambling to find a competitive response.

2.   Another common strategy is to *create systems that vitally improve convenience and efficiency for customers.* American Hospital Supply's extension of its internally distributed order-entry and inventory-control systems to 300 large hospitals frequently is cited. That this linkage to customers helped make American Hospital a top competitor is evidenced by the unsuccessful monopoly lawsuit undertaken by its corporate rivals.

3.   Many companies have *used existing technology to reach new, previously inaccessible markets.* This strategy has enabled established concerns to capitalize on earlier technological investments. J.C. Penney's use of its telecommunications-based credit management systems to serve the needs of national petroleum companies has been notably profitable. They are now planning to market their expertise in video teleconferencing.

4.   Finally, risk-taking ventures *have profited from identifying latent demand for entirely new services which could be delivered only with advanced technology.* For example, Worldwide Management Systems, Inc., a venture undertaken by a consortium of travel agencies, committed $2 million in 1981 to build a "multilingual" computer reservation system. Today they have a unique capability to serve the business travel needs of such large companies as IBM and Xerox. With immediate access to 15 airlines, five car-rental companies, and nine hotel chains, they have preempted the market from conventional agencies.

Some of these successes did not have strategic implications when they were originally conceived and implemented. Some became strategically significant and practical only because significant investment in internal systems already had been made. A scarce few were the results of careful analysis of customer needs and a decision to proceed from scratch.

All these thrusts have the common characteristic of long lead times—three to five years—from conception to fruition. Consequently, each afforded the innovator adequate time to realize excellent profits during its competitors' catch-up endeavors.

WILL THE TREND ACCELERATE?

There are several developments in technology that point to a quickening of the pace of product differentiation through network systems.

1.   *The functional value of semiconductors is appreciating and their cost declining.* This will improve the return on investment for workstation automation, and will provide incentives to increase communications capability at each station.

2.   *The quantity and quality of databases and the software packages that utilize them*

is improving due to continuing heavy expenditures by industry and government.

3. *Digital communications capacity is displacing analog* as optical fiber and digital microwave networks are put in place by common carriers. Digital transmission offers enormous firehose capacity, increased efficiency, and lower costs—especially when superimposing additional traffic on existing systems.

4. *Standards are evolving which will allow more networks to talk with one another.*

WHAT'S HAPPENING IN MARKETING MANAGEMENT?

Before the 1950s, marketing was considered to be more a subject of economic statistics and theory than a serious business function. Scholars debated whether or not it was a science. Marketing was looked upon by top management as "no more than the selling function." There were a few, however, who were beginning to understand and define the "marketing concept" which elevated consumers to the status of king and urged a pervasive business orientation toward accommodating their desires.

A decade later, marketing management's role in selecting target customers, assessing their needs and concerns, and managing resources to satisfy them was almost universally accepted. Some attention was given to the 'coordinating activity' of relating marketing to other business functions, yet there was no hint of the emergence of marketing management as a leadership role within a firm.

By 1970, marketing as a business function was assuming parity in significance with manufacturing, finance and research. As Theodore Leavitt asserts, "Business success is a matter of the disproportionate and enduring attractions of certain proportions of customers at certain levels of relative price—defines the purpose of business in terms of marketing—once again, getting and keeping the customer. This, therefore, installs marketing at the center of what's done in corporate strategic planning."

Still the idea of marketing as the prime mover—internally as well as externally—is neither clearly comprehended nor widely practiced. Further, any relationship or interdependency between marketing and information technology is dismissed with an occasional reference to marketing and the computer in problem solving. The note of the American Management Association Marketing Council meeting in 1985 reports a consensus among participants that "Marketing strategy is becoming increasingly sophisticated, especially with the rising use of the computer as an analytical tool."

It seems that marketing management has a lot to do if it is to fulfill its destiny as the prime mover in the successful integration of information technology with the strategic and tactical planning and implementation process of the corporation. Why must marketing take the leading role?

1. In an environment of intensifying international competition, deregulation, and diminishing customer loyalty, product differentiation is crucial. As Leavitt defines it, "The search for meaningful distinction is a central part of the marketing effort . . . It is about achieving customer-getting distinction by differentiating what you do and how you operate. All else is derivative of that, and only that." The increasing number of companies that have achieved product differentiation through technology is compelling evidence of the need for marketing leadership in this endeavor.

2. Marketing can help the company identify its customers' and prospective customers' satisfied and unsatisfied needs.

3. Marketing managers ought to be fully cognizant of all relevant internal operations, including management information systems.

4. The marketing function, as the prime mover of the company, requires of its managers the visionary skills and persuasive capabilities needed to initiate and sustain corporate planning and growth.

5. No other function is likely to fill this role. The MIS department is too far removed from the customers, and is rarely visionary or venturesome. The corporate development function lacks detailed knowledge of customers' needs and of the relevant internal functions. Finance is too short-term profit-oriented. Top management often does not distinguish the company's products and services from those of its rivals in the minds of its customers to the extent that marketing does.

WHAT SHOULD BE DONE?

• Marketing management must work closely with and understand in detail the firm's management information systems. What are the firm's databases? What will be added? What is the value of the databases' contents to the firm? To its customers? To vendors? To potential partners? Intensive and extensive research of this subject is mandatory, and the results should be analyzed by the most creative and perceptive marketers to be found.

The value of the database may arise from one or more of four virtues: timeliness, accuracy, completeness, and the avoidance of duplication. The timeliness of Citibank's exchange-rate information affords customers the opportunity to save money. An accessible bill of materials file, including detailed specifications of all parts and components with the latest engineering changes, gives the involved departments, vendors, subcontractors, and customers superb accuracy and thoroughness.

Remarkable improvements in efficiency can be attained. Prices, sales statistics, and inventory levels conglomorated to include multilevels in distribution channel can be utilized to derive benefits from all of the virtues listed above. It is important to understand the firm's information handling capability. Are networks in place or planned that can be expanded or modified to reach customers, prospects, or vendors? What are the fundamental economics underlying the networks?

• A parallel effort to research and document customers' and prospective customers' "wish list" is imperative. Specific individuals must be made responsible for developing comprehensive answers to these and other questions: How can the information value of current and planned products or services be enhanced? What opportunities are there for significant improvements in efficiency or convenience? Is there merit in integrating vertical and horizontal systems? The designated individuals must be imaginative, and should know about other companies' successful marketing automation systems.

• A permanent committee should be established to conduct regularly scheduled brainstorming sessions. Appropriate marketing, top management, financial, and technical executives should participate, and you should consider including executives from customer companies in pertinent discussions. In addition to identifying potentially profitable link-ups with them, you may be able to discover potential "blindsides" by competitors. For example, is the music industry vulnerable to a revolution from digitalized music transmitted directly to the home through the existing telephone networks?

• An encyclopedia of other people's success stories should be developed. Vendors of information-age technology regularly conduct executive seminars which include briefings on specific applications. Trade journals, annual reports, news articles, and advertisements frequently contain details of innovative approaches.

• Marketing must take an active, not reactive, role in advocating increased investment in and commitment to technology within the firm. Most importantly, management's thinking about computers and networks must be changed. Information-age technology must be considered a potentially dynamic earning asset rather than a budget expense item.

• Each firm should have a recruiting and staffing plan designed to markedly improve the marketing department's technology skills over time.

Based upon the results of the marketing effort, all management personnel should be taught the necessary skills to take full advantage of information-age technology. If the ultimate result is a change in the firm's strategic direction, an informed and knowledgeable management team will be crucial to successful implementation.

Frank E. Moriya is professor and chairman of the University of Bridgeport (Connecticut) department of marketing and international business. Carl M. Vorder Bruegge is senior vice-president of marketing at MCI Communications Corporation in Washington, D.C.

20.
STRENGTHEN DISTRIBUTION PERFORMANCE THROUGH CHANNEL POSITIONING

James A. Narus
James C. Anderson

In order to gain a competitive presence in the marketplace, a manufacturer needs an effective distribution network. Manufacturers often attempt to strengthen distributor performance through a complicated collection of short-term incentives, with sometimes disappointing results. The authors propose a four-step process, which they call channel positioning, that pursues far-reaching results and a sustainable competitive advantage.

To gain a strong, competitive presence in the final-customer marketplace, manufacturers must reward, cajole, and coax their distributors to take marketing actions. Uncertain of what is required for success in these undertakings, many manufacturers pursue "quick fixes" through short-term incentive programs instead of seeking long-term, strategic solutions. At best, these incentives yield temporary performance improvements. More often than not, they are received with indifference by distributors firms, which see them as little more than gimmicks. When not couched within a broader strategic plan these incentives can even bring unexpected consequences, as the following examples illustrate.

• With the intent of increasing distributor market penetration, the management of a specialty bearings manufacturing firm raised the functional discount on their product lines by 5 percent. Management believed that the added discount would motivate distributors to aggressively promote the lines and to seek out new business. Two months later, management reviewed the situation and discovered that unit sales had remained stable and that no new accounts had been established. Upon detailed investigation, management discovered that instead of capitalizing on the opportunity for added profits, distributors had merely given the discounts away in the form of lower prices to their customer, in an attempt to increase sales. Although some distributors gained added short-term sales, the consequences of their action was to trigger a price war. When all competitors matched the lower price levels, sales and market shares stabilized at their old levels. Unfortunately profit margins had eroded significantly, and distributors no longer pushed the lines in their promotional efforts.

• The top salesperson for a small computer-peripherals manufacturing company returned fresh and invigorated from a two-week vacation in Hawaii. She had won the trip in a companywide contest designed to increase sales of peripherals to computer dealers. Because a significant component of her compensation came from commissions on sales, she was doubly satisfied; the contest had resulted in a hefty boost in personal income. As she resumed her sales calls on dealers, the salesperson found that few wanted to buy more peripherals. When asked why, the typical dealers responded that the company had purchased up to three months worth of inventory to take advantage of the rebates given during the contest period. At the same time, the dealers requested that the salesperson make joint sales calls with their own sales staff and assist with product demonstrations to help clear peripherals inventory. Reviewing the situation, the salesperson found herself in a bind. If she assisted the dealers with presentations, she would have to forgo her own commissions for some time. On the other hand, if she pursued new business, she would jeopardize the loyalty and cooperation of her dealers.

• The sales manager for an electronic components manufacturer was pleased with a new distributor sales contest that he had just presented to a meeting of a distributor's salesforce. As part of the contest, each distributor salesperson was given a scorecard. Over the next four months, each salesperson would earn points. The points distributed varied as a function of the following criteria: sales to new accounts, percent of sales over quota, number of demonstrations, increase in the number of products sold per order, and number of joint sales calls made. At the end of four months, the salesperson with the most points would win a VCR. The sales manager liked the contest because he felt it would allow his company to achieve a multitude of objectives with one program. Unfortunately, the sales manager received a cool response from the distributor's sales personnel. When asked about the response later in the day, the distributor firm's president said he found little extraordinary about the contest. As a matter of fact, he pointed out, many of his other suppliers also had contests running: Two offered VCRs as prizes, five featured portable color TVs, two promised mobile car phones, and one promoted a trip to Bermuda. More important, the other contests were easier to understand, with prizes based solely on sales over quota.

In this article, we advance the concept of *channel positioning* as a coherent, strategic framework for strengthening distributor performance and thus the manufacturer's performance in the marketplace. This approach can help marketing and sales managers to avoid the unexpected consequences just described. We begin by contending that a positive, partnership philosophy necessarily precedes strategic thinking about strengthening distributor performance and leads to the formulation of the concepts of *channel position and channel offering*. Next, we outline the process of channel positioning. Finally, we furnish a disguised example of channel positioning from a manufacturer of equipment parts.

THINKING STRATEGICALLY ABOUT DISTRIBUTOR PERFORMANCE

From the start, many manufacturers are locked into the short-term incentives treadmill because their distribution philosophies are myopic, contradictory, and incomplete. Before a manufacturing firm can act strategically, its managers must think strategically. Doing so requires that the manufacturer adopt a constructive, long-term philosophy in which distributors are viewed as a resource that enables the firm to reach markets that it otherwise could not.

Perhaps the best way to achieve this end is to consider the distributor as a partner, and then to develop a relationship that genuinely reflects that conceptualization. Only then will both the manufacturer and the distributor recognize the importance of each other's contribution and well-being, and coordinate their efforts to better satisfy the requirements of the final customer.[1] Implicit in this thinking is the understanding that the manufacturer has two tasks to perform simultaneously. The first is "marketing to distributors." The second is "marketing with distributors" to the final customer. Thus, the astute manufacturer views the distributor as a partner in competition with other manufacturer/distributor pairs for sales to the final customer. Such a view logically leads to long-term, strategic efforts to improve the distributor's ability to market successfully.

CONCEPTUALIZING CHANNEL POSITION

As veteran marketers readily point out, meeting customer needs is necessary but not sufficient for success in the marketplace. Year after year, the firm must battle competitors for each final customer's business. To win, the marketer must gain a reputation for providing the final customer with superior value, perhaps in the form of lower prices or better support service. Marketers refer to this provision of superior value maintained over time as a *sustainable competitive advantage*, and to the reputation for furnishing it as a *position* in the marketplace.[2,3] For example, a manufacturer that has a sustainable competitive advantage as the lowest-cost producer in an industry is likely to pursue a marketplace position among final customers as the "low-price leader." A producer with superior technical design and manufacturing capabilities is likely to gain a reputation among final customers for its "state-of-the-art products."

Although this fact is not often recognized, the manufacturer faces a similar challenge in its dealings with distributors. Because each distributor may carry more than a hundred lines, in some cases even those of competing producers, the manufacturer must compete for the distributor's time and effort. To succeed in *this* competition, the manufacturer must provide the distributor with superior value from the resale of products or from support programs and incentives relative to those offered by other manufacturers. We call this superior value given to the distributor the manufacturer's *partnership advantage* over the competition, because it makes the distributor more dependent upon the manufacturer and thus more willing to contribute to a partnership through improved marketing efforts.

A *channel position* is the reputation a manufacturer acquires among distributors for furnishing products, services, financial returns, programs, and systems that are in some ways superior to those offered by competing manufacturers. Under ideal circumstances, this channel position should mirror the firm's marketplace position, capitalize on any of the firm's distinctive competencies, and be based on a sustainable partnership advantage. For example, a manufacturer with a sustainable partnership advantage based on giving the best technical assistance to distributors is likely to gain a channel position as the industry's "technical support leader." Alternatively, a manufacturer that furnishes its distributor with the most comprehensive and effective point-of-sale merchandising tools is likely to seek a reputation as the industry's "promotional support leader." Thus, two critical tasks for a manufacturer that markets through distributors are acquiring a sustainable partnership advantage and securing an advantageous channel position.

FORMULATING THE CONCEPT OF CHANNEL OFFERING

The realization that it must compete for distributors' efforts as well as for final customers' business leads the manufacturer to reformulate strategic thinking about the range of products and services it brings to the marketplace. It is useful to conceptualize the marketplace offering as consisting of two components. The first, the *product offering*, comprises a core product of benefits, a tangible product enhanced by packaging and features, and an augmented product of customer services and warranties.[4]

The second component, the *channel offering*, includes the bundle of services, programs, and systems directed toward distributors. It is composed of core elements (or benefits) the distributor expects from the manufacturer, distributor capability-building programs (e.g., promotional support and train-

Figure 1.
Channel-Offering Component of the Marketplace Offering

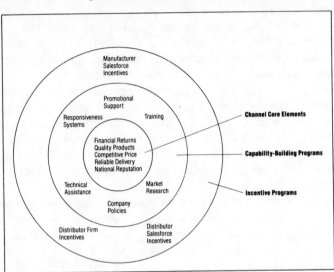

ing), and incentive programs. Figure 1 depicts this second component of the manufacturer's marketplace offering.

As a partner in marketing to the final customer, the manufacturer's efforts are directed first at devising a product offering desired by final customers, and second at creating a complementary channel offering that will reward and facilitate proper marketing activities on the part of the distributor. Clearly, these efforts require long-term, strategic thinking on the part of the manufacturer's marketing managers.

THE PROCESS OF CHANNEL POSITIONING

Channel positioning consists of four basic steps:

1. Performance expectations for distributors are determined.
2. An advantageous channel position is selected.
3. A channel offering is constructed to secure a partnership advantage.
4. The channel position is communicated and promoted to distributors.

STEP ONE: DETERMINE PERFORMANCE EXPECTATIONS

The channel-positioning process begins when the manufacturer determines what the firm expects from distributors in the way of performance. Devised after consultation with distributors, these expectations should take into account both marketplace realities and the firm's objectives. Expectations are typically formalized in oral or written sales agreements, policy statements, and annual objectives or quotas. All distributors should be made aware of these expectations through personal contacts and correspondence.

When defining expectations of distributor performance, manufacturers should explicitly state desired levels of market penetration, product augmentation, and management professionalism. Market penetration can be measured in terms of territory sales to targeted market segments, market share, new accounts developed, sales calls made on potential customers, and changes from last year's sales levels. All manufacturers want distributors to augment product offerings to some degree with services ranging from twenty-four-hour delivery to repair work. Marketing managers may require distributors to provide facilities and personnel resources, technical and marketing capabilities, and repair and service work. Finally, many manufacturers now expect management professionalism from distributors in areas as diverse as strategic planning, marketing operations management, financial management, and succession planning. These requirements should also be communicated to distributors.

STEP TWO: SELECT AN ADVANTAGEOUS CHANNEL POSITION

Next, the manufacturer must identify the most advantageous channel position to build. Naturally, selection of a channel position should be guided by a recognition of the firm's capabilities and distinctive competencies, as well as of its overall objectives and strategy. A typical sequence of activities is as follows. First, the manufacturer reviews the firm's current channel position for deficiencies caused by a failure to meet distributor requirements or to differentiate the firm, inconsistencies with the overall marketing strategy and position, and changing marketplace conditions. Second, the firm compares the channel positions of its principal competitors to distributor requirements, then attempts to isolate unfilled existing or developing gaps. Third, the manufacturer defines the desired channel position around those gaps most important to distributors and around its own capabilities.

The channel position should be observable, distinctive, and communicable to distributors. The following are examples of successful channel positions. In the "low-price leader" position, the manufacturer's lines are the lowest priced in the industry, resulting in high-volume sales for distributors. Under the "full service supplier" position, a manufacturer touts its broad range of services. Many manufacturers promote a "technical support" position in which they extol their ability to solve technical problems, provide engineering assistance, and design new products and services for distributors. With today's advancements in computing technologies, some firms are turning to "networking systems" positions, in which they emphasize computerized order entry, electronic mail, and problem-solving systems.

STEP THREE: CONSTRUCT THE OFFERING TO SECURE A PARTNERSHIP ADVANTAGE

As can be seen in Figure 1, the channel offering is composed of three major sections—channel core elements, capability-building programs, and incentive programs. To construct a channel offering, the manufacturer begins by identifying key components from each section that are required by distributors in the industry and that give credence to the desired channel position. Next, the manufacturer determines the level of each component that the firm is prepared to offer. The resulting channel offering should at least meet industry norms for each component and, at best, surpass them on critical dimensions. Although channel-offering components may vary from industry to industry, they typically contain the following.

- *Channel Core Elements.* The channel core elements are those five basics that distributors must have from all their suppliers.
- *Financial Returns.* A distributor's financial returns accumulate from three key sources—the functional discount provided by the manufacturer, volume sales and inventory turnover, and a premium for performing additional services. Today, the shrewd manufacturer enhances distributors' financial returns by supplementing the functional discount with programs designed to increase distributor sales and inventory turnover, and to enable the distributor to augment the manufacturer's products with services.
- *Product Quality.* A quality product is one that consistently meets or exceeds the minimum requirements of final customers. In the channels context, this definition must be expanded to cover the distributor's requirements for the product line, including these: the product line is in demand by final customers; the product line is as complete as possible; and the manufacturer has a record of new product development.
- *Competitive Price.* The distributor must carry lines priced in correspondence with their perceived value.
- *Reliable Delivery.* Consistently prompt, accurate, and reliable delivery is important to distributors because their business depends on getting the right product to customers quickly.
- *National Reputation.* Distributors prefer handling the lines of a manufacturer with a national reputation; therefore, a manufacturer should implement pull-marketing programs designed to generate final-customer awareness and brand loyalty.
- *Capability-Building Programs.* The second section of the channel offering

encompasses programs a manufacturer can employ to build desired distributor capabilities and, hence, long-term marketplace performance. Because competing firms typically offer similar channel core elements to distributors, capability-building programs represent the most potent, strategic means of differentiating one manufacturer from another. Ideally, such programs enhance distributor skills but are not directly transferable to the lines of other suppliers (e.g., joint sales calls for a new product application). To the extent that this is not possible, the manufacturer can achieve its end by focusing on programs that improve distributor capabilities overall (e.g., financial management courses), and by doing so build distributor goodwill.

Some key programs are as follows. To improve distributors' market-penetration capabilities, manufacturers can offer various types of *promotional support* including cooperative advertising, merchandising assistance, and joint sales calls. They can develop *responsiveness systems* to identify, anticipate, and resolve distributor needs and problems. These systems usually concern themselves with personnel training, enhanced expediting and delivery capabilities, and effective communications networks. Depending upon the type of augmentation and distributor professionalism needed, manufacturers can furnish selective *training* courses: for example, product applications, selling, technical problem solving, strategic planning, and financial management. Firms can provide *technical assistance* to distributors by hiring field technical representatives, establishing an "inside" technical problem-solving group, or implementing a computer-networked expert system.

Because distributors often have more limited financial resources or lack research capabilities, many manufacturers provide *market research* studies for them. These might range from furnishing sales leads to defining market segments to identifying "cross-selling" opportunities (e.g., the chance to sell complementary products as a package or system).

Often overlooked, *company policies* can also strengthen distributor performance. For instance, selective distribution policies typically motivate distributors to give particular attention to the lines. Also, a manufacturer can gain distributor respect and compliance by simply creating equitable policies and consistently enforcing them.

• *Incentive Programs.* Because they are tactical in nature, incentive programs should be selected *after* the other two components are selected and should be based on long-term strategy; they need to reinforce long-term strategies and generate enthusiasm. To achieve these ends, incentives are directed at three targets—the manufacturer's sales force, the distributor firm, and the distributor's sales force.

Manufacturer-Sales Force Incentives. The final type of incentive is directed to the distributor's salesperson. Manufacturers like to use these incentives for several reasons. The incentives are directed to the individual who actually sells the product to the final customer. In addition, they can create sales force enthusiasm for an otherwise indistinguishable product line. Unfortunately, these incentives are also likely to generate conflict with distributor management over control of the sales force. Among the most frequently used distributor-sales force incentives are spiffs (gifts awarded to the salesperson for increased sales) and sales contests.

Having assembled a tentative channel offering—in the form of channel core elements, capability-building programs, and incentive programs—the manufacturer should review and pretest it to be certain it will be effective. One way of accomplishing this is by informally presenting it at the firm's distributor council meeting and soliciting evaluations and suggested improvements. When incorporated, these ideas can strengthen the firm's partnership advantage.

In reviewing the channel offering, the manufacturer should be aware that certain elements are more likely than others to bring about a partnership advantage. For instance, research suggests that these core elements contribute the most to a sustainable partnership advantage: product quality (including completeness of product lines and new product development) and the manufacturer's national reputation.[5] When the industry is highly competitive in terms of core elements offered to distributors, capability-building programs (most notably technical assistance and promotional support) are the most likely sources of a partnership advantage.

Incentive programs are least likely to result in a partnership advantage because nearly all of them are tactical and can be copied by competitors. However, by following these incentive-program pointers, a manufacturer can move toward securing partnership advantage while building distributor enthusiasm for the line. First, to create a more strategic and long-lasting impact, the manufacturer should "institutionalize" programs by limiting their number to a few major efforts designed to strengthen distributor performance. By making incremental improvements in these programs each year and promoting them extensively, the manufacturer will increase distributor understanding and enthusiasm for the programs, enhance effectiveness, and instill a sense of tradition with distributors. Second, by keeping incentive programs and contests as simple as possible, the manufacturer will increase comprehension and participation. Third, the manufacturer should avoid giving its own salesforce incentives that encourage the salesperson to load distributors with added inventory rather than to generate real sales increases. Instead, manufacturers should rely on "win-win" incentives in which salesforce bonuses are tied to distributor sales. Fourth, manufacturers should design incentives that encourage the completion of tasks with long-term consequences—for example, giving sales training programs and making joint sales calls to prospective customers. Fifth, rather than relying too much on incremental functional discounts, manufacturers should try to improve distributors' financial performance through such means as increasing inventory turnover rates and helping distributors to achieve price premiums by offering services. Sixth, the greater use of distributor-firm incentives, and the avoidance of incentives directed toward distributors' salespeople, can eliminate potential conflict over control of the distributor's salesforce.

Of course, the manufacturer must weigh the costs and the benefits of its overall channel offering and, to the extent possible, of the offering's individual components. A number of the benefits, such as increased market penetration in select segments, unit sales, and gross margin, can be quantified easily. Other benefits are more qualitative, but nonetheless critical for long-term success. Examples of these benefits are as follows: improved communication about potential new applications for existing products and new product ideas, and better coordination of marketing activities (e.g., sales calls and customer problem solving). Limiting the number of programs to a few "institutionalized" ones not only enhances their impact, but also facilitates the monitoring of their benefits and costs.

STEP FOUR: COMMUNICATE A CHANNEL POSITION TO DISTRIBUTORS

Having constructed a channel offering that secures a partnership advantage, the manufacturer must now build a reputation for its channel position among distributors. Relying upon the full range of promotional tools available and appropriate to the industry, the manufacturer communicates the position to distributors. Doing this can involve anything from advertising in trade journals to sales presentations. Today, several manufacturers are using innovative communications media such as videotapes and electronic mail to build and reinforce their channel positions.

AN EXAMPLE OF CHANNEL POSITIONING

Chemparts, Inc. (a fictitious name), manufacturers a line of specialty repair parts for equipment used in the chemical-process industry. The firm has an established marketplace position of technical excellence in the production of top-quality parts for use in highly acidic or caustic applications. The lines are sold exclusively to distributors for resale.

Although Chemparts' line had distinct quality advantage, distributors' selling efforts were limited because the products required a difficult, technical sales approach that few distributors could manage. It was far easier for distributors to sell less complicated, well-known lines on price than to initiate discussions on life-cycle costs and value-in-use. For years, the firm had made half-hearted efforts to improve distributor performance, relying almost exclusively on a variety of inventive programs. Results were mixed at best, and

Table 1.
A Comparison of Industry Norms and Competitive Channel Offerings

		Key Competitors	
	Industry Norm	**MicroChem**	**CLT Equipment**
Channel Position	—————————	low price leader	computer networking leader
Channel-Offering Components			
Core Elements			
• Functional Discount	• 32% off suggested resale price	• 32%	• 32%
• Payment Discount	• 2/10/net 30	• 2/15/net 60	• none/net 45
• Quantity Discount	• 3% on orders of 50–100 units	• 4% on orders of 50–100 units	• 3% on orders of 50–100 units
	• 5% on orders of 100 + units	• 7% on orders of 100 + units	• 5% on orders of 100 + units
• Quality Measured in Life-Cycle Cost*	• $225	• $250	• $225
• Suggested Resale Price/Unit	• $35	• $25	• $35
• Completeness of Product Line (# of complementary products)	• 7 out of 12 items	• 6 out of 12 items	• 7 out of 12 items
• Reliability of Delivery	• 90% of orders filled in one week	• 85% of orders filled in one week	• 95% of orders filled in one week
• National Reputation Development	• $1 million in annual national advertising	• $750,000 in annual national advertising	• $1.25 million in annual national advertising
Capability-Building Programs			
• Promotional Support	• product literature and catalogs	• product literature and catalogs	• product literature and catalogs • sales leads • electronic mail promotions
• Responsiveness Systems	• none	• none	• computerized ordering • expert systems • electronic mail
• Training	• one-week sales course	• one-day sales course	• one-week sales course plus videotapes • three-day course on computer systems
• Technical Assistance	• 5–10 tech reps	• 2 tech reps	• 10 tech reps • portable problem-solving computers
• Company Policies: Distribution Selectivity	• 120 distributors for U.S. • few distributors/ trade area	• 250 distributors • many distributors/ trade area	• 131 distributors • few distributors/ trade area
Return Policies	• 10% of annual purchases	• 5% of purchases	• 10% of purchases
Incentive Programs			
• Manufacturer-Salesforce Programs	• commission on sales to distributors	• commission on sales to distributors	• bonus on sales over quota to distributors
• Distributor-Firm Programs	• rebates on purchases made prior to peak sales periods	• rebates	• rebates • price reductions on orders placed through computer network
• Distributor-Salesforce Programs	• spiffs • annual sales contests	• spiffs	• spiffs • monthly contests based on sales and computer utilization • blazers awarded to best salesperson of the year

* Life-cycle cost refers to the total cost of using a product, including purchase price, during its productive lifetime.

when a program succeeded, it was copied immediately by competitors. Chemparts did not engage in any pull-marketing efforts.

Then Chemparts' managers decided to take a strategic approach using channel positioning. First, the firm summarized its expectations of distributors. These included the following: selective penetration of its target market and augmentation of the products with technical design and problem-solving assistance from distributors. In addition, the firm sought increased distributor professionalism in technical selling and marketing.

Second, Chemparts' managers identified the most advantageous channel position the firm could acquire by reviewing the firm's current channel positioning and offering. They quickly discovered that their functional discount did not correspond to the required level of distributor competence and effort. Technical assistance and national advertising were also deficient. Next, they gathered industry norms for each of the channel-offering elements. Using market research and salesforce intelligence, the firm identified the components of the channel positions and offerings of its two key rivals, MicroChem and CLT Equipment (also fictitious names). This information is summarized in Table 1. Managers identified gaps in competitive offerings and contrasted these with Chemparts' capabilities. They decided that a channel position could be built around "technical support leadership" for three reasons: both final customers and distributors placed a high value on technical assistance, the position had been ignored by the competition, and the firm had strong technical capabilities.

Third, Chemparts' managers assembled a tentative channel offering by listing channel-offering elements needed to meet distributors' requirements and construct a technical support leadership position. Then the manufacturer worked to secure a partnership product quality (including completeness of product line) and new product problem-solving training programs, hiring more technical representatives and problem-solving specialists; offering sales leads and market research; and providing joint sales call assistance. Incentive programs were pruned and limited to a few that have been repeated and improved each year. The final offering is presented in Table 2.

Fourth, Chemparts communicated its channel position as the industry's technical support leader to distributors through a series of advertisements in two leading distributor publications, an elaborate presentation at the company's annual distributor sales meeting, sales calls on each distributor by the firm's distributor-marketing manager, and a policy manual presented to all distributors. The firm used all opportunities to reinforce the position through correspondence and personal contact.

As a result of its channel-positioning efforts, Chemparts simplified and gained control of its distributor programs, created a reputation among distributors as the industry's technical support leader, improved distributor technical selling and assistance capabilities, and, most important, strengthened the firm's competitive presence in the final-customer marketplace. For the past three years, Chemparts' sales of the line have grown at a rate significantly higher than their principal competitors', Micro-Chem and CLT Equipment.

In this article, we propose a four-step strategic approach for strengthening distributor performance, called channel positioning. The method strives to

Table 2.
The Channel Offering of Chemparts, Inc.

Channel Position	Technical Support Leader
Channel-Offering Components	
Core Elements	
• Functional Discount	• 33% off suggested resale price
• Payment Discount	• 2/10/net 30
• Quantity Discount	• 3% on orders of 50–100 units
	• 5% on orders of 100 + units
• Quality Measured in Life-Cycle Cost*	• $185
• Suggested Resale Price/Unit	• $45
• Completeness of Product Line (# of complementary products)	• 12 out of 12
• Reliability of Delivery	• 95% of orders filled in one week
• National Reputation Development	• $1 million in annual national advertising
Capability-Building Programs	
• Promotional Support	• product literature and catalogs
	• sales leads and market research
	• demonstration kits
	• joint sales calls
• Responsiveness Systems	• 800# for customer problem solving
	• well-trained order center personnel
• Training	• one-week technical sales course
	• three-day product applications course
	• one-week technical design course
• Technical Assistance	• 20 tech reps
	• mobile lab for demonstrations and problem solving
	• 5 problem-solving specialists
• Company Policies: Distribution Selectivity	• 80 distributors for the U.S.
	• exclusive trade areas
Return Policies	• 10% of annual purchases
	• all defective parts
	• all discontinued products
Incentive Programs	
• Manufacturer-Salesforce Programs	• bonus based on distributor sales to final customers
	• bonus based on new customers developed with distributors
• Distributor-Firm Programs	• special deals during slow sales months
	• award given to top 10% of distributors for annual sales
• Distributor-Salesforce Programs	• none

*Life-cycle cost refers to the total cost of using a product, including purchase price, during its productive lifetime.

achieve a long-term position based on the construction of a comprehensive channel offering and the acquisition of a sustainable partnership advantage. If manufacturers practice this approach they can expect improved distributor performance and an improved marketplace presence because it offers the following elements: consistency between distributor programs and overall company strategy; comprehensive programs that satisfy distributor requirements as well as surpass competitive offerings; and the creation of a long-term reputation among distributors based on the distinctive competencies of the firm.

REFERENCES

1. J. A. Narus and J. C. Anderson, "Turn Your Industrial Distributors into Partners," *Harvard Business Review*, March-April 1986, 66-71.

2. M. E. Porter, *Competitive Advantage: Creating and Sustaining Superior Performance* (New York: The Free Press, 1985).
3. P. Kotler, *Marketing Mangement: Analysis, Planning, and Control*, 5th ed. (Englewood Cliffs, NJ: Prentice-Hall, 1984).
4. Ibid.
5. R. Sethuraman, J. C. Anderson, and J. A. Narus, "Partnership Advantage and Its Determinants in Manufacturer and Distributor Working Relationships," *Journal of Business Research*, forthcoming.

James A. Narus is associate professor of Marketing at the Babcock Graduate School of Management, Wake Forest University. James C. Anderson is the William L. Ford professor of Marketing and associate professor of Behaviorial Science in Management at the J. L. Kellogg Graduate School of Management, Northwestern University.

21.
MANAGE TELEMARKETING EFFECTIVELY

John I. Coppett
Harold E. Glass

> There are no absolute management rules for telemarketing, but some
> emerging patterns provide guidelines for training, motivation and com-
> pensation, as well as handling burnout and turnover.

As new or improved technology changes the way that companies do business, so it alters the management of human resources. Nowhere is this more
evident than in the burgeoning area of telemarketing—an activity that may
create as many as eight million new jobs by the year 2000. Already more than
65% of the Fortune 500 companies use telemarketing applications to increase
profits.

Not long ago, managing people in a corporate telemarketing center usually
involved little more than mixing corporate personnel philosophy with some
common sense applied by center managers. Today the story is different.

Fortunately, better management information is now becoming accessible.

As in anything that has to do with the unique characteristics of human
beings, there are no absolute management rules for telemarketing. However,
there are some emerging patterns that provide guidelines for telemarketing
managers—in terms of hiring practices, training, motivation and compensation, as well as managing burnout and turnover. Through experience and
research, management is beginning to identify certain human resource constants and develop guidelines to help manage people in the telemarketing
center.

CENTERS DIFFER BY APPLICATION TYPE

Any discussion of human resources in telemarketing must begin with this
obvious, but often overlooked, fact: The telemarketing environment is

different from most other office environments. In contrast to most other office jobs, the telemarketing specialist is an important customer contact; the impression that he or she makes, whether good or bad, is the basis of the customer's impression of the company.

The manager must take care to recognize not only the differences between other parts of the organization and the telemarketing group, he or she must also understand how the telemarketing environment differs by the type of application involved.

Telemarketing centers can be grouped into four types of applications, each with its own set of human resource needs.

Order Processing. The most basic application is order processing. The primary function of these types of centers is to enter orders from customers who call. Direct-response consumer catalog firms are perhaps the most familiar example, but many business-to-business orders are also handled through telemarketing-order-processing centers.

In these centers, the telemarketing specialist's main responsibility is to accurately enter the order information. Depending on the center, the specialist may also have cross-selling or limited upgrade selling responsibilities. Some specialists may answer inventory queries or conduct simple market research. The primary, distinctive characteristic of this application is processing inbound calls.

Customer Service. Classic customer service activities also are well-suited to a telemarketing center. In this application, there are actually two distinct types of centers: 1) those that handle customer complaints or inquiries concerning billing, order/shipping status, or dealer location information and; 2) those that handle service/repair calls.

In the latter category, the customer service center could be helping the customer put together a child's toy, repair a washing machine, or maintain a piece of electronic equipment—all without the need for a field visit from a serviceperson.

Sales Support. A somewhat more complex telemarketing application is in sales support. Here the telemarketing specialist acts as the inside liaison with the customer, supporting the direct field salesperson in all types of customer contact. In this application, customer contact is not necessarily responsive, but frequently constitutes a company's main exposure to its customers. The center may concentrate on certain low-margin, high-volume products so that the full sales force can focus on more complicated, higher-return sales efforts.

Full Sales Role. Finally, telemarketing can be used to replace field sales visits in a full account management role. Functions can include selling, taking orders, answering inquiries, promoting new or improved products, and in general doing everything a corresponding field salesperson would do—except travel.

In each of these general categories, the defined telemarketing application can generally do the job better, more efficiently, and more effectively—*if* the

Figure 1.
Key Tasks and Job Design Factors

		Order Processing	Customer Service	Field Sales Support	Account Management
	Key Tasks	Record orders Access and provide factual information Confirm orders Provide minimal clerical follow-up Exercise minor sales discretion	Provide and Interpret factual information Diagnose problems and needs Do some problem solving	Qualify leads Take and expedite orders Service present accounts Handle complaints and problems Schedule production and/or shipments Communicate with field sales people	Service and manage accounts Prospect, qualify leads and sell new accounts Handle complaints and problems Handle rate negotiation, pricing and scheduling Communicate with field sales and service staff
Job Design Factors	**Know-How:** Technical	Low	Medium	Medium	High
	Managerial	None	None	None to low	Account Management
	Human Relations	Moderate	High	High	High
	Problem Solving: Thinking Challenge		Known solutions to known problems	Known solutions to known problems	Moderate analysis, differing situations
	Thinking Environment	Routine decisions	Clearly defined procedures	Varying procedures	Varying procedures and policy guidelines
	Accountability: Freedom to Act	Close supervision	Close supervision	Supervision of progress and results	Supervisory review

Note: Job design factors are based on Hay guide chart profile technology. Technical know-how includes all of the following: Knowledge of equipment use and order processing, selling skills, product knowledge, and market/customer knowledge. Problem solving addresses the way in which knowledge is used in the job. Accountability describes the freedom the job has to affect end results.

right people are hired, *if* they are trained adequately, and *if* they are well-managed and properly motivated.

WHAT HAS BEEN LEARNED ABOUT HIRING?

The first rule of hiring is that selection always depends upon job design. There is no universal description of a telemarketing specialist. Instead, the kind of person needed varies according to the telemarketing center's specific application.

Although all telemarketing applications have the common element of customer contact by telephone, everything beyond that is different. Required selling skills, educational levels, training needs, motivating factors, compensation, and performance measurements may all differ.

The actual description of what the telemarketing specialists is expected to do is the starting point. All too often, managers skip to a desired outcome, without looking at the actual mechanics of the job.

Of course, certain generic tasks and job-design factors are relevant to each type of center. For example, the need to analyze orders in most order processing jobs is minimal. Instead, these specialists must be able to deal with a succession of nearly identical situations.

In contrast, the account management specialist who faces several differing situations must be able to draw from several procedures, policy guidelines, and experiences. In managing these operations, it becomes apparent that order processing and customer service centers require close supervision. On the other hand, specialists in field sales support and account management centers should be given more freedom.

After determining the basic job design, some obvious decisions can be made in the area of recruitment, hiring, compensation levels, and so forth. For instance, the specialist hired for an order processing application for one or two products will be quite different from the specialist hired to handle a line of 300 interrelated technical products. Each requires different compensation and different skills, experience, and training.

Even in less extreme situations, experience and research have been able to identify some general characteristics that help create a profile of the type of person best suited for each of the basic telemarketing categories.

For example, returning to the order processing basic job definition, telemarketing managers should look for people with a low need for variety, a good attention to detail, and typing or video display terminal experience.

Selecting the right people first requires correctly designing the telemarketing job. For example, one West Coast order processing center continued to have severe day-to-day operating difficulties. The abundance of college graduates in the area had prompted company management to staff the center with over-qualified people. Turnover was high and processing errors common

Figure 2.
Selection Criteria

	Order Processing	Customer Service	Field Sales Support	Account Management
Education and Experience	High school or equivalent Typing and/or CRT experience (preferred) No knowledge of product No experience	High school or equivalent* Prior clerical experience (preferred) Usually no prior product knowledge* No experience	Some college (often) Product knowledge (sometimes preferred) No experience	College education or equivalent Some product or business knowledge Demonstrated long term potential Excellent communication and organization skills
Intelligence	Low analytical skills	Somewhat higher analytical skills*	Somewhat higher analytical skills	Developed analytical skills
Behavioral and Other Characteristics	Comfort with CRT Clear speech pattern Good listening skills Low need for variety Patience with customers Good attention to detail Ability to follow procedures Ability to handle telephone stress	Human relations skills necessary to calm and defuse angry customers Superior listening skills Ability to deal with variety and unusual situations Ability to withstand pressure from callers	Minimum selling ability Minimum computation skills Ability to follow procedures and policies Ability to deal with variety and unusual situations Moderate degree of initiative and ability to perform without close supervision Good organization and attention to detail Ability to sustain customer rapport	Full sales skills Aggressiveness, energy and drive Ability to follow and recommend procedures and policies Ability to deal with variety and unstructured situations High degree of self-motivation and independent thinking Good organization and attention to detail High ability to persuade and create customer rapport

*Except in highly technical product applications

Figure 3.
Training and Development Factors

Training Areas	Order Processing	Customer Service	Field Sales Support	Account Management
	Emphasis on equipment training (CRT, telephone), call handling—disregard procedures	Emphasis similar to order processing, with added elements of product training	Emphasis on MIS training, company procedures, some selling training	Emphasis on general sales training
Break-In Period[1]	½ month	1–3 months	1–3 months	3–6 months
Up-to-speed Period[2]	1–3 months	6–12 months	6–12 months	12 + months
Career Pathing Practice	No planning	No planning	Little planning, but informal	Informal planning
Advancement Potential	Limited potential within center	Limited potential within center, some to field customer service	Limited potential, some within center, some into field sales	Some potential out of center into field sales

[1]Break-in period: The time required for a line Telemarketer to reach basic proficiency and independent functioning.

[2]Up-to-speed period: The time required for a line Telemarketer to reach center average performance following the break-in period.

until center management stepped back, properly designed the job, and hired according to the job's requirements.

MOTIVATION AND COMPENSATION

Selecting and then training the right people is only part of the task. A more difficult problem is keeping them motivated so they continue to be productive. To meet this challenge, there are eight key motivational factors. Again, their importance differs depending on both the telemarketing applications and the individual. These include:

- Career Path. Offer the opportunity for promotion out of the entry level telemarketing specialist position.
- Job Challenge. Make the job flexible enough so that it can grow with the telemarketing specialist.
- Team Spirit. Create a sense of center identity, loyalty, and enthusiasm.
- Financial Incentives. Provide the appropriate variety of compensation vehicles, such as merit increases, commissions, incentive compensation, contest prizes, and so on.
- Recognition. Acknowledge contributions or achievements, either as an individual or as part of a group.
- Company Contribution. Communicate the sense of helping the company achieve its overall mission.
- Individual Reinforcement. Give notice of, and commentary on, an individual specialist's work.
- Working Conditions. Build in appropriate shift length, breaks, plug-out flexibility, scheduling flexibility, and working environment.

The first seven of the motivational factors tend to change in relative importance when viewed across telemarketing applications. (This in no way detracts from the importance of the eighth factor, "working conditions"; it is important in all telemarketing situations. However, its parameters are fairly constant.)

Order Processing Centers tend to emphasize factors related to team spirit and group recognition, but downplay special financial rewards. In fact, in order processing centers, incentives can be counter-productive to the development of team spirit. The primary motivational techniques in this application involve diversions and interesting side activities to maintain enthusiasm.

To one hotel services center, this means regular trips by telemarketers to other company operations. To another hotel reservation center, this translates into teaming shifts against one another in a variety of friendly job performance contests.

The Customer Service Center tends to use similar techniques for motivation. Since customer service personnel are solving product or order related problems, specialists can take pride in helping customers and feel a sense of contribution to their company.

One large customer service center finds that circulating laudatory letters from customers particularly helps foster this sense of contribution.

In *Sales Support Centers*, receiving recognition from the field sales force and feeling a real sense of contributing to overall company sales are also critical motivational elements. Most sales support specialists work closely with the sales force in qualifying leads, providing customer information, and selling the product.

Also, within a sales support center, the factors of career pathing, job challenge, and individual recognition become more important. One center even has its specialists accompany several of their respective field contacts each year.

In *Account Management Centers*, because of the direct sales role of the specialist, motivational factors differ significantly from those in other application segments. For example, team spirit is much less important. Instead, emphasis is on the internal motivation created by achieving and maintaining ongoing account relationships through selling products directly to customers. Account management specialists often view their positions as stepping stones toward career growth.

To one transportation services company, the center is so important that all field sales people must begin in the telemarketing center. Telemarketing center salespeople at a major chemical company earn as much as $60,000. Therefore, the motivational factors used in account management centers are geared toward achieving sales volume, customer conversion, and other direct sales-related performance measurements.

Compensation is an issue that is naturally related to motivation, but with the exception of account management telemarketing centers, compensation is rarely the key motivational factor. In fact, most telemarketing specialists, except those responsible for account management, are hourly employees. Also, many center managers have indicated that it's difficult to justify incentive programs—again, except in account management situations.

Most of the individuals in order processing, customer service and sales support centers are not motivated by the risk/reward trade off offered by incentives or commission-type compensation. Similarly, the basic design of their job limits the applicability of incentive-based motivation. Still, it is prudent to provide better performers with larger wage increases, lest they begin to feel that how they do their job does not matter.

BURNOUT AND TURNOVER

Much has been written about a motivational problem that cuts across all types of centers: employee burnout and turnover. Although burnout is always bad, turnover may not necessarily be. In addressing the burnout and turnover issue, the cost of retention and career development must be balanced against the cost of hiring and training.

In general, the training costs of order processing and customer service centers are minimal compared to retention costs that could be high. In these situations, burnout becomes a big problem when it is
not followed by turnover.

In contrast, in sales support and account management applications, training is comparatively more expensive; here the investment in retention programs becomes more worthwhile.

The correct motivational techniques can be used to reduce burnout, but the cost of substantially reducing turnover must be evaluated in light of retention costs. Motivated employees *are* distinctly less likely to burn out and leave. However, the cost of motivating the employees must be measured in comparison to the cost of hiring and training new specialists.

Telemarketing can do many things better, more effectively, and more efficiently if the human resources are selected, trained, and motivated properly. But how, in the end, do you know if you are doing it correctly? One of the issues that still requires investigation is the mechanisms for measuring the performance of human resource management.

From the substantial experimentation in performance measurements in telemarketing contexts, some guidelines have emerged. Although performance measurement represents one of the most sophisticated of human resource management tools, telemarketing center management seldom has a hand in the design of the measurements themselves.

All too often, the measurement requests from corporate management do not make enough sense within the environment of a telemarketing center. For instance, order processing and sales support centers are frequently measured by revenue generation, but revenue generation is dependent on the number of calls they *receive*—and that depends on factors like advertising, which may be beyond the control of the telemarketing center.

The corporate level *and* the telemarketing center level must establish realistic performance measurements, measurements that reflect the ability or lack of ability of the individual specialist and the center as a whole to perform the assigned task. That means measuring people on factors they can affect—not on those on which they have no real impact.

Telemarketing has become an effective and pervasive sales tool, but only companies that use it best will get the desired results. Proper planning and management in this people-intensive area is especially critical. Without it, companies that seek a competitive edge might not make the marketing gains that they expected. The caveat here is to avoid blaming telemarketing itself if the problem really is telemarketing management.

John I. Coppett is associate professor of Business Administration and Marketing at Drake University. Harold E. Glass is head of the Hay Group's consulting practice to information-industry clients.

Part IV
MARKETING CONCEPTS AND THE MARKETING MIX

22.
DRAWING ROAD MAPS TO HIDDEN MARKET SEGMENTS

Robert C. Ferber
Stanley I. Cohen
Ernst Mendels

The most obvious ways to segment a market may not be the best. But with the a technique called the "automatic interaction detector," marketers can learn what really makes different kinds of buyers tick.

A common problem in market analysis is finding meaningful ways to segment markets—to discover those characteristics, shared by members of a segment, that make them different from people in other segments. Sometimes, the answer is obvious, such as when a product or service meets the application needs of certain industries better than others. But in other instances, the key differences among groups may not be readily apparent.

For example, suppose a company sells an industrial product that is complicatedly related to consumer markets in 40 countries. In 22 countries the business is consistently very profitable, but in 18 it is tenaciously unprofitable. Before pulling the plug on the unprofitable markets, the company would like to know if there are some hidden differences between the profitable and unprofitable ones that can be addressed by changes in the marketing program.

Or perhaps a business marketer wants to know what characteristics are shared by buyers who put a heavy emphasis on low price, compared with those who do not. If the differentiating characteristics are observable, a program designed to maintain profit margins by emphasizing product quality and support can avoid buyers who are least likely to accept the offer. The marketers can concentrate sales and communications resources on other prospective customers.

A consumer product marketer, meanwhile, may wonder if mothers with more than one baby differ from mothers with just one baby, on any characteristics that can be referenced by a marketing appeal. If so, the marketers can address the subtle differences with the more obvious ones (income, blue- vs. white-collar, etc.) that define the heavy-user segment of baby product buyers.

The similarity among those examples is that each deals with dichotomies in the marketplace. In each instance, the marketer wants to know the difference between two subgroups, or market segments, that have different purchase behavior. The marketer may not know all the ways in which the subgroups differ, yet "hidden," non-obvious differences may have greater influence than the obvious ones.

In this article, we'll examine a statistical analysis technique called the "automatic interaction detector," or AID, designed to identify hidden differences among market segments. And we'll illustrate it with an example of actual survey research analysis.

Developed in the 1960s, AID is widely available in computer programs. But it is not a cure-all for market segmentation problems. It doesn't look at marketing programs and automatically prescribe the next step. It doesn't even do a complete job of analyzing segment differences, but is best used as a first step followed by further statistical analysis. Yet for the kind of dichotomous problem outlined above, it does a beautiful job of screening for segmentation factors deserving a closer look.

SPOTTING HIDDEN MARKETS

Suppose, for example, that a researcher examines a large number of demographic and attitudinal variables to see if any of them relate to the usage of some particular product. Among a large number of different measurements taken on each respondent—such as age, taste preference, etc.—only one variable seems to be related to product usage: the income level of the respondent.

Conventional cross-tabulation analysis finds that although usage averages 4.0 in the overall population, the total market can be split according to income into two groups that differ significantly in their usage: a low-income group averaging 3.0 and a high-income group averaging 6.0, as shown in Figure 1.

That's an important finding. The researcher may conclude that he or she has isolated the heavy-user market, identifying it as the high-income group, and has solved the research problem. But perhaps not. Will a marketing campaign focused on the high-income group and avoiding low-income consumers represent the best allocation of marketing resources? Possibly. But there may be a more substantial market, hidden within the low-income group, that represents a better marketing target that would be ignored by a program designed for high-income consumers only.

The researcher can test another two-way cross-tabulation on just the low-income group. If he or she happens to choose profession as a criterion and splits the low-income group into white- and blue-collar segments, he or she finds, as

Figure 1.
The Hidden Market

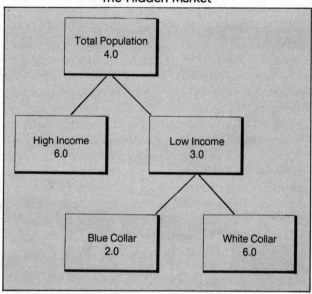

Figure 1 shows, that white-collar low-income consumers have an average usage of 6.0—equal to the high-income group—compared with 2.0 for the blue-collar, low-income consumers.

It could be that, regardless of present income, one's career outlook is associated closely with usage of the product under study. Whatever the qualitative inference, the low-income group, which at first seems unimportant because of its overall low-usage average, is found to be harboring heavy users. The consumer's line of work seems to be an additional predictor of usage.

The researcher found that the low-income subgroup was not homogenous. In fact, if he or she proceeds to test other criteria with two-way cross-tabulation, he or she may discover that the white-collar, low-income group isn't homogenous. Important product consumption differences within that group might be associated with, say, education levels, or life-style characteristics, such as a consumer's desire for conspicuous consumption.

Research in an industrial marketplace might proceed in the same way. An initial two-way split of the photocopier market might find, hypothetically, that companies with more than 1,000 employees have a significantly greater employee-to-copier ratio than companies with 1,000 or fewer employees. But further cross-tabulation analysis might find that the split between manufacturing and service companies is a better way to discriminate between heavy and light photocopier buyers. Or perhaps sales-per-employee is a better dis-

criminant. And within groups split on that basis, the ratio of clerical to technical and management jobs might prove a better segmentation standard still.

All of that involves a great deal of hypothesis testing—all of which the AID
program can do automatically, as its name indicates. By repeatedly applying
the statistical technique known as analysis of variance to the data, AID tests
the most important splits first. AID users can preset how far they want the
program to go in making significant splits. When the splits are no longer
significant on any one subgroup, the splitting stops on that one. And so the
diagram of the computer calculations looks like a tree with uneven branches.

The factors revealed as important in segmenting the market may not all
appear at first, but appear only when AID moves into split after split. For example, the job-related factor shown as important in the consumer product example above, did not show up in the analysis at the very start because AID first
examines the most important split—the one creating the biggest difference.
The statistical interaction between income level and blue-collar/white-collar
status causes the split between high and low income to be made first. That
"interaction" is "detected" "automatically" during the next step, thus revealing
the additional, but hidden, two-way segmentation criterion.

FIELD EXAMPLE

Conversely, it's very useful when a marketer learns that certain factors,
presumed to be important in market segmentation, actually are not. It can save
much useless marketing effort and allow resources to be channeled more
productively.

To illustrate the phenomenon, two of the authors conducted an AID
analysis of a limited survey replicating nationally known consumer confidence
polls. A number of organizations around the country periodically conduct such
polls. They forecast future economic conditions with surprising accuracy,
apparently because people can experience the microeconomic level of the
economy on a daily basis. They know who is hiring, who is laying off, etc.

But the polls would be more useful to marketers if they accurately forecast
consumer spending on goods and services. Alas, many a marketer who based
forecasts on them is sadder but wiser. The work on which this example is based
(and it is provided here only as an example) gives a clue as to why that might
be. A word of caution: The sample was not scientific and the conclusions
should not be considered universally valid. The poll was conducted by
telephone as an exercise by marketing students in a three-county area.

The survey questions were pretty much the same as those used by the Conference Board Inc., New York, and the University of Michigan, Ann Arbor.

- Present business conditions in your area—good? normal? bad?
- Business conditions, etc., expected six months from now?

- Available jobs in your area now—plenty? not many? hard to get?
- Six months from now—more? same? fewer?
- Guess total family income six months from now—higher? same? lower?
- Anyone in your household buying a house in next six months—yes? maybe? no?
- Car?
- Appliances?
- Vacation away from home in next six months—yes? undecided? no?
- County?
- Sex?
- Age?
- Occupation?

Researchers build a model with the results, using the answers to the first two questions as the dependent variable—the index of consumer confidence.

In other words, they determine the mathematical relationship among the answers to the first two questions and the answers to all the others. One way to combine the answers to the first two questions into a single index is shown in Figure 2.

Figure 2.
The Index of Consumer Confidence

SIX MONTHS FROM NOW \ BUSINESS CONDITIONS NOW	GOOD: 10	NORMAL: 5	BAD: 1
BETTER: 10	100	50	10
SAME: 5	50	25	5
WORSE: 1	10	5	1

To construct the index, the responses are assigned arbitrarily the values 10, 5 and 1. These are multiplied together, so that a response of "good now, same six months from now" scores 50 on the consumer confidence index for this example.

The example analysis, based on 150 responses, shows a consumer confidence index of 41.3 (the X value) for the whole group. It's an artificial index, but it illustrates the comparisons of subgroups, as shown in Figure 3.

The first split made by the AID program used the factor of "jobs now" and a two-way split of the sample, forcing the "not so many" and "hard-to-get" responses into one group (group 2) and the "plenty" responses into another (group 3). The 32 respondents in group 3, who thought there are plenty of jobs now, had a consumer confidence index of 61.1—the highest of any single group. (Of course, a recession only occurs when you have a job and your neighbor doesn't. When there are no longer jobs you can get, it becomes a depression. So far no surprises!)

Group 2 had an index of only 36.0—quite a bit less than the average for the entire sample.

The next split divides group 2 on the basis of job expectations six months hence. Group 4, expecting the "same" or "fewer" jobs, has a confidence index of 28.8, while those expecting "more" jobs (group 5) have a whopping 48.6 confidence index—a level greater than the sample overall and much greater than the index for group 2, of which group 5 is a part.

Examining the 75 respondents in group 4, AID splits them into those who think jobs now are "hard to get" (group 6) and those who say there are "not so many" (group 7), thus separating two responses that were forced together earlier.

Group 6 is really in the dumps with a 20.9 index. Group 7 has a much higher, but still depressed, index of 32.5.

Splitting group 7 on the basis of away-from-home vacation plans finds 31 respondents with no plans (group 10) and 20 who say they have plans or are undecided (group 11). Those groups have confidence indexes of 29.7 and 36.8 respectively.

Going back to group 5, and 43 people who think jobs are scarce now but expect more in the future, the analysis splits them on the basis of income expectations.

Twenty-one expecting the "same" or "lower" income have a confidence index of 42.6—still greater than the overall sample average. The 22 people who think income will be higher (group 9) have an index of 54.3, second only to the people who think there are plenty of jobs now.

In other words, for this sample, the people who are the real optimists on the economy are in only two groups—54 people out of a total of 150:

- The 32 who think there are plenty of jobs now; and
- The 22 who think there are not so many jobs now or that jobs are hard to get now, but who nonetheless expect more jobs in six months and a greater income for themselves.

That's all. If the splits made by AID do not use the answers to a specific

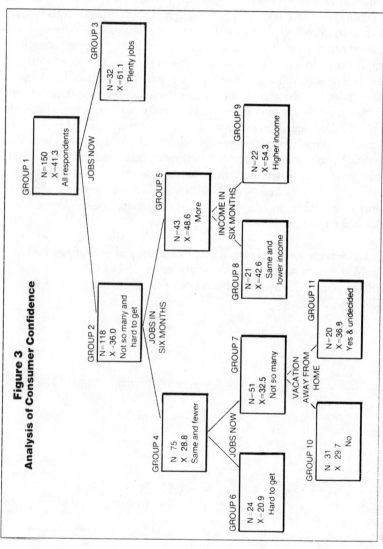

**Figure 3
Analysis of Consumer Confidence**

GROUP 1
N=150
X=41.3
All respondents

JOBS NOW

GROUP 3
N=32
X=61.1
Plenty jobs

GROUP 2
N=118
X=36.0
Not so many and
hard to get

JOBS IN
SIX MONTHS

GROUP 5
N=43
X=48.6
More

INCOME IN
SIX MONTHS

GROUP 9
N=22
X=54.3
Higher income

GROUP 8
N=21
X=42.6
Same and
lower income

GROUP 4
N 75
X 28.8
Same and fewer

JOBS NOW

GROUP 7
N=51
X=32.5
Not so many

VACATION
AWAY FROM
HOME

GROUP 11
N=20
X=36.8
Yes & undecided

GROUP 6
N=24
X=20.9
Hard to get

GROUP 10
N 31
X 29.7
No

The top number in each box shows the number of respondents in that group. The bottom number shows the consumer confidence index for that group. The abbreviations under the angles indicate the question on which that split is being made.

question, the question has nothing statistically significant to offer in explaining the differences between those with high confidence and those without.

What's the implication for marketers?

It's tempting to think that consumers' buying plans for houses, cars and appliances have a strong relationship to their marketplace "confidence." Yet those factors even have less to do with consumer confidence than their vacation expectations, which aren't all that predictive anyway. Perceived job and income expectations seem to be the basis of "confidence." Perhaps consumers buy appliances and autos when those are needed or cheaper than usual.

And people sometimes just say what's expected, or what they wish to believe. Under those conditions, no statistical significance would be expected.

But that is neither here nor there. The purpose of the example is to show what positive and negative clues one can get about marketplace behavior and attitudes. Some are intuitively obvious; others may be surprising. The advice is, invariably, to test the findings further, using other analytical techniques with the same data. When used with the proper understanding and caution, the AID technique of analysis can be a valuable first step in probing the anatomy of a market, in order to apply limited marketing resources where they'll do the most good.

Robert C. Ferber is a certified management consultant and heads the Ferber Company in New York. Stanely I. Cohen is a statistician and president of Pulse Analytics Inc., Ridgewood, N. J. Ernst Mendels is a professor of marketing at Iona College, New Rochelle, New York.

23.

PUBLIC RELATIONS AND SALES . . . THERE MUST BE A MEASURABLE RELATION

G. A. Marken

Sending out a few dozen press releases a year doesn't constitute a public relations program. To exert a strong influence on the marketplace, a company must use the full arsenal of PR tools.

Our firm asked 100 senior marketing executives in small and midsized firms in the computer/communications industry about their public relations programs. In examining the results, we found a glaring problem: For more than 60% of the firms, "public relations" boiled down to nothing more than two- to three-dozen news releases shotgunned out each year, some press kits for trade shows and a few new product announcements.

That's publicity, not public relations.

It does nothing for the company. It does nothing for the company's products. It does nothing for the marketplace.

It *does* provide income for the U.S. Postal Service.

Certainly news releases have a value. They are an inexpensive way to present routine company information and minor announcements to editors and reporters. However, while they provide information, they do not help establish the firm's position or image. They inform, but they don't persuade or sell.

SOLID MARKETING MOVES

To understand the difference between PR activities that merely publicize and those that exert a strong influence on the marketplace, we need to take a look at the advantages you gain from a solid public relations program. A strong PR program:

- *Is economical.* Because of the high cost of advertising in today's marketplace, no company has enough money to reach all of its prospects and suspects on a consistent basis. Public relations materials help a company tap into peripheral or secondary markets it otherwise would have to ignore or set aside.
- *Extends the reach of advertising.* All too often, advertising and PR departments compete against each other for money and management's attention. To be truly effective, advertising and public relations should work in concert. Public relations can extend the reach of advertising by focusing on secondary audiences. It helps a company get its message to all buying influences.
- *Adds credibility.* We all realize that an advertisement—in the form of publication space, broadcast commercial, billboard, brochure or direct mail piece—is a paid message from the advertiser with the explicit goal of selling something. We are more likely to believe a third-party endorsement in a publication's editorial columns because the editor or reporter—not the manufacturer—is telling us about the company or product.
- *Measures interest.* If the news or trade media cover a product announcement and no one responds, either there is no market for the product, or you were reaching the wrong target audience. By evaluating customer and prospect reaction to an announcement according to geographic region, job responsibility and potential application, you can decide fairly easily whether the product's appeal is universal or very narrow.
- *Generates leads.* Most management is volume-oriented. In fact, some firms have developed lead generation into a science by determining exactly how many sales will result from every 1,000 inquiries. Leads, especially those that are further qualified, are a boon to today's sales force. Few salespeople want to make cold calls. An inquiry at least provides an interested suspect—a starting point—for a sales call.
- *Builds or rebuilds an image.* A company's image is extremely fragile. Late deliveries, product recalls, rumors and innuendos can severely cripple a firm's ability to stay in business. Solid and aggressive PR efforts can counter those problems, and entice customers to give the company another chance.

BEYOND THE RELEASE

But to achieve those results, a solid public relations program must employ the full arsenal of PR tools. They can't rely simply on press releases or product announcements dropped without warning on editor's desks.

The strongest public relations programs use all of the public relations techniques, at one time or another, throughout the year. The key is to achieve just the right balance to match your company's corporate, marketing and sales objectives.

A multidimensional program should include:

• *Feature articles.* These include stories that clearly establish what your company, its management and products stand for in the market. They help the business, financial, trade and user communities develop a better understanding about where your firm fits into its marketplace and industry. Such articles can take the form of user case studies, approach-to-problem stories, industry trend pieces, technical articles, position papers and other, similar vehicles.

• *Local editorial contacts.* Don't insist on working only with a publication's headquarters staff. No matter where a major publication locates its main office, it's likely to set up local bureaus in key market areas to be closer to the news. Because bureau editors and reporters generate much of the day-in, day-out coverage, it's important to develop relationships with them.

Set up one-on-one meetings to explain the company, its management team and its products. The relationships you'll establish in those meetings will position your company as a valuable source of news about your area and market segments.

• *Editorial tours.* It is vital to give senior editors and their staffs the ability to associate your company's name with a face or faces. Without that personal identification, a company blurs into a crowd with hundreds of other good firms offering good products.

To combat that, arrange one-on-one meetings at the headquarters of major and secondary trade publications. Those sessions aren't just friendly get-togethers. They are opportunities to discuss your company, its products and product applications, its successes and future plans, and its projections for the market.

• *Market research meetings.* Too often, companies overlook market research firms when they think about who needs to be informed about the company, its products and its progress. But the sphere of influence for research firms extend well beyond the reports they produce. Prospects often call them for recommendations, and they're the first sources a publication contacts for market status or trend information. As a result, you want to make sure that research firms covering your market can discuss your company intelligently and favorably.

• *Trade shows.* Trade shows are an expensive proposition for any firm. Mounting an exhibit costs money. And more importantly, trade shows take time away from other engineering, marketing and sales activities.

However, trade shows give you the opportunity to exploit new products, programs and activities, and to highlight your company's recent successes and future direction. It's essential to take maximum advantage of industry events.

Don't stop at producing a simple press kit. Instead, work the show aggressively. Bring key editors and reporters together with your senior managers, who will be able to present your message and establish a strong interchange of information and ideas.

• *Publication special issues.* Nearly all trade publications plan their editorial calendars 6 to 12 months in advance. In a specific issue, they will give in-depth coverage to a topic or market segment.

Be alert to the editorial calendar for each publication covering your market, and ensure that your company gets its message to the person who is responsible for each special issue. Contact the publications well in advance, and give them information and ideas for that issue.

The more information you can provide—and the more you service the editor—the better chance you have of obtaining your "unfair share" of coverage.

• *Product announcement.* The time, money and effort your company spends to design, engineer and develop a new product demands that you achieve the optimal coverage and exposure for each new offering. That includes product enhancements and add-ons, which deserve their own exposure.

However, not every product requires or deserves the same amount of attention. Major products, which can provide a significant return on investment and larger profit/earning ratios, demand and deserve more exposure. Minor products, which provide lower returns and less significant price/performance advantages, will receive less exposure.

The goal for each announcement is to highlight the technical advancements and progress your company is making, and to obtain the maximum amount of in-depth, broad exposure for the new product. You'll want the coverage for each new product to run for about six months, to build recognition and interest in your company, its product and technology.

Major product publicity requires that you begin your efforts three to six months before the actual announcement.

First, you'll negotiate with publications to develop magazine cover treatment, in-depth new product features, and technical articles. About a month before those articles appear, you can work with a few other publications to get "featurette" coverage. Those articles will come out immediately after the main features but before you make the general industry announcement. Then you make the general announcement to business, financial and trade publications.

A minor new product is important to your company and its marketing effort. However, it doesn't have the unique character and totally new look or impact of a major new product. It therefore does not warrant, nor will it earn, major coverage. For minor products, you want to develop feature articles in selected publications, followed-up by the general news announcement.

MEASURING FOR RESULTS

To determine how effectively you're balancing the mix of those public relations tools, you need to measure results.

Ours is still an instant society. We eat at fast-food outlets and get our photos developed in an hour. And we expect an instant return from our public relations programs. In their rush to please management, public relations managers too often measure results by the pound or inch.

I saw one corporate activity report which proclaimed that, during the reporting period, the company mailed 10 news releases and obtained mentions in 50 different new items. To further prove that effort's value, the report emphasized the company received 4,583 bingo cards during the reporting period. The company was happy with its report.

But numbers alone have very little relevance. To get meaningful results, you must measure your public relations program on both a quantitative and qualitative basis.

Quantitative measures include public relations audits, internal and external feedback, benchmark studies, surveys and weighted audience impact studies.

At the same time, you should measure article appearance in terms of quality. For example:

- Is it a key market publication?
- Was it in the front or back of the book?
- How often was the company or product mentioned?
- Did it reinforce the company or product position in the marketplace?
- Was it a substantive and credible article?

Answers to those questions clearly help management evaluate the worth of a specific public relations effort.

Other measures that are slightly less scientific, but just as valid, include:

- How many of the key and secondary publications in the industry have written about the company?
- Has management developed a strong relationship with key editors and reporters? Are top executives asked for quotes or information about the industry?
- Is the image and message that the press conveys consistent with what the company wants to present?
- Are industry luminaries or market researchers who are quoted reinforcing the company's image and message?

Those types of factual measures add credibility to the concept that public relations is an integral and valuable part of the marketing mix. They place a tangible value on what management often considers an intangible marketing support activity.

Editors won't use every article idea and interview opportunity you send them. But by employing the fullest available mix of public relations tools, and by measuring their impact on the marketplace, you'll establish stronger relations—and higher visibility—with the key influences for that market.

That visibility reinforces the company's image, and its shows that your products are accepted. Strong, positive press coverage creates a positive image in the minds of both present and prospective customers that you are a winner.

It is here, in the shadowy reaches of the mind, that marketing and sales battles are won . . . or lost.

G. A. Marken is head of Marken Communications, a Sunnyvale, California-based public relations firm.

24.
CONSUMER DRAW—FROM MASS MARKETS TO VARIETY

Alan Zakon
Richard W. Winger

The mass market is disappearing. How can manufacturers and retailers capture the new specialized markets while maintaining the stability that comes with focussing on a mass market? This article describes how a successful competitor has met the challenge.

The mass market is disappearing. That has become a well-established truth among consumer marketers who see more and more areas splinter into specialty markets with rapidly growing varieties of new products and rapidly shrinking product life cycles. More importantly, breadth of choice is becoming a central consumer value in more markets.

But the broadening of choice, with its proliferation of brands and escalating advertising spending, operates in a zero-sum environment. Overall demand is growing slowly, if at all, and the search for innovation grinds categories into smaller and smaller markets.

Yet operationally most manufacturing and retailing companies are still geared to the mass market. They work most efficiently where they can target a limited range of products for a homogenous set of customers and sell it over a long period of time. For example, most packaged-goods companies with which we are familiar see a rich range of opportunity in specialized products, geared to small markets. But to make a national launch successful, most feel, a product must have the potential to reach roughly $100 million in sales. However, only a few ideas have a reasonable probability of making this hurdle.

As a result, consumer marketers are torn in two directions:

- Toward flexibility, variety, and small markets to stay ahead of consumer tastes; and
- Toward stability, focus, and big markets to maintain the efficiency of operations.

These crosscurrents can produce the corporate equivalent of a whirlpool effect: lots of movement but no visible progress in any direction.

The strategic challenge is to achieve both *variety and efficiency*—both *flexibility* to follow shifting consumer trends and *stability* centered around enduring competitive advantages.

This article describes how a successful competitor has met the challenge; analyzes the forces underlying the trend toward variety-based competition in many consumer markets; draws some general lessons; and develops the long-term implications for specialty marketers, department stores, and the consumer packaged-foods industry.

FROM BUYER PULL TO CONSUMER DRAW

Benetton, the phenomenally successful Italian sportswear company, succeeded in a market that is about as complex and risky as consumer markets get: an infinite variety of products in a range of styles and colors; volatile, largely unpredictable consumer preferences; and life cycles that often last less than a season. It's a market that is a notorious headache for department stores and is littered with failed boutiques and specialty chains.

What has Benetton done differently?

It operates on the concept of *consumer draw*: make only what the consumer buys. The formula is deceptively simple, but to follow it three ingredients are needed; instant feedback about what sells, absolute flexibility in manufacturing, and rapid order turnaround.

For most retailers, this is an elusive dream. Orders are finalized up to seven months in advance. When it becomes clear what sells, it typically is too late to influence the delivery flow. This traditional system must operate on "buyer pull." And because even the best buyer can't second-guess the consumer perfectly, the fashion risk is considerable and increases the more variety the retailer tries to offer. It is embodied in markdowns and sales. This introduces a fundamental constraint which has shaped the competition in retailing for many years: the more up-to-date the merchandise and the greater the variety, the higher the cost. Consumers who want broad choice among the latest fashions pay dearly.

To break this constraint and move from buyer pull to consumer draw, Benetton invested heavily in two areas:

- An *information system* which provides instant movement reports and can translate them, through a link into the factories, directly into production plans; and
- A *manufacturing operation* which is highly automated and flexible, and can switch with minimal inefficiencies between garment types, styles, and colors.

In this system, turnaround from order to delivery is only two to six weeks for U.S. stores. Therefore, nobody needs to place big bets: Store managers can go through several replenishment cycles during a fashion season. Instead of having to guess in advance, they can watch what sells and reorder only what's "hot." The factories produce only to order. Inventory in the system is minimal. Even if Benetton misses a trend, a sophisticated CAD system can convert a new design almost instantly into a full range of sizes and colors, and collapse design-to-production time to proliferate a "hot" style or fabric in mid-season.

The brand strategy is consistent with the business system. Instead of branding a specific look which could go out of fashion (and render the investment in the business system valueless), Benetton chooses to brand timeless values: color, fashion, excitement. They are embedded in looks and ambience of the stores, and supported by heavy print advertising. In effect, Benetton says to the consumer: "If these values appeal to you, come to our stores and we will produce—to your order." Founder Luciano Benetton explains, "Our method of merchandising originated with the idea of manufacturing sweaters in different colors . . . and the very simple idea of colors being something that everyone appreciates and being universal. We stuck to one product and made a wide spectrum around it, and allowed stores to sell our product only if that was all they sold."

The stores' product mixes, he adds, were designed to fit with the tastes of "a specific neighborhood, *via*, or avenue." This merchandising strategy," he says, is "tailor-made for our products."

The results? Benetton has dramatically tilted the retail function. In the traditional "buyer pull" system, cost (and prices) increase with increasing variety and fashion content. Benetton's "consumer draw" system dramatically slashes the cost of variety and minimizes the fashion risk (Exhibit 1.). As a result, it has built sustainable competitive advantage around a distinctive new value position: It has built a *stable* system that allows it to operate *flexibly*.

If history is a guide, "consumer draw" technology will revolutionize broad areas of the consumer-goods industry. It's a crucial step in the evolution of competitive advantage, a step that has been pioneered by the Japanese in manufacturing industries. In fact, the evolution of competition in retailing closely parallels that in manufacturing.

The broadline department store of the 1950s and '60s followed the same competitive principles General Motors did at the time: Offer something for everybody. Grow by appealing to as many buyers as possible.

Competition was *scale-driven*; costs would decline as volume grew. But increased volume meant increased variety and more complex operations—and complexity drives up costs. When additional volume increased complexity-related cost more than it decreased scale-related costs, the giants began to stumble.

The response emerged in the 1970s: *focused competition*. Toyota did to GM what specialty stores did to the department stores—reduced cost (and price)

Exhibit 1.
Buyer Pull and Consumer Pull

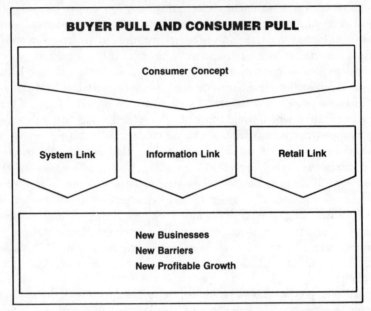

through focus. For Toyota, it meant fewer models with fewer options. For specialty stores, it meant a focus on wider selection within a few categories.

In the early '80s, Japanese manufacturers came up with another strategic twist. Observers noted that in many businesses (for example, cars, lift trucks, and motorcycles) they suddenly offered two to four times the model varieties of their U.S. or European competitors, and still maintained a price advantage of 30 to 40 percent. Somehow they had found a way to break the complexity constraint, to proliferate variety and still keep cost down.

The secret was *Kanban*—the rigorous manufacturing discipline of making only what you need when you need it. It dramatically slashes inventory, reduces direct labor costs, and increases flexibility. It allowed successful companies to move to *variety-based* competition: lower cost and more choice.

Toyota now takes this approach a crucial step further, and links its Japanese dealers into the system. The goal largely is to abolish finished goods inventory, manufacture to order, and hand the car over to the consumer within seven days after it comes off the production system. The results are a sharp decrease in inventory in the field, a drastic reduction in the roughly 30 percent of cost traditionally accounted for by distribution, and, at the same time, the ability to offer the consumer every possible combination of options. Consumer draw—an information link between the consumer and the factory, and a highly flexible production system that can adjust without friction to shifts in demand—brings us back to Benetton.

WHY NOW?

The consumer values of broadened choice and variety permeate more and more markets. Consider the supermarket: While overall sales have been rather flat, the number of items in stock in the average supermarket has doubled over the past 10 years.

This trend to diversity is here to stay. Two forces come together: On the *supply side*, the evolution of manufacturing technologies and the revolution in information technologies make business systems like Benetton's possible. On the *demand side*, fundamental demographic factors increase the number of sophisticated and affluent consumers.

One factor is the aging of the population, or the much discussed "graying of America." Indeed, the population over age 65 will grow from roughly 29 million in 1985 to 34 million by the year 2000. An equally important trend for marketers is the *maturing* of America. The fastest growing segment of all is the population between ages 45 and 65, a group that traditionally accounts for a large portion of discretionary spending. It will increase from 45 million in 1985 to 60 million in the year 2000. Together with 43 million people in the 35-to-44 age group, it will represent much of the baby-boom generation. It will carry with it the increased sophistication of tastes and desire for diversity that characterizes this generation much beyond the hard core of conspicuous "yuppie" consumption.

This trend is reinforced by a massive shift in income distribution. While demographics will make variety a more important consumer value, the shift in income distribution will create a much larger group of affluent spenders who are able to indulge this desire.

U.S. society historically has been characterized by a very broad middle-income market with a limited population at the very high-income end. This "universal middle class" was the demographic basis for the American mass market. Mass marketers concentrated on high-volume products for the average consumer, and brought them to market with a degree of efficiency that has not been paralleled elsewhere. This has distinguished U.S. consumer markets from those of Europe. Travelers often have been struck by the very low cost of average products and the relative absence of affordable luxury products in the U.S., in contrast to the relatively high cost of commodity products and the relatively greater affordability and availability of luxury products in Europe.

By the year 2000, however, America's income distribution will have changed dramatically: *The high income segment (those with annual earnings of at least $50,000) will virtually double.* This signals a massive increase in the population's ability to afford high-value products, and a concentration of growth opportunities in the premium end of markets which are characterized by value and variety (Exhibit 2).

More (and more sophisticated) consumers in the peak years of discretionary spending, and a massive increase in high-income households, together spell a

Exhibit 2.
"Consumer Pull" Stragegies

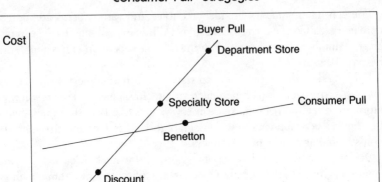

massive increase in demand for high-value items, but also a fragmentation of demand into a broad range of preferences. Variety, volatility, and unpredictability—the characteristics Benetton must contend with in the sportswear market—permeate more and more consumer markets. As a result, growth opportunities increasingly will be in specialty markets—fewer $100-million opportunities, and more $10-to-$50-million ones. The strategic challenge will be to find a way to make money in these markets.

HOW TO MAKE IT WORK: FOUR PRINCIPLES

The total Benetton answer will be inappropriate in many instances But the principles of "consumer draw" strategy can make a significant contribution to long-term success in most markets where variety has become a central consumer value.

The key principles are:

- *Consumer concept.* Build a business not around individual products, but around timeless consumer values—especially quality.
- *System links.* Orient the business system so that it is consistent with these values.
- *Information links.* Enable the system to operate as quickly as possible in response to real-time consumer demands.
- *Retail links.* Closely manage the retail presentation.

The consumer concept and the retail link provide the stable foundation; the system and information links allow flexible operations. How to translate these elements into operating principles will, of course, depend upon the characteristics of individual markets.

• *Consumer concept.* Consider the great consumer brands—Tide, Levis, Colgate, Jell-O, Maxwell House. In general, they are built around a strong product focus. Product focus is present in the deliberate development process to get it just right—in manufacturing, where dedicated lines are run efficiently at high speed; and in advertising which communicates a specific set of benefits clearly. This strategy is appropriate in mass markets, where high volume creates the basis for efficiency. But it becomes both costly and risky in specialty markets—costly, because the product volume is low; risky, because life cycles can be short. What is the value of an efficient, focused plant if the product it was designed to manufacture is obsolete?

In variety-based markets, individual products often are too small and too unstable to sustain a lasting advantage. It is much more promising to build businesses around *values*—a set of specific, but timeless, customer values which can encompass a changing variety of products. This creates a stable platform for a range of products which can shift according to changing consumer tastes.

Take the market for frozen entrees as an example. In the early '70s, competitors focused on one basic ingredient and sold mass-market products of modest quality at low prices. Then Stouffer entered the fray with its Red Box line of frozen entrees.

Its positioning was brilliant from both the marketing and strategic perspectives. From a marketing perspectives, Stouffer recognized the opportunity to upgrade a near-commodity category and create consumer excitement (and corresponding higher prices) through higher quality and new products. From a strategic perspective, Stouffer realized that this specialty approach would not be viable in the existing market structure. Separate, high-quality businesses built around chicken, beef, fish, and so on would be small, and therefore costly to operate and difficult to defend.

Stouffer decided to restructure the market and position its line *across* established product segments. The unifying themes were (and are) taste concept and variety: high-quality, contemporary favorites, and lots of choices through a broad product array, with a constant stream of introductions and withdrawals. The concept creates a stable mass-market basis for a changing collection of specialty items.

This concept approach to branding is quite different from the approaches of the past, but it is very similar to Benetton's. Benetton also chose a broad focus (sportswear) and a timeless theme (fashion, color, and excitement) to build a stable platform for a rapidly changing product collection.

• *System link.* If product linkage creates the stable base by tying formerly separate categories into a coherent consumer proposition, the supporting business system must be oriented consistently to the same consumer values.

Stouffer built its plants explicitly around the values of quality and variety: Relatively high manual-labor content assures consistent quality. Flexible assets make it possible to introduce new products with minimal new plant investment. It's not the cheapest way to make frozen entrees—an automated facility focused on a stable, narrow product range would operate at far lower cost. But it's the most cost-effective way to operate against the distinctive consumer proposition Stouffer is striking: It too does not optimize its manufacturing operation in isolation. Rather, it chose the most cost-effective manufacturing approach in the context of its overall strategy.

• *Information link.* Variety drastically increases the potential for inefficiencies along the supply chain. Consider a true mass-market product like Tide. Retailers have a stable demand history to guide ordering patterns. Even if they over-order, errors can be worked off relatively quickly. contrast that with a variety-based category, such as, for example, ice cream novelties, in which there are many more items, limited demand histories, and a strong fashion cycle. Order errors can be compounded and, once made, are not easily rectified. Operational linkage means tying the various steps into an integrated information flow from the retail outlet to the factory, so that the system operates as closely as possible to real-time consumer demand. Neither Benetton nor Toyota are dependent upon sales forecasts anymore.

• *Retail link.* The consumer concept and the links discussed earlier imply the need for a consistent marketing strategy. But in a variety-dominated environment, marketing strategy often has to go further and create a tight fit between the product range and the retail environment. That's partly because a complex brand is inherently difficult to manage at the retail level. But even more importantly, if a brand encompasses a broad range of variety, *how* it is presented becomes as important as *what* is presented. Thus, the retail environment becomes a key component of the brand image.

Specialty retailers have long recognized the power of the retail environment to create a brand identity. Banana Republic and Crabtree & Evelyn, for example, both rely on a distinctive store ambience to tie a heterogeneous range of products into a unified concept. But in a variety-driven environment, manufacturers will have to think more like retailers if they want to maintain their brand identity. Consider, for example, Ralph Lauren's Polo brand, which consists of a distinctive "look" and cuts across a number of product categories. The concept is embodied in the integrated presentation of the line to the consumer. The Polo brand would not exist without the Polo store.

The same is true for a number of other pioneers. Manufacturers as diverse as Laura Ashley, Estee Lauder, and Waterford Crystal have found it necessary to forward-integrate into retailing—directly, by opening their own stores (Laura Ashley), or leasing space in department stores (Estee Lauder); or indirectly, by insisting on consistent presentation of their lines (Waterford Crystal). In all cases, the retail presentation is a consistent element of the brand strategy, and the shopping experience is a significant part of the product's value to the consumer.

The same is beginning to be true in the supermarkets. For traditional product brands (again, Tide is an example), merchandising principles can be simply summarized: "Stock it as highly as possible, and in as visible a location as possible." But for variety-based brands such as Stouffer's Lean Cuisine frozen dinners, merchandising and shelf presentation are more important and more demanding. Much of Stouffer's enduring strength can be attributed to the minute control its sales and detail forces exercise over retail product presentation, in effect acting like retailers. Control of shelf presentation will become even more important for fresh and prepared foods, which many leading manufacturers see as a major growth area for the future.

Retail linkage forces the manufacturer to behave like a retailer. Operational linkage enables the retailer to stay in close touch with its suppliers, and *vice versa*. Strategic linkage forces both parties to orient themselves toward the same consumer-driven competitive posture. Together, the three linkages of consumer-draw strategy amount to a strong argument for vertical integration. However, this does not necessarily imply common ownership of facilities. For example, Benetton subcontracts some of its stores. The key assets are the elements that create the linkages: *strategy* (strategic linkage), *information systems* (operational linkage), and *brand name* (retail linage).

COMPETITIVE OPPORTUNITIES

Let's consider the competitive opportunities that consumer draw strategies create for marketers and suppliers in three areas: specialty retailing, department-store retailing, and packaged-goods marketing.

Specialty retailers will be among the major beneficiaries of consumer-draw opportunities. They already own a concept and control the front-end contact with the consumer. They are, therefore, in a strong position to structure the appropriate supply system.

For specialty retailers as a group, this represents a major opportunity to increase the margin of advantage over broadline retailers. But competition among specialty retailers will be affected too: The innovators have a unique opportunity to decisively strengthen their position.

Some leading specialty-retailing chains already are moving in the direction of consumer draw. They are investing heavily in information systems to capture order flow, inventory, and movement in real time. They also have begun to select their suppliers based not only on cost but also on turnaround time. The Limited's success, for example, is only partly due to any fashion genius its key executives may have. It largely is based on a sophisticated sales tracking system which, combined with its insistence on short-order turnaround from its suppliers, allows it to replenish stocks faster than the competition. But even The Limited has not yet developed its information system into an operational link between the consumer and the factory, between demand and supply.

What holds the industry back?

When you run the numbers on creating a consumer-draw system, it is easy to be deceived by traditional cost/benefit analyses, which tend to focus on manufacturing unit cost reductions. These are only a small part of the efficiencies a consumer-draw system creates. Additional benefits come from more far-reaching cost reductions throughout the system, and from significant revenue enhancements. The key *savings* come in cost elements which are either hidden or generally considered irreducible: markdowns, excess inventories, excess manufacturing capacity, and management time spent on managing the interface between supply and demand. *Revenue enhancements* come from being able to track consumer trends more precisely. There are fewer lost sales because of stockouts, and incremental sales result because of quicker adjustments to changing demand patterns.

Therefore, only a comprehensive view of cost and revenues throughout the system will reveal the magnitude of the advantage a consumer-draw strategy can create.

As farsighted competitors begin to take advantage of consumer-draw opportunities over the next several years, we expect a number of major changes in retailing:

- The innovators will significantly increase their profitability, consumer appeal, and, therefore growth potential. This will lead to consolidation. In five years, there will be far fewer brand names in shopping malls.
- Today's leaders may not be tomorrow's, because the basis of successful management will change. Today, specialty retailing is an operator's business in which the key is to make many small decisions and hope that they average out to be mostly the right ones. Many successful chains are ruled by "golden guts." Consumer draw will transform the industry into more of a strategist's business in which a few big decisions have to be absolutely right. Which of today's specialty retailing stars will be able to make this transition successfully?
- Correctly choosing one's area of specialization will become both more important and more difficult. Historically, specialty retailers defined themselves through their consumer propositions. These became the basis of segmentation in the industry. In the future, the ability to put together a flexible supply system will become a second crucial segmentation dimension.
- U.S.-based suppliers will increase their potential advantage over offshore manufacturers. Their assets will be easier coordination of strategy and meshing of systems, and greater speed of response. These will weigh increasingly heavily against offshore advantages in unit manufacturing cost.
- More and more brand manufacturers will integrate forward into retailing, either by opening their own stores or by building stronger marketing and operational links with department stores through a "store-within-a-store" approach.

- Finally, specialty retailers as a group are likely to improve their margin of competitive advantage over broadline retailers—both department stores and discount stores.

  Department stores, already under attack from the retailing malls, will have to rethink their strategies carefully. The key question will be: How can we remain *value-competitive with, but distinctive from*, the specialty retailing mall? These two objectives will take stores in different directions:

- To remain value-competitive, department stores will have to achieve, at least in their core departments, the same operational flexibility as specialty retailers. This will mean running a store as a collection of semi-autonomous specialty retailing businesses, each narrow enough to build the necessary close strategic and operational links with its suppliers.

- To remain distinctive, department stores will have to reinforce a consistent store image and ambience. As individual departments become more independent, the store concept will increase in importance as the integrating factor.

Each of these two objectives is challenging in itself. Managing them simultaneously will mean a delicate balance between decentralization and unification.

The implications for department-store brands are equally challenging. The value of operational and marketing linkage with the retail store will force them to decide between opening their own stores or building stronger alliances with department stores.

Either way, they will have to start to think and act more like retailers, and present their products not as salesmen, but as partners in merchandising and marketing.

A LESSON FOR P&G

The most important lesson Benetton can teach is to the Procter & Gambles of this world. The packaged-goods industry invented and perfected mass-marketing techniques, so it finds it particularly difficult to adapt to growth opportunities in specialty markets. The declining effectiveness of new-product development, escalating cost of brand differentiation, and fierce battles for shelf space are symptoms of a mismatch between mass marketing and the new retail environment.

The packaged-foods retailers have been most effective and innovative in following consumer preferences for variety, premium quality, and freshness. They do so by behaving like specialty retailers in more areas of the store: delis, fresh meat counters, in-store bakeries, produce, bulk foods, and prepared foods are among the fastest-growing departments in grocery stores, for example. Here, many supermarkets succeeded in creating a new form of private label, one that does not compete based on lower price, but rather on higher value for the consumer.

Now it is often the brand-name product that is the budget alternative, while the unbranded items in the specialty retailing departments are positioned as higher quality and fresher—and, naturally, they carry a higher price tag. At the same time, space devoted to packaged goods is declining. Traditionally, only about 25 percent of floor space was devoted to specialty retailing departments, with the remainder allocated to packaged foods. In many recently opened stores, the ratio is 50/50.

How did the packaged-foods retailers manage to seize the initiative?

Behind successful specialty-retailing departments in the supermarket, there generally are small-scale, "consumer-draw" business systems—system linkage, information linkage, and retail linkage. They consistently are oriented to the central consumer values the department appeals to: selection, freshness, quality. Often, the store manager or local merchandising manager has wide authority over the departments. As a result, selection is tailored to the tastes of the neighborhood. The products are supplied by local distributors, and, in the case of prepared foods, prepared and assembled locally. This short line of supply makes it possible to provide freshness at a relatively low incremental cost, and the supply can be adjusted instantly to meet changing patterns of consumer demand.

This system is easier to establish by "building backward" from the local store than by "building forward" from a national manufacturing operation. The national focus, which is a major source of efficiency for packaged-goods companies in the mass market, turns into a liability in variety-based markets.

The opportunity for specialty retailing represents a tremendous competitive opportunity for supermarkets. It will enable them to rebuild their stores' brand names based on delivering higher consumer *values*, not just lower *prices*. The reward will be higher profitability.

Can the starting advantage of the retailer be overcome? This will be one of the central strategic challenges for the major packaged-foods companies to come to grips with. The second challenge will be to build a solid presence and increase market share in the shrinking packaged-foods section. The most successful companies will not be those that learn to fight the battle for shelf space and consumer recognition on a product-by-product basis. Successful competitors will focus their efforts on staking out major positions in key departments and building unified consumer concepts which, once established, can accommodate a changing variety of new products.

Consider some of the most successful recent introductions in the supermarket: Yoplait, Ragu, LeMenu, Lean Cuisine. They have several elements in common:

- A benefit-based brand name that is broad enough to accommodate a large number of new products—the consumer concept—and an effective new

product development process that keeps the concept vital through continued innovation;
- Flexible manufacturing operations which can shift easily within the product range—the system link;
- Top-notch salesforces which can provide quick feedback about market conditions—a strong, although imperfect, information link; and
- A dominant position within their categories—the retail link.

However, even these successful brands have not yet fully come to grips with the information link. The salesforce link between the factory and the store, while useful, is tentative and does not enable them to fully exploit the opportunities of consumer draw. A key challenge for long-term success in the growing variety-based markets will be to establish and solidify this link; whoever can keep real-time tabs on how consumers behave has a tremendous starting advantage.

Today, the supermarket represents the information barrier between the manufacturer and the consumer. As consumer tastes continue to richen and create new segmentation opportunities, control of information will become a new, and perhaps dominant, strategic variable. The uneasy alliance between retailers and manufacturers will be tested around exactly this issue. It will either develop into a close partnership, or dissolve into open competition.

Alan Zakon is chairman of the board of the The Boston Consulting Group, Inc. Richard W. Winger is also associated with The Boston Consulting Group in a number of capacities.

25.
WHEN MARKETING SERVICES, 4 Ps ARE NOT ENOUGH

A. J. Magrath

> Marketing plans are usually structured around the four Ps of Price, Product, Place, and Promotion. But when it's a service that is being marketed, three more Ps—Personnel, Physical facilities, and Process management—must be added to the mix.

Since Neil Borden introduced the concept of the marketing mix in 1962 and Jerome McCarthy popularized the four Ps in 1964, marketing plans have incorporated these elements as key building blocks for marketing programs.[1,2] The four Ps of Price, Product, Place, and Promotion have become the four gospels of marketing.

But the four Ps are not enough for the marketing of services. Another three Ps, strategic elements that occupy management's attention, must be included in the marketing mix: Personnel, Physical facilities, and Process management.

THE POWER OF MODELS

By providing clarity where complexity exists, models play a critical role in the learning process. Oxenfeldt has eloquently pointed out how business executives use and rely on models of various kinds, such as analogies, checklists, matrices, charts, and symbolic models.[3]

In marketing, Ansoff's product/market expansion grid, Levitt's product life-cycle graph, and Lavidge and Steiner's heirarchy-of-effects model make marketing phenomena understandable by providing clear visualizations for abstract constructs.[4] Just as portfolio models helped provide a foundation for strategic planning, so, too did Borden's market mix analogy gain ready acceptance as an insightful concept in marketing.

The four Ps built upon this concept by providing the organizing framework for integrating diverse marketing tasks. Marketing, sales, new product development, physical distribution and other functions could be checklisted under the relevant P of the mix. This ability to classify made it possible for decision makers to bring order to activities that formerly were only loosely related.

It could be argued that, for certain markets, *packaging* (consumer marketing) or *personal selling* (industrial marketing) should be a fifth P. Each is of considerable importance in its industry. However, in most cases such key elements are still considered under an augmented notion of *product*, in the case of packaging, or *place*, in the case of personal selling.

But service businesses should consider adding three more Ps. Failure to focus adequately on *personnel, physical assets, and process management* can spell disaster for such firms. Figure 1 provides a newer model for structuring marketing plans and programs. The seven Ps are shown as part of an organic model, with cross-linkages evident among them. Ignoring these three additional Ps means ignoring elements critical to the marketing of services.

For example, in the late 1970s Harlan Sanders, the founder of Kentucky Fried Chicken (Heublein), voiced his concern for the company's future.[5] The food was frequently unappetizing, the facilities were run down, and the staff and franchisees were demoralized. Only after Heublein gave these key issues of process management, physical assets, and personnel the management attention and capital infusions they required did KFC regain its marketing vitality and return to healthy sales growth and profitability.

Figure 1.
Expanding the Traditional Marketing Mix for Service Businesses

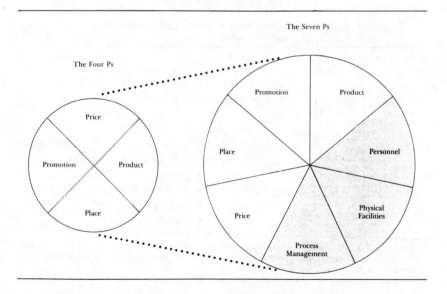

Braniff, a healthy airline in the 1970s, went broke in 1982, in large part because it had emphasized "lowball" pricing instead of streamlining its service processes, trimming its personnel costs, and focusing more closely on aircraft asset productivity.[6]

STRATEGIC MARKETING IN PRODUCT-BASED BUSINESSES

Most strategic marketing plans for product-based businesses begin by sizing up environmental and market factors (see Figure 2). Many plans are built around the notion of identifying both market share and market growth opportunities, by leveraging each of the four key marketing mix elements of Price, Product, Place, and Promotion. Critical debate and marketing decisions in such companies revolve around how each of the marketing mix elements (and subelements) can assist the firm in achieving its strategic objectives.

The four Ps are strategic weapons in the firm's market struggle against its rivals. The typical question is: If we were to alter one of these strategic factors, would it aid us in gaining an edge on our competitors? Discussion then ensues about the differentiating advantages of altering a specific element to gain new "value-added" consumer and trade appeal.

The debate is based on a thorough analysis of the consumer, competitor, channel, and the corporation's own strengths. After agreement is reached on which key marketing mix element presents the most compelling leveraging prospects, supporting marketing elements can be coordinated to reinforce and

Figure 2.
Typical Sequence for Developing a Product-Based Marketing Plan*

Discussion Sequence

      I. Situation Analysis: Environment and Market
     II. Problems and Opportunity Summary
   III. Objectives: Growth, Share, Profitability, Other
    IV. Strategies and Tactics
     V. Action Programs: Timing, Accountability, Expected Results
              Action Program Documentation:
                  • Pricing Plans
                  • Promotion Plans
                  • Product Plans
                  • Distribution Plans

*The Marketing Plan is usually embodied within the strategic plans for the corporation's business units. It does not encompass the scope, time horizon, or strategic emphasis of the strategic plan from which it is derived.

---

multiply the impact of the key element. This process is analogous to scoring and conducting various sections of a symphony in order to accent the performance of a featured soloist.

For example, if the firm sees new product features as the key to achieving market advantage, the other marketing mix elements must be orchestrated to highlight and enhance these features. Promotion and advertising may be structured creatively to draw attention to the new product benefits. Bold packaging graphics may showcase the added benefits. The sales force may require new sales aids to explain or demonstrate the new benefits. Prices may be adjusted, and merchandising deals may be promoted for both the trade and consumers to capitalize on the newly designed product. Figure 3 details some common subelements that provide the tactics for many marketing plans.

MARKETING SERVICES

Service-based marketing has been differentiated from product-based marketing, and different approaches to managing specific market mix elements have been delineated.[7] A great many service organizations have adopted the concept of marketing and have benefited from it. Successes have been documented for banks, utilities, airlines, courier companies, insurance firms, and public and private institutions (health care, education, museums), as well as for fast-food restaurants and other service franchises.[8]

When service organizations adopt marketing principles, they frequently organize their marketing plans around the four Ps. For example, a group of dentists may research their target market and decide that the keys to success are discount prices and convenient services. They may execute a plan to achieve their objectives by structuring appealing fee schedules and hours of operation and opening their office in a convenient suburban shopping mall.

Even sports teams have discovered the benefit of marketing principles; they merchandise products with their trademarks, use the broadcast media aggressively, and "sell" their teams (their "brands") with dynamic uniforms, attractive cheerleaders, animated mascots, and enthusiastic booster clubs. They use target-direct-mail marketing to build season ticket sales, and they price their product differently to various market segments by scaling ticket prices.

THE 7Ps AND SERVICE BUSINESSES

When service businesses try to develop marketing and tactical programs around the four Ps, one fundamental difficulty they encounter is making the four Ps fit the nature of their operations. The four Ps ignore important service marketing realities: namely, personnel, physical assets, and process

Figure 3.
Elements of the Market Mix that Generate Strategy and Tactics for Product-Based Businesses

The Four Ps of Marketing	*Subelements of the Four Ps*
Product	Product-line width, assortments, "families" Packaging New-product development Product naming, logos, trademarks Product quality Product warranties Product servicing after sale
Promotion	Brand positioning Advertising spending levels Chosen media, schedules Creative theming Sales promotion, coupons, contests, dealing Publicity
Price	Price level changes Quantity discounts Payment terms, cash discounts Published prices Pricing intelligence, bidding Trade discounts
Place	Forward vertical integration Channel selection, concentration Channel supports Customer service (delivery, ordering) Inventory and warehousing issues Direct marketing Personal selling

Adapted from A. W. Frey, *The Effective Marketing Mix* (Hanover, N.H.: Amos Tuck School, Dartmouth College, 1956).

management. These three Ps are interconnected and represent vital marketing elements in the management of service businesses.

Personnel is key to the creation of the service and its delivery to the consumer in a consistently acceptable fashion. Services represent personnel producing intangible deeds or efforts. Customers identify and associate the traits of service personnel with the firms they work for. A testy flight attendant, a rude mechanic, or a careless cook can seriously affect repeat business for an airline, a service station, or a restaurant.

Physical assets are important in facilitating the enhanced marketing and delivery of services. A consumer must experience a service. This experience is greatly affected by both the setting that is visible to customers and the physical assets hidden from view but critical to providing the service. For example, visitors experience Disneyland by what they see, but the hidden, below-ground support machinery is essential for the park's fantasy fulfillment.

Process management assures service availability and consistent quality, in the face of simultaneous consumption and production of the service offered. Without sound process management, balancing service demand with service supply is extremely difficult. Services cannot be inventoried or stored, so ways must be found to handle peak loads and optimize different customer needs with varied expertise levels within the service company. Banks try to channel "cash-only" customers or customers desiring after-hours service to automated teller machines, freeing up expert help to handle more complex customer needs during normal working hours.

PUTTING THE THREE Ps TO WORK

To illustrate the key role played in the marketing of services by personnel, physical facilities, and process task management, consider a modern fast-food restaurant chain that caters to families with small children.

The traditional four Ps would put primary emphasis on:

- The *pricing* of menu offerings;
- The *promotion* of the restaurant chain in the media, backed up by point-of-sale merchandising;
- The selection and production of appealing menu choices (*products*); and
- The creation of viable network of outlets with capabilities (eat-in or eat-out) and supporting facilities (for example, warehouses) to cover the target-market needs (*place*).

The addition of the three Ps makes a significant contribution to completing a tactical marketing plan.

PERSONNEL

A key to positioning the restaurant is image, which is very much influenced by personnel. Their friendliness, their prompt response to diners, their dexterity in filling orders and handling payments, their ability to keep the line moving despite temporary order backlogs, their ability to be enthusiastic and calm even when the job is boring or routine and the customers are noisy and impatient—all are key to the restaurant's success.

So the fast-food restaurant expends considerable effort in selecting and screening personnel who display the right combinations of enthusiasm, courtesy, and initiative. The restaurant trains and supervises the staff closely to ensure that personnel can handle peak demands with the utmost finesse and dexterity. The restaurant managers motivate the staff with contests, recognition awards, praise, job rotations, and other meaningful forms of support.

Staff are coached on how to handle difficult orders and unruly customers. Uniforms or dress codes are usually required, as is personal cleanliness, proper language, and good posture. Staff are also given numerous duties to keep them industrious during lulls. All of these tactics assure a consistent image of quality.

PHYSICAL FACILITIES

Physical facilities are crucial to the fast-food restaurant. They influence convenience of their service, the diners' enjoyment of the meal, and the efficiency with which large numbers of customers are served at busy times.

Location affects a variety of marketing concerns: the availability of parking, road access, visibility of signs and logos, and attractive buildings and grounds. Location determines the size of the trading area the restaurant will serve, as well as the nature of its clientele.

Internal facilities add ambience to the service. They are coordinated with the market image portrayed in advertising—from colors, fixtures, and lighting to location of exits, refuse containers, washrooms, and counters with condiments.

Even plants and dividers, cleverly placed, convey an impression of privacy or spaciousness, deflect and absorb noise, and allow for cleaning around dining furniture. These physical factors help to build a "personality" (intimacy, cleanliness) for the location where the service is provided.

PROCESS MANAGEMENT

The seventh P, process management, involves the task schedules, routines, and supervision of activities involved in meal preparation, packaging, and serving.

Much thought and planning goes into the design of order forms, preprogramming of cash registers, routines for handling nonstandard orders, and forecasting demand for menu items in anticipation of cooking needs and salad bar replenishment.

Policies are clearly written down for the handling of food, ideal cooking time, disposal of waste, and coping with customer complaints and other contingencies, from kitchen accidents to customer health emergencies.

In planning both the flow of activities and mechanization of the service, nothing is left to chance. Services marketing depends on meeting the pre-sold expectations of customers about how their orders will be handled, how they will look, taste, smell, and how hot they will be.

CORPORATE EXAMPLES

We have looked at the three Ps of personnel, physical assets, and process management as they apply to a hypothetical fast-food restaurant. But, once we leave the realm of theory, how do the three Ps work in actual practice? To answer that question, let us look at two corporate examples: Emery Air Freight and Beverly Enterprises.

EMERY AIR FREIGHT

In an interview in *Planning Review*, John Emery, CEO of Emery Air Freight, highlights the strategic importance of the three Ps of personnel, physical assets, and process management in successfully marketing "predictable, reliable and dependable air cargo service."[9]

Emery talks about several critical aspects of *personnel* in the marketing of his company's service. The company maintains an upbeat and enthusiastic environment so that "the sum total of the staff working together is greater than the power of any one individual." Handsome bonuses reward key managers for their marketing initiatives. The firm listens constantly to personnel in the field, who are closest to the actual service interaction with customers.

As to the crucial role of *physical assets* in marketing a service, Emery has kept ahead of competition by upgrading its aircraft with new low-noise engines that meet tougher government regulations. It has automated cargo sorting with state-of-the-art, large-scale computer systems. Without this commitment to upgrading both aircraft and computer assets with heavy capital outlays, Emery could not seize marketing opportunities that are resulting from deregulation and changing customer needs.

Process management is given high priority at Emery so that the next-day promise of delivery can be met. Each night, Emery puts 1.5 million pounds of cargo through a three-hour sorting process that creates three categories: letters and envelopes, other small packages under 70 pounds, and heavier material. Only then can trucks and planes leave for their arranged destinations from the central Dayton, Ohio, sorting facility and arrive at the customer's doorstep by 10:30 the next morning.

Emery is also installing computer terminals in its customers' offices so that airbills can be printed on customers' premises, saving end-users time and money. The terminals also tell customers the whereabouts of any shipment and its status in the Emery System. Being married to customers by computer is, according to John Emery, a strategic marketing advantage, an advantage provided by the company's process management expertise.

Emery Air Freight sees these three Ps of *personnel, physical facilities and process management* as critical to its service marketing success. These three Ps allow Emery to live up to its *promotion* promises (each year Emery spends in excess of $20 million in media advertising), expand its market coverage (*place*) to new airports, offer new international services (*product*), and remain *price* competitive on services provided.

BEVERLY ENTERPRISES

Beverly Enterprises is this country's largest nursing home operator, with 75,000 nursing home beds in 643 homes.[10] By paying attention to the marketing implications of the three Ps of personnel, physical facilities, and process management, this firm has been able to price its service competitively, enhance the basic services it offers to patients, and expand its geographic scope across the U.S.

Beverly has concentrated on *personnel* in marketing a better service, providing, better training for its medical nurses, and hiring a creative, dynamic director of patient activities. In all of its various homes across the country, Beverly's quality assurance staff of 75 trained nurses controls compliance with medical standards and regulations. Its creative program director has launched a host of programs aimed at giving patients and families more input into nursing home activities and conditions.

Beverly Enterprises' efficient *physical asset management* is considered the finest in the industry. Four service-care programs are marketed: (1) garden apartments at $1,500 per month; (2) $900 efficiencies; and other rooming arrangements for either (3) severely ill patients or (4) patients requiring minimal care. Its asset management includes managing its own laundry facilities, which cut these costs by 50 percent.

Process task management includes skillfully centralized food purchasing, which gives Beverly Enterprises savings of 15 percent over its competitors. Another innovation is Beverly's toll-free hot line, where head office management deals directly with patient or family complaints.

Beverly has recognized that its basic services marketing, pricing plans, and promotion programs are all tied to successful attention to the three Ps of personnel, physical assets, and process management.

Services marketing planning and execution should focus attention on seven Ps: the traditional four Ps plus three additional market mix elements that are crucial to service success—personnel, physical assets, and process management.

Whether the service entity is a Las Vegas casino, an engineering consulting service, or a financial service conglomerate, these additional three Ps greatly influence product line and promotional possibilites. They dramatically affect the pricing and actual physical distribution of the service.

Services are often called "credence" purchases because customers are asked to believe a service marketer's promises.[11] The credibility and reliability of many service companies hinge on understanding this broader notion of a services marketing mix.

REFERENCES

1. Neil Borden originated the concept of the marketing mix in "The Concept of the Marketing Mix," *Science in Marketing*, ed. George Schwartz (New York: John Wiley & Sons, 1965): 386-97.

2. E. Jerome McCarthy popularized the use of the four Ps in *Basic Marketing: A Managerial Approach*, 2nd ed. (Homewood, Ill.: Richard D. Irwin, 1964): 38-40.

3. Alfred R. Oxenfeldt, *Cost Benefit Analysis for Executive Decision Making* (New York: Amacom, 1979). See especially Chapter 4.

4. See Igor Ansoff, "Strategies for Diversification," *Harvard Business Review*, September-October 1957: 113-24; Theodore Levitt, "Exploit the Product Life Cycle," *Harvard Business Review*, November-December 1965: 81-94; and Robert J. Lavidge and Gary A. Steiner, "A Model for Predictive Measurements of Advertising Effectiveness," *Journal of Marketing*, October 1961: 59-62.

5. *The Wall Street Journal*, March 19, 1981: 29.

6. David W. Cravens, "Strategic Marketing's New Challenge," *Business Horizons*, March-April 1983: 19.

7. Good survey articles of the various aspects of the marketing mix include G. Lynn Shostack, "Breaking Free from Product Marketing," *Journal of Marketing*, April 1977: 73-80; G. Lynn Shostack, "Designing Services That Deliver," *Harvard Business Review*, January-February 1984: 133-39; William R. George and Leonard L. Berry, "Guidelines for the Advertising of Services," *Business Horizons*, July-August 1981: 52-56; Christopher H. Lovelock and John A. Quelch, "Consumer Promotions in Service Marketing," *Business Horizons*, May-June 1983: 66-75; Steven Unwin, "Advertising of Services, Not Products, Will Be the Wave of the Future," *Advertising Age*, May 27, 1984: 39-40; Donald Light and George Warfel, Jr., "Distribution Strategies for Services," *Standard Research Business Intelligence Program*, Report #698, Winter 1983-1984; Theodore Levitt, "A Production Line Approach to Service," *Harvard*

Business Review, September-October 1972: 41-52; and William R. George and Hiram E. Barksdale, "Marketing Activities in the Service Industries," *Journal of Marketing*, October 1974: 65-70. An excellent summary of various aspects of the marketing of services is Christopher H. Lovelock, "Classifying Services to Gain Strategic Marketing Insights," *Journal of Marketing*, Summer 1983: 9-20.

8. A variety of such industries are profiled in *Marketing of Services* (Chicago: AMA Proceedings Series 1981), eds. James H. Donnelly and William R. George. Included are articles on services marketing by banks, retailers, professions, leasing companies, educational institutions, health-care services, and so on. For an overview of service business marketing strategies practiced across different industries, see V. A. Zeithaml, A. Parasuraman, and L. L. Berry, "Problems and Strategies in Services Marketing," *Journal of Marketing*, Spring 1985: 33-46. See also their "Quality Counts in Services, Too," *Business Horizons*, May-June 1985: 44-52.

9. "Flying Anything Door-to-Door," a Robert J. Allio interview of John C. Emery, *Planning Review*, November 1984: 8-12.

10. Thomas Moore, "Way Out Front in Nursing Homes," *Fortune*, June 13, 1983: 142-50. A profile of Beverly Enterprises.

11. Connie Cox, "Marketing Business Services," *Business Marketing*, June 1985: 72.

A. J. Magrath is manager of market planning and research for the Canadian subsidiary of a Fortune 500 diversified manufacturer. He is coauthor of Marketing Channel Management: Strategic Planning and Tactics.

26.
STRATEGIC MARKETING TAKES A BOW

Frederick J. England, Jr.

> In both hard and soft markets, sales volume is enhanced when anorganization has a detailed marketing plan, or "Strategic Marketing Process," to follow.

No architect in his right mind would think of constructing a building without a blueprint. Yet, according to surveys conducted by the Independent Insurance Agents of America (IIAA), most agencies do not have a formulated marketing plan even though they dream of the day when increased premium volume will come rolling in, and even though they are sure they could handle more business with their current staff and facilities.

Whether markets are hard or soft, increased premium volume doesn't materialize out of a magicians's hat. It is a direct result of the effectiveness of the sales effort, and that effort is enhanced when the agency has a detailed marketing plan to follow. Guidelines scheduled to be released to IIAA members suggest that the Strategic Marketing Process can be divided into five phases: the situation analysis, market segmentation, evaluation of alternative marketing strategies, development of the formalized marketing plan, and monitoring of the program.

The first step in the Strategic Marketing Process is to undertake a situation analysis assessing the agency's strengths and weaknesses so the agency can determine what direction it should and can take in the future. The analysis begins with a determination of exactly what type of business the agency currently writes—personal lines, commercial lines, or both? Is insurance sold as commodity based on price or is the agency's expertise and advice the principal concern of its customers? Is life/health insurance included in the product mix? Is the product sold primarily to existing clients or new accounts? Is selling important, or is most of the business generated from renewals and order-taking?

The agency also should review the financial data over a period of years, paying particular attention to any period in which significant changes occurred. An analysis of these changes could provide valuable insights into what has been successful or unsuccessful in the past.

Additionally, the agency should look at productivity, developing measures that include commission income per employee; commission income per producer; staff count compared with commissions; and income per principal. It will also want to evaluate the effectiveness and efficiency of support function, including workflow and processing of insurance transactions; automation support; and general and administrative expenses.

Next, the agency needs to look at its existing accounts in terms of premium size, commission income, and annual number of service transactions. This provides a good indication of which accounts generate the most income with the least amount of association expense. The number of policies per account and historical retention should be analyzed, as well.

The agency also needs to examine the companies it represents vis-a-vis its relationship with each company and each company's competitive posture in the industry. This will help determine whether there is a fit with some or all of the companies and whether new relationships need to be developed or current relationships need to be changed. The analysis should look at the service provided to the agency by the company; the compensation arrangements the company has with the agency; and the marketing support provided by the company, including its products, advertising, market coverage, and market expertise.

The final step, and one of the most important, is to look at the agency's principal competitors to determine where an agency can best use its particular strengths to take advantage of a competitor's weaknesses.

Once the situation analysis has determined what is being sold and to whom, it is time for the agency to decide whether its current clientele represents the type of market it wishes to continue to penetrate or whether other areas offer better opportunities. In this market segmentation phase, the agency determines the "marketing mix" of its target market and the relative emphasis placed on price, product and promotion by the target market so the agency can match its effort to that marketing mix.

For a relatively small number of agencies, the total marketing approach, in which a general marketing mix attempts to satisfy all segments, might be appropriate. This demands a combination of competitively priced products, expertise in all lines, and significant promotional dollars, which is virtually unattainable for most agencies.

The market segmentation process permits an agency to use its particular strengths to reach an audience for which these items are crucial. A number of strategies can be adopted, including:

• *Specialization based on strength.* For many agencies, this is an obvious way to·go. Under this strategy, the agency directs all of its marketing efforts toward those markets where it is strongest, even if it means abandoning other segments to competitors. This process offers the advantage of placing the agency as the expert in a specific field, assuring a stronger image than that of competitors in that particular area.

• *Specialization based on potential market.* This strategy involves going after a market that appears to have potential, and it probably will require acquisition of resources in order to build the agency's expertise in the field. This approach would be taken by an agency that has determined from its situation analysis that other alternatives are less attractive. For example, it may have found that it lacked the strengths of its competitors in its current field, leaving it highly vulnerable, or perhaps a new competitor is threatening its principal line of business.

• *Diversification.* This is an alternative form of specialization in which the agency adds new, insurance-related products to its current mix of business. The advantage of this strategy is that it protects the agency against disaster if one area goes sour. On the other hand, it turns the agency into a more generalist-type of entity, making it possible for competition to specialize in one area and steal away business.

• *Segmentation without specialization.* This ambitious strategy involves identifying a large number of target markets and developing an individual strategy for each target. It requires a broad range of expertise and normally is feasible only for larger agencies where an ample staff permits the assignments of particular individuals to each market segment.

Once the agency has determined its target, it must decide how it is going to reach that target. It is reasonable to start with advertising in trade books for that particular market segment or some sort of institutional advertising, with follow up by mail. Direct mail also can be useful. To make sure it accomplishes its objectives, the agency will want to set up a monitoring system that involves review of marketing activity.

Much press has been give to alternative marketing as the savior of the independent agency system. However, no system exists that can save an agency which fails to market its product. In fact, some alternative systems could imperil the independent agency system by playing away from its strengths, which primarily come from the entrepreneurial, intelligent, professional, caring, service-oriented and people-oriented individuals who make up the system. Those qualities lead to the strong client/agent relationships that characterize the system.

An agency that has a formalized business plan, including an aggressive sales/marketing strategy, will prosper. Alternative marketing systems can enhance these business plans if they mix well with the basic overall strategic thrust of the agency, and they should be considered only if the agency is sure that its basic marketing strategy is working.

Among the alternatives agents might consider are joint ventures, group marketing, telemarketing/sales centers, direct-mail-response marketing, and exclusive agency approaches. In each instance, the alternative system should be evaluated with the bottom line in mind:Can the agency make a profit if it embarks on a particular strategy?

Too often an agency adopts an alternative system out of a fear that if it doesn't do so, its competition will. While this is neither a good nor bad reason in and of itself, it becomes a terrible reason if the marketing venture proves unprofitable and vice versa if the venture answers all the agency's wildest dreams.

Just as was done in the segmentation process, the alternative system should be analyzed to see if it is an effective way to reach the agency's target. It also should be monitored on a regular basis to determine if it really is bringing in new business that would not otherwise be obtained through traditional channels.

The marketing plan is the blueprint for the agency's total sales effort. It should incorporate all of the decisions that were made in the first three steps of the Strategic Marketing Process and should also involve a delineation of the agency's planned market area (geographic), market segment, products, distribution, suppliers and penetration rate.

The marketing plan should contain individual product plans for each product the agency plans to sell. The product plan should include:

1. An executive summary briefly stating the main facts and recommendations contained within the plan.
2. A situation analysis giving background on the marketing of the particular product thus far, along with a forecast of opportunities and threats.
3. Objectives and goals that are measurable, time-bounded, realistic, understandable, and results oriented.
4. A strategy statement setting forth the strategy (plus any alternative strategies) intended to achieve the stated goals.
5. An action program listing the tactical initiatives that will be taken to achieve the overall strategy. Specific activities by month or even week should be included. The program provides a general framework, but should be considered malleable if new probelms and opportunities arise.
6. The supporting budget for the operation needed to achieve the goals and objectives, broken down into detail if possible.
7. A monitoring system projecting budget and sales quotas by month or quarter for each producer and in total. It should be reviewed regularly so trouble spots can be spotted and corrective action taken.

Once all the pieces are in place, a system should be set up to review the overall strategy on a regular basis, quarterly at the very least. This allows an agency to spot problems quickly before they have a serious impact on the bottom line. The monitoring system should be designed to look at each aspect of the marketing plan to determine what is and what is not working so that new-found strengths can be expanded while weaknesses can be corrected.

Frederick J. England, Jr., is president of Hastings-Tapley Insurance and president of the Independent Insurance Agents of America.

27.
WORD OF MOUTH: THE INDIRECT EFFECTS OF MARKETING EFFORTS

Barry L. Bayus

Word of mouth is an extremely important factor in a consumer's purchase decisions. The author discusses the significance of word-of-mouth information and suggests ways to adjust a company's marketing efforts to take advantage of it.

The fact that consumers obtain information about products and services from other people, particularly family members, friends, and neighbors, is well documented in the marketing literature. As Gordon Weaver, executive vice president of marketing for Paramount Pictures, said, "Word of mouth is the most important marketing element that exists."

The literature suggests that word of mouth is an extremely important factor in the consumer's final purchase decisions; sometimes even more influential than other promotional methods. While the mass media is generally effective in generating product awareness, in many instances consumers more often rely on word of mouth when making their actual purchasing decisions.[5]

Several studies in diverse purchase situations document the pervasive influence of word of mouth. For example, one study found that over 50 percent of a large sample of durable goods buyers consulted their friends and relatives for advice.[27] This same study also found that over one-third of the buyers bought a brand or model which they had seen at someone else's house. In a study on the diffusion patterns of air conditioners within neighborhoods, they found further evidence that visual influences can be as important as verbal communications.[55] Other empirical research presents evidence that personal influences are important in the purchase of food and household products, in movie selection, and fashions; in choosing dental products and services and physicians; in farming practices; and voting; in the purchase of razor blades, and automobiles; and in the purchase of new products.[28,48,14,3,29,31,47, 41,44] Arndt reviews several other studies.[5]

257

Aside from these academic studies, the business community is also keenly aware of the power word of mouth carries. Firms compete to become sponsors of various activities and events. For example, several thousand dollars have been invested by firms to become "the official Olympic" candy, shoe, camera, airline, etc., (e.g., Alsop.)[2] Running-shoe companies give hundreds of dollars worth of equipment to running clubs, hoping to gain favorable exposure with local joggers and corporations sponsor athletic events.[33] Peters and Waterman cite several companies which have built their reputations around providing services to the customer. These companies (e.g., IBM, Maytag, Frito Lay, Caterpillar) go to great lengths, sometimes ignoring substantial economics, to ensure a strong reputation, and thus larger profits in the long term.

Negative word of mouth, on the other hand, can have disastrous consequences.[4] J. Arndt, for example, found that negative word of mouth retarded sales of a food product more than twice as strongly as positive word of mouth promoted sales of that product. Other studies have confirmed that unfavorable information is stronger than positive information.[54,39] Thus, it is perhaps even more important for the firm to be aware of negative word of mouth about its products. For example, Procter and Gamble has spent a lot of time and effort to quell a rumor that they had dealings with Satanists.[49] Poor word of mouth has also led to the failure of many motion pictures.[26] Several studies have appeared which investigate the effects of company policy on how consumers' complaints are handled.[52,43,51] The Technical Assistance Research Programs (TARP) presented evidence that the effective handling of consumer complaints had significant effects on future purchasing behavior. TARP concluded that given the high cost of mass media campaigns, it is often cheaper to satisfy old customers than to win new customers.

The power word of mouth can carry has been observed and noted by several researchers. Consider, for example, the case in which one company in a highly competitive consumer products area regularly spent considerably less on advertising than its leading competitors.

It would be overstating the case to say that this was a planned strategy, but investigation revealed that the apparent reason for their ability to succeed with relatively little advertising was the fact that their brand received vastly more word-of-mouth activity than did the two other brands which had about the same market share. The other brands were moved by muscle. The word-of-mouth brand had developed an advertising program which apparently aroused curiosity which, in turn, stimulated some of the information seeking.

This example summarizes the impact word of mouth can have, and at the same time sums up the way personal influences are used in practice—i.e., as a desirable side effect. These effects are not systematically or consistently included in the formulation of marketing policies by academicians or practitioners.

J. F. Engel and R. D. Blackwell have suggested that an integrated view of the mass media and personal influences be taken.[22] As they put it, "If a marketing organization understands how mass media and personal influences interact, it may be possible to develop an *integrated marketing program* including these influences even though they are not controlled by the marketing organizations."

Thus, we see the need for further research and development in this area. The purpose of this article is twofold. First, we introduce a new conceptual structure which bridges the gap between earlier fragmented studies. Second, we provide empirical evidence for this model.

This data is organized as follows. In the next section we present a brief review of the structure of aggregate marketing models which have appeared in the literature and discuss the limitations of these models. A new conceptual model is then proposed and empirical evidence presented. Implications for marketing strategy are also outlined.

PREVIOUS RESEARCH

The structure of a general marketing system can be represented as shown in Figure 1. The arrows in the diagram represent directions of influence. We note that these influences can take several forms, including both verbal communications and visual impressions. Furthermore, these influences can be positive, negative, or neutral.[37]

In general, personal influences can occur between three different groups: buyers, the target market, and other influential populations. The target market is composed of potential customers, including leaders and followers. We note that, for the most part, sales come from the target market. Other influential populations can include reference groups not part of the target market (and thus not considered to be potential sales). A good example would be parents' influence in their children's future educational and occupational choices.[32] Marketing efforts then impact this system.

The fact that buyers influence potential customers is well established in the literature.[5,44] For example, people with product experience can reduce the perceived risk associated with a purchase decision.[15,56] The importance of opinion leaders and their influence within the target market is also well documented as is the influence of reference groups.[5]

In general, most modeling efforts have focused on some smaller part of this marketing system. Two types of aggregate modeling efforts can be identified in the literature: marketing response models and new-product diffusion models.[7] Details of these can be found in Sethi[46] and Little[34] who review advertising models, Zoltners and Sinha[57] who review sales-force models, and Mahajan and Muller[35] and Gatignon and Robertson[23] who review first-purchase diffusion models.

The basic structure of aggregate marketing response models is shown in Figure 2. Here, marketing efforts impact some identified target market; individuals from this target market then eventually become sales. We note that

Figure 1.
Word of Mouth and Marketing Efforts in a Marketing System

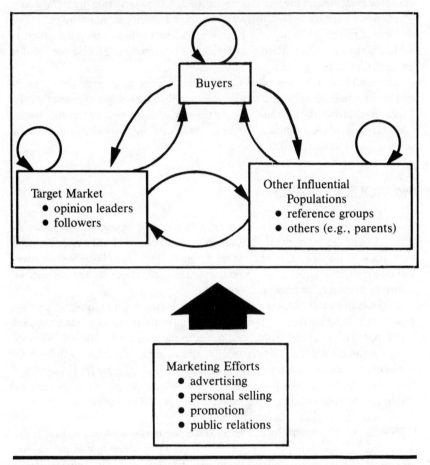

such a model does not make any provisions for personal influences. The new-product diffusion models, on the other hand, do include word-of-mouth effects, but only the personal influences between buyers and the target market. The basic structure of these models is shown in Figure 3. Here, the marketing efforts impact some identified target markets, who, in turn, eventually make a purchase. In addition, buyers can influence prospective customers.

Two key assumptions underlie these aggregate models: (1) marketing strategies are limited to the target market, and (2) when included, word of mouth is operationalized only as a function of cumulative buyers. Comparing the structures of these models with that of the general marketing system shown in Figure 1, we find that other interesting marketing phenomena have not been adequately modeled. In particular, the possible strategy of directing marketing

Figure 2.
Structure of Marketing Response Models

efforts to the other influential populations (who can, in turn, influence those in the target market) does not result from an analysis of existing aggregate models.

A NEW MODEL STRUCTURE

Let us now consider a paradigm in which word-of-mouth activity is also a state variable of the system (see Figure 4). From our discussion so far, existing aggregate marketing models consider the current level of sales to be the only relevant state variable of the system. Marketing efforts are an input variable (i.e., controllable influence), and, where included, word of mouth is modeled as a function of cumulative sales. In this new model structure, sales impact the level of word-of-mouth activity in the marketplace (i.e., buyers participate in word-of-mouth conversations). Word of mouth, in turn, influences the amount of final sales. Marketing efforts impact sales directly and also can affect the level of word-of-mouth activity. We note that the effects of these system variables can be expressed in various ways, including both direct and indirect influences. For example, the influences of word-of-mouth activity on sales can be direct product recommendations, as well as indirect endorsements from visual displays. Thus, our concept of word of mouth is not limited to only verbal communications. Furthermore, our aggregate conceptualization of word of mouth includes the personal influences between all relevant individuals or

Figure 3.
Structure of New-Product Diffusion Models

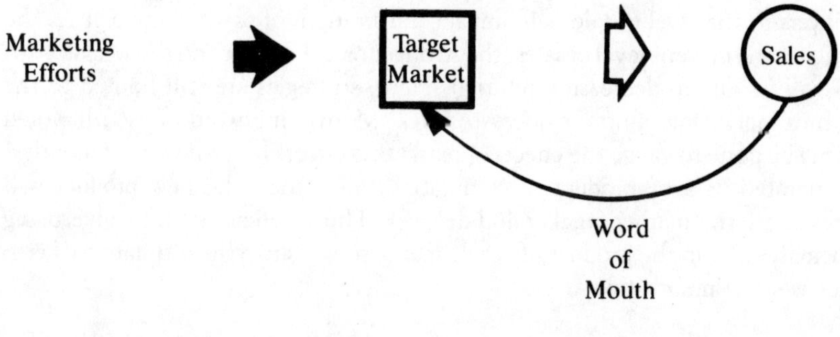

Word
of
Mouth

Figure 4.
The Conceptual Model Structure

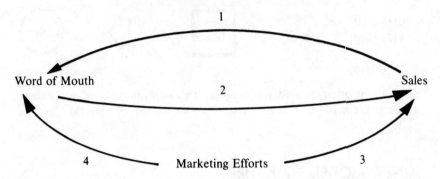

groups, as well as the nature of the influence (e.g., positive, negative, brand specific, etc.).

Viewing the marketing system in this way opens up new avenues of insight into marketing behavior. Consider the case cited earlier in which a company was able to spend considerably less on advertising than its competitors, yet retain approximately the same market share.[14] Such a scenario is possible in the proposed paradigm. Under certain conditions, the influences between word of mouth and sales can set up a homeostatic or a positive feedback (growth) situation. Thus, promotion may not be required to sustain market share, or even possibly to increase market share.

Research has generally concluded that word of mouth affects sales (path 2). Much research has centered on path 3—i.e., the effects of marketing efforts on sales.[1] These efforts, however, do not provide any useful guidelines concerning marketing strategies which combine personal influences and marketing efforts. Furthermore, the structure in Figure 4 points out the possibility of interaction between word of mouth and marketing efforts. The effectiveness, for example, of a particular resource (e.g., advertising) may be critically linked to the current amount and type (i.e., positive or negative) of word-of-mouth activity in the market.

New-product diffusion models have added path 1, the feedback link from buyers to the level of sales will impact the strength of paths 1 and 3 (i.e., the higher the current level of sales, the stronger path 1 will be and the weaker path 3 will be due to decreasing returns). Here, strategies are still limited to the firm's marketing efforts to increase sales. Monitoring word of mouth would only be done to gauge the effects of marketing efforts (e.g., if word of mouth is generated as a by-product of cumulative sales, then the new product will penetrate the market quicker and deeper). Thus, policies such as advertising heavily early in the product life cycle makes sense, since the ultimate goal is to let word of mouth take over.

Adding path 4 enriches the model considerably. This link presumes that the firm can affect word of mouth. It is well known that advertising copy has differential effects on sales.[11] This suggests that the firm, in targeting its marketing efforts to increase word of mouth, may use different copy than it might otherwise use to influence the target market. In fact, within our word-of-mouth conceptualization, three different populations exist—each possibly requiring different marketing approaches. Included are potential efforts by the firm to influence: (a) the target market to seek information through personal channels; (b) other influental groups to actively discuss, display, or endorse the firm's product; and (c) buyers to recommend the firm's product to potential customers. In all three instances, word-of-mouth activity has been increased. Here, the level of word of mouth will impact the strength of paths 2 and 4 (i.e., the higher the level of word of mouth, the stronger will be path 2 and the weaker will be path 4 due to decreasing returns of marketing efforts). It is this link which we will explore further.

MARKETING EFFORTS AND WORD OF MOUTH

Although not rigorously demonstrated, the notion that marketing efforts can affect word-of-mouth activity has been suggested by several researchers. They found that people who heard about President Roosevelt's death from the radio were more likely to tell others than those informed by word of mouth. Others, however, found the opposite results in the case of Senator Taft's death. In the Project Revere studies, emergency conditions were simulated by dropping leaflets from planes, instructing people who found the message to inform other members of their community. Researchers found that message diffusion was related to stimulus intensity (number of leaflets dropped per person) and the number of repititions (airplane drops). H. B. Cox and S. M. Cunningham found that those exposed to advertising of a consumer product talked more about the product than a control group; although the people who purchased the product had an even higher incidence of word of mouth. Other research found that sampling was associated with product-related conversations. As already mentioned. D. F. Cox cites a case in which advertising for a certain household product was able, over several months, to increase word of mouth about the product but provides no supporting evidence for his claim. G. S. Day also suggests that advertising can trigger word of mouth. In the case of established convenience products, he found that advertising stimulated the needs for more information about the product. The research of Bayus, Carroll, and Rao discuss an experiment involving word of mouth and movie attendance.[7] Their research indicated that direct methods to influence word of mouth (i.e., direct mail and prescreening for identified opinions leaders, and the use of paid messages spreaders) were largely unsuccessful.

The positive effects of marketing resources on word of mouth are summarized

Figure 5.
The Impacts of Marketing Efforts on Word of Mouth

	Stimulate Positive Word of Mouth	Retard Negative Word of Mouth
Increase	Trigger need for more information.	Provide information/ handle complaints, rumors.
Decrease	Trigger need for information from other sources.	Reduce public visibility of firm.

Marketing Efforts (row label)

in Figure 5. In the case of positive word of mouth, increasing marketing expenditures can stimulate the amount of word-of-mouth activity in a market by triggering the need for more information. Catchy slogans and clever advertising copy are other ways to increase personal conversations.[19] In addition, firms can encourage recommendations through promotional activities (e.g., giving a bonus to current customers providing recommendations and/or new sales). Decreasing marketing efforts can also lead to more word of mouth in certain situations. For example, face-to-face contact with a salesperson is an important source of information for high-involvement purchases.[22] Absence of such interpersonal influence may result in more conversations with friends and relatives before the final purchase decision.

In the case of negative word of mouth, public relations activities can be used to retard consumer complaints, rumors, and editorials by providing accurate and truthful information. In some instances, however, the firm may choose to decrease marketing efforts in order to reduce its public visibility (e.g., the Tylenol scare), allowing the negative information to decay over time.

The possibilities presented in Figure 5 are intuitively appealing and speculative. We next turn to an empirical investigation of the impact of marketing efforts on stimulating positive word of mouth.

THE CASE OF MILITARY ENLISTMENTS

Enlistment recruiting for the military services has received considerable attention from marketing researchers.[40],[24,25,12] The military "purchase" decision is a high commitment situation which provides an ideal setting to examine our proposed model structure (Figure 4), since personal influences and marketing efforts are important sources of information.[45,7,25,12] In this context, marketing efforts include advertising and the recruiter's salesforce; word-of-mouth conversation can generally take place between potential recruits and their parents, friends, and/or people in the delayed-entry program (where new recruits are allowed up to 12 months before they must report to boot camp). We note that parents are not part of the target market, and individuals in the delayed-entry program represent sales.

We note that empirical evidence for links 1, 2, and 3 in our proposed model was found in the military enlistment context and is documented by B. L. Bayus.[7] Our focus here will thus be on examining the effects of recruiting resources on word-of-mouth activity.

The Data. The empirical data for this research came from a large-scale marketing experiment conducted in conjunction with the U.S. Naval Recruiting Command in mid-1978. The unit of analysis used in the experiment was the Area of Dominant Influence (ADI), since it offered the most reliable way of executing and measuring the changes in media advertising. Based on the media-use patterns of sampled households, the electronic media-rating services assign individual counties to one of over 200 ADIs in the United States. A subset of all ADIs was selected for experimental treatment and observation. Both increased and decreased conditions of recruiter strength levels and national advertising expenditures were considered. Treatment markets were matched on the basis of previous levels of military enlistments and the Navy's share of those enlistments. In general, the design and objectives of this project were met extremely well. Independence, variance, and measurement were obtained, and conformity to planned levels was achieved. Details of this project and the ensuing analyses can be found in two studies conducted in 1984 and 1985.[12,7]

As part of this experiment, 12 markets were part of a two-wave survey program. Three markets in each of four combinations of increased and decreased levels of national advertising expenditures (+/- 50 percent) and recruiters salesforce numbers (+/- 20 percent) were involved in the design. Data was collected from the general target population (17- to 24-year-old females) through a random-digit-dialing telephone-survey procedure. Questionnaires were completed in the summer of 1980 (wave 2), nine months into the experiment. Details of the sample design and response rates are in reference number 8. A comparison of respondent profiles between waves 1 and 2 revealed no major differences.

Information collected from respondents included whether or not they had discussed the military with anyone (e.g., family, friends) in the previous six months. We will use this survey variable as a measure of word of mouth; unlike the new-product diffusion studies which consider word of mouth to be a function of cumulative sales.[6] We note that certain limitations do exist, however, and include: (1) the assumption that positive information is involved, and (2) these discussions are concerned with military enlistments. Some support for making these assumptions is available.[37]

Results. Impacts of the various treatment conditions on word-of-mouth activity for selected segments of men and women is shown in Table 1. We find that word of mouth can be stimulated by increasing or decreasing marketing efforts under various circumstances.

Even with changes in the marketing variables, we would not expect word-of-mouth activity among all individuals to be affected. In particular, respondents who have already made up their minds (positively or negatively) about military enlistment are expected to be the least responsive. It is the people who are unsure about whether they desire to enlist that will want to discuss the possibility with family, friends, teachers, etc. Detailed analyses supporting this are contained in reference number 7.

Table 1 suggests that the advertising copy in place during the experiment triggered the need for more information among men who were unsure about military enlistment. Frequently repetition of advertising describing the potential of Navy enlistment may have caused individuals to discuss it further with family and friends. For women, on the other hand, decreasing advertising expenditures was associated with increased word-of-mouth activity. Results from a segmentation study discussed offers a possible explanation.[8] They found that the Navy's national advertising campaign in place during this time was not generally appealing to women. However, one segment of women accounted for over 40 percent of Navy contracts. These women (called "achievers") tended to be highly motivated individuals desiring to acquire a skill and obtain a position of leadership. Thus, with less frequent exposure to advertising citing such opportunities in the Navy, these individuals might be expected to seek advice and information from other sources since military enlistment is an important option.

Responses to the recruiter resource shows a similar pattern. Decreasing the number of recruiters in a market (and thus the available time and effort for personal selling activities such as high school lectures, visits, etc.,) is associated with a higher proportion of the individuals who are unsure of enlistment in the military. Military enlistment is a high commitment decision; interpersonal communications play a critical role. The results for both men and women suggest that an unavailability of face-to-face recruiter contact may lead individuals to seek other available sources of advice and information. The relationship between increased recruiter levels and word-of-mouth activity is interesting. In this case, young men with positive intentions of enlisting in the military, but not in the Navy, can be persuaded to seek more information from other informal sources because of an increase in competitive Navy salesforce activity. Thus, the Navy recruiter can possibly point out opportunities previously unknown to the individual, leading to a need for more information before the final decision.

Table 1.
The Effects of Advertising and Recruiters on Military Discussions

	Wave 1		Wave 2			
	N_1	% discussions	N_2	% discussions	χ^2	p
Men:						
Increased Advertising[1]	22	22.7	13	53.8	3.51	0.06
Decreased Advertising[1]	24	54.2	23	60.9	0.22	0.64
Increased Recruiters[1]	18	38.9	20	55.0	0.99	0.32
Decreased Recruiters[1]	28	39.3	16	62.5	2.20	0.14
Increased Recruiters[2]	35	51.4	60	68.3	2.68	0.10
Decreased Recruiters[2]	37	71.3	44	75.0	0.23	0.63
Women:						
Increased Advertising[1]	13	30.8	6	33.3	0.01	0.91
Decreased Advertising[1]	8	25.0	8	75.0	4.00	0.05
Increased Recruiters[1]	13	38.5	8	50.0	0.27	0.60
Decreased Recruiters[1]	8	12.5	6	66.7	4.38	0.04

[1] Individuals who were unsure of whether they would enlist in the Armed Forces.
[2] Individuals with positive intentions of enlisting in a branch of the Armed Forces other than the Navy.

CONCLUSIONS AND IMPLICATIONS

The importance of word of mouth is widely acknowledged. Numerous academic studies have appeared in the literature documenting the impacts of personal influences in diverse purchase situations. The business community is also cognizant of the pervasive effects favorable word of mouth carries and of the disastrous consequences negative word of mouth conveys. However, the effects due to personal influences have not been systematically or consistently included in the formulation of marketing strategies by academicians or practitioners.

Previous modeling efforts make two key assumptions: a focus on the target market and a limited operationalization of word of mouth. A broader conceptualization of the salient influences in a marketing system was outlined. This led to the formulation of an aggregate model structure which integrates word-of-mouth influences and the effects of marketing efforts. The key concept in this model involves viewing the aggregate level of word-of-mouth activity as a state variable of the system. This model has three main components; the effect of sales on word-of-mouth activity; the effect of marketing efforts on sales; and the effect of marketing efforts on word-of-mouth activity.

The significance of this model structure comes from the marketing phenomena which it can generate. Several observations have been made in the literature about situations where a firm was able to take advantage of positive word-of-mouth activity by reducing expenditures associated with marketing efforts. Such a scenario is possible in our paradigm. Under certain conditions, the feedback effects between word of mouth and sales can set up a homeostatic or a growth situation. Thus, marketing efforts may not even be required to sustain market share. In addition, our structure shows that the firm can affect sales directly through the traditional use of marketing resources and, indirectly, by targeting its efforts to increase positive word of mouth or retard negative communications.

In the context of a field marketing experiment involving the military enlistment decision, empirical support for stimulating positive word of mouth was presented. Changes in advertising and salesforce levels were found to be associated with increased word-of-mouth activity among individuals who have not finalized their career decisions and who can be influenced by formal and informal sources.

These results have important implications for marketing strategy. Our findings indicate that advertising may be an effective means of stimulating word-of-mouth communications. Thus, it is clear that a firm should be attentive to the existing word-of-mouth activity in the marketplace. By adjusting its marketing efforts (through, for example, copy directed beyond the target market), a firm may be able to alter its market position by taking advantage of the power of word of mouth.

Several future research directions also surface. Our research has only considered the effects of marketing efforts in stimulating positive word of mouth. Further empirical work is needed to examine the possibilities outlined for retarding negative word of mouth. Another limitation of our empirical study concerns the measurement of word-of-mouth activity. Identifying the separate influental groups (e.g., in the case of military enlistment, family and college-bound friends) and examining the relationship between marketing efforts and word of mouth in each of these populations may provide greater insight. Finally, the notion of product-category word of mouth and a product-brand word of mouth arises. In our empirical context, changes in marketing efforts were related to a specific brand (i.e., the Navy), while personal discussions were generic. A question not addressed in our research concerns the effects of marketing efforts on brand-specific word of mouth. Furthermore, interesting questions can be asked about the effects of product-category marketing expenditures on word-of-mouth activity in general and for particular brands.

REFERENCES

1. Aaker, D. A., and J. M. Carman, "Are You Overadvertising?" *Journal of Advertising Research 22*, 4 (1982): 57-70.
2. Alsop, R., "Study of Olympics Ads Casts Doubts on Value of Campaigns," *The Wall Street Journal*, December 6, 1984.
3. Arndt, J., "Word of Mouth Advertising: The Role of Product-Related Conversations in the Diffusion of a New Food Product," Ph.D. dissertation, Harvard University, 1966.
4. ——. "Role of Product-Related Conservations in the Diffusion of a New Product." *Journal of Marketing Research*, 3 (1967)a: 391-295.
5. ——. *Word of Mouth Advertising: A Review of the Literature*, New York: Advertising Research Foundation, 1967b.
6. Bass, F. M., "A New Product Growth Model for Consumer Durables," *Management Science 15*, January 1969: 215-227.
7. Bayus, B. L., "Word of Mouth and Marketing Strategy: A Model Integrating the Effects of Marketing Efforts and Personal Influences for One Time Major Purchases," Ph. D. dissertation, University of Pennsylvania, 1984.
8. ——. Carroll, V. P.; and A. G. Rao, "Harnessing the Power of Word of Mouth," In *Innovation Diffusion Models of New Product Acceptance* J. Wind and V. Mahajan, eds., 1985.
9. ——, and V. P. Carroll, *User's Guide and Codebook to the Navy Field Marketing Experiment: The Wharton Administered Navy Tracking Survey*, Wharton Applied Research Center Technical Report, University of Pennsylvania, 1983.

10. ——. Carroll, V. P.; H. L. Lee; and A. G. Rao, "Market Segment Response Through Field Experimentation." Paper submitted for publication, 1985.

11. Bloom, D.; A. Jay; and T. Twyman, "The Validity of Advertising Pretest," *Journal of Advertising Research 17*, 2 (1977): 7-16.

12. Carroll, V. P.; A. G. Rao; H. L. Lee; A. Shapiro; and B. L. Bayus, "The Navy Enlistment Marketing Experiment." Paper submitted for publication 1984.

13. Coleman, J.; E. Katz; and H. Menzel, "The Diffusion of an Innovation Among Physicians," *Sociometry*, December 1957: 253-270.

14. Cox, D. F., "The Audience as Communicators," in *Toward Scientific Marketing*, Proceedings of the American Marketing Association, S.A. Greyser, ed. Chicago: American Marketing Association, 1963.

15. Cox, D. F. ed., *Risk Taking and Information Handling in Consumer Behavior*, Boston: Harvard University Press, 1967.

16. Cox. H. B. and S. M. Cunningham, "Chicken Sara Lee Team Report," Unpublished paper. Graduate School of Business Administration, Harvard University, 1961.

17. Day, G. S., "Attitude Change, Media and Word of Mouth," *Journal of Advertising Research 11*, 6 (1971): 31-40.

18. DeFleur, M. L. and E. D. Rainboth, "Testing Message Diffusion in Four Communities: Some Factors in the Use of Airbourne Leaflets as a Communication Medium," *American Sociological Review 17*, (1952): 734-737.

19. Dichter, E., "How Word of Mouth Advertising Works," *Harvard Business Review 44*, 6 (1966): 147-166.

20. Dodd, S. C., "Diffusion Is Predictable: Testing Probability Models for Laws of Interaction," *American Sociological Review 20*, (1955): 392-401.

21. ——. "Formulas for Spreading Opinions," *Public Opinion Quarterly 22*, (1958): 537-554.

22. Engel, J. F. and R. D. Blackwell, *Consumer Behavior*, New York: Holt, Rinehart and Winston, 1982.

23. Gatignon, H. A. and T. S. Robertson, "Integration of Consumer Diffusion Theory and Diffusion Models: New Research Directions," in *Innovation Diffusion Models of New Product Acceptance*, J. Wind and V. Mahajan, eds. 1985.

24. Goldberg, L., "Recruiters, Advertising and Navy Enlistments," *Navy Research Logistics Quarterly 29*, June 1982: 385-398.

25. Hanasens, D. M. and H. A. Levien, "An Econometric Study of Recruitment Marketing in the US Navy," *Management Science 29*, October 1983: 1167-1184.

26. Harmetz, A., "Hollywood Is Joyous Over Its Record Grossing Summer," *New York Times*, September 9, 1981.

27. Katona, G. and E. Mueller, "A Study of Purchasing Decisions," in *Consumer Behavior: The Dynamics of Consumer Reaction*, L. H. Clark, ed., New York: New York University Press, 1955.

28. Katz, E. and P. F. Lazarfeld, *Personal Influence*, New York: Free Press, 1955.

29. ——. "The Social Itinerary of Technical Changes: Two Studies in the Diffusion of Innovation," *Human Organization 20*, (1961): 70-82.

30. Larson, O. N. and R. J. Hill, "Mass Media and Interpersonal Communication in the Diffusion of a News Event," *American Sociological Review 19*, (1954): 426-433.

31. Lazarfeld, P. F.; B. Berelson; and H. Gaudet, *The People's Choice: How the Voter Makes up His Mind in a Presidential Campaign*, New York: Duel Sloan and Pearce, 1944.

32. Levine, A, "Educational and Occupational Choice: A Synthesis of Literature from Sociology and Psychology," in *Selected Aspects of Consumer Behavior*, R. Ferber, ed., Washington, D. C.: National Science Foundation, 1977.

33. Lisko, M., "The Road Race: An Untapped Promotional Tool," in *Marketing Theories and Concepts from an Era of Change*, J. Summery et al., eds., Chicago: American Marketing Association, 1983.

34. Little, J. D. C., "Aggregate Advertising Models: The State of the Art," *Operations Research 27*, 4 (1979): 629-667.

35. Mahajan, V. and E. Muller, "Innovation Diffusion and New Product Growth Models in Marketing," *Journal of Marketing 43*, 4 (1979): 55-68.

36. Market Facts. *Youth Attitudes Tracking Study*. Report prepared for the Department of Defense, 1979.

37. Midgley, D. F., "A Simple Mathematical Theory of Innovative Behavior," *Journal of Consumer Research 3*, 1 (1976): 31-41.

38. Miller, D. C., "A Research Note on Mass Communication," *American Sociological Review 10*, (1945): 691-694.

39. Mizerski, R. W., "An Attribution Explanation of the Disproportionate Influence of Unfavorable Information," *Journal of Consumer Research 9*, 3 (1982): 301-310.

40. Morey, R. C. and J. M. McCann, "Evaluating and Improving Resource Allocation for Navy Recruiting," *Management Science 26*, December 1980: 1198-1210.

41. Newman, J. W. and R. Staelin, "Repurchase Information Seeking for New Cars and Major Household Appliances," *Journal of Marketing Research 9*, 3 (1972): 249-257.

42. Peters, T. J. and R. H. Waterman, *In Search of Excellence*, New York: Harper and Row, 1982.

43. Richens, M. L., "Negative Word of Mouth by Dissatisfied Consumers: A Pilot Study," *Journal of Marketing 47*, 1 (1983): 68-78.

44. Rodger, E. M., *Diffusion of Innovations*, Glencoe, IL.: Free Press, 1983.

45. Rothschild, M. L., "Marketing Communications in Nonbusiness Situations or Why It's so Hard to Sell Brotherhood Like Soap," *Journal of Marketing*, 43 2 (1979): 11-20.

46. Sethi, S. P., "Dynamic Optimal Control Models in Advertising: A Survey," *SIAM Review*, 19(October 1977): 685-725.

47. Sheth, J. N., "Word of Mouth in Low-Risk Innovations," *Journal of Advertising Research*, 11, 3 (1971): 15-18.

48. Silk, A. J., "Overlap Among Self Designated Opinion Leaders: A Study of Selected Dental Products and Services," *Journal of Marketing Research*, 3, 3 (1966): 255-259.

49. Solomon, J. B., "Procter and Gamble Fights New Rumors of Link to Satanism," *The Wall Street Journal*, November 8, 1984.

50. Stafford, J. E. and A. B. Cocanougher, "Reference Group Theory," in *Selected Aspects of Consumer Behavior*, R. Ferber, ed. Washington, D.C.: National Science Foundation, 1977.

51. Technical Assistance Research Programs (TARP), *Consumer Complaint Handling in America: Final Report*, Washington, D. C.: White House Office of Consumer Affairs, 1979.

52. Technical Assistance Research Programs (TARP), *Measuring the Grapevine—Consumer Response and Word of Mouth*, Atlanta, GA: The Coca-Cola Company, 1982.

53. Turnbull, P. W. and A. Meenaghan, "Diffusion of Innovation and Opinion Leadership," *European Journal of Marketing*, 14, 1 (1980): 3-33.

54. Weinberger, M. C.; C. T. Allen; and W. R. Dillon, "Negative Information: Perspectives and Research Directions," in *Advances in Consumer Research*, 8, K. B. Monroe, ed., Ann Arbor, MI: Association for Consumer Research, 1981.

55. Whyte, W. H., "The Web of Word of Mouth," *Fortune*, 50 (November 1954): 140ff.

56. Woodside, A. G. and M. W. DeLozier, "Effects of Word of Mouth Advertising on Consumer Risk Taking," *Journal of Advertising*, 5, 4 (1976): 12-19.

57. Zoltners, A. A. and P. Sinha, "Integer Programming Models for Sales Force Allocations," *Management Science*, 26 (March 1980): 242-260.

Barry L. Bayus is a member of the Corporate Operations Research Group at RCA.

28.
ANOTHER CHANCE FOR THE MARKETING CONCEPT?

H. Michael Hayes

> Several decades after the introduction of the marketing concept, we
> have the opportunity to learn from the past and to take a betterapproach
> to marketing—one in which top management assumes the responsibility
> for establishing the marketing concept as its pervasive business
> philosophy.

Today the term *marketing* is so well-established in our vocabulary and as a
business function that there is little appreciation for its newness as a business
philosophy. Yet it was less than 40 years ago that marketing burst into the field
of management thinking as a new way to orient and organize business
activities. The premise of the marketing concept was both simple and appealing—business results would be enhanced if satisfaction of customer wants and
needs became the starting point of all business activity, and if profits, not
volume, became the organizational goal.

For two decades, marketing and the marketing concept flourished. Led by
consumer packaged-goods manufacturers, followed by consumer durable
manufacturers, and then by industrial-goods manufacturers, countless firms
established marketing organizations. The marketing concept was adopted
more slowly by service industries, and ultimately, by not-for-profit
organizations. But by the late 1960s, marketing was well-established
throughout the United States and was beginning to take root in Europe.

And then—just as marketing and its promises seemed to validate its
premises—signs began to develop that marketing was not, in fact, delivering.
Creation of marketing departments and increased expenditures on marketing
activities were not necessarily accompanied by either increased sales or profits.
Intra-organizational conflict increased as some marketers attempted to impose
their will on the organization, taking as their authority their new charter or
responsibility for customer satisfaction.

Marketing, as a way to determine business objectives and enhance business
results, gave way to strategic planning. Overnight—or so it seemed—vice

presidents of strategic planning were appointed, and strategic planning systems were installed. Seminars on strategic planning became an "in" activity. Books on strategy and strategic planning moved to the best-seller lists. For firms in high-growth industries, preoccupation with the customer seemed less important than the problems of technology and finance. For firms in low-growth industries, business development—a euphemism for mergers and acquistions—was the new emphasis. Marketing, the focus of management enthusiasm in the fifties and sixties, had moved out of the limelight.

Now, in the mid-eighties, with many high-growth industries experiencing maturation of markets, with mergers and acquisitions becoming increasingly expensive, and with the problems of managing mergers and acquisitions of widely disparate businesses becoming increasingly evident, there is growing evidence that marketing has reclaimed center stage. Articles in *Business Week* and *Fortune* suggest that marketing is the new priority and that the nature of markets is, once again, of paramount importance to business. *The Wall Street Journal* has inaugurated a column devoted to marketing. Major organizations are seeking experienced marketing executives to guide their marketing activities or, in some instances, to take over the helm as president and CEO.

For those engaged in marketing, this re-emergence may seem to be a highly appropriate state of affairs. But thoughtful managers may have some critical questions. Given the apparent failure of marketing to live up to its earlier promises, is it reasonable to expect that it will deliver on them now? Or, will management once again make larger commitments in support of marketing activities only to be disappointed in the results and turn, as before, to some alternative approach? Answers to these questions may well depend on what we have learned from our previous marketing experiences.

THE RISE OF MARKETING

Heralded by General Electric's avowal that it had become a marketing company (see The Marketing Concept at General Electric), and assisted by the rapid growth of business school enrollments and the attendant outpouring of academic thought, the 1950s saw marketing enter the consciousness of American corporate thought and, subsequently, public awareness. As described by Robert J. Keith, chief executive officer of The Pillsbury Company, it was a revolution—that meant not merely adoption of the marketing concept but demanded that a firm become a "marketing company"—a company where marketing would increasingly influence long-range policy, and where, more than any other function, marketing would be tied to top management.[1]

Despite the inherent appeal of marketing, the revolution was neither instantaneous nor universal. The term itself did not receive instantaneous acceptance. The authors of a leading marketing text, for instance, titled the

1951 editions of "Sales Management: Policy and Procedures," in the belief that neither the business community nor marketing teachers would accept "Marketing Management," a title that had to wait for the second edition, published in 1960.[2] Few firms embraced marketing for its intrinsic philosophical appeal. Most, according to marketing expert Philip Kotler, turned to marketing only as a remedy for sales decline, slow sales growth, significant change in buying patterns, increased competition, or rising costs of market-related activities.[3]

By the early 1960s, however, marketing was well-established. A survey of 273 large- and medium-sized manufacturing firms found a majority with marketing departments headed by a chief marketing executive at the same level as the chief manufacturing executive and reported to the president.[4] Marketing research departments were commonplace, and most marketing departments had at least some responsibility for new product development. To many, this was evidence of a marketing orientation. As was pointed out, however, the survey reported only what had happened to the organization charts. It could not determine the extent to which the marketing concept had permeated management thinking. As later events were to suggest, the apparent widespread acceptance of marketing fell far short of Keith's revolution and, in most instances, was not accompanied by major changes in management attitude.

THE RISE OF STRATEGIC PLANNING

Even as the 1960s saw general acceptance of the marketing concept and the addition of marketing departments to most organization charts, concerns were developing. Disenchantments with the ability of marketing to deliver promised results, and conflicts between marketing and other functions, fueled growing interest to think about business management in new ways. Strategic planning, with its multifunctional emphasis, portfolio concepts, new analytical techniques, and sophisticated models, held the promise to dealing with problems beyond the scope of marketing and providing better business results; not necessarily better than those promised by marketing, but better than those that marketing had been able to deliver. If the decade of the 1960s belonged to marketing, the decade of the 1970s came to belong to strategic planning.

To describe the shift to strategic planning as the demise of marketing would greatly overstate the case, but there was no question that in the 1970s marketing no longer led in the determination of corporate objectives. Marketing inputs to the strategic planning process were important, of course, but sharp focus on the customer, the hallmark of the marketing concept, gave way to a broader focus on the firm's total environment; an environment that included but did not accord the customer more importance than competitors or broad economic, social, political, and technological trends. Strategy was formulated in new ways. Implementation of strategy, formulated by others, became the major role for marketing.

Today another shift is taking place. There is growing concern that lack of sharp customer focus is a serious deficiency of strategic planning. In some instances, strategic planning procedures have become bureaucratic to the point of stifling innovation. In others, the size of strategic planning staffs has become burdensome. Strategic planning, per se, is still important, but its new emphasis is on integration of market leadership with technological capability. Once again, marketing is the emphasis of management attention. This renewed emphasis, however, may be inappropriate without some thought as to the reasons for its decline in the 1970s.

WHERE MARKETING WENT WRONG

Despite all that has been written about the marketing concept, there is no simple definition that leads to easy understanding. For instance, many companies wanting to adopt the marketing concept confused marketing with advertising, and even in the 1980s were still learning that there is a difference.[5] Others simply equated annual sales forecasts with marketing planning.[6] Most important, however, many failed to recognize that simply satisfying customers' needs was not enough, and that the real requirement of the marketing concept was to provide the marketplace with a product of superior value.

In many instances, top management either did not understand what was required to become a marketing company, or failed to take appropriate action. Marketing in industrial firms, it has been asserted, failed to measure up to expectations "because management concentrated on the trappings of marketing rather than the substance."[8] That is, the emphasis was on speeches, new organizations, new administrative mechanisms, and increased marketing expenditures instead of on a fundamental shift in thinking throughout the company.

In other instances, however, those in marketing either failed to understand the requirements of the marketing concept or were unable to articulate an appropriate role for marketing in the organization. The "conspicuous decline in the role of the chief marketing executive since the late 1960s" was blamed on the old chief marketing executive's bull-in-the-china-shop style—using force as a weapon and unable to verbalize his logic.[9] As late as 1983, there was still the concern that the marketing profession had failed to penetrate corporate America and was unable to convince top management that sophisticated marketing techniques coupled with the latest marketing concepts and methods would enhance strategic business unit and corporate decisions.[10]

Much concern has been expressed about the relationship of marketing to innovation. The marketing concept, it is argued, has contributed to the death of true product innovation in North America. Contrast—said this view—marketing innovations such as new-fangled potato chips, feminine hygiene deodorants, and pet rocks, with technological developments such as the telephone, laser, and transistor.[11] In a similar vein, it is held that a marketing orientation has led us to new, improved lemon scents instead of technological innovation and market development.[12] And, where technological innovation is the name of the game, there is far more confidence in technological capability than in marketing capability.[13]

Of increasing concern have been the successes of the European and the Japanese, suggesting that they are better at implementing the marketing concept than are its American inventors. According to one author, Americans could learn a lot from the Europeans about identifying niches, differentiating products or industries, as well as how to achieve better product durability and quality.[14] Kotler hailed the Japanese as "world champion marketers." They have, he says, an adroit sense of market segmentation and sequencing that is accompanied by market flexibility, and they are adept at using a multiplicity of competitive weapons—price, product quality, product features, service, distribution, promotion, and product-line stretching—with varying degrees of emphasis to penetrate and win markets. Their skills, presumably, are superior to those of U.S. marketers.[15]

Much has been written recently about the need for keeping "close to the customer." The notion is not new, however. In a 1980 speech, Lewis Young, then editor-in-chief of Business Week, asserted that "probably the most important management fundamental that is being ignored today is staying close to the customer, to satisfy his needs and anticipate his wants. In too many companies the customer has become a bloody nuisance."[16] In a similar vein, Delorean's description of General Motors, as an organization that believed there was no problem that could not be overcome by a good sales pitch—and that a hard sell would persuade customers to buy power boats in Death Valley—seemed to be the norm in many business enterprises.[17]

From a broader perspective there were other concerns. Certainly, among consumers there is no great enthusiasm for marketing—at least for marketing as they understand it, that is, as synonymous with advertising. In fact, in its efforts to provide relevant information to carefully selected market segments, marketing has succeeded in greatly irritating all the others for whom the message is not relevant, but who get it anyway.[18] The rise of consumerism, after 20 years of rhetoric about marketing and customer satisfaction, suggests that, in fact, not much true marketing was being practiced. As Peter Drucker put it, "Consumerism is the shame of marketing."[19]

This list of concerns, criticisms, and disappointments could be greatly expanded. In the final analysis, any judgement about the success or failure of the marketing concept will, inevitably, be a subjective one. For some firms, the marketing concept is well established, generally with superior results. For management that is disappointed with marketing results, however, the question is not so much "what is wrong with marketing?" as it is "why did it go wrong?" Hard evidence to answer this question is difficult to obtain. However, after reviewing criticisms of marketing and patterns of marketing success and analyzing the GE experience (see The Marketing Concept at General Electric), four principal reasons emerge:

- An assumption by those in marketing that marketing was the superior business function.
- An assumption by those in the rest of the organization that only those in marketing need be concerned with the customer.
- A failure to change principal measures of performance.
- A lack of top management commitment.

Marketing, the Superior Function: With the clarion call "the fundamental purpose of a business is to serve the wants and needs of the customer," and the subsequent establishment of marketing departments, it was easy for those in marketing to view themselves as something special. While it was not the intent at General Electric to give marketing people excessive clout, it was not difficult for them to interpret the company's 1952 annual report to mean that they were now in charge and could call the shots. To the extent that they did so because of some presumed higher authority—derived more from their new status as keeper of the company purpose than for their persuasive presentation of the customers' point of view—antagonisms were raised in the other functional departments. Energies that should have been devoted to serving the customer and gaining competitive advantage were squandered on Pyrrhic turf fights.

Turning the Customer Over to Marketing: The converse of marketing as a superior function occurred when marketing was seen to have sole responsibility for the customer interface, thus allowing those in engineering, finance, and manufacturing to "do their own thing," spared the inconvenience of having to respond to unreasonable (or so they were perceived) customer demands. Here conflict seldom occurred, not because the organization was debating how to serve the customer well, but because there was little communication between marketing and the other functional departments. Principal marketing activities were advertising and personal selling. What marketing research was conducted served primarily to find ways to enhance the persuasiveness of marketing communications.

Inappropriate Performance Measures: A third explanation of the failure to achieve a true marketing orientation lies in the performance measures used to evaluate managers. The emphasis of the marketing concept on satisfaction of customer wants and needs strongly suggests that a firm's performance in this dimension should be measured and that managers should be evaluated on their contribution to customer satisfaction as well as to profit. Few firms, however, attempt to measure customer satisfaction directly. For most firms, the sales billed, orders received, backorders, and market share are the key measurements of success. These are certainly important measures, but changes in the economy or competitive actions may influence them as much or more than customer satisfaction. Hence they do not unambiguously indicate how well the firm is meeting its standards for customer satisfaction; nor do they suggest the nature of corrective action when results are below expectations.

Lack of Top Management Commitment: Finally, a marketing orientation is unlikely without broad acceptance of the most profound aspect of the marketing concept—that profit, or achievement of other similar internally focused objectives, is the derivative of customer satisfaction; not vice versa. For most managers steeped in profit-focused measurement systems, making the transition to putting customer satisfaction ahead of profit is difficult, to say the least. Customer satisfaction is a nebulous concept compared to the normal measure of managerial performance. Hard evidence that unswerving commitment to delivery of specified levels of customer satisfaction pays off in profits is difficult to obtain (although studies using the PIMS database indicate that quality, as perceived by the customer, is strongly and positively correlated with return on investment).[20]

To a large degree, therefore, the marketing concept is an act of faith. Hence, it is not enough to create a marketing department or appoint a marketing vice president. Embrace of the marketing concept requires conversion to a new faith, a faith that puts commitment to customer satisfaction equal to or ahead of profits, that requires definition of customer satisfaction in customer terms, not the firm's, and that requires fundamental changes in values and beliefs throughout the organization. The responsibility for shaping these values and beliefs rests with top management. It cannot be delegated.

ON BECOMING A TRUE MARKETING ORGANIZATION

The foremost lesson to be learned from disappointments with marketing is that the marketing concept is too important to be delegated solely to the marketing department. Certain activities, of course, are logically assigned to the marketing department; sales, advertising, and market research are the obvious ones. In many organizations, such activities as physical distribution and after-sales service are also functions of the marketing department. But the marketing concept—the notion that the firm as its primary purpose is the satisfaction of customer wants and needs—is the responsibility of top management. If this philosophy is to become ingrained in the beliefs and values of the organization, top management must define it in organizationally relevant terms and must constantly reiterate and reinforce it.

DEFINING ORGANIZATIONAL PURPOSE

Kenosuke Matsushita, founder of Matsushita Electric, the Japanese consumer electronic giant, describes his business philosophy—his view of the relationship between purpose and profit—this way: "The purpose of an enterprise," he says, "is to contribute to society by supplying goods of high quality at low prices in ample quantity. Profit comes in contribution to society." "Thus," he goes on to say, "profit is a result rather than a goal. An enterprise in the red will make all cooperating people and, ultimately, the whole society poor. If the enterprise tries to earn a reasonable profit but fails to do so, it is because the degree of its social contribution is still unsufficient."[21] This idea articulated again and again by Matsushita at countless meetings with managers and employees alike, now permeates the organization and conditions the behavior of everyone in it.

The same idea is expressed somewhat differently by Renn Zaphiropoulos, president and one of the founders of Versatec, Inc., the world's largest manufacturer of electrostatic printers and plotters. He prefaces his business philosophy by saying: "The only way you can succeed in a business is to satisfy need at a profit. If you satisfy a need at no profit, that's philanthropy. It you satisfy no need at a profit, then you're a crook."[22]

This idea, articulated by Zaphiropoulos in every employee orientation meeting and in hundreds of informal interactions with members of the organization, conditions the behavior at Versatec and is the foundation on which that company's marketing orientation is built.

But for top management, the responsibility for the marketing concept does not end with an expression of a business philosophy. The organization also needs to know the dimensions of customer satisfaction and the strength of commitment to its delivery.

DEFINING CUSTOMER SATISFACTION

It may be trite to say that no one can be all things to all people. But if "satisfaction guaranteed" is to be more than an advertising slogan, then customer satisfaction needs to be defined in specific and precise terms—terms that can guide it will compete and, ultimately, provide the basis on which it can be measured.

The marketing department can provide the information about opportunities that exist in the marketplace, but top management must decide which ones are key to a firm's success and how they will be measured. For Matsushita Electric, it is, above all else, quality, and low price. For Versatec, it is, above all else, flexibility of product features to meet a wide range of applications. At GE's Meter Department it is, above all else, customer service, with 22 specific measurable areas of performance, including deliveries from stock, shipping promises met on nonstock items, and after-sales service. Challenging quantitative performance levels are established for each area. Performance is measured monthly and reviewed by all the functional managers and the general manager. Areas of performance and target levels of performance are reviewed frequently.

The nature of the customer satisfaction opportunity, then, is identified by the marketing department. Top management, however, decides its final dimensions in the context of the firm's overall strategy. Once defined, the critical task is to ensure commitment to specified levels of customer satisfaction.

ENSURING COMMITMENT TO CUSTOMER SATISFACTION

In some organizations the commitment to customer satisfaction is so much a part of corporate culture that its delivery is built into the organization's reflexes. At UPS, for example, a few days before Christmas in 1982, its Chicago office received a call from a railroad official confessing that a flatcar with two UPS trailers had unaccountably been left on a siding in the middle of Illinois. The UPS regional manager paid for a high-speed diesel to get the flatcar into Chicago, and ordered two 727 jets from the UPS fleet diverted to Chicago, in order to get the trailer contents to Florida and Louisiana in time for Christmas. Interestingly, despite the high cost involved, the regional manager neither asked permission nor informed headquarters of his action.[23]

The UPS example may be an extreme case of reflexive response to customer needs and commitment to customer satisfaction. Some organizations may be reluctant to delegate as much authority as apparently exists at UPS in order to provide customer satisfaction. For most firms, however, the question is not one of overacting to customer needs. Rather, the challenge is to develop a pervasive sense that responding to customers' needs is imperative.

In small organizations such as UPS and Versatec, the dimensions of customer satisfaction and management's level of commitment to it are easily communicated and reinforced through informal discussions, the nature of the reward system, and a visible pattern of management decisions. This level of commitment, built into the corporate culture when the firm is small, cannot be taken for granted as the firm grows.

It is not taken for granted, for instance, at Matsushita Electric, which has constantly emphasized its basic values since the founding of the firm. Discussions at monthly and annual meetings and daily recitation of these values by all employees have created and reinforced a belief system for the thousands of people who work for the company. This philosophy, "a human value beyond profit, to which their productive lives are dedicated," provides a basis of meaning beyond the products they produce. Translated into marketing terms, initial and ongoing training emphasizes that what counts at Matsushita is knowing the customer and getting marketable products to the point of sale at minimum cost.[24]

Nor is it taken for granted at IBM, where customer service is a key corporate commitment. Customer satisfaction surveys, at both corporate and division levels, are taken as often as once a month. These surveys determine how customers view IBM as a company with which to do business: how satisfied its customers are with the company's marketing approach; how satisfied they are with the product itself, in terms of both quality and reliability; and how satisfied they are with service support in terms of quality and timeliness. The results of the surveys are widely disseminated and are used to measure the effectiveness of the company's constant efforts to improve customer satisfaction on an overall basis and to guide focused actions in areas that need immediate attention.[25]

Many firms, however, may have no long tradition of defining and delivering customer satisfaction. In others, early traditions may have become lost due to management preoccupation with other aspects of the business. This was the situation in 1977 at Kentucky Fried Chicken (KFC). After years of enviable growth in sales and earnings, the situation turned sour. Sales per store fell as customers were turned off by poor quality and service. Earnings were further eroded by low productivity. Faced with this situation, KFC launched what turned out to be an enormously successful turnaround strategy. Definition and measurement of a number of elements of customer satisfaction were integral to this strategy. A mystery shopper visited each store monthly and rated the store on various measures of quality, service, and cleanliness (including such fine points as the temperature of the chicken at the time of service). Each quarter the monthly scores were averaged. Store managers had to achieve a minimum average level of customer satisfaction for the quarter before becoming eligible for incentive compensation. Although performance has improved dramatically since 1977, measurement of customer satisfaction is still an integral part of the company's evaluation system. According to Dick Mayer, chairman and CEO of KFC, measurement of customer satisfaction and its impact on incentive compensation continues to positively motivate the entire organization. In an environment of high employee turnover, measurement of customer satisfaction is a powerful tool to indoctrinate new employees. In 1985, KFC tested a "quality hot line" as another way of measuring its delivery of customer satisfaction.[26]

MARKETING WITH A SMALL "m"

If the commitment to customer satisfaction is clear, and if its dimensions are well spelled out, top management still needs, as Levitt says, to "push the marketing concept into every nook and cranny of the organization."[27] Even if the corporate culture and reward systems encourage customer satisfaction, there is still the problem of ensuring that everyone, not just a select few, has the right reflexes.

As previously noted, the marketing department often makes it possible for others in an organization to pursue their interest, unencumbered by customer demands. In this vein, one top executive recently said, more than a little seriously, "Perhaps we should do away with the marketing department. It would send a powerful message to the rest of the organization that the customer is everyone's responsibility."

In a less extreme vein, at General Electric, where top management now is calling for a marketing renaissance, and where marketing has become a strategic thrust for the consumer products sector, Paul Van Orden, sector executive, says, "It's essential to note that when I say marketing I do not mean marketing with a capital 'M,' I mean marketing as a focus—a rigorous external focus on the marketplace by the *entire organization* [emphasis added]. This means that the enterprise must continually strive to better understand customers, then respond with innovative products and services that provide solutions relevant to their problems."[28] At the company's Video Products Division this new emphasis has, among other things, put video design engineers in direct contact with consumers (a practice that has long been standard for most Japanese consumer electronics manufacturers). As Jacques Robinson, vice president and general manager of the division, says, "Engineers working at the drawing board are getting their directions from customers. The whole business is oriented toward bringing technology and consumer demands together."[29]

ROLE OF THE MARKETING DEPARTMENT

While it is up to top management to articulate the idea of marketing with a small "m," those in the marketing department will play the pivotal role in making the idea work. They will, of course, have to continue to be proficient in various forms of promotion and marketing research. They will also have to deal with top management's concerns, which include the perception that marketing managers are not sufficiently entrepreneurial and are generally financially unsophisticated.[30] But this will not be enough. Those in marketing will also have to recognize that a marketing renaissance does not mean that those in marketing are, in some magical way, once more elevated to the top of the organizational hierarchy. It means that they must rely on skilled communication—as skillful as that used to communicate with customers—to represent customers' wants and needs to others in the organization, and to constantly reinforce the importance of the basic commitment to customer satisfaction. It also means that those in marketing will have to recognize that they are not solely responsible for customer contact. In the truly outstanding marketing organization, the customer does not belong exclusively to the marketing department. Design engineers and manufacturing and finance people are all extensively involved with customers, both in the field and in customer factory visits. Not only is the importance of nonmarketing involvement with customers recognized and encouraged, but those in marketing look for and identify heroes in other parts of the organization; heroes who then get credit for their contributions to sales breakthroughs, new product successes, and other achievements, normally credited to the marketing department alone.

CONCLUSION

As *Business Week* suggested, we are living in an era when business seems to be preoccupied with the fad of the moment. For many firms, the renewed interest in marketing may stem more from their hope that the marketing department will provide a quick fix for current and pressing sales problems, than from an appreciation of the marketing concept as a fundamental, and very different, business philosophy.

Implementing this philosophy is difficult. It is inextricably interwined with corporate culture, which cannot be changed overnight. Putting the customer and customer satisfaction ahead of profit will involve some risk, at least for short-term results. The experience of firms such as General Electric, Pillsbury, Matsushita, Versatec, UPS, Kentucky Fried Chicken, IBM, and many others, however, is evidence that adopting the marketing concept is feasible and that focus on customer satisfaction as the primary organizational goal has great potential for long-term rewards.

In the 1980s we have the opportunity to learn from the past and to take a new approach to marketing; one in which top management assumes the responsibility for establishing the marketing concept as its pervasive business philosophy; one in which the marketing department shares its responsibility for the customer with the rest of the organization; and one that establishes carefully designed measures of customer satisfaction, which are as important as the more traditional measure of return on sales and investment.

Table 1.
The Marketing Concept at General Electric

Marketing at General Electric, 1944-1982

General Electric is widely credited with pioneering the marketing concept in the United States in the early 1950s. As with Mitsui, International Harvester, Sears Roebuck, and others, signs of marketing at General Electric were manifested much earlier. Owen D. Young, the company's chairman from 1922 to 1940, certainly captured the spirit of customer orientation when he told employees that if they felt grumpy they should blow up a GE plant rather than bark at a customer. "We can rebuild a plant," he said, "but we can never get back the lost goodwill."[1]

More formally, marketing as a business philosophy emerged when a company committee on marketing was formed in 1944, and the marketing concept was introduced and tested at two subsidiary companies. By 1949 a marketing guide had been written, and in 1950 the first marketing vice president was appointed. During 1951 and 1952 a companywide implementation program was initiated to develop understanding and gain acceptance of the marketing concept.

As described in GE's 1952 Annual Report:

"In 1952 your Company's operating managers were presented with an advanced concept in marketing, formulated by the Marketing Services Division. This in simple terms would introduce the marketing man at the beginning rather than at the end of the production cycle and would integrate marketing at each phase of the business.

"Thus marketing through its studies and research, would establish for the engineer, and the manufacturing man what the customer wants in a given product, what price he is willing to pay, and where and when it would be wanted.

"Marketing would have the authority in product planning and production scheduling, inventory control, as well as the sales, distribution and servicing of the product. This concept it is believed will fix responsibility while making possible greater flexibility and closer teamwork in the marketing of the company's products."

During the rest of the 1950s, marketing continued to develop a strong hold on General Electric's management practices. Marketing was established as one of five natural business functions (in addition to engineering, manufacturing, finance, and employee community relations), and each of over 100 product departments or profit centers had its own marketing departments. In 1954, Fred Borch, later to become president of the company, was appointed vice president of marketing services, responsible for extensive consulting and marketing education activities. By 1960 marketing was well-established, not just on the organization charts, but as a mainstream legitimate business function with its own heroes, customs, and folklore.

Marketing as it developed and was practiced at General Electric has been widely chronicled in business and academic literature and in cases written for classroom teaching purposes. With few exceptions, the company's marketing practices received favorable attention. In a particularly glowing report, the November-December 1967 issue of *Marketing Forum* asserted that "General Electric is the complete marketing company. The marketing concept pervades the company from top to bottom. How they do their work and how they train their people rates study by all marketers."

Seemingly the 1960s should have been a decade in which the company reaped a reward for its commitment to marketing. And yet, in 1970 and 1971, GE's management described the decade as one of profitless growth and the job of marketing vice president was abolished.

For General Electric, as for many companies, the marketing concept held out more promise than it had delivered. While pockets of marketing excellence remained, strategic planning became the new intellectual force that guided the company's activities. Throughout the 1970s strategic planning flourished and, again, the company's practices were widely reported and generally praised in both academic and business literature. But in 1982, following significant reductions in strategic planning staffs and practices, a vice president of marketing was once again appointed. His major challenge: "Leading General Electric in a marketing renaissance."

1. Donald D. Holt, "The Hall of Fame of Business Leadership," *Fortune*, 23 March 1981, 110.

REFERENCES

1. Robert J. Keith, "The Marketing Revolution," *Journal of Marketing*, January 1960: 35-38.
2. D. Maynard Phelps and J. Howard Westing, *Marketing Management*, 3rd ed. (Homewood, Illinois: Irwin, 1968).
3. Philip Kotler, *Marketing Management: Analysis, Planning and Control*, 5th ed. (Englewood Cliffs, New Jersey: Prentice-Hall, 1974): 23-24.
4. Richard T. Hise, "Have Manufacturing Firms Adopted the Marketing Concept?" *Journal of Marketing*, July 1965: 9-12.
5. "Marketing: The New Priority," *Business Week*, 21 November 1983.
6. Philip Kotler, *Business Week*, 28 July 1975.
7. Roger C. Bennett and Robert G. Cooper, "The Misuse of Marketing: An American Tragedy," *Business Horizons*, November-December 1981: 51-61.
8. B. Charles Ames, "Trappings vs. Substance in Industrial Marketing," *Harvard Business Review*, July-August 1970: 93-102.
9. John A. Howard, *Marketing News*, 22 June 1984.
10. Yoram Wind, *Marketing News*, 16 August 1985.
11. Roger C. Bennett and Robert G. Cooper, "Beyond the Marketing Concept," *Business Horizons*, June 1975: 76-83.
12. Robert H. Hayes and William J. Abernathy, "Managing Our Way to Economic Decline," *Harvard Business Review*, July-August 1980: 67-77.
13. John F. Welch, Jr., "Where Is Marketing Now That We Really Need It?" Presentation to the Marketing Conference of the Conference Board, New York, 28 October 1981.
14. Ralph Z. Sorenson, II, "U.S. Marketers Can Learn From European Innovators," *Harvard Business Review*, September-October 1972: 113-23.
15. Philip Kotler and Liam Fahey, "The World's Champion Marketers: The Japanese," *Journal of Business Strategy*,: 3-13.
16. Quoted in Thomas J. Peters and Robert H. Waterman, Jr., *In Search of Excellence*, (New York: Harper & Row, 1982).
17. J. Patrick Wright, *On A Clear Day You Can See General Motors*, (New York: Avon Books, 1980): 164.
18. Theodore Levitt, *The Marketing Imagination*, (New York: Free Press, 1983).
19. Peter F. Drucker, *People and Performance*, (New York: Harper & Row, 1977): 91.
20. Robert D. Buzzell, "Product Quality," PIMSLETTER, no. 4, Strategic Planning Institute, 1978.
21. "Matsushita Electric," Harvard Business School Case Study, No. 9-481-146 (Boston: HBS Case Service, 1981): 14.
22. "Renn Zaphiropoulos," Harvard Business School Case Study, No. 9-480-044 (Boston: HBS Case Services, 1980): 2.

23. *Business Week*, 6 June 1893.
24. Richard Tanner Pascale and Anthony G. Athos, *The Art of Japanese Management*, (New York: Warner Books, 1982): 73.
25. Personal communication with Yupin Wang, IBM, 22 February 1984.
26. Personal communication with Richard P. Mayer, KFC, 16 October 1984.
27. Theodore Levitt, "Marketing Myopia," *Harvard Business Review*, July-August 1960: 24-47.
28. *General Electric Monograph*, Summer 1983: 6.
29. "Listening to the Voice of the Marketplace," *Business Week*, 21 February 1983: 90.
30. Frederick E. Webster, Jr., "Top Management's Concerns About Marketing: Issues for the 1980s," *Journal of Marketing*, Summer 1981: 9-16.

H. Michael Hayes is professor of Marketing and Strategic Management and director of Graduate Programs at the University of Colorado at Denver.

Part V
TACTICAL
APPROACHES

29.
MANUFACTURING MARKET SHARE

W. J. Kaydos

The importance of manufacturing to achieving market share is not generally understood. Manufacturing capabilities can be a powerful weapon in the ever-present battle for market share. By understanding what the market wants and directing the manufacturing organization to maximize the related performance measures, a company's ability to market its products will be improved.

In the brief span of a decade or two, the Japanese have been able to dominate markets all over the world with a dazzling array of products. Although other factors are also involved, there is no question that manufacturing prowess has been critical to their success. Japanese firms obviously understand that the manufacturing end of a business can contribute more than simply meeting shipping deadlines and keeping costs within acceptable limits.

According to leading experts, reflecting on the role of manufacturing in the corporation:

"Unfortunately, manufacturing is the least understood among the functions governing business productivity . . . yet, without a strong and highly productive manufacturing base, companies will find it difficult to respond to, much less anticipate, changes in the marketplace."[1]

The Japanese know how to use manufacturing to enhance their marketing efforts by producing high-quality, competitively priced products and by responding to changing market conditions. The efficiency, versatility, and reliability of their production systems have enabled them to become leaders in certain product lines and to maintain this position by continually introducing new products to the marketplace.

But Japanese companies aren't the only ones that understand the importance of a strong and productive manufacturing base. Many American companies do, too, and they tend to be quite successful even in a weak economy. These firms can be found in many industries and competitive markets.

A prime example of a thriving company in a severely depressed industry is Nucor Corporation, a well-known manufacturer of steel, steel joists, joist girders, steel deck, and other products. By using vertical integration, decentralized production facilities, and an innovative compensation system, Nucor is able to produce quality products at prices below those of foreign competitors. In addition, its flexibility and responsiveness to its customers' needs have enabled it to continually improve its market share and operate quite profitably in spite of the current economic recession.

Other examples can be found in such corporate giants as Kodak and IBM. Surely, technological innovation and well-developed marketing skills have contributed significantly to their success; but without a responsive manufacturing system could IBM have entered the personal computer market so quickly and with such success? Would Kodak's reputation for quality and consistency in its photographic products be possible without a well-developed manufacturing capability?

Although it may be argued that larger firms play in a different field, a recent survey of companies in the $5-$50 million range indicates that manufacturing capability is at least as important to them as to their bigger brothers. Consider the following examples:

- A small apparel manufacturer lost a large portion of its sales because its customers went out of business. The flexibility of its production system enabled the company to enter new markets, and it purposely became more responsive to market fashion trends, enabling it to recoup most of the lost sales within a year.
- Another apparel firm has seen its customers lost to foreign producers. Since it cannot compete on the basis of price or quality, it sees as a viable strategy becoming more efficient at producing smaller lots, increasing its profit margin by charging higher prices for this specialized service.
- A manufacturer of Christmas ornaments has prospered by continuously introducing new products that are superior in terms of quality and cost relative to the competition. This has been accomplished by custom designing its production machinery, adapting processes from other industries. The policy of its president is that marketing will never by constrained by manufacturing.
- A producer of stamping dies installed a scheduling system that reduced its order lead-time from six to two months. Besides significant inventory reductions, the competitive edge of the reduced lead-time resulted in rapid expansion of its market share.
- A manufacturer of valves entered a market dominated by more than 100 competitors that had well-established positions. By making some design improvements and vertically integrating production to give rapid response to customers' needs, it has acquired a significant portion of the market in a few years and expects this trend to continue.

This is not to say that cost is not important, because in most cases, the respondents indicated that other factors being equal, cost would become the deciding factor, given a large enough differential. However, not one of the companies viewed itself as the low-price leader in any market segment.

If manufacturing capabilities can be so important to increasing market share, and if cost is not necessarily the most important factor, why is so much attention typically given to manufacturing costs and relatively so little to other factors? Perhaps it is because costs are easier to measure than other factors and can be handled on an income statement. Or it may be that sufficient consideration is not given to the possibility that other performance measures may be more important than cost. Indeed, the competitive strategies used by the more successful companies seem to have evolved more out of a general awareness of the marketplace and an intention to build a better mousetrap rather than a formalized strategy. Most of the CEOs interviewed had a very clear picture of what made their company successful but had to reflect on the relative importance of manufacturing performance measures. One stated: "I don't think I've ever been asked to rank these factors before, but now that you ask, quality and availability are much more important than cost to our customers. We have just always operated this way because we knew what our customers needed and wanted."

IMPROVING MANUFACTURING IMPORTANCE

From this survey, it is reasonable to conclude that for a large number of businesses where manufacturing is a significant portion of the total operation, it is likely there are opportunities to effect changes in the manufacturing system which would enhance the marketing of their products. A company seeking to increase its share of the market should identify the desires of its present and potential customers to determine if there are areas where improvements in manufacturing performance can increase the perceived value of the firm's products. Characteristics such as order lead-time, on-time delivery, availability, customizing capability, quality, consistency, cost, and ability to respond to changing market needs are some possibilities for gaining a competitive edge. Market research can assist in clarifying these issues if they are not presently known. After the product and service characteristics that will facilitate marketing efforts have been identified, the next step is to modify the manufacturing system to improve those factors.

A manufacturing system can be viewed as a physical system of machines and processes which creates the products and a management system that controls and allocates resources to the physical system. The management system in turn, consists of three elements:

- The management information, or reporting system;
- The operations management, or resource allocations system; and
- The human, or acting system.

When manufacturing operations are viewed as a set of four subsystems that interact and overlap, it becomes clear that desired improvements to performance will involve more than short-term development programs.

Changing one component may necessitate changes throughout the system, but this shouldn't be interpreted as meaning that the entire manufacturing system needs to be turned inside-out to achieve beneficial results. On the contrary, significant improvements can frequently be achieved by modifying the management system without materially affecting the production process. For example, the stamping die manufacturer achieved remarkable results by changing the shop scheduling system. In my experience, simply defining accountability for the key performance measures and related causal factors can produce remarkable results if consistent measurement and feedback takes place.

A comprehensive analysis of manufacturing operations and the management system will identify those areas that are likely candidates for improvement. But to be effective, the analysis must objectively look at the production, management information, operations management, and human systems simultaneously and consider their interactions with each other and the external environment. This exercise is both time-consuming and demanding, but will generate options for improvement which would not be recognized by other means.

A good example of what can be discovered is illustrated by a manufacturer of components for the HVAC industry that had consistent delivery problems. Although it was largely presumed that the inventory control system was at fault, a detailed analysis clearly demonstrated that production and purchasing problems were the real issue and that an effective scheduling and control mechanism was needed.

Regardless of how the desired results are obtained, it is clear from this survey that manufacturing capabilities can be a powerful weapon in the ever-present battle for market share. By understanding what the market wants and directing the manufacturing organizations to maximize the related performance measures, a company's ability to market its products will be improved. Although cost is often the primary consideration in manufacturing, it is well-evidenced by this survey that other factors, such as quality, often are more important than cost. By focusing too heavily on cost at the expense of other issues, opportunities for increasing sales are probably being missed by many firms. Modifying the management system to improve the critical performance factors of manufacturing can often produce positive benefits without altering the production process. A comprehensive and objective analysis of the productions and management systems will usually uncover opportunities that would not be recognized in the normal course of business.

One final note became quite apparent to me in the course of the survey: The somewhat old-fashioned virtue of providing value to the customer has considerable merit. Knowing what your customer wants and being better than anyone else at giving it to him is still an important factor to business success.

W. J. Kaydos is a consultant in operations and manufacturing management.

30.
IF AT FIRST YOU DON'T SUCCEED, REMARKET

Michael Gershman

> Many products that eventually became household names originally ex-
> perienced tough sledding in the marketplace. Partial failures can become
> successes with some tinkering—that's what remarketing is all about.
> These successful strategies are used by marketers to reposition products
> and make them thrive.

Marlboro cigarettes were born with red and white "beauty tip" filters to
tempt women, Philip Morris's target audience in the 1920s: They bombed.

John H. Patterson, hailed internationally as a pioneer in selling and sales
training, introduced NCR cash registers with the first large-scale direct-mail
campaign; it earned a catastrophic .00007-percent response.

Smirnoff vodka, "the drink of Tsars," came to America with a 100-year
history as a favorite throughout Europe; after 21 years of abject failure here, it
became partially successful only briefly—when it was mislabeled as whiskey.

Because these products are so firmly entrenched in our homes and in our
minds, we tend to think of them as Immaculate Conceptions—products that
were successful immediately—such as the likes of Bic pens, Kodak cameras,
and Reynolds Wrap aluminum foil.

Nothing could be further from the truth.

These products and dozens of other household names—Buster Brown shoes
and Borden's milk, Kotex napkins and Kleenex tissues, Timex watches and
Tupperware—are really Second Comings, products that were (to be kind) less
than successful at the outset and needed imaginative remarketing to overcome
resistance with both consumers and retailers.

Whole categories like low-calorie beer and ballpoint pens were marketing
disaster areas until manufacturers found ways to "accentuate the positive" in
their remarketing campaigns. Lite Beer managed to reposition diet beer by
having former athletes endorse it in the context of "beery environments,"
humorously making the point that regular guys like Boog Powell and Dick
Butkus drank low-calorie beer. Patrick Frawley Jr., the genius behind Paper

Mate, made everyone forget how ballpoint pens had smudged their jackets, slacks, and dresses by getting a less-known group of celebrity endorsers—school principals and bank presidents—to praise the wonders of the Paper Mate.

More recently, Yoplait and Post-it Notes have overcome disastrous introductions with packaging expertise and product demonstrations. Dow Chemical Co. has revitalized Saran Wrap's slumping market share by touting the fact that, unlike other plastic wraps, it can be used in microwave ovens. Johnson & Johnson has overcome the damaging effects of two nearly catastrophic Tylenol scares by repackaging its pain reliever as a combination capsule and tablet it calls a caplet.

Of course, not every remarketing effort has been successful. Procter & Gamble is still trying to make Jif peanut butter a leader after 25 years and has made four separate and thus far unsuccessful attempts to remarket Pringle's potato chips at a reputed cost of more than $100 million. Similarly, in 1977, Schlitz executives tried to remarket their beer by substituting cheap corn syrup for costly malt and putting all their "Gusto" into advertising, with disastrous results.

There are also limits to what even successful remarketing campaigns can do. In many cases, changing the product, the package, the price, the point-of-sale or the promotion or all of the above can give a product a temporary lift, but it can't hide basic flaws.

Consider three airlines that remarketed themselves in the 1970s. Quantas, BOAC, and Braniff. Commercials featuring a koala bear changed the perception of Quantas from no-name airline to major carrier. Similarly, using twinky-eyed actor Robert Morely transformed stuffy BOAC into "fun" British Airways. On the other hand, however, the remarketing pizzazz Mary Wells Lawrence and Wells/Rich/Greene brought to Braniff (Pucci uniforms for flight attendants and planes painted by artist Alexander Calder) couldn't solve underlying basic management, personnel, and finance problems which eventually forced the airline into bankruptcy.

And remember Corfam? This synthetic material was created in the 1950s by Du Pont and appeared to have the potential of other Du Pont innovations like nylon, Teflon, and Mylar. With leather prices rising, the company decided to make Corfam into nonstretching shoes and produced several thousand pairs for employees and consumers to test. Even though both groups complained that the shoes were hot and uncomfortable, Du Pont targeted upscale audiences for Corfam shoes, running full-page, four-color ads in *Vogue, Harper's Bazaar, The New Yorker, and Esquire.*

Unfortunately for Du Pont, consumers had become accustomed to shoes that stretched; those that didn't were perceived as being †tight fitting'—even if they fit perfectly. After thinking things over, Du Pont decided to remarket Corfam by urging consumers to buy slightly larger sizes. In *Management Mistakes*, Robert Hartley says, "This idea met the irrational psychological fact that few people wanted to admit having bigger feet." Seven years and $150 million worth of Du Pont losses later, Corfam was eventually sold to the Polish government. (Remarketed as cheap footwear for working men, it sold like hotcakes, so well in fact that it was eventually imported into the United States.)

WIDE APPLICABILITY

For every failure that can be laid at the door of remarketing, there are many more successes because of its applicability to a wide variety of situations. It's relevant to:

Every part of the marketing process. Remarketing success stories abound in design (Cuisinart), packaging (Yoplait), promotion (Buster Brown), positioning (Wheaties), distribution (Life Savers), point-of-sale materials (Timex), etc.

A wide variety of industries. Such campaigns have been successful in soft drinks (Pepsi-Cola), soft dolls (Cabbage Patch Kids), soft soap (Softsoap), hard liquor (Smirnoff), hard candy (Life Savers), and hardware (NCR cash registers).

Old products as well as new ones. Forty-six years after its introduction as a kid's shampoo, Johnson & Johnson's Baby Shampoo became a hit with adults as the result of a remarketing program. Similarly, Alka-Seltzer nearly doubled its sales by replacing the old familiar glass tube with foil packs containing two tablets, urging consumers to use two at a time with its "Plop plop fizz fizz" campaign.

Worldwide marketing. Tang failed when introduced in Germany, because it means "seaweed" in Germany. Remarketed as Seefrisch ("sea-Fresh"), it became a roaring success. Similarly, Coca-Cola's initial efforts to market Coke in China produced a set of characters that meant "bite the wax tadpole." It's sold a lot better since with a new set that means "happiness in the mouth."

As with Coca-Cola's initial failure in China, many products that fail when first introduced in a specific market are not mistakes on the level of Corfam; they're only partial failures and can still become successful with a little tinkering. That's what remarketing is all about, although I first heard the term used in a different context. I interviewed Moreton Binn, the self-styled "Baron of Barter" for a book called *Smarter Barter.* Describing what he did to make a living, Binn said, "We're in the remarketing business, when products fail, for whatever reason, we remarket them."

He meant that he could salvage part of a manufacturer's investment by selling precisely the same product (same package, same everything) in different marketing arenas, such as: supermarkets in foreign countries; company stores owned by American corporations; U.S. Armed Forces PX's; direct sales through TV telemarketing campaign; and the premium and incentive market.

For example, Binn took unsold $1,000 Leica cameras and discounted them to a New York City bank which used them as premiums to attract new depositors. In another case he took lawn mowers and traded them for broadcast advertising time; several radio stations got the mowers and gave them away as prizes, the manufacturer got radio time to push a different product, and Binn got his commission; everybody won.

This kind of remarketing may be the only way to get some return of investment from discontinued lines or obsolete merchandise; however, from the manufacturer's standpoint, such a policy means writing off a considerable investment in R&D, consumer research, raw materials, labor, production, sales training promotion, and distribution.

DUMPING IS NOT REMARKETING

Dumping a product is the very opposite of remarketing, which is a way of reviving it, giving it a second chance, a second life, in football terminology, making a second effort. The actual nuts-and-bolts process could be defined this way: *The original marketing plan the knowledge gained from actual experience in the marketplace the basis for a remarketing campaign.*

Remarketing involves a step-by-step review of every component in the marketing process, including:

the basic idea behind the product;
its target market and supportive research;
the pricing and packaging philosophy behind it;
the product's positioning in a given category;
its distribution pattern;
the promotion and advertising surrounding it.

That's the hard part—finding the flaws. You can't cure the patient, eliminate the mysterious rattle in the back seat, or find the murderer without the correct analysis. Using Corfam as an example, consumers told Du Pont what was wrong with the product; the company just didn't act on the evidence and, consequently, didn't solve this remarketing problem.

This sounds like a very logical approach to marketing consumer products—which can appear, at least, to be a very illogical business. Marketing is a very rational process, but there is a tendency to confuse the irrationality of sales appeals with the rationality of marketing. For instance, Michelin recently ran a series of TV commercials which exclusively feature babies and tires. Was this a rational campaign? Absolutely. It took advantage of parent's natural concern for child safety in automobiles and women's growing decision-making interest in and financial impact on replacement purchases and came up with a sales appeal no tire company had used before. The appeal may have been emotional, but using it in marketing Michelins was supremely logical.

MID-COURSE CORRECTIONS

Remarketing, then, is a rational process which re-examines the key decisions made in launching a product, identifying and correcting the mistakes made, and aggressively relaunching the product. From a managerial standpoint, such mid-course marketing corrections involve bruising egos, affecting morale adversely, and possibly even damaging careers. Yet, even factoring in this human element leaves manufacturers of new products or providers of new services with only two choices: They can settle for a minor return on what may have been a major investment in money, time, and effort simply by disposing of their inventory through a barter company—getting a little something instead of nothing—or, they can risk more time, effort, and money and try to remarket the product.

That's not the gamble it appears to be for four very good reasons. Remarketing, among other things:

1. Protects often substantial investments already made in time, market research, trademark searches, and test marketing;
2. Requires less time for internal sales training and motivational efforts than marketing totally new products;
3. Creates less confusion for distributors and retailers, and,
4. Is *a whole lot cheaper than starting all over again.*

Consider two real-life examples from the disposable paper business—ScotTowels and Kleenex. Scott Paper Co. was established in the toilet paper business when Arthur Scott, the son of the company's co-founder, received a shipment of paper too wrinkled to be converted into its primary product. Coincidentally, he read a newspaper article about a Philadelphia schoolteacher who had lowered absenteeism because of student illnesses by replacing the cloth towel her pupils had previously shared with simple cut-up squares of paper.

Scott turned his unsaleable toilet paper into paper towels and was immediately successful in the industrial world, selling to plants and factories; however, initial sales to consumers were disappointing. Housewives thought the price (200 sheets for 25 cents) was too high by 1907 standards, and grocers considered the unproven product "avant garde," according to company documents. Angered at the retailers' reaction, Arthur Scott lowered the price and decided to sell his paper towels without them—door-to-door and by mail order. When a handful of female demonstrators were able to show housewives how useful the towels could be, ScotTowels quickly caught on with a minimal investment and became a household name.

Similarly, in 1930, Kimberly-Clark discovered the right sales approach for Kleenex at a cost of $650. Transformed from filter material for World War I gas masks into disposable "cold cream towels," Kleenex originally traded on the public's fascination with Hollywood glamor by posing movie stars with the product. Sales were "encouraging, but by no means sensational," according to company literature. On the other hand, Kimberly-Clark kept receiving letters from consumers who said they had a more practical use for Kleenex—blowing their noses.

Ultimately, the company decided to test which of the two appeals was more popular by using a split-run copy test. Kimberly-Clark ran ads in two newspapers in Peoria, Illinois of identical size and layout, each offering a free box of Kleenex. One headline stated, "We pay to prove there is no way like Kleenex to remove cold cream." The other said, "We pay to prove Kleenex is wonderful for handkerchiefs."

When a decisive 61 percent of the readers said they were using Kleenex as handkerchiefs, advertising was changed to "Don't put a cold in your pocket," and sales doubled the first year.

Even though it affects diverse areas like product size, package shape, pricing, and promotional activities, remarketing seems to boil down to even simpler matters like addition, subtraction, and substitution. Companies with failed product introductions should ask, "What should we add? What should we dump? What should we change?" Kleenex substituted a new primary sales appeal, embodied it in a copy line, and increased sales dramatically. Scott temporarily substituted a different method of distribution for ScotTowels until it could show hard evidence of consumer demand to retailers.

Making a small addition or subtraction can be just as spectacular a remarketing ploy. Joshua Lionel Cowen, the creator of Lionel Trains, invented an "electric flowerpot" and originally intended to sell it as a novelty for florists. Restaurant-owner Conrad Hubert bought it, discarded the flowerpot, and turned the remaining bulb-and-battery into something he called the Eveready flashlight.

Similarly, the Peter Paul company had tried to sell milk chocolate-covered coconut candy bar for 14 years without success. Even worse, its Dream Bar was almost exactly the same product as the company's dark chocolate covered Mounds bar. Then a marketing manager suggested adding whole almonds to change the bar's taste and look: The new ingredients differentiated the product from Mounds and, as Almond Joy, it quickly became a success.

Naturally, not all products can be revived by such simple adding, subtracting, and substituting. The remarketing saga of one product— Pepsi-Cola—involved all of the above, began before Franklin D. Roosevelt took office, and continues today. In 1931, Pepsi was reeling from its third bankruptcy in the space of eight years. By 1987, after changes in flavor, packaging innovations, promotional wizardry, and repositioning, Pepsi had become a corporation with annual sales of $6 billion and led all colas in U.S. supermarket sales.

It was created in 1893 by North Carolina pharmacist Caleb Bradham as a cure for dyspepsia and prospered steadily until Bradham got whipsawed in the commodity crunch in 1920; when sugar he had bought at 22 1/2 cents a pound in May was worth just 3 1/2 cents in December, he declared bankruptcy on March 2, 1923. Bradham sold Pepsi-Cola Corp. to Wall Street financier Roy C. Megargel. It went bankrupt again in 1925 and filed a third petition of bankruptcy on May 18, 1931.

The very next day, a shrewd entrepreneur named Charles Guth decided to buy Pepsi—out of spite.

Guth had gained control of the Loft's Candy Store chain in 1930 and had immediately noticed that Loft's was selling lots of Coca-Cola at its 115 soda fountains—31,000 gallons of Coca-Cola syrup in 1930 alone. He felt entitled to buy at the wholesaler's price, but Coca-Cola turned him down in a series of increasingly bitter meetings. Enraged, Guth inquired about doing business with Pepsi, discovered the company's abject financial condition, and agreed to loan Megargel $10,500 to buy its assets at a bankruptcy sale.

Loft's replaced Coke with Pepsi at all its outlets, but Pepsi's financial fortunes didn't improve; from 1931 to 1933 Pepsi sold only $100,000 worth of syrup, nearly all of it to Loft's. Sales were so poor that Guth even offered to sell out to Coke at one point; his offer was firmly declined.

Since he couldn't sell the company, Guth searched for a way to differentiate Pepsi from Coke and the other colas. On the theory that bigger was better, he bottled it in used 12-ounce beer bottles as opposed to Coke's six and a half ounces, and sold the bigger Pepsi for the same dime that Coke charged. When that didn't work, he made the decision most responsible for making Pepsi a viable soft-drink company: Taking advantage of Depression-era economics, be based his entire remarketing strategy on price and began selling 12 ounces of Pepsi for a nickel.

As of September 1933, Pepsi drinkers began getting nearly twice as much soda for their money as Coke drinkers did. Consumers immediately began buying Pepsi in unprecedented numbers, and Guth bought 91 percent of the stock as sales doubled in 1934 and doubled again in 1935. By 1936, Pepsi was showing a $2-million profit, and things looked rosy for Guth. As it turned out, however, he had bought stock with money "borrowed" from Loft's and was eventually ousted in a stockholder's suit by Walter Mack.

Even though Pepsi had become profitable, it still could not match Coke's advertising reach or the other leading soft drinks: Mack's 1939 ad budget was $600,000, while Coke's was 10 times that amount. What tipped the scales that September and finally made Pepsi a power in beverages was a jingle which capsulized Guth's remarketing strategy in a fresh new way. For $2,500, Mack bought an updated version of an English hunting song, *D'Ye Ken John Peel*; it became the most famous jingle in advertising history:

Pepsi-Cola hits the spot
Twelve full ounces, that's a lot
Twice as much for a nickel, too
Pepsi-Cola is the drink for you.

Two years later, the jingle had been broadcast an astounding 296,426 times in a number of versions. It was given a Latin beat for Hispanic audiences, a twang for country music fans, and Mack even aired it on New York's leading classical station. (It was played sedately on a solo celeste.) At the beginning of World War II, another catch advertising phrase, "More bounce to the ounce," gave Pepsi yet another image boost, and it finally passed Seven-Up, Royal Crown Cola, and Dr. Pepper to become second only to Coke in soft-drink sales.

From World War II to the present, the remarketing of Pepsi has continued with increased distribution, the momentum engendered by the Pepsi Generation campaigns of the 1960s, which repositioned Coke as "out of touch" and, most recently, the Pepsi Challenge. Nevertheless, it is clear that without the key moves made by Guth and Mack in pricing, packaging, and promotion in the 1930s, Pepsi could never have lasted into the 1980s.

Michael Gershman is a Westport, Connecticut-based freelance writer specializing in the field of marketing.

31.
TELEMARKETING: PUTTING BUSINESS ON THE LINE

Bernard R. Cohen

> Telephone sales are now being refined by modern marketing techniques and new call-management technologies to bring people together in new and efficient ways. Regardless of the transaction, information can be shared, problems can be prevented, responses can be given, and decisions can be made.

The technology of telephone marketing has come a long way. In 1956 Pan American World Airways had personnel sitting in front of telephones 24 hours a day to receive incoming telephone calls for consumer reservations. The unsophisticated universal call distributor which was used to assign the incoming calls to operators was large and cumbersome. To incorporate the benefits of hands-free operation, each sales agent used a bakelite mouthpiece attached to a heavy headset—noted for giving the wearer a headache.

In the 1960s and 1970s the telephone started to be used along with direct mail, catalogs, radio and television as an effective method to promote products and services. In 1969, the Sheraton Corp. became the first company to combine the Bell system's 800 number in a national campaign with direct mail.

Today, the telephone is being incorporated into marketing strategies. Advertisements with an 800 number pull 20% more than ones without. Automatic-call distributors are the easiest telephone equipment purchase to cost-justify. A modern automatic-call distributor improves the productivity of a phone answering force by 20% to 40%, cuts line costs by 10% and boosts customer purchases. Automatic-call distributors had been used only by airlines, rent-a-car companies, and hotels. Now they're for everyone because everyone takes orders on the phone and answers customer complaints or inquiries.

That's on an inbound basis. Outbound, there are automated-call management systems which can boost completed call rates by as much as 300% by keeping telephone communicators on the line all of the time. The systems automatically survey the prospect database and dial out. When a voice response is detected, the live call is forwarded to a communicator, eliminating wasted time. At the same time, the prospect's record is displayed for the representative, allowing immediate order entry and record keeping. "No answer" and "busy" calls are recycled for later attempts. By forwarding only answered calls to a live communicator these automated call management systems increase productivity. It's like having your prospects call in to the telemarketing center.

Improvements in technology, which translate into profitable strategies, have encouraged many insurance companies and agencies to use telemarketing extensively. Descriptions of the following telemarketing strategies are based on interviews conducted, of course, by telephone.

TARGET MARKETING

Lisa Fleischman, marketing director for Crowder Insurance of Tampa, Florida, described the agency's business prospecting center, a formalized system designed to accomplish three goals: (1) gather X-dates from target markets; (2) set appointments for the agency's producers, and (3) monitor the performance of producers.

A key to the success of the center is target marketing. First, the types of businesses which have the greatest potential are identified. This is done by consulting the underwriting manager or marketing manager of the various carriers the agency represents to determine the type of risk they wish to pursue. Once the target market has been established, the agency develops prospecting sources and experiments with three or four submissions to see if their recommendations are on target. The Crowder Agency's main prospecting source in Tampa is Contacts Influential. A secondary source, which is the next best source available, and which is available everywhere, is Dun & Bradstreet.

Next, target prospects are identified. A target prospect is defined as someone who meets fixed criteria, which include a minimum potential of $500 commission. Target prospects are then contacted to obtain their expiration dates. Due to both careful targeting and a carefully written phone tract which structures the telephone call, Crowder is obtaining expiration dates on virtually 100% of the people contracted. After the phone contact, a letter is sent to the prospect, thanking him for his time and telling him that the agency will get back to him at the appropriate time.

As the X-date approaches, a phone call confirms that the prospect still meets the criteria (about half the prospects are eliminated because of changed conditions, which are detected in this final screening). After this final exclusion, about 70% of the people contacted make appointments. A confirming letter from the business prospecting center indicates who the sales representative will be and reminds the prospect to have his insurance file available when the producer arrives.

The system itself is nothing magical. Crowder Insurance made a strong commitment to the concept of a business prospecting center and did what was necessary in its development and support.

QUALIFICATION PROGRAM

The concept of a telemarketing center at the agency level is strongly advocated by Continental Insurance. Walter Tarver, vice president of marketing for Continental, said that his company has gone one step further by offering a telemarketing program to qualified independent agencies.

The Tel Sel program was developed centrally, but is implemented locally by qualified agencies. The key to its success is the qualification of the agencies which ultimately use it. Continental's highest-volume agents were informed that Tel Sel was available to them. Their inquiry about the program becomes the first step in the screening process. After investigation to assure that Continental is able to offer competitive services and products which are appropriate for sale by telephone, Tel Sel personnel meet with the management team of the agency in an orientation session. They describe both the role of the telemarketing manager and telemarketing communicator training and what the two-day courses will cover. The training, conducted on the agent's premises, covers the basics of etiquette, selling skills on the telephone, and telemarketing applications training. The applications focused on are X-dating, with qualified prospects using a prepared script; renewals with existing customers, where less-structured call guides are used; and collecting over-time accounts, which also uses call guides.

INBOUND AND OUTBOUND MODES

Both Continental Insurance and the Crowder Insurance Agency emphasize the use of Telemarketing technology in the outbound mode. Montgomery Ward's direct marketing program for auto insurance incorporates the telephone in both an inbound mode for response and an outbound mode for follow up to qualified prospects and direct mail. Jill Meyer, assistant vice president-telemarketing, explained that the cornerstone of the operation includes the piloting or testing of all components from direct mail pieces to telephone communicator scripts. Also important are highly motivated and well-trained, licensed communicators, a list of qualified prospects, a willingness to quote and bind directly on the telephone and, of course, a highly competitive offer.

Montgomery Ward sends a direct-mail package which encourages phone calls on a toll-free "personal service" phone number. These packages are mailed to Montgomery Ward charge-card clients who reside in the states in which the company is licensed. People who respond either by mail or by telephone become qualified prospects.

The next step is the telephone. The idea is to provide a quote 15 to 45 days prior to the X-date of the prospect's current policy. Licensed communicators will calculate the quote and bind the contract directly on the telephone. There is no need for a signed application. The policy is mailed with the bill. It is honored when paid within 30 days. The company even provides the policy number over the phone.

Results show that the direct-marketing center binds 15% of inbound calls and 4% of outbound follow-up calls. Those prospects who don't take a policy are put on an automatic recall follow-up system for requotes every six months for two years.

All work stations have CRTs as well as telephones. Although software incorporates scripting, this is not a crucial feature. A more important benefit is direct access to the database, which gives communicators the ability to calculate and provide quotes quickly, to input orders and policy number assignments, and to combine this information with automatic recall for follow up for outbound calls.

Using this technology, Montgomery Ward can duplicate much of the personal two-way communication inherent in face-to-face selling, at less cost. The company is able to pass these savings on to its customers in the form of lower premiums.

BEYOND CUSTOMER SERVICE

Telemarketing technology has traditionally been used for marketing basic products, or for customer service, but General American Life, St. Louis, has had great success using its system as a tool to aid in underwriting. The system was described by Dick Condon, vice president of General American:

"It is the function and responsibility of an insurance company's underwriting department to make informed decisions concerning the risk involved in the creation of a policy. To perform this function, it is necessary that underwriters be provided with complete and candid information resulting from applicant interviews."

Traditionally, data needed for the underwriting process has been obtained by commercial reporting agencies and supplemented by attending physician's statements. Such reports were effective, but they were also costly, time-consuming, and they did not include personal contact between the client and the home office.

General American decided to develop a program where applicant interviews would be conducted almost entirely by telephone, rather than by face-to-face methods. The company believed that telephone interviews employed by General American would be conscientious in collecting information and that applicants would be inclined to give factual information by telephone directly to the insurance company with no third party involved.

First, a 90-day trial program was set up for applicants applying for less than $25,000 coverage. The original program's major objectives were to collect information comparable to that of an outside investigative agency, at less cost and in less time. As the program evolved, some startling facts emerged.

The company was delighted to find that in-house telephone interviewing was actually more successful than a reporting agency. In fact, interviewers were able to elicit four times as much usable underwriting information. The cost and time objectives were also exceeded. The time to process an application was reduced from two weeks to 48 hours in 80% of the cases. And the cost was approximately two-thirds of that charged by an outside investigative agency.

The personal history interview program was so overwhelmingly successful that General American gradually increased the limit on the amount of policy coverage to a present limit of $1 million. The program is now operating with a team of personnel hired specifically for telephone applicant interviewing. Medical history reports have now been incorporated into the program, eliminating the need for an attending physician's statement in routine cases, which saves the company an additional $75,000 yearly.

Insurance companies will always require usage of investigative agencies in certain situations, but for the routine investigation of potential policyholders, telephone interviewing works.

The preceding examples show that the same principles that guided old-fashioned telephone sales are now being refined by modern marketing techniques and new call-management technologies to bring people together in new and efficient ways. Regardless of the transaction, information can be shared, problems can be prevented, responses can be given, and decisions can be made.

Bernard R. Cohen is telemarketing manager of NYNEX Business Information Systems.

32.
HOW TO TELL WHEN
SEGMENTATION WORKS

Editorial Staff of Marketing News

> Segmentation studies are most likely to succeed under eight con-
> ditions. Informal surveys suggest that only half of all segmentation studies
> are useful, often because of attempts to differentiate segments that are not
> really there.

Are segmentation studies successful? "By this I do not suggest that a study
yields different segments," said Seymour Lieberman, president of Lieberman
Research Inc., New York. "I'd like to use a tougher criterion, and this is: 'Was
the study useful?'"

Lieberman said that an informal survey he conducted showed that only half
of all segmentation studies are useful.

Studies are likely to succeed under eight conditions, Lieberman said. Four
are market conditions:

- When there are real, not phony, differences between brands in a given
  product field. The automobile industry, with cars ranging from luxury
  models to sports cars, has real differences.
- When there are real linkages between the properties of products and the
  needs and desires of people, as in the toilet soap field. Cosmetic brands
  featuring skin-softening ingredients, deodorizing brands with deodorizing
  ingredients, and others are hybrid brands that purport to soften and
  deodorize at the same time.
- When the same product category can serve two or more different
  functions. The toothpaste field has some brands that promise whiter
  teeth, others offer fresher breath, and others promote prevention of
  decay.
- When different people use the same product category for different
  reasons, as with cosmetics. "Marketers sell alluring shades to the
  flirtatious sexpot," Lieberman said, "subdued shades to the sophisticated

lady, and natural shades to the girl next door. They wisely ignore the sloppy homebody because she does not use cosmetics all that often."

There are four company conditions under which a segmentation study has a good chance of succeeding:

- When a company is willing to direct its brand entry at a portion of the market rather than against the whole market.
- When a company has an existing brand aimed at one market segment and is interested in targeting a new brand against another market segment.
- When a company has the economic clout and determination to develop several products and target each of them to the different segments that compose the market.
- When the company has the vision to realize the potential of an emerging market segment.

Lieberman presented several case studies to illustrate why some segmentation studies failed. He called one "the case of the inappropriate segments," which involved a study of the nondandruff sector of the shampoo market.

"The marketing and research people recognized that there were not many real or functional differences in cosmetic shampoos that were being marketed, so they opted to base the segmentation on personality traits of respondents," Lieberman said. "They reasoned that hair had deep psychological meanings for people, so they thought that segmenting on the basis of personality traits might yield meaningful market segments."

The study uncovered three segments, successful, confident people; outgoing, sociable people; and withdrawn, isolated people.

"The only problem was what did these segments have to do with the shampoo field?" Lieberman said.

The study had respondents rate the importance of a few key shampoo qualities and benefits, but these ratings turned out to be unrelated to the three personality segments, Lieberman said.

The study also measured brand use, but the results also were not related to the personality segments.

"The marketing and research people realized too late that the personality segments were inappropriate for the shampoo field, and the study was quietly interred," he said.

Another study, dubbed "the case of the commodity market," was done in a category in which the brand entries were virtually identical.

"The brands had the same product attributes, so there was little room for benefit differentiation," Lieberman said. "The product was a simple functional food additive, like salt or sugar, so there was not much room for image differentiation. And the products were all priced about the same, so there was not much room for price differentiation."

Nevertheless, the marketers persisted in requesting a segmentation study, and "the study fell flat on its face as the research struggled in vain to differentiate segments that were not really there," Lieberman said.

"The problem was that the benefits and attributes studied were too present-oriented and were not sufficiently future-oriented," he said. "The benefits and attributes studied were old ones that already existed, and not enough attention was paid to new ones that might serve as a basis of product differentiation."

One segmentation study almost failed, but ultimately succeeded. Lieberman called it "the case of the compressed segments."

The study was conducted for a major chain of women's clothing stores. The study revealed four fairly distinct segments, defined by the types of clothes that appealed to women.

The groups were: trendy women, who wanted to wear "way-out" apparel; stylish women, who wanted the latest clothes, but not too "far out"; elegant women, who wanted to look chic and sophisticated; and basic women, who wanted functional comfortable wardrobes.

The merchandising people accepted the four segments, but they had a problem: Space in the stores was limited, and they did not have enough room to stock clothes for four distinct apparel sections.

A solution finally was reached. The four segments were compressed into two. The trendy customers and stylish customers were contained in a contemporary-customer segment. The elegant and basic customers were placed in a conservative-customer segment.

The contemporary section was stocked primarily with the latest fashions, "with a few way-out items to add pizzazz," Lieberman said. The conservative section contained mainly basic items, with a few elegant pieces for special social occasions.

The chain's middle-of-the-road orientation allowed the collapsing of four segments into two, Lieberman said.

"The first two segments had certain qualities in common, as did the last two segments," he said, "so the collapsing was sensible as well as practical. For example, the first two segments both tended to have younger women, while the last two segments both tended to be composed of older women."

The segmentation study almost failed, Lieberman said, "but due to some nimble footwork on the part of the merchandising and research people, it ultimately succeeded."

33.
MARKETING IN THE ELECTRONIC ERA

George Nordhaus

Electronic marketing is a new marketing method that promises to be the major distribution revolution in the history of insurance and financial products.

For the last 200 years, since the days of Benjamin Franklin, the insurance product has been distributed primarily one way: through one-on-one distribution. Physical distribution connotes my selling to you, your selling to me, our selling to others. An agent looked at the customer, face-to-face, to make an individual sale.

In the 1960s, a new way of selling called "mass merchandising," "group marketing," "franchise selling," and various other titles became popular. The idea was to sell to more people at once, making one sale to insure a number of individuals or businesses. Mass merchandising has captured about 10% of the market.

In the late 1970s and early 1980s, a new way of marketing—electronic marketing—came along. It promises to be the major distribution revolution in the history of marketing insurance and financial products. The development of electronic marketing can be attributed primarily to the advent of the sophisticated buyer, a person who understands the value of money. Consumers who have been exposed to all types of media, who understand the fact that one must use money to make money, represent this new era of consumerism. Sophisticated buyers have grown up in a world where mass media have exposed them to the fact that a responsible adult manages more finances than his parents or his grandparents did. The average college graduate today has been bombarded by all types of media—newspapers, magazines, billboards, radio, television and audio-visuals of every variety—for an average of 15,000 hours.

At the same time, the development of new electronic means of conveying financial services advertising messages has had an impact on practically every consumer, not just the sophisticated buyer. The development of this technology is escalating so rapidly that we find it difficult to comprehend.

There is no question that the more sophisticated buyer understands that he can get the financial services product cheaper or quicker, and that automation technology will make it easier than ever to switch over to other, more sophisticated financial providers. The key issues for the insurance industry are (1) Will visitors to financial institutions use electronic technology to buy insurance? (2) Will visitors to retail establishments set aside enough time to inquire about insurance? (3) Will people utilize the other flexible distribution channels that electronics brings to the marketplace? These questions must be answered by every insurance organization, insurance company and financial services distributor (agent or broker) that intends to survive and prosper into the 1990s and the 21st century.

But will one-on-one selling disappear during this "electronic revolution?" What will be the relationship between "high-tech" and "high-touch" as consumers use automation technology to buy insurance? Only time will tell, but analyzing electronic distribution methods in terms of a "Four C's" model may provide valuable insights.

THE FOUR "C's"

The Four C's of electronic distribution are convenience, customer base, credibility and collection mechanism. The first "C," Convenience, is vital, as shown by the success of such old-line carriers as Aetna Life & Casualty, Allstate, John Hancock, Hartford, Metropolitan and SAFECO in developing new methods of distribution based on convenience.

Electronic technology offers a number of innovative methods to market the insurance product. The first is the automated teller machine (ATM). Some 145,000 are expected to be on the market by 1990. ATMs already are being used to market such coverages as accidental death and dismemberment, auto, homeowners, hospital cash and Medicare supplemental income, with more products sure to follow.

Point-of-sale systems (POS) that let consumers use debit cards (as opposed to credit cards) will proliferate over the next decade. While only 2,500 POS debit-card systems were operating at the end of 1984, that figure should grow tenfold to 25,000 by the mid-1990s. Many of them, no doubt, will be offering insurance and financial services products. These systems will be everywhere—in airports, convenience stores, supermarkets, gas stations and even shopping malls.

Videotex will be available in practically every home in three to four years. Videotex involves using a television set or computer at home (more than 90% of homes will have "cable-in" and "cable-out" capability by 1992), or some other method of using an interactive video display to order products. The first "electronic mall" based on videotex technology is now open. Metropolitan, Equitable, Bank of America and E. F. Hutton are among the 42 vendors that have signed one-year leases as tenants in this "shop at home," on-line computer service.

A variation on videotex technologies is the kiosk, which will allow the consumer to access an agent or underwriter from a video screen in practically any location (such as a mall) and deal one-on-one with that person.

We are entering the era of "control group marketing," with aggressive marketers tapping employee credit unions, utility company files, phone directories and every other source of customers. Seminar selling is becoming a growth industry, driven by the ability to utilize larger customer bases and gather more people in one location, rather than dealing with them one-on-one.

THE CUSTOMER BASE

Target marketing forms an integral part of the electronic environment. The need to pinpoint the customer is more apparent than ever. Knowing what, when, where and how much we sell them will be far easier now that automation gives us the ability to access names on a pinpointed basis. The old axiom of "the more you know about me, the better your chances for a sale" will be more applicable than ever. One organization, National Information Systems, has 80 million names in its database and can overlay these names to learn practically everything possible about these potential consumers.

The era of telephone sales also has arrived. One study predicts that by the year 2000 telemarketing will provide more new jobs than all other occupations combined. The ability to combine telephone and automation technology with direct mail will create an entirely new method of marketing financial services. For example, some systems not only can call prospects but also allow prospects to call in for quotes (produced electronically) for practically any financial service or product.

CONSTANT CONTACT

We clearly are living in the age of constant contact. Every individual in the United States will be contacted time and time again, to the point where it will be impossible to escape the barrage of salespeople letting the consumer know, electronically, that "I can get you a better deal—and get it for you cheaper."

This is the age of positioning: determining a niche for oneself in the marketplace and making that slot known to one's customers and prospective customers. The third "C," credibility, comes into play here. Positioning will be more important than ever if agents are to reach a higher percentage of the consumer base for insurance and financial services products.

Our competitors—Sears, American Express, Citicorp, MasterCard, Prudential—have the electronic technology and the money to blanket the country. We may not like to think about it, but the fact is that no one, no matter how isolated, will be able to escape this advertising/marketing barrage.

In this period of instant availability, the alert consumer will be shopping the marketplace. A case in point: 40% of insured car owners last year considered alternatives to their existing coverage. One out of seven switched. People who are looking to get the product better and cheaper will be swayed by these electronic media.

EASE OF COLLECTION

Ease of collection (the fourth "C" in our scenario) also will play a vital role in the marketing of financial services. Premium financing, automatic premium withdrawal from bank accounts and electronic funds transfer all will be commonplace within the next 15 years. According to one expert, by the end of this century more payments will be handled electronically than by paper check.

How the product is paid for will be as important—perhaps even more important—than the amount of money charged for it. The competition will be using pay-by-the-week plans, package policies, and every other feasible method to make collection as easy as possible. The insurance and financial services provider who finds a way to use electronic technology to ease the collection procedure will have a giant leg up on the competition.

The insurance manufacturers (insurers) and distributors (agents/brokers) who will survive and thrive in this era of electronic distribution will be those that follow these guidelines:

- *Understand the sale.* Successful salespeople and marketers are going to begin to understand the selling process more thoroughly than ever. This includes traditional selling methods, as well as the sophisticated techniques of the future. Old methods of selling, such as X-dating and direct sales, still have their place, but they will work much more effectively when combined with the techniques and technology of electronic marketing.
- *Understanding the distribution force.* Insurance companies will need to understand their distribution force if they want to compete, and agencies will need to begin to understand themselves. Agents and brokers will have to study financial management to learn how to analyze their balance sheets and profit and loss statements.

Among other figures the agents will need to acknowledge are that it costs $2.57 to produce every $1 of new business, and 40 cents for every $1 of in-house commission to service the business on the books. It takes 5.66 years for a personal lines policy and 4.27 years for a commercial lines account to break even.

Once agents begin to understand these facts, they will be able to run their agencies better. That applies just as well to insurance companies, which have yet to figure out that keeping customers on the books is every bit as important as getting new ones because 80% of insurance companies' and agents' business comes from renewals.

THE PAPERLESS ERA

Agents also will have to understand that they are living in the era of the computer. The totally paperless, computerized insurance agency office is a reality—even now. In a few short years, agents and companies alike will be using computers in ways they cannot even conceive of today.

- *Recognize the role of market planning.* Both agents and companies will have to plan their marketplace entry much more effectively than they have in the past. Most agencies are not utilizing the planning materials and information available to them. For example, less than 5% of the agency forces has a five-year written plan. That few companies have long- or short-term plans is evidenced by the disastrous results of insurers over the past few years. As the electronic future develops, neither companies nor agents will thrive without sound planning.
- *Prepare for the era of relationship selling.* It will be necessary to identify specific clients, corporate or personal, with whom we plan a long-term relationship, rather than simply trying to meet the client's immediate needs. In both personal and commercial lines, the only long-term answer to a relationship selling situation (and the only long-term defense against the electronic media barrage) will be insulating or isolating a customer—turning that customer into a client. The only way to insulate or isolate a client is to sell him more than one product. One of the most effective methods of insulating clients is the package-type policy, such as the Continental PCP. But that's only one approach. There are other ways, primarily focused on total account selling.

We would add three more "C's" to make our point even more clearly. The fifth "C" might be called "client rounding;" the sixth, "creativity;" and the seventh, "commitment." Things really are not more difficult today than in the past. The distributor actually has it much easier in several respects. To begin with, he or she has access to a wide array of marketing and management tools. Agents can use electronic technology to develop their prospects into customers and their customers into clients.

A LITTLE EDUCATION

Second, the body of marketing expertise is growing more rapidly than ever. There's nothing wrong with most company and agency marketing programs that a little education couldn't cure. Such a variety of educational facilities are available—many of them an out-growth of electronic technology—that there is no longer any excuse for poor marketing performance.

Third, the growth of premium volume will give the industry the resources we need to bankroll our marketing thrust. In 1984 the industry did $119 billion in property/casualty premium volume. The Future One Report predicts a mind-boggling $245 billion by 1990. With that kind of growth—which essentially means that agents and companies will be twice as big in five years as they are today simply by keeping their market share—what excuse can we possibly have not to progress? Progress we will, because of the free enterprise system, because of motivated and aggressive management in companies and agencies, and because we will be utilizing the biggest gun in the distribution revolution—electronic technology.

George Nordhaus is president and founder of Insurance Marketing Services and Nordhaus Professional Marketing, Santa Monica, Calif.

34.
CRACKING THE 'TRANSPLANT' MARKET

John H. Sheridan

Sheller-Globe Corporation, a major auto industry supplier, has been successful in unlocking the door to the increasingly important market segment of foreign companies who manufacture products in the United States.

Albert H. Grava is president of a large company headquartered in Toledo, Ohio. But that isn't where you'll find him on a typical workday.

Sure, he has an office in Toledo. But Al Grava's primary base of operation is a modestly appointed office in a sprawling, three-building complex in Detroit just a few blocks from Tiger Stadium. He lives—and spends about 90% of his time—in the Motor City.

Not because he's a Tiger fan—which he is—but because that's where the customers are. The traditional customers, anyway.

His company, Sheller-Globe Corp., is one of the nation's largest auto industry suppliers. It employs 10,000 people and operates 23 manufacturing plants, including two in Europe. The company, whose roots date back to the early 1900s, does about $800 million a year in sales of steering wheels, instrument panels, door panels, body-sealing systems, and other interior components—just about everything that goes inside an automobile—"everything except the seats."

It's only logical that Mr. Grava, a 35-year veteran of the automotive business, should be situated near the hub of the market his company serves.

Shifting Market. But that market isn't what it used to be. By 1991, analysts estimate, Japanese-owned or operated assembly plants could be producing 2 millions cars and trucks a year on U.S. soil. So, while the big Three—General Motors, Ford, and Chrysler—still constitute the bulk of the market for U.S. suppliers, the new kids on the block are becoming a factor to reckon with.

But the Japanese "transplants" haven't created sales bonanzas for most American auto parts manufacturers. Instead, they have tended to rely on their traditional Japanese suppliers for many of the parts for their U.S.-built cars.

317

However, supplier relationships have been changing—and Sheller-Globe is in the vanguard of firms shaping that change. A subsidiary of Knoll International Holdings Inc., Sheller now counts all of the Japanese transplants among it customers. Once all of the transplants are up and running, Mr. Grava calculates, this new market segment will account for "close to 10%" of Sheller-Globe's annual sales.

That percentage is likely to keep climbing. Chester Devenow, Sheller's chairman and CEO, anticipates that the transplants eventually could represent 15% to 20% of his firm's business. "Within the next five years," Mr. Devenow says, "we'll see the Japanese making 2 million passenger cars a year in the U.S. That will be the equivalent of another Ford Motor Co."

What to do? Sheller-Globe's executives concluded several years ago that dramatic marketplace shifts signaled a need to respond. The automotive market, Mr. Grava observes, "was not only being eroded by imports, but it was obvious it was also going to be impacted by the number of foreign cars produced in this country—and that we were either facing a shrinking domestic-car build or we had to find a way to become a suppler to the various transplants that were being put here in the U.S.

"Then it became a question of what do you do and how do you do it?"

So a corporate policy committee conceived a strategy. And Mr. Grava, then Sheller's executive vice president, was charged with implementing the strategy.

"We've had some successes and some defeats," acknowledges Mr. Devenow. "But we're delighted with the progress we've made. And a lot of that is due to Al Grava's ability to put the program together."

If you ask Mr. Grava what the key to success was, you may get a detailed discourse on the importance of quality—and the lengths that his company goes to in assuring it. He'll tell you about Sheller-Globe's continuous quality program, a company-wide effort ranging from statistical process control and quality audits to "feedback systems" and an award-winning employee-involvement program.

Building Liaisons. But before Sheller-Globe could demonstrate its prowess in producing quality components, it had to get the ear of key decision-makers in the Japanese target firms.

"Basically," Mr. Grava says, "we started by putting together an organization of people whose dedicated mission was to get to know the various people who were building assembly plants here in the U.S.—and to work with them, both here and in Japan on the product lines that we produce."

Beginning in late 1985, Sheller established two sales/engineering teams—one in Tokyo and one in the U.S.—charged with cultivating new relationships. The Tokyo office is staffed with five Japanese nationals: four engineers with automotive experience and a secretary. This team's mission was to develop links with the parent companies on their turf—to serve as "contact people." Meanwhile a three-person U.S.-based team, comprised of Japanese-

Americans, was instructed to establish liaison with key people in the U.S. heading up construction and operation of the transplant facilities. Relying on Japanese nationals and Japanese-Americans helped to overcome any potential language or cultural gaps.

The strategy clearly has paid off. While Mr. Grava declines to discuss specific dollar amounts, he notes that Sheller has been awarded contracts to supply Mazda, Toyota, Nissan, NUMMI (the GM-Toyota plant in California), Honda, and Diamond-Star (the Chrysler-Mitsubishi joint venture in Bloomington, Ill.).

These successes undoubtedly figured heavily in the decision early last year to promote Mr. Grava to president of the company.

Getting Started. In conceiving the strategy, Mr. Grava notes, Sheller executives concluded "that it was going to take time, and that it was going to require the establishment of relationships with the various foreign manufacturers—getting them to know us and our capabilities.

"I think the real issue," he says, "comes down to their evaluation of the manufacturing process—your plants, your quality, your people, your manufacturing systems, and the technical support you are able to provide. And cost is a very important factor."

Influencing the vigorous move to woo the transplants was a related decision to concentrate on the automotive market. Until early last year the automotive segment represented only 60% of Sheller-Globe's business. But after the firm divested office-products and industrial-products units, the figure climbed to about 90%.

"We decided," Mr. Grava says, "that the automotive business was really the business that we were in—and since we had become part of a larger holding company, that diversification in the overall corporation would occur at that level."

Mr. Grava, who held a number of engineering and management posts at Chevrolet from 1953 to 1973, was vice president for production at Rockwell International when Mr. Devenow hired him in 1984. He has several personal goals for the company he now runs.

He wants to see Sheller-Globe continue on its course of becoming a "worldclass quality supplier." He wants to continue the firms's expansion into Europe—it now has a steering-wheel plant in Birmingham, England, and is involved in a joint venture to produce window/body sealing systems in Mesnel, France.

And he hopes to expand into the Far East, perhaps through joint ventures, to enhance the company's stature as a global supplier. (Sheller-Globe is now engaged in a joint venture in Shelbyville, Ind., with Japan's Ryobi Ltd. to produce precision aluminum die castings for the auto industry.)

Design Expertise. Internally, Mr Grava is determined to "continue to enhance our technical capability in order for us to become a total-systems supplier capable of taking on total design of modular componentry."

Toward that end, Sheller-Globe has dramatically enhanced its engineering and design capability. Its Detroit complex now features 23 sophisticated CAD workstations and, over the last three years, it has expanded its engineering staff from six people to 60.

"We want to do the engineering as well as the manufacturing. That will allow us to move to a more modular systems approach."

Sheller-Globe seems to have the ingredients of a sound strategy. But as it cements its ties with foreign-based car-makers, it is keeping a wary eye on overseas auto suppliers.

They, too, have been moving to the U.S. (A Goodyear publication notes that 314 foreign auto suppliers—134 of them Japanese—have already set up shop here.)

That trend is worrisome, Mr. Grava admits. "But I think we're going to be able to compete. I think we have employee relations that enable us to be as competitive as anyone."

Further, he adds, Japanese automakers with U.S. facilities are becoming increasingly receptive to the idea of doing business with American suppliers.

"There are a lot of reasons for that," he says. "And one is that they are finding that there does exist in America capable, competent, quality suppliers to the automotive industry."

35.
NEW TOOLS FOR ENHANCED SALES FORCE PRODUCTIVITY

Diane Lynn Kastiel

Computer-aided marketing should produce better sales force efficiency, giving salespeople more time to make sales.

Back in mid-1983, Westinghouse Electric Corp. decided that, to stay competitive, it had to increase its sales force's productivity and efficiency.

Now, almost three years and $10 million later, the Pittsburgh-based electronics giant is ready to roll out a new, state-of-the-art computer system it developed to do just that. And, despite some start-up problems, Westinghouse says it has a winner.

Based on feasibility studies it performed and the results of a two-month test run in its Framingham, Mass., sales office, the company is convinced that "we'll get at least 2 1/2 times the payback on this" as soon as the system is in operation, says Bob Rhen, general manager of the Marketing Services Division of Westinghouse's Industries and International Marketing Group. "And, I really think that's a conservative estimate."

That payback primarily should come in the form of better sales force efficiency, giving salespeople extra time to make more sales. Plus, the system will let customers and salespeople place orders immediately, check the status of their orders instantaneously and determine whether the products they want are in stock.

Called WesMark, the complete office automation system is composed of three subsystems: order processing, electronic communications and "advanced negotiation." Each subsystem allows the company's 800 salespeople and 1,200 sales-support personnel to perform myriad computer tasks without switching terminals.

Order processing enables users to check on the availability of stock, enter orders and determine the status of an order. The communications system, known as CEO ("comprehensive electronic office"), allows users to send and receive inter- and intraoffice communications, send telegrams and devise spread sheets. It also creates an electronic filing system and has word processing capabilities for writing letters.

With advanced negotiation, salespeople can develop quotations for "engineered" products—those built to customer specifications—simply by entering the desired product's special characteristics into the computer.

But the pinnacle of WesMark, Westinghouse says, is its ability to let users switch from one subsystem to another instantaneously, using a desktop or laptop computer. That integration means a salesperson can go from writing a letter, for example, to checking the status of an order, "pick up" his or her electronic mail and messages, and then go back to writing the letter, all from one terminal.

"We're buying the ability to flip from process to process with the push of a button," says Lionel Rickford, manager of field office systems for Westinghouse's Marketing Services Division. "In the old world, some of the functions weren't available, or if they were available, you had to get up from your desk, and go to different machines to perform different tasks."

The "old world" to which Mr. Rickford refers was inhabited by a Raytheon Co. system, Westinghouse's computerized order processing system that WesMark replaces.

The system, which Westinghouse used for eight years, "was out of horsepower for what we wanted to do," Mr. Rhen says. "We wanted to tie the sales system together with the marketing, engineering and, ultimately, the manufacturing systems, so we'd have a completely integrated system."

WesMark, which is compatible with all other computerized systems at Westinghouse, can accomplish that goal, Mr. Rhen says. In fact, that capability was one of the main reasons Westinghouse chose Data General Corp., Westboro, Mass., out of the 22 vendors it considered, to supply WesMark's hardware and help create its software.

In addition to its versatility and compatibility, WesMark is more powerful than Raytheon; the system servicing the Framingham, Mass. office alone has more capacity than the entire Raytheon system, which served 800 terminals in sales offices nationwide, Mr. Rickford says.

And, unlike the Raytheon system, which equipped medium- to large-sized offices with seven or eight terminals, the WesMark system calls for 40 to 50 terminals in those offices, not including the portable computers to which all offices will have access.

Westinghouse planned to begin installing WesMark in February, placing it in four to five of its 109 U.S. sales offices each week and completing installation by the end of the year.

All sales offices will receive access terminals, printers and facsimile machines. However, some smaller offices will share the central processing unit of "host offices." That setup will make changing the data base or operating system simpler and less expensive, Mr. Rickford says.

Most personnel will have their own terminals on their desks, and everyone will at least have access to one. In addition, salespeople will be able to take portable lap-top computers, complete with their own printers, on the road.

"Using the lap-tops, they can dial into their office and get hooked into the (main computer) system just like they were sitting at their desk," Mr. Rhen says. "So, they'll be able to take one on a trip and check their mail, do stock checks and write letters from a hotel room. They'll be able to sit in a customer's office and work up a quotation or enter an order right there."

Westinghouse initially intended to begin installing WesMark in 1985, after the trial in its Framingham office. The company selected the Framingham office for several reasons. It's close to Data General headquarters and it's within easy "shuttling distance" of Westinghouse's corporate headquarters. It's also a medium- to large-sized office, with 112 sales personnel representing all three of the company's selling groups: electrical utility, industrial and construction.

However, shortly after it was installed, the system started slowing down. "It was not as fast as Raytheon," says Aubrey S. Engle, district administration manager of the Framingham office. Because of a flaw in the software, "You had to perform more functions, hit more keys, to do the same job," he says. "It was also slow in response time."

Specifically, response time—the time it takes a computer system to execute a command—should have been about two or three seconds. Instead, it was at least five seconds—no faster than the Raytheon system. And total throughput—the time it takes a system to perform such duties as transmitting information from one location to another—was at least three hours, not 30 minutes, as it should have been.

Ironically, the software problem was exacerbated by frequent use of the system, indicative of employees' enthusiasm for it.

"People were using the system at more than triple the rate than we expected in all our studies," Mr. Rhen says. "It really blew our minds."

In response to those problems, Westinghouse shut down the system, revising the software so it could accommodate the frequent use it is bound to have.

"Rather than continuing to muddle along, we chose to pull it back and rewrite it," Mr. Rhen says.

But, now that the new system seems to be on the right track, Westinghouse is confident its sales offices will be markedly more efficient than they were in the Raytheon days.

"They're two completely different concepts in systems," Mr. Rickford says.

During the testing period, Westinghouse's Productivity and Quality Center—which performs quality-control and ergonomic studies for all the company's divisions—developed user profiles on each Framingham employee. Those profiles served as benchmarks against which salespeople could measure their use of the WesMark system. Other sales offices will have the option of having users profiles developed for their employees, Mr. Rhen says. The company will update the profiles periodically to compare work patterns and detect trends in the way people use the system.

"We wanted to give people an opportunity to evaluate how they're using the system," Mr. Rhen says, adding that "we think people are smart enough" to want to monitor their performance. "But we're definitely not building a spy network."

Part VI
RESEARCH, MODELS AND CONSTRUCTS

36.
PERFORMANCE ADVERTISERS PRACTICE WHAT THEY PREACH

David Perry

> Top marketing professionals are increasing their emphasis on four factors to achieve measurable results from their advertising campaigns: strategic planning; an international perspective; involvement by ad agencies; and creativity.

Karl Kaufmann of 3M calls it "the benefit of achieving critical mass." Steve Trygg of the Anderson & Lembke agency stresses an "increased productivity orientation." Du Pont's Dan Motz emphasizes "communications quantification," and Bob O'Brien of Polaroid calls it "advertising payoff."

What are those four distinguished marketing people discussing? They're describing the No. 1 priority in business-to-business advertising today: the need to achieve measurable advertising results.

During recent conversations with 14 leading marketers—seven professionals working for advertisers and seven ad agency people—I found that there's a unanimous, nationwide agreement on the need to maximize the return on advertising.

To reach that goal, the marketers say that four predominant factors are receiving an increased emphasis:

- strategic planning;
- an international perspective;
- involvement by ad agencies; and
- creativity.

None of those represent something new under the marketing sun. But it's critical that marketers are embracing them for their ability to contribute to a profit statement, in a practical—as opposed to theoretical—manner.

STRATEGIC PLANNING

Remember the old Andy Hardy movies, in which Mickey Rooney jumped up and yelled, "Hey kids, let's clean out the barn and put on a show!"? The approach too many business-to-business marketers use when they establish advertising strategy is comparable. Marketing Mickey Rooneys jump up in their offices and say, "Hey staff, we've got a slumping product here. Let's slap an ad together and see if we can put some zing into the sales curve!"

However, in response to the need for continuous, long-term results, some of the nation's better marketing managers are discarding the Andy Hardy ad hoc advertising approach. Instead, they're using a well planned strategic emphasis.

"In the past, business-to-business advertisers were very seat-of-the-pants," states Nola Anderson, senior vice president at Hill, Holliday, Connors and Cosmopolus Inc. Advertising in Boston. If a product came along, and ad would be made—which may or may not have been consistent with the overall image and message that was projected by the company as a whole.

"It wasn't integrated into the marketing scheme of things, and you ended up with a company that communicated a lot of unrelated messages and identities. Now that's changing quickly, as advertising is being utilized as a critical part of the long-term planning process."

Bob O'Brien, advertising manager for Polaroid Corp., in Cambridge, Mass., agrees. We're driving toward a strategic approach to advertising that makes it part of the long-term marketing plan. In order to maximize ad productivity, our strategic aim is this. Before we'll place a live salesbody in front of a prospect, we want that prospect to be as highly qualified as possible. And to achieve that demands a focused, unified effort between all phases of the ad mix.

"General advertising, such as print ads, is used to create an overall environment of customer interest. More targeted techniques, such as direct mail and telemarketing, build on this interest by establishing specific appeals that create desire and action, or sales, on the part of the customer.

"While that may sound simple, the coordination of this multistep approach demands planning time and effort, in order to get great results. It's definitely not an overnight, seat-of-the-pants approach to advertising."

The strategic planning at St. Paul, Minn.-based 3M Co. is an example of the evolving approach.

Karl Kaufmann until recently was 3M's manager of corporate marketing communications. He now heads Karl Kaufmann Is a Consultant, a St. Paul-based consulting firm. As one of the most respected members of the business/industrial advertising profession, he practices strategic advertising.

In an interview conducted while he was at 3M, Mr. Kaufmann described how that company tries "to create a critical mass for ourselves and our customers" through the strategic approach.

"For example, by looking at the needs of automotive industry customers, we noticed that 12 separate 3M divisions were independently serving that single customer base: 12 divisions, 12 ad strategies, one customer.

"So we stepped back, evaluated our situation, and sought to maximize our effectiveness and efficiency. For instance, a 24-page, four-color advertorial was prepared for automotive customers which combined all of 3M's automobile-related products into one piece. That piece was put into double-duty (in *Ward's Auto World* magazine), and as a handout brochure for our salespeople.

"The benefits of that streamlined, strategic approach were multiple: Customers perceived us as a full-line, single-source problem solver, rather than a fragmented supplier. We generated the highest readership score ever recorded by *Ward's Auto World*. And by combining the advertising efforts of 12 separate divisions into one, our overall production costs were reduced.

"All told, that strategic approach made it easier for our customer to do business with us, and it cost us less to serve them. We achieved maximum impact and cost effectiveness through strategic planning."

THE INTERNATIONAL PERSPECTIVE

All of the marketers I interviewed recognized the impact of strategic marketing on sales and profits. However, an international perspective toward advertising was noted by fewer than 40% of the professionals.

Popularized over the past few years as "global marketing" by Theodore Levitt of Harvard University's business school, marketers are increasingly melding the international perspective into their advertising strategies—but at a cautious pace.

According to Steve Trygg, president and creative director for Anderson & Lembke, an internationally oriented agency in Stamford, Conn., the international perspective should be adapted at an even faster pace.

"To make a transition to global advertising isn't as complex or risky as it appears, because the needs for industrial products are the same worldwide.

"For example, nuclear reactor purchasers are all concerned with safety, durability, cost, and so forth. What appeals to a buyer in one country pretty much appeals to most others. A common or similar message translates well in any language.

"In addition, because of the similarities of purchaser profiles worldwide, your message can be communicated over a broader customer base, resulting in a higher exposure/lower production cost situation. It's an effective way to reach the most buyers with the lowest per-exposure costs."

Mr. Trygg developed a model that shows how complex industrial products have common denominators in different global markets (see Figure 1).

Bob Crittendon, director of communications for Fullerton, Calif.-based Beckman Instruments Inc., agrees with Mr. Trygg.

"An international approach provides an outstanding avenue for maximizing advertising results," says Mr. Crittendon. "In the last few years, we've all been forced to take off the domestic blinders, and reevaluate our advertising effec-

Figure 1.

According to the global marketing model designed by Steve Trygg of the Anderson & Lembke agency, a product has greater appeal across different international markets as it falls further to the left with complex industrial products. Industrial offerings like Product A tend to be more amenable to globally similar advertising appeals than are the similar consumer products on the model's right side. Offerings with large numbers of buyers are more susceptible to local differences—and therefore more subject to segmented appeal.

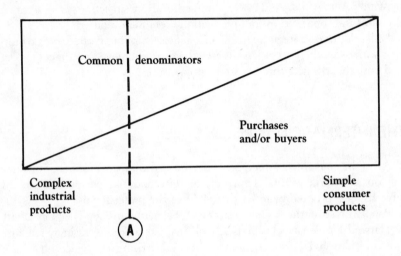

tiveness. At Beckman, we've responded by finding a basic message and appearance that's accepted and well received by all countries where we operate.

"Although it was a challenge to settle on a globally acceptable image and approach, the consistency of purpose, clarity of communications—and in the end—cost economies that we experienced made it well worthwhile."

It's not unusual for consumer marketers to associate themselves with mass-appeal events to promote their products. However, business-to-business marketers with products of limited appeal rarely associate their offerings with broad-reach audience vehicles. But at the 1988 Summer Olympics in Seoul, South Korea, 3M will promote both its industrial products and consumer offerings. The company will sponsor the event with makers of consumer-oriented offerings, such as Coca-Cola and Fuji film.

"As far as we know, we're one of the first industrial companies to use a worldwide sporting event to leverage a product," said Mr. Kaufmann. "The reasoning is this: The Olympics are perceived positively throughout the world. In fact, they are one of the few things with universal acceptance. And while the advantages of consumer-goods sponsorship of the games are obvious, our expanding awareness of business-to-business customers leads us to believe that it's good sense for our industrial products to be associated, also."

We no longer view industrial buyers as purely rational robots. They have emotions just like everyday consumers. So a tie-in between the Olympics and 3M products has a positive impact worldwide for all of our products. Whether it's Scotch tape, or automotive tape.

AD AGENCY INVOLVEMENT

If you think about my earlier comments on the Andy Hardy School of Ad Planning, you'll find that an inherent aspect of that approach is that the agency is viewed as an afterthought. Or, in less positive terms, a dubious expense.

But marketing experts say that perspective is changing drastically. An increasing number of marketers view their ad agencies as business partners, or expanded staff, who can contribute to attaining better marketing results.

The importance of that relationship wasn't mentioned only by ad agency people. Of the marketing professionals I interviewed that identified agency involvement as a marketing success factor, 42% worked for an advertiser.

For example, Kirk Jewitt, vice president-advertising at Pitney Bowes Inc., Stamford, Conn., says that last-minute agency involvement is "just not an effective" way to advertise. "When your agency is a part of the team—a true member of your planning process—you'll always get better results."

"The need for greater agency involvement is largely due to corporate America's changing customer perspective," explains George Cohan, president of Fletcher/Mayo/Associates Inc., a Chicago-based agency. "In the past, a lot of marketers developed programs that would stimulate short-term returns or transactions: a sale here, a sale there.

"But now, marketers are increasingly recognizing the need to build long-term customer relationships to protect market share and profits. And to do that, you need the help of an agency to maintain constant, consistent customer communication.

"To achieve advertising results, meaningful effective customer communication and cost effectiveness requires a close relationship with your agency. And that demands involvement with the overall planning process," adds Mr. Kaufmann.

"To do that at 3M, we created a Centralized Communications Center, which consolidates all advertising activity into one area. The center acts as focal point, working closely with the marketing departments to achieve an optimal customer approach. An integral part of the center is our ad agency. We rely on their judgement—not only for advertising, but also for developing our overall strategy. They've become a critical element in 3M's marketing process."

FOCUS ON CREATIVITY

Creativity is a highly subjective, hard-to-measure quality that's more often associated with consumer, rather than industrial advertising.

But 85% of the business-to-business marketers I interviewed say that creativity is extremely important in achieving quantifiable results.

Professionals at two outstanding advertising organizations explain why.

"There was an increasing 'sameness' about most industrial advertising in the past that caused a prospect to turn the page on your product," states Bob Williams, managing director of external affairs at E. I. du Pont de Nemours & Co., Wilmington, Del. "We've revised our advertising guidelines to allow greater creative freedom.

"Increasing competition, changing economies, and a perspective of industrial buyers as people—not just rational professionals—has led us to expand on the emotional side, beyond a 'just-the-facts' approach, to reach the *whole* individual. By broadening our guidelines and adopting some consumer techniques, we feel that we're more effective."

Joe Hoke, president of Mintz & Hoke Inc., an Avon, Conn.-based agency, says that "we're working to be more provocative—using better strategies, more color, better execution and fresh ideas to express a sales message. Heavy competition and a more worldly economy are factors.

"But there's also an increase in product parity that didn't exist in the past," he continues. "With technology and advanced tools available to nearly every manufacturer, the truly unique product or breakthrough is getting harder to sustain in the marketplace. Today's breathtaking innovation can be quickly matched by competitors, and it fast becomes tomorrow's norm.

"So a company needs to draw attention to itself in ways other than product or feature superiority. That's where 'image' as in consumer marketing, becomes the critical edge. And that's the reason for the increasing role of creativity in business-to-business advertising: to provide an edge that, in the past, a superior product could provide."

"We're getting away from the 'magnificent black box' syndrome, and treating the customer as a person," Mr. Kaufmann adds.

"That means that you, I and our customers consist of emotional and intellectual motives that are interwined, inseparable.

"3M's advertising appeals to both elements," Mr. Kaufmann adds. "While we haven't fully embraced consumer-goods methods, we try to combine the best of business-to-business and the best of consumer advertising to reach those 'intelligent emotions' of industrial buyers. We attempt to create well-executed, high-impact advertising that's built around providing a solution to customer problems."

The current industrial business environment—characterized by unparalleled competitive levels, increasing product parity, a shifting economic balance and expanding perceptions of customer motivations—has a strong impact on industrial marketers. Smart marketing professionals adapt one or more of the four predominant approaches to achieve measurable advertising results.

3M practices one of the most expert responses to the marketplace's dynamics. The company integrates all four approaches into its advertising strategy, and is well-poised to maximize sales and profit growth—now and in the years ahead.

David Perry is a product planning manager for Motorola Inc., Schaumburg, Ill.

37.

THE FAILURE OF
MARKETING RESEARCH

David C. Lehmkuhl

To be relevant to the marketing/media community, research must begin to be more reflective of today's marketplace. This is a difficult assignment for an industry steeped in tradition and resistant to change. The author offers four ideas that will make marketing and media research information a truly valuable tool in the decision-making process.

Are our research services failing to provide us with suitable information with which to make informed marketing decisions? I think the advertising/marketing community would respond with a resounding, "Yes!" In spite of the hundreds of thousands of dollars we invest in research information each year, it just does not reflect the current marketplace.

The syndicated services to which we subscribe seem to ignore the fact that over the last several decades such important variables as how we buy products, how we consume media and who is making the purchase decisions in the family, have all changed dramatically. The market/media researchers continue to use methodologies and assumptions that reflect a much simpler time when family roles were clearly defined and media consumption was limited to but a handful of options.

Nielsen, the "bible" of television audience research, for example, is capable of measuring only the broadest of viewing options and the broadest of demographic audience groups. This is a throwback to the time when television was viewed in a familial situation and the number of viewing options was severely limited. Despite major changes in the number of viewing choices and the growing trend toward TV viewing being a one-on-one experience, research continues to ignore this and employs a methodology that is some 20 or more years old.

Similarly, SMRB and MRI, the two leading purveyors of marketing information, measure only the primary shopper when it analyzes package-good types of products. This again is a throwback to a time when the women stayed home with the children and made virtually all of the family purchase decisions. In today's world of working women, smaller households, larger family incomes, etc., this simple demarcation is no longer valid. The purchase of many products is highly segmented and the primary shopper could, in fact, be responsible for as little as 40% of what the family purchases.

Perhaps even more noteworthy, this simplistic approach to marketing research completely ignores the importance of product influencers. These people may not make the final purchase, but they certainly have an important effect on the selection of the products and/or brands purchased. While these important factors have assuredly changed dramatically in just the past several years, the research community continues to provide the same information based on the same assumptions they provided years ago when things were much simpler and family roles were much more clearly defined.

To be really relevant to the marketing/media community, research must begin to be more reflective of the marketplace *today*. This is a difficult assignment for an industry steeped in tradition and with a history of "digging in its heels" to resist change. I would like to offer four suggestions to begin turning this situation around and making our marketing and media research information a truly valuable tool in the decision-making process.

1. *Become an observer of societal trends.* Most trends in society take many years to unfold and just as long to be reflected and tracked by the syndicated services. It is important, therefore, that we detect these trends early and begin to include them in our marketing plans.

    The growth of working women, the increased political and purchasing power of the elderly, the growth in leisure time availability, and numerous other trends have been in the press and making headlines for over a decade. It is the astute, aggressive marketer who has picked up these trends early and made them part of his marketing plan—even before the syndicated research services began to reflect them.

2. *Aggressively support new research findings.* I am certainly not suggesting that we blindly support any new idea that is offered, but we must encourage new research. For some reason a wait-and-see attitude is pervasive among media people. This is usually the attitude with new magazines and new ideas and is certainly the attitude toward new research. Just look at the difficulty MRI and AGB have had getting broad industry support for their new ideas; and Starch's new ideas for media and marketing research were met with such apathy they scrapped the whole proposal. We must realize that moving into a research field is an expensive proposition and it is the rare organization that can fund a test or offer a full-blown research tool entirely on their own with no promise of support. Thus, by taking the ever-safe, wait-and-see attitude, the existing research organizations have no threat of competition and service and improvement are usually sorely lacking. If we want new and insightful marketing research information we

must offer our support, both financial and moral, to those organizations who are offering "the better mouse trap."

3. *Get tripartite support to move research in one direction.* It is one thing to complain about the research tools we presently have; it is very different to offer clear direction and new insights into just what it is we want from research. It has long been the role of advertisers and agencies to throw stones at the existing research, but to offer no real help in just what it is we need. If we are to get the kind of research data we want, it is for the buyer to specify what information it required. This will necessitate that the agencies, the advertisers and the media join hands and commit to what is needed. This technique seems to work well in most European markets and would most likely be successful in the States. We should at least give it a try and eschew the constant criticism we now endure.

4. *Use the tools made available to us.* Many of the media have, over the years, brought us useful information, at no cost to us, that has gotten very little use. The *Newsweek* "Eyes on Television" studies, the "Influence of Purchase" study done by *TV Guide, Reader's Digest, Sports Illustrated*, et al., and the *Seventeen* study of the growing importance of teens as supermarket shoppers are but three examples that immediately come to mind. Rather than using the valuable insights these studies provide, the marketing/ media community has, for the most part, chosen to dismiss and ignore them. This is disturbing not only because it puts to waste some very good marketing information, but it also sends a message throughout the industry to not provide any new research data—it will just be discarded anyhow.

No doubt about it, our research services are not providing us with the kind of information we need to make informed decisions in today's marketplace. If we are to expect anything different we, the users of the data, cannot accept the status quo. We must take the lead and demand marketing research information that reflects the marketing nuances of the period.

David C. Lehmkuhl is a vice president and group media director with N. W. Ayer, Inc., New York.

38.
MARKETERS TRADE OFF FOR RESEARCH PRODUCTIVITY

Tom Eisenhart

> Computerized trade-off interviewing—also known as adaptive conjoint analysis—is a relatively new marketing tool. Marketers using the technique find they can quickly zero in on the key factors that entice customers. But will the advantages diminish as more companies jump on the bandwagon?

Thanks to advances in microcomputer technology and the increasing use of micros by business, market researchers are dramatically boosting their productivity with computerized interviewing. A sophisticated research technique called trade-off analysis illustrates those gains.

Among the companies that use the computerized application of trade-off analysis—also known as adaptive conjoint analysis—are such *Fortune* 500 giants as IBM Corp., Xerox Corp. and Dow Chemical U.S.A.

The technique operates on the premise that buyers weigh their options in any purchasing decision, giving up one attribute to get another. A marketer using the technique develops a series of choices to determine which features buyers value most, then incorporates those tradeoffs into its product or service design, pricing strategy, packaging, promotion and distribution.

"Trade-off analysis is like infrared radar, looking into minds and coming back and pointing out the best way to go," says Harris Goldstein, president of Trade-Off Research Services Inc., Studio City, Calif.

Computerized trade-off analysis is relatively new, although marketers have long used conjoint analysis to examine buyer preferences. John Morton Co., a Chicago-based research firm, developed software in the early 1970s that computerized the trade-off technique and offered the package to its clients. Sawtooth Software Inc., Ketchum, Idaho, bought rights to the software, refined it, and introduced it commercially in 1985.

Using the software, marketers first select the product or service features that they think interviewees will value. They then divide each attribute into "levels" of, for example, four different prices or six product brands.

Once the program includes that information, an interviewee can use a microcomputer to respond to questions about which levels are acceptable. Based on those choices, the software generates a series of trade-offs, each of which includes two opposing attribute combinations.

As the respondent makes selections, the software "adapts" to the responses by eliminating the interviewee's least desired choices from further trade-offs. The entire interview usually takes between 20 to 30 minutes.

Marketing executives who use computerized trade-off surveying say it has several advantages over more traditional research methods. First, because the technique is still relatively new, interviewees tend to be more interested in responding. Second, it eliminates the bias inherent in a personal interview.

And because a computer interview "can push an hour interview into 20 minutes," it alleviates respondents' fatigue, says Peter Zandan, president of Intelliquest, an Austin, Texas-based market research and consulting firm.

Computerized trade-off interviews also are attractive because they can be conducted through the mail. Researchers who mail interview diskettes can get response rates that are dramatically higher than those for pencil-and-paper surveys.

For example, Mr. Zandan's firm mailed about 30,000 diskettes for 50 client surveys last year. He says that a 40%-50% response rate is typical for diskettes sent without prescreening. With telephone prescreening, the response rate jumps to between 60% and 80%.

The novelty of computer trade-off surveys and the fact that many of Intelliquest's clients are in the computer industry contributes to the high response rate, Mr. Zanda explains.

Other marketers find that combining computerized trade-off surveys with focus group sessions lets them zero in on pertinent questions. Because the trade-off interview responses are on diskettes, results can be quickly compiled via computer just before a focus group session. Moderators armed with the computerized survey results can pinpoint questions that reflect highly valued attributes.

Marketers also can conduct trade-off analysis through telephone interviews. And for small surveys, a researcher with a lap-top computer can conduct trade-off interviews in person.

One company that combines computerized trade-off interviews with focus groups is Fujitsu America. The San Jose, Calif.-based company uses the two techniques to design its cellular telephone products.

One research project identified features that Fujitsu will include in two cellular products it plans to introduce early this year. The findings of that project also led Fujitsu to redesign its Commander cellular telephone. It launched the Commander II in August 1987.

"Normally engineers sit around and dream up designs," says C. P. Shanker, group director of strategic marketing and business development for Fujitsu's telecommunications product group.

But, he warns, trade-off analysis isn't a panacea for all of a marketer's problems. Instead, it's "a *starting* point in designing a sellable product," he says.

Trade-off research allowed Fujitsu to examine how end-users valued different attributes. But the company still had to weigh those choices against its technical, cost and time limitations.

Fujitsu hired Trade-Off Research Services to conduct its research in 1986. First, Mr. Goldstein at Trade-Off developed a list of two groups: those interested in buying a cellular phone and those that already owned one. In New York and Los Angeles, four focus groups, divided according to ownership status, identified relevant features.

The focus groups allowed Fujitsu to determine how end-users described features of the company's products. "Our words for describing features are sometimes different than users,'" explains Mr. Shanker.

Based on feedback from the focus groups, Mr. Goldstein's firm entered product features—including price, weight, handset size, power, color, warranty and antenna type—into the trade-off software at different "acceptance" levels.

Finally, Trade-Off Research Service conducted computerized trade-off interviews in shopping malls, screening interviewees by the same parameters used for the initial focus groups.

The research showed that Fujitsu should design a slimmer handset for the Commander II. Survey respondents also favored an amber phone key pad over the green color used in the old Commander model.

Mr. Shanker adds that Fujitsu based its "flexible" price guidelines on the survey results. Company officials say they need price flexibility because Fujitsu imports its cellular components from Japan, and the yen's value rose rapidly between the survey's completion in 1986 and the Commander II's launch in 1987.

Beyond product features and price, the survey changed Fujitsu's distribution tactics. Interviewees preferred "one stop shopping"—offered by the regional Bell operating companies (RBOCs)—over department stores and such electronic specialty shops as Radio Shack. Fujitsu distributed some products through those stores before the research.

The company now devotes its distribution solely to the RBOCs, which include product sales, financing, installation and phone service in their sales packages. Fujitsu distributes through four RBOCs, selling the cellular phone under the regional company names and the Commander II label.

Mr. Shanker declined to say how much the research cost. However, he believes the additonal expense for the initial focus groups was necessary to develop the right questions. "Trade-off is a very sharp tool, but if you ask the wrong questions, you can screw up the entire business," he explains. It does seem that Fujitsu asked the right questions. The company projects sales of $30 million for the Commander II for its fiscal year ending March 31.

SELECTING DISTRIBUTION

In a 1981 research project, ISU International also combined focus groups with computerized trade-off interviews. But unlike Fujitsu, the franchisor of independent insurance agents and brokers used trade-off analysis before focus group sessions, to identify what type of insurance distribution system small businesses like most.

"We wanted to find out how they would look at an independent as part of a national organization," says Thomas J. Ryan, president of the San Francisco-based firm.

ISU defined small-business owners as those who pay from $2,000 to $200,000 in insurance premiums annually. The company hoped to find that those owners favored the system of independent agents within a national organization the ISU introduced in 1980.

The company also wanted to know how the attributes of its system stacked up against three others: independent agents without a national affiliation; exclusive company agents; and national insurance brokers, such as Rollins Burdick Hunter Co.

ISU started by conducting computerized trade-off interviews at eight meetings in major cities around the United States. Twelve to 18 small-business owners attended each meeting. ISU used software developed by John Morton Co. for its meetings.

During those interviews, respondents first went through a series of trade-offs to determine what influenced their selection of a broker or agent. The attributes included price, availability of automated quote information, product knowledge and personal interest in a client's business. The company then asked respondents how they related those attributes to the four types of distribution systems.

The computer surveys showed that small business owners gave the lowest ranking to independent agents. That didn't surprise ISU: Over a 20-year period prior to the survey, independent agents lost 2% market share each year, down to 43% in 1987.

Exclusive company agents were twice as attractive as independents, and national brokers scored six times higher. However, the combined attributes of ISU's system—an independent agent's high personal interest with a national broker's capabilities—scored twice as high as national brokers.

The personal interest attributes "was much more important than we originally thought," says Mr. Ryan. "Small businesses don't think the large national brokers will get excited about their business."

And contrary to ISU's initial expectations, the trade-off research and subsequent focus group sessions also showed that price was not the ultimate factor in a respondents's purchase decisions. "If people have a choice, they want the best value," Mr. Ryan notes.

That value message has become the basis for ISU's marketing thrust.

According to Mr. Ryan, customers want an agent to examine all available in-surance carriers and recommend a policy that represents the best value. The company's television commercials now say, "Let the ISU agent conduct a value search for you."

Using the perceptions it identified in the combined trade-off/focus group research, ISU has grown from zero to about 400 franchises in 40 states. Franchisee revenues for fiscal 1987 were $2.36 billion.

TRACKING BUYER ATTITUDES

A third firm, Ashton-Tate Inc., mails out computerized trade-off interviews as part of its ongoing studies to track buyer attitudes. Last year, the Torrance, Calif.-based software publisher sent about 20 diskette surveys to a variety of software purchaser decision makers and influencers. The firm also conducts computerized trade-off interviews over the phone.

"We're so thrilled by the response rate and data quality that we rarely send out a paper survey," says Todd Kort, Ashton-Tate's senior market research analyst. He says that prospects return the mailed diskette surveys at a response rate of better than 50%. And when Ashton-Tate uses phone trade-off inter-views—which are less complicated than the mail surveys—90% of the contacts either answer the questions immediately or arrange a call back.

Late last year, Ashton-Tate completed a tracking study that examined attitudes among managers of management information systems (MIS) toward the company's 6-year-old dBase software package vs. 12 competitive products. The software publisher uses such information to design future generations of its products.

To conduct that project, Ashton-Tate worked with Intelliquest and mailed diskettes to 400 MIS executives. The managers first entered such information as their name, job duties and software products they currently used. Then respondents indicated their level of involvement in product purchase decisions. The trade-off program offered five involvement categories.

At that point, the program bypassed the survey's trade-off section if the managers did not fall within the top three involvement levels. Those 150 managers were asked demographic questions about their organizations.

The program included the other 250 MIS managers in the survey's trade-off section. Some of the attributes were price, processing speed, customer support and documentation.

Results of the trade-off confirmed Ashton-Tate's expectations, based on previous surveys of other audiences. Generally, MIS managers put a high value on software that offers a lot of features, extensive documentation and high processing speed. Attributes such as price and manufacturer's reputation ranked low.

The dBase survey took respondents about 20 minutes to complete. Cost to

Ashton was around $30,000. Compared to a paper survey, "It was a little more expensive up-front because of diskette duplicating costs. But since we didn't have to keypunch the information, we recouped that cost at the end," says Mr. Kort.

Computerized trade-off interviews may never totally replace the paper survey. However, the technique's higher data quality, quicker compilation and higher response rate indicate that it's a strong alternative to traditional surveys. And computerized trade-off interviews also seem to be worthy adjuncts to their research methods.

Of course, computerized trade-off interviewing is still a relatively new tool. So it remains to be seen whether the advantages it provides will diminish as more companies jump on the trade-off bandwagon. But for now, marketers using the technique find they can quickly zero in on the key factors that entice customers.

39.
ACTIONABLE RESEARCH NEEDED
WHEN MARKETS CHANGE
Editorial Staff of Marketing News

> The various publics have changed and are continuing to change with regard to purchasing behavior, attitudes, and lifestyles. This situation has major implications for the business world, and that is why research is more necessary and more in demand now than ever before.

Strategic research covers a wider area than most people think, according to Allen Sorkin, president of Sorkin-Enenstein Research Services Inc., Chicago.

"It is my belief that all research is strategic in nature if it is part of the overall company plan that aids in attaining long-term business objectives," he said.

Sorkin said all projects qualify as strategic research planning "if they are organized, orchestrated, and integrated to maximize the success of the company."

"A strategy is dependent on clearcut business objectives, and strategic research is based on the translation of those business objectives into research objectives," he said.

Although most research is technically sound, much of it fails because it doesn't relate to business objectives very well or the analysis isn't translated into business recommendations, he said.

Sorkin outlined five steps to ensure that research is actionable:

- Business objectives must be clear and explicit, and translated into research objectives.
- Management and researchers must develop a good rapport and work together effectively.
- Management and researchers must have a true understanding of what research can and cannot do.
- Researchers must learn to communicate in good business English, remembering that although the majority of research is technically sound, improvements are possible in interpretation, analysis, and business recommendations.

• Tracking over time is essential for long-term company survival and gain, and certain types of research—such as market structure, gap research, segmentation, and configuration analysis—are valuable in this type of project.

"There is an important principle that should be mentioned, which we have named the Sorkin 80-20 Principle," he said. "Eighty percent of what research finds out, management will already know. If we are really lucky we will develop 20% new information to augment and extend management's base of knowledge."

But the research is needed because the results reduce the risk factor in making decisions, he said.

"We are able to quantify common sense and previous business experience through our research findings so that management attains the ability to respond faster and in a more sensitive way to the public's needs and to competitive threats."

Almost everyone needs research nowadays, Sorkin said. Because markets are changing, research is necessary to track new needs, different attitudes, altered life-styles and consumer opinions about various companies, brands, and products.

If the research is to be strategic, he said, it cannot be compartmentalized. Management must participate more fully from the beginning and in the plans of action derived from the results of research.

"One way for this to be accomplished in the initial phases of a project is to identify what each component of the research does with regard to specific business objectives, so that management can be sure that the research is on track," Sorkin said.

Managers don't have to be technicians, he added, but they should use their skills to ensure there are no "negative surprises at the end of the project."

Research is used more widely and is more practical than in the past because of changing markets. Sorkin's company has conducted various types of research for such industries as banks, telecommunications, retail gasoline sales, health care, and food products.

Common among these industries, especially during the last several years, is the excess of products in the marketplace, Sorkin said.

"There are many companies competing," he explained. "The various publics have changed and are continuing to change with regard to purchasing behavior, attitudes, and life-styles. This situation, I believe, has major implications for the business world, and that is why research is more necessary and more in demand now than ever before."

The fierce level of competition and the availability of products have made consumers more sophisticated and demanding, he said.

Research that Sorkin's firm conducted for Unocal Corp. was designed to meet business objectives, which were translated into research objectives.

Figure 1.

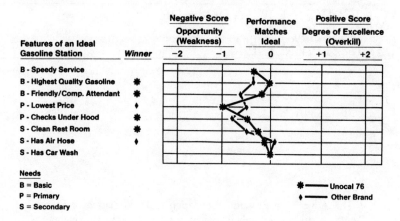

NON-USERS AWARE OF BRAND   GAP SCORES   (BRAND MINUS IDEAL)

Features of an Ideal Gasoline Station	Winner	Negative Score Opportunity (Weakness)		Performance Matches Ideal	Positive Score Degree of Excellence (Overkill)	
		−2	−1	0	+1	+2
B - Speedy Service						
B - Highest Quality Gasoline	✳					
B - Friendly/Comp. Attendant	✳					
P - Lowest Price	♦					
P - Checks Under Hood	✳					
S - Clean Rest Room	✳					
S - Has Air Hose	♦					
S - Has Car Wash						

Needs

B = Basic
P = Primary
S = Secondary

✳ ——— Unocal 76
♦ ——— Other Brand

Those objectives were to identify priorities and attitudes of the retail gasoline market, identify target markets, measure purchase behavior, evaluate Unocal's position in the marketplace, and track changes.

The business objectives were to increase Unocal 76's share of the market, select the most profitable target markets, turn deficiencies into opportunities, place the company in the most positive position against other oil companies, and respond with a feasible strategic plan to changes in the marketplace.

"From the outset, we identified what the research could accomplish and what it could not accomplish," he said. "That is probably one of the most important and difficult tasks to achieve."

Gap research deals with how consumers make decisions, and allows a company to zero in on the needs that have the greatest impact on its success, he said.

The performance level of the Unocal 76 attendants (see Figure 1) appears to be more satisfactory than the competition's. This feature is basic to the marketplace and to success.

40.
WHERE'S THE ARF/ABP STUDY VALUE?

M. E. Ziegenhagen
Fergus F. O'Daly

> The Advertising Research Foundation and Association of Business
> Publishers study is certainly not a panacea; no research of a communica-
> tion form as dynamic as business advertising can provide indisputable
> answers. But the study goes a long way in guiding us toward more informed
> decisions.

ADVERTISER: CREDIBILITY IS IN THE MIX

Why is the ARF/ABP study getting a tepid reception, and what, if anything,
should we advertisers do about it?

The ARF/ABP two-year, $390,000 study is by far the most thorough and
ambitious effort ever made to measure the effectiveness of business paper
advertising in terms of sales. It has great potential for helping us use business
papers advertising more effectively.

Why, then, isn't it getting the credit it deserves?

To me, the explanation boils down to a single word: *credibility*. A smart
marketing manager just can't swallow the flat assertion that the more you
advertise the more you sell & profit. Promoting the study's results that way is
unwise overkill.

But that's the way it's billed by advertising proponents. Cloaking a claim like
that with $400,000 worth of authority from the Advertising Research Founda-
tion, and feeding it to ad people, incites them to use it in a way that hardens the
very attitudes the study seeks to change.

Consider this realistic scenario:

Mac, the marketing communications manager, and Al, the agency account
executive, review their proposed annual budget with Bill Williams, a division
marketing manager.

Williams is an able and experienced guy with a good feel for the whole area of marketing communications. He consults with Mac and Al each year while preparing his marketing plans, giving them sound guidance for product positioning, program timing with sales and distribution, and selection of communications media.

Mac runs through the entire proposed marketing communications program. Williams makes occasional suggestions but seems pleased. Mac and Al have high hopes as Mac winds up with the usual comparison of the proposed budget for each product and market area with that of the previous year.

Williams, who generally likes what he's heard, has one main question: "I note you've added some business paper advertising for two or three lines where we couldn't justify it last year. And you bumped it up 10% or 15% for most of our other major lines. Fill me in on your reasons for that."

DATA IN ACTION

Mac and Al had anticipated the query. With a nod, they agree it's time to put the ARF/ABP study to work. Al gives it a good build-up and hands Williams a sheet listing the highlights of the study, taken from a mailer promoting it. "We think you'll agree our advertising has done a good job for us in the past, and this explains why we feel an increased budget will pay off next year," Al explains.

Williams takes a quick look and smiles. "Are they telling us that if we double our ad budget we'll double our sales?"

Mac laughs and passes that off, "Naw, they aren't claiming any straight-line effect—just that the more you advertise the more you sell and profit."

"That's still a pretty strong claim," Williams replies. He spies a couple of stunning sales increases cited in the study. "Wow! Are they claiming they got this 390% and this 630% sales increase just by running these ads?"

Al has anticipated that too, and explains how ARF research experts made sure that all other factors were held constant during the study so that any sales increase could be attributed to the advertising.

Williams shakes his head in disbelief. "If they were able to freeze everything else—and I wonder about that—you can bet your boots that those other factors that were held constant included some real lulus—like a hot new product, a very low sales base and light competition."

Mac shifts uneasily in his chair and feels the need to move to some common ground. "Sure, Bill, the sales increase you get is bound to vary all over the lot depending on the specific product and market situation. All they're saying is that—in general—the more you advertise the more you sell and profit."

"More profit too?" Williams asks. "If I could believe what you just said I'd want a lot bigger ad budget than you've recommended. But wouldn't I reach a point where I'd stop getting my seed money back and start *hurting* our profit?"

"Oh sure," Al interjects. "There's a limit to every good thing. But we're sure our proposed ad budgets aren't anywhere near that limit."

"Maybe not," Williams smiles. "But you'll have to do a better job of convincing me. I feel, as you do, that our past advertising has paid off. But I think it paid off because we have all realized that—as Mac just said—the payoff varies all over the lot depending on the specific marketing situation.

"We've always worked to tailor the amount of advertising to the facts of life of each situation—the potential market; the profit potential of the product; the strength of our selling proposition as compared to that of competitors; the support we can expect from field sales; the need for a smart balance between advertising and the supporting media that help make it pay off. And other things, including how well we think your advertising does in putting across our selling prosposition.

"I'm comfortable," Williams continues, "when we apply that kind of thinking to the selection of all the communication tools we use. But I'm very uncomfortable when you use this study to justify increased advertising right across the board—as if it could sweeten every kind of marketing situation in terms of sales and profits.

"True, the study shows that advertising *can* boost sales. But that doesn't change things for us. We've always known that and have concentrated on the tough job of *making sure it does.*

"So I'm asking you to reconsider your recommended advertising budgets," Williams concludes, tapping his desk top for emphasis. "If you can use those marketing facts of life to justify the increases, fine, I'll buy them.

"And, fellas, if you then *guarantee* that we can bump up sales on any of our major lines by 15% to 20% by adding still more business magazine advertising, just let me know and I'll get the money for you!"

THE PROBLEM

Unqualified parroting of the promotion surrounding the ARF/ABP study—phrases such as "Here, finally, is quantitative proof that the more you advertise in business publications the more you will sell, and profit"—creates the credibility problem, even among marketers like Williams who have a healthy respect for the potential of business magazine advertising.

To tap the full potential of that trail-breaking study, we must avoid the half-truths and tell the whole story to management as we know it. Here are a few suggested guidelines to follow in using the findings of the ARF/ABP study:

- Don't ever let anyone think you're saying that the advertising boosted sales and profit *all by itself.*

    You're just asking for an argument you can't win. Business and industrial marketers won't believe it—and darn well shouldn't.

You'll do much better by simply saying that the study shows that business publication advertising produces more sales than would occur without advertising—and that increased advertising will usually produce even more product sales.

That's the way it's stated in a summary of the study. That's true, and putting it this way leaves room for some more truth—that the other marketing factors held constant during the study no doubt did as much or even more than the advertising to boost sales. It's a smart retreat that still leaves you with a very strong claim, and the facts to back it up.

So don't be greedy. Give the advertising its fair share of credit but leave a lot of it for the other functions that deserve it.

- Don't treat business paper advertising as if it were a commodity.

When agencies pitch an account they point out—correctly—that some ads can be 10 times more effective than others, and that creative effectiveness makes the difference. Business marketers find that quite easy to believe and hope it will give them a competitive advantage.

So they question the motives of the agencies and the publishers who turn around and use research to show that advertising effectiveness depends primarily on advertising tonnage, the number of ads they buy. They wonder, "Are these guys selling me a unique creative product or a plain old commodity like bricks that can be piled atop each other until they yield the desired level of sales?"

Here again, just tell the truth. Tell the marketing manager that an adequate schedule is very important. But tell him that the creative effectiveness of the ads is also very important, and should be considered along with other factors in deciding how many pages to buy. Tell him that, while the creativity may come from the agency, the main elements that make it *effective* must come from the company side.

- Tell the marketer that the effectiveness of his business magazine advertising is primarily determined by the strength of his message.

Tell him he has to have *something to say*—a strong message that's important and helpful to customers and prospects. Then he can get a great deal from every page of advertising.

But, by all means, be honest and tell him that if his ad is so-so or me-too-message, he'll get at best a marginal payoff.

And if it's weak, he's wasting his money.

And if it's phony, he'll just speed the rate at which he disappoints and loses customers and prospects.

Marketing managers know those things. They may not be advertising experts, but they didn't get where they are without some common sense.

The marketing communications facts of life acknowledge the great gap between what business magazine advertising can do when it is part of a strong marketing mix and what it does in a vacuum. Facing up to the difference, we will be striking at the problem that prompted the ARF/

ABP study in the first place. We will help motivate marketing and general managers who don't believe in advertising, to provide the kind of marketing mix that justifies more advertising.

AGENCY: REAL VALUE FOR CLIENTS

How does an advertising agency use the ARF/ABP study to help its clients and itself?

My agency is deeply involved in business-to-business advertising, and its future is dependent upon understanding the specialized business of business marketing communications. I can say unequivocally that the study conducted under the auspices of the Business Advertising Research Council of the ARF has been very useful to our agency and very valuable to our clients.

Clients expect their agencies to have the wherewithal to plan and select the right media in order to achieve their marketing objectives. But, all too often agency recommendations fall victim to *subjective* client reasoning—gut reactions based on very little fact.

For instance, at a recent presentation our media director recommended to a client that about 25% of his space budget for a high-priced industrial tool be spent on dealer advertising. Our recommendation was based on our experience that dealer advertising is a very important part of any end-user product promotion.

But the client said "Why should we spend money on dealer advertising? We have all the dealers we need and those that we'd like to attract know all about us and our new product. Let's concentrate our space budget where it counts: on the buyer . . . the end-user."

However, the new study clearly shows that it pays to advertise to both dealer and end-user when you promote a new product—*even when you only want to sell the end-user.*

In fact, in the Association of Business Publishers' Fact Sheet No. 9, the study's high dealer/high end-user ad weight cell for the commercial transportation product clearly shows that the greatest sales reported were achieved when both the end-user and the dealer were exposed to a heavy advertising schedule. Sales increased to 321% of the base level, compared to 157% when only end-user advertising was executed.

Suppose that our media director had had the study findings in hand when he recommended dealer advertising. You can almost hear him telling that client:

"Let me warn you that if you do not include dealer advertising in your approved plan, you can kiss off an additional 164% gain in sales."

The client asks, naturally enough:

"Says who?"

Our response: "Says the Business Advertising Research Council's study, specifically designed to measure the impact of specialized business publication advertising on sales and profits."

That's the crux of it; the study is unbiased and independent, as all good research should be. It's not a publisher talking, or an agency or an advertiser. It's an industry funded research project which also has the financial support of 45 generous sponsors. It's hard to argue with it, although like 99% of all research, it too has had its critics.

CYNICS INTO BELIEVERS

As an agency, what Poppe Tyson likes most about the study is the way it covers a lot of important marketing bases: Fact Sheet No. 1 says "more advertising means more sales." Those words are near and dear to any agencies' executive's heart.

But now you have a solid document. When it says the difference between a) running six black-and-white pages and one four-color two-page insert in a single publication, and b) six black-and-white pages and 11 two-page four-color inserts in the same publication, could mean a 153% boost in sales, that should be dear to a client's heart.

And when the same comparison can be translated into 80% more profit, that should be dear indeed to a CEO's heart.

Excellent advertising is advertising that *sells*—advertising that produces a profit for the client who's willing to invest in it.

Many elements must come together in order to create excellent advertising: planning, creativity, execution, etc. All play an important part. But the first element that's needed is a belief on the part of a business product advertiser that advertising really works. And that is the vitally important point that the ARF/ABP study makes. It should turn cynics into believers.

Another important part of the study deals with leads. The clients we service today are more interested in leads than ever before. New computerized inquiry handling systems, desktop publishing and telemarketing are the modern quick-response tools of today's business marketers. And leads fuel those new response and sales systems.

The average industrial sales call today costs more than $230, so a qualified lead is a very valuable thing. Again, the ARF/ABP study quickly proves that advertising, when it is reasonably invested, can pay for itself and a lot more.

Take the 2.22 inquires per 1,000 circulation that were documented in the high cell on the transportation product. One can then assume that an ad in a book with 50,000 circulation might then produce 111 inquires.

Those 111 sales calls could cost more than $25,000. But a buyer's interest level in a product is a lot stronger when a salesman calls after an ad has called first. The study makes a strong argument for print advertising as a way to reduce the high cost of sales calls.

POWER OF COLOR

My favorite part of the study is Fact Sheet No. 4, titled "It takes four to six months to see the results of an advertising program." I have the cover of that fact sheet out for gold leaf framing.

There's an old adage in the agency business that says, "Just about the time the customer is starting to notice your ad, the client wants to change the campaign." It would be funny if it were not so true.

ARF/ABP study results indicate, at least to me, that executing a good business advertising campaign calls for patience, because it takes from four to six months before a good business product campaign starts to pay off. And it takes up to six months before it starts to die.

Of equal importance is the opportunity to refer to the study when we recommend full-color vs. black-and-white ads. The study dramatically indicates just what color buys an advertiser.

Last year we had a classic disagreement with a client that we probably could have won if we had had the study in our hands. We recommended that six full-color pages be inserted over a six-month period in each of three publications. The client asked, why not nine black-and-white ads in each book, since that would give the campaign greater frequency?

I commented that I thought the name of the game was sales. He had a warehouse full of product, so I said, "Why not sell as many as we can as fast as we can?" Then I quoted a well-produced piece of research executed by a major publisher, which said color delivered up to 50% more readership and would therefore deliver 50% more inquires—and color would deliver the inquires faster.

He smiled and in so many words said, "I didn't think you were the kind of agency that believed everything a publisher printed."

I sent this same client a copy of the ARF/ABP study write-up and politely asked him to read Fact Sheet NO. 5, entitled, "Four-Color Advertising Can Dramatically Increase Sales."

Thanks to all of those responsible for the study, next year our client will have a much more difficult time disagreeing with our recommendation. That, too, is one of the important reasons why I think this study will serve agency people well. It will allow us to help document a lot that we have learned from experience—and learned from the experience documented in this new study. It will help turn subjective reasoning into reasoning based on research.

And it will allow our clients and ourselves to make fewer mistakes. The ARF/ABP study is certainly not a panacea; no research of a communication form as dynamic as business advertising can provide indisputable answers. But it goes a long way in guiding us toward more informed decisions, so agency people can be right more often and clients can make fewer mistakes.

BIBLIOGRAPHY

Abell, Derek F. and Hammond, John. *Strategic Market Planning: Problems & Analytical Approaches* (Englewood Cliffs, NJ: Prentice-Hall, 1979).

Agarwal, Manoj K. *Readings in Industrial Marketing* (Englewood Cliffs, NJ: Prentice-Hall, 1986).

Alsop, Ronald and Abrams, Bill. *The Wall Street Journal on Marketing* (Homewood, IL: Dow Jones-Irwin, 1987).

Ames, Charles and Halvacek, James D. *Managerial Marketing Industrial* (New York: Random House, 1983).

Anderson, Patricia and Rubin, Leonard G. *Marketing Communications* (Englewood Cliffs, NJ: Prentice-Hall, 1986).

Anderson, Paul and Ryan, Michael. *Scientific Methods in Marketing* (Chicago: American Marketing Association, 1984).

Axelrod, Nathan. *Selected Cases in Fashion Marketing* (Indianapolis, IN: Bobbs Merrill, 1968).

Baeujeu-Garnier J. and Delobez, A. *Geography of Marketing* (New York: Longmans Inc., 1979).

Baier. *Elements in Direct Marketing* (New York: McGraw-Hill, 1985).

Bair, Frank E. *International Marketing Handbook Supplement* (Detroit, MI: Gale Research Company, 1986).

Beaumont, John A. *Your Career in Marketing* (New York: McGraw-Hill, 1976).

Berry, Leonard L. *Emerging Perspective on Service Marketing: Proceedings* (Chicago: American Marketing Association, 1983).

Bloch, Thomas M. *Services Marketing in a Changing Environment: Proceedings* (Chicago: American Marketing Association, 1985).

Bobrow, Edwin E. and Bobrow, Mark. *Marketing Handbook* (Homewood, IL: Dow Jones-Irwin, 1985).

Bonoma, Thomas V. and Shapiro, Benson. *Segmenting the Industrial Market* (Lexington, MA: Lexington Books, a division of D. C. Heath, 1985).

Boone, Louis E. and Johnson, James C. *Marketing Channels* (New York: Macmillan, 1977).

Bradway, B. M. and Frenzel, M. A. *Strategic Marketing: A Handbook for Entrepreneurs & Managers* (Reading, MA: Addison-Wesley, 1982).

Buell, V. P. *Handbook of Modern Marketing* (New York: McGraw-Hill, 1986).

Czepiol, John and Backman, Jules. *Changing Marketing Strategies in a New Economy* (Indianapolis, IN: Bobbs Merrill, 1977).

Dalrumple, Douglas J. and Parsons, Leonard J. *Marketing Management: Strategy and Cases* (New York: Wiley, 1983).

Davidow, William H. *Marketing High Technology: An Insider's View* (New York: Free Press, a division of Macmillan, 1986).

Dawson, John A. *The Marketing Environment* (New York: St. Martins, 1979).

Degen, Clara. *Communicator's Guide to Marketing* (New York: Longmans Inc., 1987).

Elam, H. and Paley, N. *Marketing for the Non-Marketing Executive* (New York: AMACOM Books, 1981).

Evans and Berman. *Essentials of Marketing* (New York: Macmillan, 1984).

Fenno, Brooks, Jr. *Helping Your Business Grow: One Hundred One Dynamic Ideas in Marketing* (New York: AMACOM, 1982).

Ferrel, O. C. *Fundamentals of Marketing* (Boston: Houghton-Mifflin, 1981).

Forman, A. *Marketing in Action: Readings & Cases* (Reading, MA: Addison-Wesley, 1986).

Foxall, Gordon. *Corporate Innnovation: Marketing & Strategy* (New York: St. Martins, 1984).

Frazier, Gary L, and Sheth, Jagdish. *Contemporary Views on Marketing Practice* (Lexington, MA: Lexington Books, 1987).

Gibson, Christopher and Schiffman, Leon. *Principles of Marketing* (New York: Random House, 1984).

Gould, James. *Marketing Anthology* (St. Paul, MN: West Publishing Co., 1979).

Govoni, Norman A. and Jeannet, Jean-Pierre. *Cases in Marketing* (New York: Wiley, 1984).

Hardy, Kenneth and Magrath, Allan. *Marketing Channel Management* (Glenview, IL: Scott-Foresman, 1987).

Hartley, Robert F. *Marketing Fundamentals* (New York: Harper & Row, 1983).

Harvard Business Review. *New Tactics in a Changing Environment* (New York: Wiley, 1985).

Hoel, Robert F. *The Dynamics of Marketing: Current Happenings in the Marketplace* (New York: Harper & Row, 1982).

Holtje, Herbert F. *Schaum's Outline of Marketing* (New York: McGraw-Hill, 1980).

Holtz, Herman. *The Secrets of Practical Marketing for Small Business* (Englewood Cliffs, NJ: Prentice-Hall, 1982).

International Marketing Data & Statistics 1986, llth Ed. (Detroit, MI: Gale Research Company, 1986).

Kaminski, Peter, and Rink, David R. *Applied Marketing Problems* (Reading, MA: Addison-Wesley, 1986).

Lovestock, Christopher H. *Services Marketing: Texts, Cases & Readings* (Englewood Cliffs, NJ: Prentice-Hall, 1983).

Luck, David J. and Ferrel O. C. *Marketing Strategy & Plans* (Englewood Cliffs, NJ: Prentice-Hall, 1985).

Mason, R. and Rath, P. M. *Marketing Practices & Principles* (New York: McGraw-Hill, 1985).

McCall, J. B. and Warrington, M. B. *Marketing by Agreement: A Cross-Cultural Approach to Business Negotiations* (New York: Wiley, 1984).

Murhpy, J. M. *Branding: A Key Marketing Tool* (New York: McGraw-Hill, 1987).

Nash, E. L. *Direct Marketing: Strategy, Planning, Execution* (New York: McGraw-Hill, 1982).

Neidell, Lester. *Strategic Marketing Management* (New York: Macmillan, 1983).

Nickels, William G. *Marketing Communications & Promotion* (New York: Wiley, 1980).

Paczkowski, Thomas. *Principles of Marketing: Study Guide* (Englewood Cliffs, NJ: Prentice-Hall, 1986).

Posch, Robert J. *What Every Manager Needs to Know About Marketing & the Law* (New York: McGraw-Hill, 1984).

Rapp, S. and Collins, L. *Maximarketing: The New Direction in Advertising, Promotion, & Marketing Strategy* (New York: McGraw-Hill, 1987).

Reibstein, David, J. *Marketing, Concepts, Strategies & Decisions* (Englewood Cliffs, NJ: Prentice-Hall, 1985).

Ries, Al and Trout, Jack. *Marketing Warfare* (New York: McGraw-Hill, 1983).

Robicheaux, Robert A. *Marketing: Contemporary Dimensions* (Boston: Houghton-Mifflin, 1984).

Rodgers, Buck and Shook, Robert L. *The IBM Way: Insights into the World's Most Successful Organization* (New York: Harper & Row, 1986).

Sachs, Laura. *Do-It-Yourself Marketing for the Professional Practice* (Englewood Cliffs, NJ: Prentice-Hall, 1986).

Schere, Frederic M. *Industrial Market Structure & Economic Performance* (Boston: Houghton-Mifflin, 1980).

Sheth, Jagdish N. and Ram S. *Bringing Innovation to Market: How to Break Corporate and Customer Barriers* (New York: Wiley, 1987).

Wind, Yoram J. *Product Policy: Concepts, Methods and Strategies* (Reading, MA: Addison-Wesley, 1982).

Yoshino, M. Y. *Japanese Marketing System: Adaptions and Innovations* (Cambridge, MA: MIT Press, 1971).

Zikmund, William and D'Amico, Michael. *Marketing* (New York: Wiley, 1984).

INDEX

Western Electric Company,
6, 321
    productivity &
    quality center
    of, 323
Wheaties, 297
White, John R., 75
White, Marcus, 73
Williams, Bob, 332
Wind, Tom, 72
Worldwide Management
    Systems Inc., 186

Xerox Corporation, 186, 337

Yoplait, 240, 296, 297
Young, Lewis, 277
Young, Owen D., 284

Zakon, Alan, 72
Zandan, Peter, 338
Zaphiropoulos, Renn, 280